BADDEST MAN

BADDEST MAN

The Making of
MIKE TYSON

MARK KRIEGEL

PENGUIN PRESS   NEW YORK   2025

This book is for Jenny Lumet.

BADDEST MAN

PROLOGUE

Tennis Dad

A copper-skinned girl in tennis whites works diligently on her forehand, a teaching pro feeding her a basket of balls. There's a beat to their ritual: a happy velvet thump.

One's gaze can't help but be drawn to the solitary figure in the bleachers. He sits still as a sculpture.

It's been so long he may have forgotten how his mere presence inevitably distorts the setting, how things rearrange themselves around him. As the scene is related to me by another young pro, an unmistakable aura emanates from the man in the bleachers. A shimmery gasoline haze, I imagine from the description. Or smoke? Maybe he lit a fatty? No, I'm assured. His was the practiced gaze of a tennis dad. It didn't swivel with the ball but remained fixed on the girl's determined stroke. She is the sixth of his seven surviving children. His stance—elbows on quads, clasped hands supporting that great Roman urn of a head—suggests a compact *Thinker*. But the elements apparent on closer inspection—that sad slice above the eye, a nose and mouth from which could be cast a mask of Melpomene, and the tattoo that emerges under the shadow of his baseball cap—might evoke a kind of gargoyle.

Of course. He was a monster, not just ours but his own, too. The tattoo was meant to acknowledge and signify exactly that, a surrender to his supposed fate. But in the years since, his attempt at mocking self-disfigurement has become, of all things, a logo, the markings of his brand. Mike Tyson has reconstituted himself as an avatar of bro culture.

It's the greatest comeback I've ever seen—not his booming, eponymous marijuana business or the fawning celebs who appear on his podcast, but the idea of him *here*, so at home in the land of wealth and whiteness, a grand duchy of eternal sunshine and good dentistry, elective surgeries and German cars.

Like most of the locals, he's become an avid devotee of self-care. His morning constitutionals take him on a trail overlooking the very edge of America, a vista that soars past equidistant palm trees to the aptly named Pacific. His mental-hygiene regimen calls for periodic psychedelic trips on the venom of warted frogs. I don't quite understand what it is that he claims to have seen during these journeys, God or Death. But I do know that psychic distance pales in comparison with the vastness he's traveled to arrive here from the point of origin, the place that birthed his dirty shadow self, Brownsville, Brooklyn.

In 1988, the year of his first public crack-up, I was a general-assignment reporter at the *New York Daily News* and trying, without much success, to write a novel. It was about a kid—an ambitious thug who makes it big and tries to outrun his fate, which he finally meets with the aforementioned ocean at his back, by the Ferris wheel on the Santa Monica Pier. As my protagonist also hailed from Brownsville, I fancied myself retelling the story of Murder, Inc., as a parable of what would come to be known as the hip-hop generation. Never mind that I didn't yet have the skill to write such a book, or that today it would qualify as an act of cultural appropriation. Eventually, my agent broke the news (more gently than some of my colleagues) that the conception itself was a nonstarter. All perps weren't created equal. Italian gangsters? He could sell that for sure. But Black kids from Brooklyn? They didn't sell.

There was a name for those kids—that ilk, if you will—all of them inevitably lumped together, as if they constituted an urban phylum. You'd hear it in the police precincts, in the newsroom, and the bars where we'd retire after putting the paper to bed: *Piece a shit.*

They were chain snatchers, pickpockets, muggers, dope slingers, and vandals. They prowled the subways and Times Square, armed with box cutters or posing as bait for chicken hawks, and were typically alumni of the notorious Spofford Juvenile Detention Center, 1221 Spofford Avenue, Bronx, New York.

They were Tyson.

Before he was *Tyson*, of course.

He was a Grandmaster Flash lyric come to life. Tyson *was* "The Message."

If Bernie Goetz had capped him on the 2 train, no one would've much cared. Actually, more likely there'd have been a smattering of applause.

And don't let anyone tell you he was saved by the nice old white man. That, too, was a form of commerce, an existential bargain. The old man was a kind of wizard, half sage, half kook. He didn't merely make the delinquent child his ward but inhabited his innermost thoughts, making the boy believe he was "a scourge from God." In return, Tyson was to consecrate his reputation, allowing the old man to live forever.

"And did I not?" Tyson tells me. "As long as people know my name, they're going to know his. My existence is his glory."

Glory is a long shot in any boxing story. I cover fighters, and all but the rarest of them feel as though they were born to be destroyed. They tend to get used up—physically, neurologically, financially, and spiritually. I don't know if it's because they're typically born into violence or because their craft itself is violence, albeit an artful form. Whatever the case, fighters who end up ruined seem the rule, not the exception.

Even as Tyson became boxing's greatest-ever attraction, his doom seemed a lock. In fact, before too long it was the very prospect of impending doom that became the attraction itself. At any juncture in his career, the smart bet on Tyson's mortality was always the under.

I've written more than my share of nasty things about Tyson—many of them justified, some of them not, some of them shameful. But I've also learned it's better to judge fighters not on their record but by what they've survived. And by that measure, the image of him watching his daughter smashing forehands, so steadfast in her task, grabs at my throat.

Tyson has withstood most of the urban plagues, those particular perils endemic to a time and a place. But also the death of a mother and the absence of a father.

Incarceration.

Molestation.

Booze.

Coke.

Boxing.

Don King.

The death of a child.

And perhaps most treacherous of all, fame. His wasn't the kind that got you a good table at Elaine's. Rather, it was a lethal dose of a peculiarly American disease, a form of insanity whose victims include Elvis, Marilyn, and Tupac.

But Tyson lives, ever defiant of the prophecy that foretold his early demise.

And that brings me, in a roundabout way, back to the kid I tried to invent in 1988. He would make it out of Brownsville (an impossibility, I was assured) only to die at the edge of America.

Compared with my stillborn novel, Tyson's was the meanest of fairy tales, full of dungeons and wizards, archvillains, wicked witches and fairy godmothers. There would be lion tamers and movie stars, warriors and whores, pimps and spies. And still the erstwhile piece of shit—I mean that with unvarnished admiration—forges ahead. He is at once the victim and the victimizer, a convicted rapist beloved in the age of #MeToo, the monster transformed into a tennis dad with a goldendoodle, whose morning walks afford him an ocean view.

Tyson surpassed my capacity to imagine. Well, not just mine, but ours. His own, too. What follows began as a kind of essay—an attempt to explain the Tyson phenomenon—and became, perhaps inevitably, biography. There's a distinct anatomy to his fame. For even among those with no recollection of his prime, the sheer idea of him, the planet's Baddest Man, remains as potent as ever.

Which brings me back to my informant, the twentysomething tennis pro. He finds Tyson in the parking lot with his daughter. She's almost twelve. At her age, Tyson was locked up. But this girl has the face of an Egyptian princess.

Is she *beaming* at him? Not sure. Let's just say she has delighted eyes.

"Dude," says the awestruck pro.

Dude. Jesus.

Beneath the shade of his brimmed cap, Tyson's squint dissolves into a grin.

"Dude. Much respect."

1

I f there's a miracle here, a cosmic uncoupling of the fates, it's embodied in that almond-eyed girl, his tennis-playing daughter.

Some kids are state raised, as the phrase goes. She was incarcerated in utero. I'm way ahead of myself, of course. But for now it's enough to know that so was her father.

"When I was born," Tyson writes of his mother, "she was working as a prison matron at the Women's House of Detention in Manhattan."

Jail dehumanizes everyone, captives and captors alike. It's difficult to imagine Lorna Mae Smith an exception, or that prison life had a salutary effect on the incubation of her youngest child. By the time he was born in the summer of 1966, the House of D, as it was called, was the most infamous women's prison in the country: a twelve-story vertical fortress, darkened over decades until the lower rungs looked like a burnt brick furnace. It was Gotham City in the heart of the Village, bordered on two sides by Greenwich and Sixth Avenues.

"No matter how long I remain here, I'll still see something every day that'll make me want to cry," wrote a social worker employed there in the late 1950s. "This place is a snake-pit."

The House of D was chronically overcrowded (it was not uncommon to have three women in a seven-by-six-and-a-half-foot cell) and disproportionately Black (65 percent, per a 1959 article in *The Village Voice*) but attracted relatively little notice until 1965, when a Bennington College freshman named Andrea Dworkin was remanded there following her arrest for protesting the Vietnam War. She was subjected to pitiless rectal and vaginal examinations during which the prison doctor asked her how many Bennington girls were virgins. The matrons, she observed, appeared oblivious to the sexual subjugation all around them. Dworkin recalled for the *New York Post*'s James Wechsler the time her friend Lisa Goldrosen "woke up one morning with two girls holding her down and a third climbing on top of her."

The jail came in for more bad press with the 1967 publication of *Hellhole*, an exposé by the former social worker Sara Harris. In 1969, Afeni Shakur—one of twenty-one Black Panthers indicted for plotting to bomb police stations—landed in solitary after declining the often hemorrhage-causing exams upon intake. She managed to sleep through the House of D's initial humiliations—"the rats, the isolation, the Spam"—and eventually found some comfort with older inmates on the eighth floor. They washed her clothes and told her to apply Vaseline to avoid stretch marks, as she was pregnant with a son eventually known to the world as Tupac, who would be, for too brief a time, famous friends with Mike Tyson.

The following year, Angela Davis spent nine weeks in the Women's House awaiting extradition on murder and kidnapping charges. Davis would recall inmates, sane and otherwise, routinely dosed with Thorazine—as Tyson himself would be, later that same decade. She remembered the nightly swarm of rodents that swept between the bars, infesting cells like a nocturnal tide, and the marital hierarchies around which prison life was organized—husbands and wives, butches and femmes. "Homosexuality is bound to occur on a relatively large scale in any place of sexually segregated confinement," wrote Davis. "I was not prepared, however, for the shock of seeing it so thoroughly entrenched in jail life."

If such mores came as a revelation to America's emerging class of feminists and self-styled freedom fighters, they couldn't have surprised the institution's everyday denizens—prostitutes, thieves, addicts, and matrons. Sex was power. Incarceration was misery. These aren't merely the universal postulates of prison life but, as it would transpire, of Tyson's life, too. It wouldn't much matter if that prison were in Manhattan, the Bronx, Indiana, or an island off Queens.

At 11:15 a.m. on Sunday, June 13, 1971, the last of the Women's House inmates were bused off to the city's new prison complex at Rikers Island. As they departed, the jail's deputy superintendent paraphrased a line from Oscar Wilde's "The Ballad of Reading Gaol," a poem Tyson himself would one day recite, at the behest of a famous filmmaker, for a feature-length documentary on his life.

"Now our girls will have a broad view of that tent of blue called the sky," said the deputy superintendent.

Sentiments such as those might've drawn applause at, say, Bennington. But despite all the jail's horrors, for single mothers like Lorna Mae Smith, it was also a *j-o-b*. It came with a regular city check and benefits. What's more, she and her three children (Rodney, the oldest; the middle child, Denise; and Mike) were clearly better off when she still had it.

LET'S GET TO IT, THEN, AS A FIGHT ANNOUNCER MIGHT SAY, THE official particulars.

Per the 1930 U.S. Census, Lorna Mae Smith was born January 4, 1927, the youngest of four children born to John and Bertha Smith in Brooklyn, New York. Originally from Mecklenburg County, North Carolina, Lorna's father was a laborer, her mother a cook. They rented an apartment for forty-five dollars a month at 61 Clifton Place in the neighborhood of Clinton Hill. They owned a radio set.

Lorna was thirty-nine when she delivered her youngest son—Michael Gerard—at Cumberland Hospital on June 30, 1966.

They lived in Bed-Stuy. It was not nearly the poorest of New York's Black neighborhoods, nor was it a sign that Lorna and her children were ascending in the world. They were not.

The surname *Tyson* comes from Percel Tyson, listed on Mike's birth certificate as his father.

The boy was told—as his siblings were before him—that Percel Tyson was a Jamaica-born cabdriver. More likely he was American, born in Morven, Anson County, North Carolina, on July 12, 1923. This Tyson worked on the Pennsylvania Railroad before serving in the Marines between 1943 and 1946. He lived for a time in Brooklyn and died in 1983.

Percel Tyson gave Lorna's children a surname only, and will not be mentioned again.

The Tyson kids were informed that their actual father was a man named Jimmy Kirkpatrick. He, too, came from the Charlotte area. He went by the name *Curlee.*

People said he was a pimp.

Mike was good with that: "I so desperately wanted to be the son of a pimp."

CURLEE'S FIRSTBORN SON, JIMMIE LEE KIRKPATRICK, HAS TRACED the family line to a slave named Sam, born around 1853 on the Kirkpatrick Plantation, in a then-rural part of Mecklenburg County.

Sam became a sharecropper during Reconstruction. In the 1890s, he bought land from which he fashioned the family home on Skyland Avenue, and donated an adjacent parcel for the building of a church, Antioch Baptist. His great-great-grandson, Curlee—born March 25, 1924—grew up in that home and worshipped at the church.

"He knew what being a Christian was," Jimmie Lee says of his father. "He knew Scripture. He knew what it meant to preach and sing in quartets. But he was also a big, strong country boy. He had sisters he protected. You didn't mess with him."

Curlee was about five ten, two hundred pounds in his prime. He wasn't fast, but he was thick with muscle, able to generate a violently efficient torque when turning on a baseball. "A legendary power hitter," says Jimmie, referring to his father's reputation in the local Negro sandlot leagues.

He had other reputations as well. Curlee never fell to the plagues that Jimmie saw riddle so many men of his father's generation. It wasn't his father's nature to submit, certainly not to alcoholism or depression. But that nature would remain a dichotomous one, as Curlee Kirkpatrick ever straddled that line between responsibility and pleasure, the sacred and the profane. "He knew everyone from the straight to the wicked," says Jimmie Lee. "He was in them streets."

In retrospect, Jimmie Lee sees his father as a kind of archetype—"a rolling stone," he has said, not unlike the protagonist of the Temptations' 1972 hit. "I grew up with a lot of people like that," he says. "They strayed: Friday, Saturday nights—they're out there hustling. Then, first thing Sunday, they're back in church."

This son doesn't specify the nature of his father's hustle or the manner in which he strayed. But by the time Jimmie was eleven, his father had crossed a line. "He had to get on up north," says Jimmie Lee. "To get away from some issues with the po-po.

"I was devastated. Everybody knew me as 'Little Jimmie.'"

The next time he saw his father, it was in Bed-Stuy, Brooklyn, somewhere around Quincy Street, as Jimmie recalls.

"When I first went up there, he was playing softball in the park—on the cement." *See*-ment. "He was still a very good athlete.

"As I got a little older, he would take me to some of his spots. I think he had a little pool hall, a little gambling thing where he ran some numbers."

He also had a new woman, Lorna Mae. Curlee's sisters had gone to school with her, attending Friendship College in Rock Hill, South Carolina. Apparently, Lorna was studying to be a teacher. Another account had her attending South Carolina State and Maryland State. "She was very well educated," says Jimmie Lee. "According to my aunts, sometimes on holiday, when Lorna couldn't afford to go back up to the city, she would come and visit at my father's house. There wasn't any relationship started then. But when he moved up to New York they evidently reconnected."

Across the years, during his trips "to the big city," as Jimmie calls it, he met their children—his half siblings—first Rodney, then Denise. But he has no recollection of the youngest. "By the time Mike came along, I had gone off to college," he says. "I was doing my own thing, and I kind of lost touch with Pops during that time."

If he can't quite pinpoint the last time he saw his father's second family, he nevertheless associates the occasion with a couple of man-made disasters. It was during the time of either the Newark riots or the murder of Dr. Martin Luther King Jr. Or maybe it just felt like that, as Curlee and Lorna's brownstone apartment had acquired an air of doom.

"Things weren't going well," says Jimmie. "Lorna was really drinking."

Thunderbird and Gordon's gin. She'd dose little Mike when he was a baby, help him stop crying and get to sleep. Something had fractured inside Lorna Mae, something irreparable. It wasn't merely her schoolteacher's ambition but her heart. She knew. Curlee was about to leave.

IN 1965, AS A RISING SENIOR DURING THE PAINSTAKINGLY SLOW desegregation of the Charlotte school system, Jimmie considered leaving Second Ward High School in the hamlet-ghetto of Grier Town for the "white" school, Myers Park. The decision, he knew, would subject him to the ire of Blacks and whites alike. "Screw them," said his sister. "When was the last time you saw a scout at Second Ward?"

A college scout, she meant. From a white college.

After all, he'd averaged more than ten yards a carry as a junior.

"I have big, broad shoulders and a big head," says Jimmie, noting his physical similarities to Mike. But the athleticism they inherited from Curlee began in the lower extremities: quads, hamstrings, and glutes. "There was no going after his legs," a Second Ward quarterback recalled of Jimmie. "He was too muscular."

On June 30, 1965—exactly a year before his brother was born—Jimmie made headlines in *The Charlotte Observer*: NEGRO GRIDDER KIRKPATRICK TO ENROLL AT MYERS PARK. In the coming months he'd be spit at, cursed, and punched in the bottom of pile-ons. Though his coach would recall Jimmie as "the greatest I have ever seen"—scoring nineteen touchdowns, still a school record, in an undefeated season—he was snubbed for the

Shrine Bowl, the annual all-star game between North and South Carolina. Julius Chambers, the attorney who sued to integrate the event, was among four local civil rights leaders whose homes were firebombed on a single night that November.

Jimmie matriculated at Purdue, in West Lafayette, Indiana, where he recalls the few Black students being effectively barred from fraternity life, and athletes forbidden to wear Afros or facial hair. As a sophomore, he led the Big Ten in kickoff returns. Junior year, he was averaging more than five yards a carry when he blew out his knee.

The injury initiated a journey, both inward and away. First he relinquished his scholarship. Then there was the commune in Berkeley, stints on shrimp boats and in lumber mills. Eventually, there'd be more college, then grad school. Jimmie Lee Kirkpatrick spent decades in the Portland, Oregon, public school system as a teacher and an assistant principal. Then he worked for a time as a counselor in the state's juvenile prison system.

Jimmy "Curlee" Kirkpatrick holding a photograph
of his estranged son, 1988

Ultimately, he'd reconnect with his father. By the 1980s, Curlee Kirkpatrick had become a deacon at the Metropolitan Baptist Church in Brooklyn. He had yet another family: a wife named Ada and three more kids. He said he'd been saved. It must've been 1985, that day Jimmie had his father on the phone. There was a hot new heavyweight. Jimmie had already seen him a few times: just nineteen, bullnecked, with legs like jet engines and knocking out grown-ass men on the television.

"What you think about Mike?" asked his father.

"Mike?"

"Yeah, Mike's fighting."

"Mike who? What you talking about?"

"You know: *Mike*, Lorna's boy."

2

n December 2013, not long after the publication of Tyson's autobiography, *The Wall Street Journal* asked him—along with forty-nine other distinguished writers, academics, artists, politicians, and CEOs—to name their favorite books of the year. Among Tyson's selections was a Kindle book, *Alexander the Great: The Macedonian Who Conquered the World.*

"Everyone thinks Alexander was this giant, but he was really a runt," wrote Tyson, who nevertheless, at the height of his own megalomania, commissioned a seven-foot likeness of Alexander (along with congruently sized statues of Genghis Khan and the Haitian revolutionary Jean-Jacques Dessalines) by the pool of his Las Vegas home. "Alexander, Napoleon, Genghis Khan, even a cold pimp like Iceberg Slim—they were all mama's boys," wrote Tyson. "That's why Alexander kept pushing forward. He didn't want to have to go home and be dominated by his mother."

Boxing is permeated with every variety of Oedipal construct. In the last decade or so, the prevalent strain is fighters not merely driven by their fathers but actually trained by them. These dads tend to be street guys who may or may not have boxed themselves. And while the fighter inevitably wants to surpass all paternal expectation, he (or, yes, she) also wants to make Daddy proud. And rich.

Then again, I still see plenty of fighters who just want to kill their fathers, typically for abandonment. Mike might've fallen into this category, at least judging from his recollection of Curlee:

> He and my mother never spoke to each other, he'd just beep the horn and we'd just go down and meet him. The kids would pile into his Cadillac and we thought we were going on an excursion to Coney Island or Brighton Beach, but he'd just drive around for a few minutes, pull back up to our apartment building, give us some money, give my sister a kiss, and shake me and my brother's hands and that was it. Maybe I'd see him in another year.

So much for the paternal side of the equation. But it's the true mama's boy who seems to me the most dangerous kind of fighter. Again, there are a couple of kinds: those who've been pampered, those who've been provoked, and those who've been by turns both babied and baited. The most strategically sadistic fighter I know was an obscure contender when he traveled from his home in Omaha to fight the world champion, a Scotsman, in Glasgow.

"You ain't shit," his mother told him, quite pointedly, as he left. "You just gon' get you ass kicked."

The fighter in question, Terence Crawford, easily beat the Scotsman for his first of many titles and now, more than a decade later, sits atop boxing's pound-for-pound rankings. Not only does his mother remain a ringside fixture at his fights, but he considers her the wellspring of his greatness.

Apologies. I stray. But you will see a procession of mama's boys come to share the stage with Tyson. They have but one trait in common: an authentic belief in the self or, if you want to get Macedonian about it, one's destiny.

Lorna Mae isn't the source of Tyson's strength, though, but his vulnerability. Tyson was neither pampered nor provoked. As best I can tell from his own descriptions, he was occasionally upbraided but mostly neglected.

There's a photograph of Lorna Mae, one of only two that exist in the entire digital universe. Tyson posted it on his Instagram account on June 2, 2020, the day he first saw it. His mother is twenty. The year is 1947. She has full, painted lips. One might call her a handsome woman, as there's something both sturdy and attractive about her. Statuesque? Perhaps, at five seven. She's dressed, too: a saucer-like chapeau, hoop earrings, a double-stranded necklace, and a deco-styled pin on her amply lapeled coat. Apparently, she knew Malcolm X, Miles Davis, and the original Globetrotters. Tyson wrote in the caption: "I'm proud to be the son of Lorna May Smith."

But his was an unrequited pride and, perhaps more traumatic, an unrequited love.

"Did you ever get the chance," an interviewer once asked, "to tell her that you loved her?"

"We didn't have that relationship," he said.

Tyson's not always a reliable narrator. None of us are. But he's revealed, like the rest of us, in the stories he tells himself. The woman in the photograph—the fine, worldly aspiring schoolteacher—is the mother he wanted. But Lorna had limited opportunity, frustrated ambition, and no agency at all.

Twenty years later, Deacon Kirkpatrick would offer something like an explanation. He was working as a construction worker, he said: "I was a little wild back then. . . . I think Mike was about 2 years old. I had a heart attack . . .

"When I went into the hospital things changed. I wasn't able to support them. I wasn't able to do the things I should've. And I couldn't marry her. She just went her way and I went mine. We just split up. All I remember about Mike then was that he was a husky baby."

Why, exactly, Curlee couldn't marry Lorna is left unsaid. It's more accurate to say Curlee went his way and Lorna went down. "Straight to hell" doesn't seem much of an exaggeration. The booze was part of it, a likely symptom at first, and later a cause. Lorna smoked Kool 100s and threw a lot of parties at the apartment on Quincy Street. There was dope smoking, a lot of drinking (with her eventual boyfriend, Eddie Gillison, she'd water down store-bought liquor and sell it as shots), and plenty of fornication. "My mother's friends were prostitutes," Tyson would recall, "or at least women who would sleep with men for money."

When Mike was seven, two years after the House of D had shut its doors, amid a recession and the city's mounting financial crisis, Lorna and her kids were evicted from their Bed-Stuy apartment. For a time, she worked as a nurse's aide. But their existence became nomadic, each move taking them deeper into Brooklyn and poverty. They slept in their clothes for lack of heat. Fires from adjacent apartments were a constant threat, as tenants or squatters lit them for heat and landlords for the insurance money. "My mother would do whatever she had to do to keep a roof over our heads," recalled Tyson. "That often meant sleeping with someone that she didn't really care for. . . . This is what I hate about myself, what I learned from my mother—there was nothing you wouldn't do to survive."

Eventually, they found a place they'd call home, 178 Amboy Street, apartment 2A, in Brownsville. It was built in 1930, when the neighborhood was still occasionally referred to as "Little Jerusalem." Back then, Brooklyn's most densely populated community was packed primarily with immigrant Jews, nonunion factories, storefront *cheders*, and the *shtarker*s later glorified—*branded* might now be the preferred term—as Murder, Inc. The building was four redbrick stories with fire escapes facing the street, a little three-step stoop, a tile-floored vestibule, and an alleyway, a teeming artery of garbage running underneath. As reconstituted in the early seventies, under the auspices of a nonprofit, Colony–South Brooklyn Houses, it was among several adjacent buildings intended to shelter imperiled single mothers.

"Amboy was *nice*, yo," recalls Lloyd Daniels, an eventual basketball prodigy, raised next door at 176. "Them was good buildings."

Apartment 2A was big enough that Rodney, five years Mike's senior, and Denise, two years older, each had their own rooms. If Mike was "husky," his siblings were prone to obesity. Rodney, by one account, was

280 pounds by age twelve. A born nerd in Mike's estimation, Rodney kept a coin collection and an assortment of test tubes and beakers for his science experiments. Nevertheless, he wasn't above beating Mike's ass when the urge hit. Denise was Mike's favorite. They watched kung fu movies (dubbed Shaw brothers epics like *Five Deadly Venoms* and *The 36th Chamber of Shaolin*), wrestling on "the Spanish station," UHF channel 47 (Mike was partial to Bruno Sammartino, Gorilla Monsoon, and Superstar Billy Graham), and hospital soaps, one of which inspired them to conduct an "operation" on the sleeping Rodney, with Mike slicing into his forearm with a razor. When Rodney came to, Mike hid behind his mother.

He slept in his mother's bed, too, not that it afforded much in the way of protection. It was a violent household. Lorna's boyfriend Eddie Gillison wasn't above smacking her around. Then again, Lorna would smack right back. Once, Mike tried to intervene. Eddie punched him in the stomach, maybe the first time he went down from a body shot. Anyway, you needed more than a lisping mama's boy—a "little fairy," as Mike was already being called on the streets—to subdue Eddie, a stocky guy who worked at an industrial laundry. You needed teamwork—like the time Lorna managed to tackle him to the floor. Denise and Mike each went at Eddie's head, beating on him with Rodney's platform shoes. Rodney's black lab jumped in, too, taking bites where he could, while Rodney himself beat Eddie around the ankles with a baseball bat.

Still, the incident most frequently recalled began with Eddie knocking out Lorna's gold tooth, a graduation gift from her father. Mike remained engrossed in wrestling on the Spanish channel as Lorna prepared her retaliatory strike: a pot of boiling water. Mike would recall the slimy blisters that rose from Eddie's face and neck. Denise tended to Eddie's wounds. Then Eddie went to the liquor store. A peace offering for Lorna. That's how it was with them.

"They'd drink, fight, and fuck, break up, then drink, fight, and fuck some more," Mike would recall.

And if it wasn't Eddie, it would've been another guy.

And maybe little Mike would be in bed alongside her. It happened at least once. Maybe Lorna thought he was sleeping. Or she was just too drunk. For Mike, it all became part of the same nocturnal soundtrack: "I knew what it was like to hear people scream in the middle of the night, getting mugged. I saw people get shot. I heard my mother get fucked a lot. So I knew about the world."

I recall apartments like Tyson's at 178 Amboy, a kind of set piece in the life of a general-assignment reporter: the smell of fry grease, the piss in the hallways, the water stains, the flaky pipes, the mice. There always seemed to be a little girl oblivious to everything but the cartoons. You'd express the greatest, most sincere white man's sorrow to the blankest of faces. Then you'd look through the dead kid's room. Maybe there'd be a trophy. A cadet badge. A certificate of attendance. Any artifact you could present to an editor on the city desk and argue that the kid had been some kind of honor student.

Then the little girl abruptly turns from her cartoon.

Mike Tyson, age nine

"You know Tupac ain't dead," she says. "He in Russia."

Meanwhile, the dead kid's mom is eyeing you because she, too, knows about the world.

I wonder how a young Alexander the Great would have fared in apartment 2A.

3

I n 1940, William O'Dwyer, the district attorney who became famous for prosecuting Murder, Inc., declared that Brownsville was responsible for "spawning more gangsters and criminals than any other section in the city."

The roster of hit men who hung out at Midnight Rose's—an all-night candy store at the corner of Saratoga and Livonia Avenues, just blocks from Amboy Street—reads like half a minyan: Reles, Goldstein, Strauss, Tannenbaum, Levine, and Nitzberg. They were stars on the street. "They swaggered," writes historian Albert Fried, ". . . with their vassals and hangers-on, wore the best, or loudest, clothes, and had the girls and cars of their dreams."

Gangs and their corresponding turf were often designated by street name, among them the Bristol Street Boys and the Herzl Street Boys (one hopes the father of modern Zionism would've been flattered). But none were more famous than a fictional crew, the Amboy Dukes. If the street itself seemed unremarkable—prior to the Dukes, it was best known for America's first birth control clinic (at 46 Amboy, an offense for which Margaret Sanger was jailed and held on five hundred dollars bail)— Irving Shulman's 1947 novel enshrined it in popular culture. From the jacket of my ninety-five-cent paperback, which boasts five million copies sold: "a searing novel of a street gang, their girls, their 'whores,' their crimes . . . Charged as obscene upon its publication, *The Amboy Dukes* now stands as a monument of stark truth. . . . This powerful novel serves to warn all of us about the depths of juvenile depravity."

Ah, the good old days. In 1972, upon the reissue of the Pocket Books edition, and shortly before the Tysons' arrival on the block, *The New York Times* dispatched a correspondent to gauge the condition of Amboy Street and found that the dense rows of tenements had been replaced with "brick-littered lots looking much like ground zero in a successful bombing run." Some of it had been razed to make way for the Marcus Garvey Model Cities project, and much of it had been consumed by arson. Worth noting is New York's patrician mayor, John Lindsay, coining the term *Bombsville.* By the 1970s, Brownsville wasn't merely burned out but also blessed with the greatest concentration of housing projects in America, more than one hundred buildings in a square mile. Belying their names— Tilden and Van Dyke, Seth Low and the aforementioned Marcus Garvey, to name just a few—they were drab and menacing and, seen from

Amboy Street, 1972

any objective distance, Soviet. Brownsville wasn't a case of urban blight; it was full-on dystopia.

No surprise, then, that gang life had evolved accordingly. Again, the *Times* cited no less an authority than Irving Shulman himself. "Compared to the psychopathic killers we have today," he said, "the Dukes were like the Bobbsey Twins."

Mike Tyson's first encounter with Brownsville's criminal aristocracy would've likely been in 1973, when Ronald Fields, better known as "Kato," pulled up on Amboy Street with a friend, a Puerto Rican kid now long since passed, and started shooting.

"Pistols blazing like crazy," Kato recalls. He had a .38, the Puerto Rican kid "one of those little automatics." They were shooting at another guy on the roof, who, by this point, was shooting back at them.

How the scene resolved itself is less clear than the actual moment, or the way it seared itself in Tyson's memory. Kato was eighteen then. Mike would've been seven. Many years later, when they were reunited, Tyson would remind him of that day. Kato was well into his sixties by then, having just been released after serving almost three decades on a federal drug charge.

"I bet you don't remember," said a giddy Tyson, recalling that gunfight almost half a century gone.

Kato had his recollection, of course. But not in the wide-eyed way Mike did.

"*Everybody* remembered me," says Kato. "They used to call me the Godfather."

In fact, the *Daily News* would identify him as the "Supreme Godfather" of the Tomahawks, then Brownsville's most powerful gang, when he was picked up on a homicide charge later that year. Kato would beat the case, but what really pissed him off was missing out on his Hollywood debut, as he was set to star in *The Education of Sonny Carson*. The movie, whose real-life subject was then out on bail facing his own murder charge, had already begun filming on location in Brooklyn. In an effort to achieve "authenticity," Paramount Pictures decided to use real gang members, who eventually claimed three quarters of the film's speaking roles. One might reasonably assume that the movie people had other authentic concerns. When Kato's number two—a former Black Spade called "Champ"—had been arrested several weeks before, Kato went to the set "and started kicking over the cameras and the lights and stuff."

The producers then promptly produced Champ's bail.

"I got him out of jail," says Kato. "He didn't do none of that for me."

After nineteen months on Rikers Island, Kato returned to Brownsville, whereupon he escorted Champ to the bank, demanded his lost wages and, for good measure, Champ's wages, too. "*All* the money," he says.

Looking back, the romance in Tyson's recollection of pistols blazing seems to obscure the real lessons of life in a place like Brownsville, or at least what I gleaned from my conversations with Kato. Underneath the successive iterations of gangster mythology—from Yids to brothers, Italians to Puerto Ricans, and ever on, through all the gangster pictures, be they brilliant or bullshit, and the hip-hop lyrics they spawned—were a couple of inexorable truths. First, the hustle never ended. The hustler could reinvent himself, sure, but he remained a hustler. Take Champ, for instance, who acquired some cachet riding a horse around the projects, posing as a kind of outlaw gunslinger, only to return years later as Akbar Allah of Akbar's Community Services. By then, he was packing a 9-millimeter, sporting a gold incisor with the letter *A*, and shaking down contractors in the name of racial justice.

Labor racketeering. The crew at Midnight Rose's would've kvelled.

But the second postulate of criminally minded life is more disturbing. It infected every relationship: your friend, your lieutenant, even those who called themselves family. Everyone was trying to get over.

"In every way they can," says Kato, pausing: "I'm just wanting to understand that we—that *you*—understand where I'm coming from."

He has made himself clear. You could never really trust anyone.

"Right," says Kato. "Listen to me: From your women to your brothers to your cousins. Everything and everyone."

They were all capable of fucking you.

And it was into this world, and onto those streets, that a lisping, unkempt child was sent forth.

———

I MET LLOYD DANIELS IN THE SUMMER OF 1989 AT THE FAMOUS playground at West Fourth Street and Sixth Avenue in Greenwich Village. It was just a few months after he'd been shot. Lloyd was a basketball genius, six eight, with an unlikely game that could evoke, at its best, both Magic Johnson and Larry Bird. If he was unique, he was also the latest in a line of archetypes—certainly in cities like Philadelphia or Chicago or New York (yes, *especially* New York): the fallen schoolyard star, that greatest kid who never was. The men in his family were mostly alcoholics. His mother died of cancer when he was three. "She was a beautiful person," he tells me. "To this day I still know she prays over me." Among the gifts Lloyd believes her prayers bestowed was the apartment on Amboy Street, where he was raised by his grandmother.

Unfortunately, there's only so much a mother can do looking down from heaven. Much like Tyson, Lloyd got by on a combination of guile, inimitable talent, and the shamelessness of those in a position to exploit it. Lloyd had attended at least four high schools and one junior college before matriculating at the University of Nevada at Las Vegas, where, despite being dyslexic and able to read at only a third-grade level, he made the honor roll. That didn't seem to bother anyone in Vegas. When he was busted buying drugs, though, *that* was a problem.

Daniels returned to New York, whereupon he became a full-blown crackhead and on the evening of May 11, 1989, was shot three times over an eight-dollar drug debt in Queens. According to the *Times*: "One bullet passed through his chest and punctured his lung. A second ripped through the right side of his neck. A third lodged in his left shoulder."

The lead fragments were still there that day when he showed up at West Fourth Street. It was 102 degrees that afternoon. He was twenty-one and already making his fourth or fifth comeback. Writing about Lloyd somehow led me to writing a sports column, and he became one of my go-to heroes. If that sounds cynical, it's still glorious and life-affirming for me to know that Lloyd ended up actually playing in seven NBA seasons. More cynical is the sportswriter's need for villains. And if you were writing for a New York paper in the nineties, no one—likely no athlete ever—fit the bill better than Tyson. What's more, for my purposes, placing each of them, athletic prodigies, at the Amboy Street starting line made for a perfect comparison: the victim and the victimizer, good and evil, Lloyd "Swee' Pea" Daniels, who never hurt anyone but himself, and Tyson. If he was really the "Baddest Man on the Planet," then how come Buster Douglas put him down? Lloyd took those bullets and rose. Lloyd was tougher than the best day Tyson ever saw. Or so I argued.

But now, on a summer afternoon thirty-three years removed from that one at West Fourth, I get Lloyd on the phone. He's born again, coaching kids in Jersey and making a case for Tyson that Tyson could never make for himself. He's telling me, quite inadvertently, that my comparison was bullshit.

He takes me back, in his mind's eye, to a corner near the subway stop at Rockaway and Livonia Avenues. "Mike be hanging there all night," he says. "And I ain't gonna lie, them niggers be grimy."

And?

"You know, Mike do what he had to do. He had to rob a motherfucker. Stick somebody up. He do it.

"Mike had to eat, yo. Wasn't no groceries in his house. Come on, man. Hard for a kid to live like that. That shit ain't easy."

You weren't snatching purses, I remind him.

Lloyd explains that he wasn't built for that kind of life, as it inevitably meant spending time in detention facilities. "I ain't never been in no prison," he says. "They take your manhood in them type of places."

So what was the difference, I ask, between him and Mike?

"I had family," he says.

Compared to Mike, at least, Lloyd considered himself rich with family. He had the grandmother, another grandma in Queens, and the drunk uncles. Then there was the ghost of a mother he could feel praying for him. It's been forty years since Tyson's mother died, but there's never been even a suggestion he felt her praying over him.

"Mike had no family," says Lloyd. "Mike's family was the street."

THE STREETS OF BROWNSVILLE, LIKE OTHER SWATHS OF THE CITY, were then dominated by confederations of teenagers identified by the patches on their sleeveless denim jackets or leather vests. Their arsenals included lengths of industrial strength chains, 007 knives, and the occasional .38, though many disputes were still resolved by proxy, with gangs designating champions for hand-to-hand combat. Perhaps the best known of these gladiators was Mitch "Blood" Green in the Bronx. He was a Black Spade. In the Bronx, it's the Black Spades and the Savage Skulls who seem most prominently remembered. In Brooklyn, they still talk of the Tomahawks and Jolly Stompers, the Outlaws and various sects of Bachelors, including the T & T Bachelors and the Latin Secret Bachelors. By 1974, the NYPD had identified forty-eight gang headquarters in the predominantly Black and Hispanic neighborhoods of northern Brooklyn.

The clubhouses were usually located in buildings that had been abandoned or condemned—*condemned*, such an apt designation for brick husks so plentiful and otherwise populated with zombielike armies of junkies, winos, and bums. "Them buildings," says Kato. "That's where all the hell was."

For decades, "the gang problem" had been viewed in sociological terms—disaffected youth, poor, predictably angry, and wanting to belong. But now they were the province of law enforcement, of 1 Police Plaza. Hordes of erstwhile urchins were organizing, a postlarval stage of criminality from which the most enterprising and ruthless would hatch, emerging as full-fledged gangsters.

On February 25, 1974, on the front page of *The New York Times*, amid datelines from Washington, Saigon, and Lahore, was a story headlined GANGS TERRORIZING BROOKLYN MERCHANTS. Not only were the Tomahawks, Jolly Stompers, and Outlaws shaking down movie houses, roller rinks, and just about every haberdasher on Pitkin Avenue, but they were meeting and coordinating their activities under the auspices of B'nai Zaken, a sect of Black Hebrews with a temple at 237 Buffalo Avenue in Crown Heights.

B'nai Zaken, which had some affiliation with a Chicago gang, the Blackstone Rangers, operated in a quasi-political universe, requiring members to join New York's Liberal Party. "They said they were controlling the gangs," says Kato. "But what they were really doing is trying to get the government to give them money."

If so, it was an elaborate hustle, one that kept members in dashikis, turbans, and tallits and required them to keep kosher. Rabbi Chaim Ben Israel bridled at the suggestion that B'nai Zaken was distributing guns to the gangs. "We are like godfathers to the gangs," he told the *Times*. "They respect us because of our knowledge of the Torah. . . . If someone messes with us, we know how to handle them—a bat in the mouth or we break two shins. Who needs guns?"

Among the ranks of B'nai Zaken were Chief Simeon, given to sermonizing on King David's stoicism, a correctional officer from the Tombs and an expert karate fighter who, like Kato, would recall Mike Tyson as a ballsy apprentice in the street life.

"I guess Mike looked at me like an older brother," says the martial artist Yoel Judah.

Just the same, the kid was unreachable.

"I'd check him, like, 'Yo, stay out of trouble,'" Judah recalls, "and he'd just look at me like I'm crazy."

VARIOUS ACCOUNTS OF YOUNG TYSON—DIRTY MIKE, AS HE WAS called—identify him as an apprentice Tomahawk or a Jolly Stomper. He would become a thief, pickpocket, purse snatcher, mugger, burglar, even chicken hawk bait. He was ten, working for a guy named Boo, a junkie who'd call him "baby": "He'd have me lure guys who wanted to fuck a little boy into a room and he and his friends would be there to smash him and take his money," Tyson recalled.

Mike would do more than his share of smashing himself. He'd become a terror, which is to say that he trafficked in fear. The infliction of fear—the very panic it would arouse, the constricted breathing in a victim's chest—would become Tyson's most potent weapon, first on the street, then in the ring. But who has the most intimate knowledge of fear? Not the bully but what he had been: the vic, the bitch, the punk, the kid who'd been had. One didn't become the Baddest Man on the Planet despite being traumatized but because of it.

"I always imagined that the people I was fighting were the people who had bullied me when I was younger," he said.

There were so many. The kids who smacked him around for the lisp and for being unwashed and a "little fairy" or a "little fag." The kids who went through his pockets, who stole his hot school lunch, who taunted him, playing salugi with his glasses. It was second grade, and those glasses were an endless source of shame and dread. They were stomped on in front of his face, thrown in a gas tank, or tossed in the street.

"I just stood there and did nothing," Tyson recalled, "like a fucking dummy."

Then, a little later on, there were the guys who hung him upside down from a tenement roof.

And the Man.

Mike was seven. It would've been around the time he saw Kato pull up on Amboy Street and start shooting. Mike had just landed in Brownsville, its terrain still alien and foreboding. The Man seems spectral, his presence admitted to only incrementally, across decades. In one telling—a single sentence on page 16 of a 581-page autobiography—he's "a guy" who merely *tried* to hurt him. A year or so later, in a radio interview, he's an "old man."

"He snatched me off the street," said Tyson. Three years hence, promoting another book on ESPN, Tyson stated more clearly, "I was molested as a child" and allowed that the experience was a seminal source of his rage. As for his attacker, he never saw him before or since. No idea who he was or where he came from. The Man—or perhaps the idea of him, of what or whom he represents—always appears in the same place, though. Symbolic or factual, I'm not sure. But it's always an abandoned building.

AROUND THE TIME OF TYSON'S VICTIMIZATION, MARILYN MURRAY and her husband had a thriving business in Scottsdale, Arizona, dealing

Abandoned buildings, Brownsville, 1971

in artwork and artifacts of the American West. She was blond, blue-eyed—"put together," she recalls of the impression she made—a steadfast presence at her church, along with daughters named Missy and Jinger. Then the headaches began, accompanied by digestive issues and pain in her back. It was relentless, to the point where Murray—despite a daily regimen of "25 tablets of Excedrin, 125 milligrams of Elavil, and 8–10 tablets of Alka-Seltzer, plus a bottle of Fiorinal (a strong pain medication) a week"—began to consider suicide. As suicide was a sin in the eyes of her church, she finally resorted to intensive therapy, whereupon she learned that the source of her pain was a repressed memory. In 1944, as an eight-year-old in Wichita, Kansas, Murray was sexually brutalized by a gang of soldiers.

The experience led Murray to become a therapist herself, specializing in childhood trauma. She has worked extensively in prisons and with sex offenders. In 1999, Mike Tyson became her patient, as per a court-ordered requirement following his release from a Maryland jail for a road rage incident.

What follows is an excerpt of Murray's 2020 interview with Eileen Murphy, senior editorial producer for ABC News. The interview was conducted with Tyson's consent.

"When I first met him, he did not cry at all. He was really tough and really hard and, 'I don't want to be here and this sucks,' and et cetera, but certainly as time went by and we really began to work on these early childhood issues, yes, tears started to come, and I've had sessions in which he just sobbed.

"One of the things that I teach is that every person is the person they were created to be, which I call your original child. And Mike has a really big original child. That's a part that comes out and he's really funny and silly and all those things. But then everybody has a pool of pain of some degree and intensity. And Mike's . . . His pool of pain is just huge. That I call your sobbing child.

"He had a kind of a high-pitched voice and a lisp. He said, at school, in the neighborhood, he was really bullied and teased a lot. . . . He said to me, 'I never had a safe place.' . . .

"His baseline for normal was a lot of violence, a lot of alcoholism. Oh, and he said that his mom, on Saturdays, usually on the weekends, would hook up with some guy and bring him home. And they were usually both drunk. And, oftentimes, his mother would get beat up. And then that he would watch them having sex. And so violence, sex, alcoholism, abuse of women, those were his baseline for normal. . . .

"When I worked in the prison with rapists and child molesters for seven years or eight years, I think it was, eight years, eighty-two percent of them had sexual abuse. . . .

"He's extremely intelligent. He has an incredible memory. . . .

"I remember there was a time that it seemed like every time I saw him, he was carrying the same book. It was about the history of Alexan-

der the Great. Alexander the Great's one of his heroes, but he was reading and reading and rereading that book."

By 2002, Murray's practice was taking her for extended periods to
Eastern Europe. She suggested a new therapist for Mike, one whom she
had personally trained and vetted. Tyson said he'd trust her recommendation, but there was something else on his mind.

"I'm realizing right now I need a mom," he said. "Would you be
my mom?"

4

I t's the spring of 1974. I'll give it a soundtrack: the Hues Corporation, TSOP, B.T. Express. Boom boxes tuned to WBLS. We find our eight-year-old protagonist set against that labyrinth of perilous ruins, through which scamper rodents and children.

"You could go in a hole in one building," recalled Tyson's childhood friend Dave Malone, "keep walking, and come out a block away."

Or not come out at all.

That's what Mike was thinking when three older kids jumped him, going through his pockets with the refrain—familiar to a time in the city—"All we find on you we keep." They found nothing so instead marched him to an abandoned building.

"Go to the roof, Shorty," he was told.

Again, Tyson was on the bitch side of this equation. Would they hurt him? Or worse? "I didn't know if they were going to kill me," he said.

There was a box of captive pigeons on the roof. The thugs were building a coop, and Mike had just been drafted into servitude as their lackey: cleaning pigeon shit, finding errant birds on adjacent roofs, and going to the store for feed. He loved it. He loved the pigeons.

Most New Yorkers consider pigeons flying vermin, an endless source of crusty, ash-like excrement coating rooftops and windowsills. But to the aficionado—an ever-dwindling strain of urban male—they remain a source of wonder, pride, and vicarious thrill, an emancipation from the strictures, physical and emotional, of city life.

"On the roof, none of my insecurities mattered," Tyson would write. "As I watched the birds soar above me, in that moment I was free just like them. . . . I didn't have to worry about the other kids trying to bully me or make fun of me."

The birds, he went on, "were totally dependent on me for food and shelter, and I felt honored to be needed."

Pigeons are woven into the mythology of the gangster class. In *On the Waterfront,* the real price Marlon Brando's character pays for testifying against the mob boss is the massacre of his pigeons. In the real world—or something like it, the federal prison in Talladega, Alabama—Kato found himself walking for hours around the track with an aging mafia don, wistfully talking pigeons. To this day, Kato helps Tyson and Dave Malone with their birds. It's not too much to say that, despite the putrid mounds they leave behind, the birds remain a source of sanctity in their lives.

"Being on the roof is a whole different place," says Kato. "You're in your own little world with them. You stick 'em, and you wind up developing."

Stick them? I ask.

Build them a home, he explains: plywood, wire screen, feed, and a feeling somewhere between responsibility and actual love. "You take time and you work with them," he says. "Sometimes it feels good to take care of something else. Gives you a little more meaning in life."

It's easy to understand the attraction, especially for a kid like Mike. Unlike people, pigeons wouldn't play you. They wouldn't punk you.

"No deceit at all," says Kato.

Amid the eternal hustle, the constant predation, pigeons represented something pure—and something worth fighting for. It was pigeons, after all, who gave Tyson his first dose of courage.

He's told the story many times, but never with less apparent guile than he did for *The New Yorker* in 2011: A crew of bigger, older kids found his coop and came to steal his pigeons. "I was screaming for my mother: 'Mommy, Mommy, they're taking my birds,'" he said.

One of the thieves had a purloined pigeon under his shirt.

Tyson told him to give it back.

"You want it back?" asked the kid, who twisted the pigeon's neck, decapitating the bird and throwing it back at Mike. Tyson remembers blood on his face.

Someone called forth from the gallery, a provocateur in all likelihood, and probably an amused one at that, suggesting that the punk-ass dirty boy fight back for a change. "I couldn't fight," Mike would recall, "but I was flailing away. I hit him more than he hit me. So I guess I won."

BY THE AGE OF EIGHT, TYSON WAS ALREADY SMOKING WEED AND drinking—Mad Dog 20/20 and Bacardi 151 were his go-tos—with the same kind of gusto that had ruined his mother. Still, despite already being a grade-school dropout (the torment he endured over the final pair of glasses was apparently the final indignation), he was a dedicated, enthusiastic apprentice in the criminal arts, especially those requiring deception and stealth.

"Mike be boosting clothes from every store on Pitkin Avenue," says Lloyd Daniels.

"He could steal your underwear without ripping your trousers," his sister, Denise, would brag. "He was simply the best pickpocket in the whole wide world."

"I learned how to rob houses," Tyson would recall, with nothing more than a random key. "We just kept playing with it until the motherfucker opened. . . . I was able to open over ninety percent of the locks."

His pigeons were purchased with ill-gotten gains. In the *New Yorker* version, he had just bought seven hundred dollars' worth of birds with his take from a burglary. In his autobiography, it's a hundred bucks. Either way, it made for a very Brownsville day in the life, as the drunk he paid to help him haul the crate of pigeons gave him up to the bullies. The details are less important than his purposeful delineation of the story. Tyson is nothing if not conscious of his own narrative. The pigeon's decapitation followed by his righteous revenge marks a clear transition, a line of demarcation separating the kid who was bullied from the bully himself, the punk from the predator. Mike was a huge, hulking presence for his age, and a good mimic. In a later version, he stood over the kid pretending to skip rope and trying his version of an Ali shuffle, as that's what he'd seen from a guy who boxed at the local Police Athletic League. And who could blame him for celebrating? This was an epiphany. Mike Tyson had discovered his natural facility for beating people up, for hurting them. Before too long, he, too, would become scary. And while violence could be gratifying, fear was a reward unto itself. Fear was power. Fear went toward your reputation, and reputation—more than gold chains, Cortefiel coats, sheepskin jackets, and Pumas, even cash money—was the most precious commodity on the street.

Mike began salvaging his reputation by hurting the kids who had picked on him. The intent wasn't physical pain so much as shame. The kid who put his glasses in a gas tank, for instance? "I beat him in the streets like a fucking dog for humiliating me," he said.

Sometimes his friends would join in, throwing punches and tearing at the erstwhile bully's clothes. In some respects, that was the point of these exercises. Now he *had* friends. And respect.

"Everyone was afraid of him," Denise remembered. "His name stopped being *Mike*. It became *Mike Tyson*. Boys would come to the door and say, 'Mrs. Tyson, is Mike Tyson home?'"

In time, guys—many of them grown men—would come from other neighborhoods to fight him for money. Bets were placed and bouts configured like games of cee-lo—but instead of dice, an adrenalized human ring formed around the fighters themselves. Fighting in front of an audience changes everything, as the spectators' take is even more valuable, and certainly more intoxicating, than the prize money itself. The gallery becomes the collective arbiter of reputation. Mike had already lost enough in that abandoned building—his own temple of memory and imagination—that there was relatively little to fear here. Fear is anticipation, and by then he'd already taken enough ass whuppings that they no longer held much mystery for him. He could win even by losing.

"Fuck. You're only eleven?" they would say.

That was a victory. That went to his standing in the street.

"We were famous before we were famous—on our four corners," says Gordy Keelen, who earned his own measure of juvenile celebrity as an expert pickpocket. "I mean, if Mike walked on the corner of Rockaway Avenue and, say, Dumont, he was, like, *Mike Tyson*. He was 'Dirty Mike.' That's just what people called him."

The conversation among these precocious criminal cliques would segue seamlessly—from kung fu movies and superheroes to pimps, drug dealers, and gangsters, who might as well have been real-life superheroes. "We didn't talk much then," Tyson would recall. "We performed."

Gordy Keelen would become a member of Tyson's entourage in the nineties. He recalls the various extravagances in the Las Vegas mansion where Tyson lived across the street from Wayne Newton: Kenya the tiger, the statues of "Genghis Khan and them," and the professional pressing machine in Mike's master bedroom closet. Among Keelen's duties was laying out Mike's clothes for the following day, something neither of them could have envisioned back in Brooklyn. With that in mind, I asked him what was better—more potent, more intoxicating—the fame Tyson had then or the more meager dose of neighborhood notoriety, being famous on the corner.

Not even close, says Keelen: "If you ain't got street cred, you got nothing. Look at TV. Look at rap. Look at movie stars. Their whole swagger is trying to be street."

If there was a guy who personified these supposed virtues, whose juvenile rep would endure undiminished in Tyson's mind, it was a stickup kid from Nostrand Avenue: Darryl Baum, nicknamed "Homicide." Gordy Keelen can still see him as he was at fourteen: wearing two-tone British Walkers and a matching knit shirt. Wasn't a big guy. "But a beast on the streets," says Keelen.

———

"EVERYBODY HAD A DIFFERENT WAY OF THE HUSTLE," SAYS KATO. "There were guys who'd snatch ladies' pocketbooks. Guys who'd rob drug dealers. The Undertakers, over on Rockaway and Dumont, they would rob delivery trucks."

"My crew was a pickpocket crew," says Keelen, speaking for the younger set. "Then there's a crew that sells drugs, and a crew that knocks people out and takes their money. Then there's Dirty Mike's crew. They do it all. They pick pockets. They rob. They stick up. Everything."

While young Tyson had a talent for jostling the unaware mark on a bus or snatching someone's gold chain just as the subway door was about to close, no one ever thought of him as an evolving criminal mastermind. "Even as a little kid," says Kevin Barry, then a bus driver with a city contract to deliver the Amboy Street kids to their free hot breakfast at local churches on weekends, "he was always a follower."

The guy he followed most devoutly was a thief named Barkim. Though Barkim was just a few years older, Tyson would later call him his "Fagin," his tutor in the criminal arts. It was Barkim who finally told Tyson to wash his ass. It was Barkim who hooked him up on Delancey Street (where all aspiring street guys seemed to get their sheepskins and AJs, double-knit slacks with stitched piping down the inseam, the height of fashion back then). And it was Barkim who used Mike to crawl through windows too small for himself. Then there was Boo, the junkie who used young Mike as chicken hawk bait. But for all the felonious wisdom they were able to impart, it did not include the maxim not to shit where you eat.

Tyson became the burglar in residence at 178 Amboy. When Lorna's girlfriends came by for a drink, he'd scamper out the fire escape and rob their houses, helping himself to everything from cash to baby food. He stole his mother's girlfriend's boyfriend's wallet after the man had fallen asleep. Upon waking, the man beat the girlfriend mercilessly. Mike didn't care.

As for his mother's "boyfriends," they were also prone to falling asleep, drunk and disrobed. "I would cut their pockets and rob their money," said Tyson, ostensibly blind to the Oedipal subtleties involving the men in his mother's life.

The most damning appraisal of Tyson's criminal life came from a man he wouldn't meet until he was thirteen, a boxing trainer who was then an apprentice himself. "His real crimes, which very few people know about, were against old ladies," wrote Teddy Atlas, who'd come to know him well. "He'd go up to them in the projects when they were carrying bags of groceries and ask them in that sweet lispy voice, 'Can I help you, ma'am?' . . . When these old ladies would say, 'Yes, thank you, young man,' he'd carry their bags into the elevator and after the doors closed, he'd knock their teeth out and take their money."

Atlas has a long-held grievance, actually several, against Tyson. Still, the idea that Tyson's maraudings were confined solely to weakened and wounded prey is itself too confined. He could be brazen, even death-defying, in the risks that he took. And he learned how to take a beating.

"Mike was tapping off guys' birds like crazy," recalls Kato.

Tapping? I ask.

"Going up on the roof and breaking into a guy's coop," he says. "Mike was doing that real young."

Eight, nine, ten years old. Some of the injured parties, those higher up in the criminal hierarchy, would've killed him if they had caught him. Fortunately for Tyson, he was a pretty good pigeon thief. "He took some ass whuppings, though," says Kato. "Few times they took him out of his house. Tried to throw him off the roof."

Mike remembered being caught with an accomplice. The retribution began with a beating. "We started to scream and they put cloth in our mouths and then they tied my hands behind my back and smacked me on the face very hard," he remembered. "I was crying and having diffi-culty breathing and they hanged my friend by the neck from a fire escape and my friend pissed and shit on himself and I spat out the stuff I had in my mouth and started to scream at the top of my lungs, and some neigh-bors heard me and came around and really saved our lives."

That didn't stop Tyson from stealing more pigeons or taking more beatings. But the worst of the beatings, at least in his telling, were from his own mother. Tyson's autobiography is replete with examples of her revulsion for him. Perhaps he reminded Lorna Mae of her own failure—even as he gave her money, his ill-gotten gains helping to feed the family. Maybe his arrival represented the coup de grâce for his mother and Jimmy Kirkpatrick. Whatever the case, she beat him in ghetto grocery stores, police precincts, courtrooms, in front of his friends and hers: "Afterwards, her and her friends would get drunk and she'd talk about how she beat the shit out of me. I'd be curled up in the corner trying to shield myself, and she'd attack me. That was some traumatizing shit. To this day I glance at the corners of any room I'm in and I have to look away because it reminds me of all the beatings my mother gave me."

A mong the essential Tyson stats is his claim of thirty-eight arrests by the time he was thirteen. It's conceivable, though, like most things having to do with him, subject to debate. "I think it's fair to say he didn't have thirty-eight priors," says Barbara Trathen, one of the prosecutors in Tyson's 1992 rape case, who based her sentencing recommendation, in part, on a presentencing investigation that included his juvenile arrest history.

Trathen concedes Tyson's "unfortunate history," though nothing she'd consider exculpatory or out of the ordinary in his juvenile record. "I'd remember that," she says, as thirty-eight arrests would've made for a hell of an argument with the judge and a lot more time in jail.

"I probably would've danced a jig," she says.

A 1999 sentencing memo from his road rage case in Maryland refers to six juvenile cases between April 14, 1976, and April 11, 1979—two robberies, an attempted grand larceny, a grand larceny, a burglary, and an assault. But that, too, seems incomplete and ambiguous.

"Back then, if you were under fifteen, your mother could pick you right up from the precinct," says Gordy Keelen, a frequent guest at Brownsville's Seventy-Third Precinct and the Seventy-Fifth in East New York. There's no reason to doubt Tyson's account of his mother once beating him with sufficient vigor that the arresting officer didn't bother writing up the case.

More certain is that Tyson was sent to a "600 school"—another failed if well-intentioned municipal experiment for delinquents and truants. Begun in 1947 with a pledge to be staffed only by teachers who "really love children," the 600 program was expanded after a Brooklyn judge complained that "hundreds, maybe thousands of wild animals are occupying rooms where decent kids go for an education." By the time of Tyson's court-ordered matriculation, it was part special ed, part juvie. Tyson would recall being dosed with Thorazine but still mugging teachers and students alike. Then there were various stays at group homes and Mount Loretto, a Catholic Charities facility on Staten Island that would become notorious for the physical and sexual abuse of children. But the true rite of passage for the young criminal set was a trip to the Spofford Juvenile Detention Center.

Spofford was a dirty-white edifice with two wings—one six stories, the other four—in the Hunts Point section of the Bronx. It was a jail—

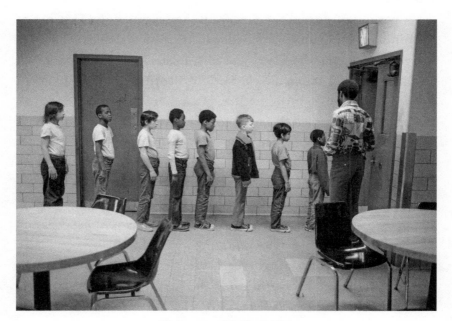

Lining up at Spofford, 1973

stained walls, peeled paint, and thin, yellowed mattresses regularly overturned in search of weapons and contraband. Just the same, it was a jail festooned with children's adornments. For a time, there was a handmade sign in the reception room: GOD BLESS OUR HAPPY HOME. Another, made of glue and glitter and once spotted by a reporter during a tour of the cells, read LOVE ME.

"You couldn't be street without going to Spofford," says Gordy Keelen. "You *had* to get there."

Tyson was just eleven or so on his inaugural visit, having been picked up in a Times Square porn theater for snatching a prostitute's purse. But his stays there became so habitual he'd eventually liken Spofford to the sitcom *Cheers*, "where everybody knew your name."

There had been discussion of closing Spofford since at least 1969, when the *Daily News* ran the first installment of a series, "Spofford: A House of Horrors." The exposé began not unlike any number of exposés on the House of D, or any jail for that matter: "an institution overcrowded, understaffed and beset with violence, narcotics and homosexuality."

A perusal of newspaper clips from the seventies gives a sense of Spofford as a fair approximation of hell. There's a maintenance worker charged with raping a fourteen-year-old inmate. A nine-year-old raped by a fourteen-year-old in a locked cell. A Board of Ed security guard charged with endangering the welfare of a minor and facilitating a criminal act after he "locked the doors for privacy" so that two boys could have their way with another. In 1972, teachers stopped escorting inmates to classrooms—effectively striking—after a rash of teacher assaults requiring hospitalizations. In 1977, the year Tyson first arrived, there were 130 escapes (in a facility with bed capacity for 286) and an inmate rebellion in the B-2 "dorm" that required a crew of Bronx precinct cops and a tactical unit from Queens to quell.

Even when Tyson was in his early twenties and still loath to admit any vulnerabilities, he'd admit that the first day there was "nerve-wracking." He remembered being asked what size sneakers he wore. He even let the kid try them on. That's how it starts, of course—except the kid said Tyson's feet were too big and gave them back.

The next morning, he woke drenched in sweat. The panic apparently continued until he was recognized.

Mike Tyson!

Yo, Mike Tyson!

Friends from home. He had kicked their asses on the street, some of them, but here, inside, they were bosses. In that way, jail was like the real world, or at least Mike's real world: a cast composed entirely of various felons, just more densely packed and, in a peculiar way, more intimate. Again, one's reputation was the most important commodity.

As per Tyson's recollection, his single Spofford loss came at the hands of a Puerto Rican kid, some kind of boxer: "So I waited one morning when he was brushing his teeth, and when his brush was in his mouth, I hit him and he was fucked up. We became good friends after that. . . . The same thing happened with most of my friends in Brownsville. I got my respect by fucking them up."

Street cred was like a commissary account on which one could draw. "If anyone had the idea to rape you or rob you or do something crazy," he recalled, "then you could whip his ass, or better yet they would be warned by your friends to lay off: 'Bro, that's my man.'"

Gordy Keelen, slightly built and by his own account probably a loser in as many street fights as Mike won, remembers being surrounded his first day in Spofford. He was wearing Jordache jeans and a pair of gray-and-black suede Pumas.

"Yo, take off the sneakers."

Gordy was about to decline the command, already anticipating where the razors would come from, knowing that the intention was to zipper his face, when he heard his name called.

"Gordy! Yo, wassup?"

It was Darryl Baum, aka Homicide.

The surrounding kids backed off, reconsidering Gordy with a look he translates as "Yo, B, we sorry." Next, Darryl engaged Gordy in conversation, ostensibly catching up on street gossip. Darryl wasn't really speaking to Gordy, though, but to the audience. It was all a bit of jailhouse theater.

"Darryl was, like, the king of every jail I ever went to," says Gordy. "He was my angel."

ON THE EVENING OF JUNE 24, 2000, IN GLASGOW, SCOTLAND, TYSON dispatched a contender named Lou Savarese in a mere thirty-eight seconds. What followed, though, remains better remembered than the bout itself: a postfight rant whose phrasing Tyson drew from comic book villains, kung fu movies, and pro wrestlers. He cited Alexander the Great, Sonny Liston, Jack Dempsey, and Allah. Most famously, Tyson vowed to eat Lennox Lewis's children.

The tirade has become another Tyson calling card. After all, who doesn't love watching a madman? But the truth is Tyson spoke less from anger or insanity than out of grief. His mood had darkened considerably two weeks prior to the fight when Darryl Baum, just six months out of prison, was fatally shot on the corner of Marcy Avenue and Quincy Street. Tyson and Baum had been partners going back to Spofford, when twelve-year-old Mike tried to rob another inmate of his gold chain. Only this kid wasn't having it and punched Tyson right in the face. "Then Hommo just jumped on him, boom, boom, boom, boom," Tyson recalled. "We beat that nigga's ass and took his jewelry."

Now, at the dawn of a new millennium, moments after the Savarese fight, Showtime's Jim Gray began the interview by asking, "Mike, was that your shortest fight?"

"I bear witness that there is only one God and Mohammad blesses and peace be upon him as his prophet," said Tyson. "I dedicate this fight to my brother Darryl Baum, who died. I'll be there to see you. I love you with all my heart."

6

Bobby Stewart attributes much of his success as a fighter to sparring with Eugene Hart. Known as "Cyclone," Hart would eventually be ranked number sixty-one in *The Ring*'s compendium of all-time hardest punchers. In his hometown of Philadelphia, a city that prides itself on tough fighters with great left hooks, it's been said that Cyclone, and not heavyweight champ Joe Frazier, had the best hook in town.

In the early 1970s, when Hart was still a young pro, his manager sent him to train under Cus D'Amato, then semiretired from the pro game and living in Catskill, New York. Part crank, part iconoclast, D'Amato was a shaman-like figure whose idiosyncrasies and contradictions made him a darling of the sport's literati, writers like Norman Mailer, Gay Talese, and the newspaper columnist Pete Hamill. But Stewart's admiration for D'Amato had less to do with the narrative arts than with the results of training in his gym.

"Gene was one of the biggest reasons I won the nationals," says Stewart, who beat a future heavyweight champ, Michael Dokes, to win the 1974 Golden Gloves title at light heavyweight, 175 pounds. "The hardest I've ever been hit was by Gene. Nice guy, but vicious in the ring. Most sparring, you hit a guy with a hard shot, you back off"—the goal of the session being practice, not pain—"but Gene would beat you down. He'd knock you out if he could. I guess that's just how they were in Philly."

Bobby Stewart grew up in Tribes Hill, New York, a small town about forty miles from Albany. His father was a state trooper, his mother a secretary. His great goal—to be that guy from a little town upstate to win the nationals—was already in his sights by the time he showed up at the Catskill Boxing Club. Problem was, when Bobby arrived at the tournaments and inevitably sized up his competition, many of them tough guys from big cities, he felt intimidated and alone.

Then one day, probably after Cyclone Hart beat him up, Stewart found himself a captive audience. D'Amato, as was his wont, was holding forth on the subject of intimidation.

"You mean scared?" Bobby asked.

Exactly, Cus responded.

They must've been alone, because Bobby blurted out what he otherwise wouldn't have said: "Geez. I'm scared, too."

"You are?" asked Cus, his eyes wide with mock surprise. "Do you think that's wrong?"

"Sort of," said Bobby. "Kind of embarrassed about it."

"Don't be," said Cus. "If you weren't scared, there'd be something wrong with you."

The trainer, then in his mid-sixties, went on to deliver his most familiar sermon, the fundamental tenet of his preachings and cause for his writerly friends, in need of quotable philosophies, to keep showing up, first at his Gramercy Gym on Fourteenth Street in Manhattan, then in Catskill, on Main Street, right above the police station. "Fear is a part of life," D'Amato began. "You just have to learn how to deal with it. If you weren't scared, you'd walk straight into traffic. Why do you think a deer jumps twenty feet when he hears a gunshot? Fear. What you have to realize is the other guy is as scared as you. It's the fighter who goes out there and handles it the best who wins."

An oversimplification, perhaps, as it doesn't allow for disparities in talent. But D'Amato's alliterative maxim—that the fighter must turn his fear into fire—was likely among the reasons that Mailer gave him his

Bobby Stewart's handwraps adjusted by
Matt Baranski, who'd become Tyson's cutman

copy of *Zen in the Art of Archery*. What's more, it worked for Bobby Stewart. If he didn't care much for Zen, he certainly learned how to handle his fear. While the rounds with Cyclone Hart were scary, they also came to fortify him: "I knew I'd never fight anyone like Gene in the Gloves."

Stewart recalls one day in particular: He suddenly jolted awake to find himself behind the wheel of his blue truck, more than sixty miles from the gym, just minutes from his exit on the New York State Thruway.

"I was scared to death," he remembers.

Stewart went home, took a shower, and called Cus.

"What happened today?" he asked.

"You don't remember?"

"No."

"We just got back from the hospital," said Cus. "You hit him with a left hook. Gene had broken ribs."

Though the nationals sated his boxing ambition, Bobby wound up turning pro anyway. He finished 13-3 with nine knockouts on mostly local cards. I'm sure there was no shortage of people telling him how rich he'd be. What he had, after all, being a good-looking white kid, was in perennially short supply. But Stewart's heart wasn't in it.

"I've never been a money guy," he says.

After retiring in 1977, Stewart started tending bar. One of the places he worked was called Russo's, which seems apt, as I can imagine him as a character in a novel by Richard Russo, who, in fact, was born in Johnstown. Anyway, after a couple years bartending, Stewart heard about good state jobs with benefits at Tryon, a medium-security residential facility for youthful offenders, just minutes from his home. Give it a shot, he figured. The first cottage he was assigned, Briarwood, proved an intensely dislikable experience. It was anarchy, recalls Stewart: the way the staff let the kids run wild, the strong ones bullying the weak, taking their cigarettes and sodas and God knows what else. He much preferred Elmwood Cottage, which housed only the most incorrigible kids. There was something about Elmwood he liked. There was respect for authority and, more than that, a chance to achieve something of meaning.

The administration even let Bobby set up a boxing program. The kids couldn't fight each other, for fear of the endless beefs that would ensue, so it was decided they'd all get in the ring with him. To qualify, juvenile offenders had to be at "level three," the cottage's highest behavioral tier: chores completed, homework finished, no fighting.

"We're going to do it right," Stewart told them. "You're going to go the full three minutes, and you're not going to quit. If you quit, I will beat you down."

He had no such intention; he just wanted to scare the shit out of them. And though these were mostly big, tough kids, they were terrified. Just the same, they each understood, perhaps at a subconscious level, that it was better to have survived a full round in a fair fight with Mr. Stewart than to keep talking shit and remain wondering if you really could. Word got around. Before long, kids *wanted* to go to the lockdown cottage.

"It worked," says Stewart, some forty-three years later. "For about five years we didn't have a single fight in Elmwood. That was by far the best job I've ever had."

Among the reasons why was Tyson. He was locked by himself in one of the cottage's "secure rooms"—one couldn't call them "cells"—when Stewart made his acquaintance late one night in 1979. He was twelve.

TYSON ALL BUT BRAGGED OF HIS GRADUATION FROM SPOFFORD TO state custody: "I had a reputation of being a killer. . . . They'd taken me in the middle of the night from Spofford and shipped me somewhere upstate to a place I couldn't escape from. So I just wanted to terrorize the new, faraway place. And I would do anything: throw bottles, hit the staff, hit other inmates . . . just be a nut, treacherous and mean with everybody. So now they took me to Elmwood. It was a locked cottage where you were not free."

Tyson recalled being sent there after picking a fight with a kid who apparently disrespected him by touching his hat. "Those huge redneck guards would fuck you up," he says of Elmwood. "For me it was a badge of honor."

But my conversation with Bobby Stewart suggests Tyson was more evolved as a con: brighter, more manipulative, but also more vulnerable than anyone had cared to notice: "He told me a million times he got sent there on purpose. He wanted to fight, to train. He asked the staff at Briarwood, 'How do I get to Elmwood?' They said, 'Just keep acting like an idiot.' So supposedly, the next day he started some trouble and assaulted a kid."

Sometime that afternoon, Stewart saw Tyson being marched through the yard, flanked by Tryon's two biggest counselors. Bobby was working on the other side of the cottage but kept checking by phone with the admitting staff, who put Tyson in isolation. Backup had even been requested for fear that Tyson would start a riot.

"He's fine," the counselors reported. "Everything's 'yes, sir,' 'no, sir.' Says all he wants to do is talk to Mr. Stewart."

Tyson had never boxed before, nor was he a boxing fan. He was, however, enthralled by Muhammad Ali, who had appeared at Spofford following a screening of his 1977 biopic, *The Greatest*.

"It's not that I wanted to become a boxer after hearing him," he'd recall. "I just knew that I wanted to be famous."

It was a fantasy. Then again, the rare sources of nourishment in his life came from the lands of make-believe: wrestlers and comic books and kung fu movies. What was Ali but a superhero who had tripped into the real world? And a Black one at that, with street cred. Shit, there was no harm dreaming—at least not until the door to his room came crashing open. It was maybe 11:15 p.m., and Bobby Stewart got right in his face.

"WHAT DO YOU WANT WITH ME?"

"I want to be a fighter."

"So do the rest of these assholes," Stewart growled. "If they really wanted to be fighters, they wouldn't be here."

Stewart sized him up: one of the bigger twelve-year-olds he'd ever seen, built "like a chubby little football player"—five six, 196 pounds when they first weighed him—"but he couldn't even look me in the eye. One of the most insecure kids I've ever met."

"I really want to be a fighter," Tyson said again, still looking away.

Stewart told him that would require wholesale change.

"I want to," said Tyson. "I want to change. I want to be a fighter."

Stewart recalls thinking: *Probably never going to amount to anything, but I think he really means it. He wants to better himself. If you help one kid the whole time you're in a school like that, it's worth it.*

The next afternoon, Stewart returned to Tryon, checked the log, and found that Tyson had already been removed from isolation. He asked for an update. Same thing: *Yes, sir. No, sir. When can I speak to Mr. Stewart?*

I don't care if he flunks every subject, Stewart told himself, *as long as he tries.*

Over the next couple of weeks, Tyson became a model student-prisoner. Stewart, for his part, began studying the report that had arrived with him from Spofford.

Were there really thirty-eight arrests? I wonder.

"The number always gets bigger," says Stewart. "Maybe he started with eight arrests. Now it's thirty-eight. Next time you call me it'll be a hundred and thirty-eight. Look, if he had thirty-eight arrests, he wouldn't have been in Elmwood. He'd have been in a secure facility like Goshen."

Goshen. Where they kept Willie Bosket, who, as a fourteen-year-old in March 1978, went on a subway murder-robbery-shooting spree that led Governor Hugh Carey to convene a special session of the state legislature. The resulting statute, known as "The Willie Bosket Law," enabled prosecutors to try juveniles as adults.

Tyson was no Willie Bosket, says Stewart: "He was big and strong, don't get me wrong. But so insecure. If somebody turned and yelled at him, he would've run the other way."

What Stewart most remembers about the report, though, was the designation "borderline retarded," which, it soon became clear, Tyson clearly was not. He remembers reading that Tyson had been to school only "a day or two" in the last several years. Tyson had never attended class long enough to learn how to functionally read or write.

"How do you term the kid 'retarded'?" Stewart asked Tryon's social worker.

"The tests," she said.

"How can you give him a test? He can't read or write properly."

Again the social worker mentioned Tyson's test scores.

"Ask him a question," Stewart implored. "I'm telling you, he's smart as a whip."

She continued, undaunted, explaining where his numbers fell on the slope of the aggregate scores.

Finally Stewart became exasperated: "*You're* retarded if you believe he's retarded."

He got written up for that one.

IN ANTICIPATION OF TYSON'S FIRST SPARRING SESSION, STEWART'S boss called Stewart into the office.

"I know you're in good shape," he said. "But this kid's bigger than you. We can't have staff getting beat up by the kids."

"Don't worry," said Stewart.

Apparently, Tyson had been telling his fellow Elmwood residents that he'd boxed before. He talked such a good game, in fact, some of them thought they'd get to see Mr. Stewart get his comeuppance.

"I just kept making him miss," Stewart remembers. "One time he just fell on his face and the kids started laughing. It was perfect."

Still Tyson kept at it. "I played with him for a month or two," Stewart remembers. "But every time we boxed, I'd show him something that he did wrong and how to do it right."

The following day, the guys on the overnight shift would report back: "Bobby, he was up to three in the morning."

"Any problem?"

"No. He's just practicing."

They were little things, mostly, Stewart's early admonitions: keep your hands up, move your head, slip and roll. Still just twelve, Tyson would be up most of the night, working in the dark.

"Tell him ten push-ups, he'd do a hundred; tell him twenty sit-ups, he'd give you two hundred," says Stewart. "He was the hardest-working kid I ever saw."

After a while, Stewart started thinking about bringing him to Cus. In fact, he started teaching Tyson little bits of D'Amato's famous "peek-aboo" style. "I taught him stuff I knew would catch Cus's eye," he says. It wasn't that Stewart considered Tyson a future pro; he just didn't want him going back on the street and getting locked up again. What's more, Cus was already known for taking on troubled kids, many of them right out of juvenile facilities or prisons. One of them, from Brooklyn, an alum of both the 600 schools and an upstate reformatory, had become the youngest heavyweight champion of the world. His name was Floyd Patterson.

IT WASN'T A SPARRING SESSION SO MUCH AS AN AUDITION, A PER-formance that began with Bobby and Mike gloving up at the Catskill Boxing Club in the spring of 1980. Cus arrived with his pal Don Shanager, a former bookmaker from Queens, and Teddy Atlas, an apprentice trainer but also the brightest and most fierce of D'Amato's disciples. Atlas had a prominent vertical scar on the left side of his face, from eye level down to his jaw, left by a 007 knife. Cus, then seventy-one, his eyebrows like puffy white clouds, liked to introduce Atlas as "the young master."

"It was so good," Stewart recalls of the way Tyson began the sparring. "He was really, really pressing me."

Tyson understood what was expected of him. Among his several talents, though the least mentioned, is an intrinsic feel for what a given audience wants. Just as he understood what Stewart wanted from him, so did he understand what his prospective patrons standing on the ring apron were looking for. He might've been raw, but he was also quick and relentless and eager to show what a good and obedient student he was. Tyson wasn't merely hungry. He was starving.

"I had to keep him off me," says Stewart, explaining why a twenty-eight-year-old former national champion bloodied a thirteen-year-old's nose. "I don't know if it was a left or a right, but it looked worse than it really was, the blood all over his face."

At the end of the second round, Atlas declared the session over, saying that "we"—he and Cus—had seen enough. Tyson then lisped his protest: "No. Mr. Stewart won't let me quit. We have to go three rounds."

"It was *perfect*," says Stewart. "I looked over at Cus. His whole head turned red."

Like he was blushing? I wonder.

"Just excited," says Stewart.

Atlas insisted that the sparring end after that second round—a none-too-subtle way of declaring that he was going to be in charge of the new kid. But Stewart distinctly remembers a third round with Tyson. When it was done, Stewart offered his gloves to D'Amato, so that they could confer while he unlaced them.

"No one believes he's thirteen," said Cus. "And no one believes he never had a fight."

Stewart said he could prove it with records from Tyson's file at Tryon.

No need, said D'Amato. "If you tell me, Bobby, I believe you."

"So what do you think?"

"I see the heavyweight champion of the world," said Cus. "He'll be the youngest heavyweight champion of all time."

They talked a bit more. By the time they were done, Tyson was waiting in the cab of Stewart's truck for the drive back to Tryon.

"Remember when I told you about Floyd Patterson?" said Stewart.

"He thinks I'm a failure," said Tyson.

"Stop this crap," Stewart cut in. "You think too negatively. He said you'll be the heavyweight champion of the world."

A thug from Brownsville, yes, but in that moment a kind of male ingenue. "He did not," said Tyson.

Stewart grabbed him. "C'mon. We're going back in to ask him."

"No, no," said Tyson. "I can't."

His eyes were welling up with tears.

"Heavyweight champion of the world," Stewart repeated. "And you can stay down here, too, after you get out of Tryon."

"Really?" Tyson might as well have said, *Golly, jeepers, thank you, Mr. Stewart.*

"Really. But only if you stay out of trouble."

Tyson went from disbelief to wide-eyed giddiness to a kind of ecstatic state. By the time they hit the freeway, he was sleeping.

And then it was Stewart holding back the tears. Actually, he'd felt like weeping with joy since Cus had taken off his gloves. Was the kid going to be a champ? Who the hell knew? Not even Cus, for whom the line separating brilliance from bullshit was obscure. That same year, D'Amato had shown up at the house of an old friend, a retired sportswriter, with a forty-two-year-old truck driver. The guy was seven foot two. Cus told the sportswriter that he would be the oldest and tallest heavyweight champ ever.

That he remained only a tall truck driver shouldn't have prejudiced anyone against Tyson's chances. To Stewart's way of thinking, it wasn't about winning a title. The kid had a shot. That was enough. Shit, *that* was a miracle.

Even more improbable, though, might've been Stewart himself. He would keep driving from Tryon to Catskill, even after Tyson was released. He will also remain the single person in this story never to ask anything in return—nothing to suckle his ego, nor a percentage of anyone's purse.

Stewart never asked, nor did it occur to him. "I was being paid by the state," he says. "It was my *job*."

Then again . . .

What? I ask.

"I would've loved it if they gave me five hundred dollars for gas," he says. "But no one ever offered."

Tyson in boxing gear, Catskill, New York, March 1981

7

Pete Hamill's facility with words included a gift for writing famously persuasive letters. Among his most effective missives was the one asking Bobby Kennedy to reenter the 1968 presidential race. "If a 15-year-old kid is given a choice between Rap Brown and RFK, he *might* choose the way of sanity," he wrote. "Give that same kid a choice between Rap Brown and LBJ, and he'll probably reach for his revolver."

Back in 1959, Hamill's letters to the editor of the *New York Post* had been good enough to get him hired as a reporter. Around that same time, at the dawn of a new decade, he wrote to the recently deposed heavy-weight champion, Floyd Patterson. It concerned Hamill's kid brother, Brian, thirteen years his junior, who wept when Ingemar Johansson knocked Patterson down seven times in the third round of their title fight, on June 26, 1959, at Yankee Stadium.

The tears were a brief if unexpected respite from the facade young men were then expected to maintain in his Park Slope neighborhood. "Every day," Brian recalls, "you had to prove yourself."

At fourteen, Brian was already immersed in the local gang scene, groupings of Irish or Italian kids in the zip-gun era: the Gremlins, the Jokers, the Undertakers, the South Brooklyn Boys, and his own crew, the Skid Row Boys. "Pete was worried about me getting pinched because some of my friends were already doing time in the youth house," he says. "Twelve-twenty-one Spofford Avenue. I still remember the address."

It wasn't long before Brian answered what he thought was a crank call: "Ma, this guy says he's Floyd Patterson."

Turns out it *was* Floyd Patterson, and he asked Brian to spend a few days in Newtown, Connecticut, where he was training for the rematch with Johansson. "I liked Floyd immediately," Brian says. "He was a kind, wonderful man, almost like he didn't have the temperament to be a fighter."

Still, for all his supposed docility, the undersized Patterson was about to become the first heavyweight to win back his crown, knocking out the guy who had knocked him out, leaving Johansson out cold, his left leg quivering on the canvas at the Polo Grounds. In a matter of weeks, an inspired Brian Hamill showed up at D'Amato's gym on Fourteenth Street. "After Floyd told me about Cus, I wanted to go up there," he says, recalling the tableau in animated detail: the pendulum arc of the slip bag, fighters wrapping their hands, D'Amato's German shepherd police dog, and D'Amato himself, already white-haired at fifty-two, his elbow resting on the ring apron as he studied the sparring fighters. Brian felt frozen for a moment, at the threshold of an initiation that began with those rickety steps up to the second-floor landing.

Over the years, the stairs themselves would be mythologized. They'd become an expression of D'Amato's best self and a touchstone for generations of writers. From D'Amato grew a tree with distinct roots, both pugilistic and literary, an advertisement for itself. From the opening of Pete Hamill's much-anthologized "Up the Stairs with Cus D'Amato":

> In those days, you had to pass a small candy stand to get to the door of the Gramercy Gym on East 14th Street. The door was heavy, with painted zinc nailed across its face and a misspelled sign saying "Gramacy Gym," and when you opened the door, you saw a long badly lit stairway climbing into darkness. There was another door on the landing, and a lot of tough New York kids would reach that landing and find themselves unable to open

the second door. They'd go back down the stairs, try to look cool as they bought a soda at the candy stand, then hurry home. Many others opened the second door. And when they did, they entered the tough, hard, disciplined school of a man named Cus D'Amato. . . .

I wasn't a fighter, but I came up those stairs almost every day in the late '50s and early '60s, and in some important ways I learned as much from Cus D'Amato as the fighters did.

Five days a week, Brian Hamill took the D train from Brooklyn to Broadway–Lafayette Street, then the 6 to Union Square. Gradually, boxing at the Gramercy helped unlock better and more useful parts of himself, as it would for hundreds of other kids who came up those stairs to receive the old man's indoctrination. He became less concerned with *proving* and eventually found his way, not to Spofford or the Brooklyn House of Detention but to the Rochester Institute of Technology. Brian traveled. He became a photographer. But he always kept in touch with Cus, even after D'Amato left the city for a self-imposed exile in Rhinebeck, New York, not far from Bard College, where, in 1969, Brian and a couple friends, all wearing their hair long, attended a Johnny Winter concert.

Brian decided to look him up and found the old man, then sixty-one, in an apartment just off Route 9G.

"He came out with a fucking rifle in his hands," says Brian.

"Who's that?" barked Cus.

"Cus, it's me. *Brian*."

"Who?"

"Brian. Brian Hamill."

"Brian?" he asked. "Well, what the fuck are you doing with the hair like that?"

It was a good visit, after Cus put away the rifle. But it brings to mind his most interesting maxim: "Nothing is as bad as your imagination will have you believe. Not even death." D'Amato was part strategist, part spiritualist, the pope of his own religion. But what of *his* imagination? What of *his* ghosts, nemeses real and imagined?

More than a decade later, even a mere thirteen-year-old from Tryon couldn't help but notice: "Some of these enemies of his are dead already and he's still talking about killing them."

It would take more than a rifle, though.

It would take Mike Tyson.

CONSTANTINE D'AMATO WAS BORN JANUARY 17, 1908, IN THE BRONX, the third of four brothers born to Damiano and Elisabetta D'Amato, immigrants from the southern Italian town of Toritto. His father delivered ice and coal in a horse-drawn cart. His mother died when he was five, a fact to which D'Amato attributed his early sense of independence, though not, curiously enough, his fascination with death. When he was six, the now all-male family moved to the Frog Hollow section of the Bronx, a predominantly Italian neighborhood still known for spawning a Jewish gangster, Dutch Schultz.

Cus's father beat him, sometimes with a bullwhip. Still, per a 1958 *Sports Illustrated* profile, he spoke with "love and affection" for his father and "reverent admiration" for the whippings he administered: "the bullwhip crashing across bare shoulders, the boy shuddering at bedside, waiting for the next stroke of the lash and refusing, after each stroke, to say he would not do it again."

"I would not give in," said D'Amato. It made him the man he was.

What's more, D'Amato shared these stories with Tyson, who wondered if it was because Cus knew that Lorna had beaten him, too. "We had those horrific experiences as a bond," Tyson noted.

As a twelve-year-old, D'Amato recalled, a grown man hit him with a stick, causing him to lose sight in his left eye. "One of those men who push kids around because they know they can't push men around," he once told *Sports Illustrated*.

I don't doubt that it happened. But his telling seems incomplete and abstract, as if it had happened in the abandoned building of Cus's mind. Unlike Tyson, however, who merely and quite reasonably presumed an early death for himself, D'Amato's preoccupation with mortality was explicit. "What you might call a religious interest," he once said. He'd follow funeral processions as a child. It should come as no surprise that D'Amato considered the priesthood and very early on found sanctity in self-denial.

He forswore all worldly pleasures, telling Gay Talese, "The more pleasures you get out of living, the more fear you have of dying."

As a kid, he'd fast for days. As a teen, he dropped out of Morris High School after his sophomore year. At twenty-one, he opened the Gramercy Gym, 116 East Fourteenth Street, with a couple of friends. In 1941, after working with fighters for a couple of years, he managed to enlist in the army despite his bad eye. He loved every minute of his military service: shaving with cold water, standing at attention for hours, sleeping on the barracks floor. "I was prepared to die," he said of the army.

After the war, D'Amato returned to the Gramercy. It was there that he found his first prospective champion, Rocco Barbella, a teenage thug who had already done time with an even more egregious delinquent, Jake LaMotta. Barbella and LaMotta were of a piece: tenement Italian, the violent offspring of violent fathers (when kids stole young Jake's sandwich, his father slapped him for coming home crying and gave him an ice pick), jailed as children and young adults, brutal fighters whose bouts tended toward bloody theatrics, each amenable to the mob and eventually immortalized in movies. LaMotta's star turn came later in life, courtesy of Robert De Niro and Martin Scorsese in *Raging Bull*. That guys my age (I was eighteen when it was released in 1980) found the script so drunkenly quotable ("Pretty kid, I don't know whether to fight him or fuck him") obscures the film's unlikely majesty. I do, however, remember one old head's bemused recollection of the now-glorified LaMotta being somewhat less regal—a guy who'd steal tip money off the bar.

As for Barbella, his Hollywood star turn came in 1956 when Paul Newman played him, or a version of him, in *Somebody Up There Likes Me*. The movie contains no mention of the trainer he betrayed, or the painstaking hours D'Amato devoted toward Barbella's development. Trainers and managers have long been admonished not to fall in love with their fighters. D'Amato couldn't help it. Barbella left him anyway—*ghosted him* might be more accurate—found a better-connected, mobbed-up manager, changed his name to *Rocky Graziano*, and won the middleweight title.

Not long after I became a newspaper columnist, when I began to write regularly about boxing, Teddy Atlas began to educate me on a variety of subjects, among them Graziano's cowardice, stories related to him by Cus. The night before a big fight, Graziano would make it a point to be seen at every joint in town, drink in one hand, a cigarette in the other.

"Make it look like he hadn't trained," said Teddy. "So he'd have an excuse."

It's not a beating that the fighter fears. It's humiliation. It's shame. Atlas made sense of that for me, just as Cus must have done for him—and Tyson, too. "Cus never forgave Barbella," writes Tyson in his second autobiographical volume, *Iron Ambition: My Life with Cus D'Amato*. "Cus would rail against him as a double-crossing coward. Cus really took his disloyalty personally."

GRAZIANO WAS ONCE SUSPENDED FOR REFUSING TO REPORT A BRIBE, and LaMotta, more famously, threw a fight to get his title shot. Doing business with Mafia gangsters wasn't a distinction particular to New York fighters or Italian ones. It was part of the job back then. The business of boxing made for some dramatic congressional hearings and drove the noir-like depiction of the sport, much of it written by Budd Schulberg, another friend of Cus's who nonetheless likened him to a "medieval archbishop." There were any number of real fighters who had good cause to moan, "I could've been a contender," as Schulberg's most iconic character, Terry Malloy, did in *On the Waterfront*. There were also plenty of gangster managers bribing busted-out newspapermen and leaving ruined fighters in their wake, the basic construct for Schulberg's novel *The Harder They Fall*. By the time it was released as a film—starring Humphrey Bogart and Rod Steiger and featuring the logline "The only thing that's on the square was the ring itself"—boxing was a vast consortium of criminality under the aegis of a former Murder, Inc., hit man, Frankie Carbo, known as "Mr. Gray." Carbo's agents included a Philadelphia gangster, Blinky Palermo, and their conspirators in the ostensibly legit world: the International Boxing Club of New York, better known as the IBC; its president, Jim Norris; and a slew of arenas, beginning with Madison Square Garden, which then featured twice-weekly televised bouts. The enterprise began with the IBC signing would-be successors to Joe Louis's heavyweight crown. As Justice Department lawyers noted in a subsequent antitrust case: "Control of the heavyweight championship is usually the most lucrative source of revenue in boxing."

If the feds eventually—perhaps reluctantly, given J. Edgar Hoover's insistence that there was no such thing as the Mafia or organized crime—saw boxing as an endeavor requiring some oversight, D'Amato saw himself in more grandiose, even messianic terms. Not only would he avenge the theft of Graziano, but he'd deliver the sport's abused proletariat—the fighters themselves—from their corrupt paymasters. It was a role that could've been written by Schulberg, not unlike Father Barry's fearless work with the longshoremen in *On the Waterfront*. And like Father Barry, Cus would need a little help. "I couldn't fight them myself," he'd say years later, looking back on his career. "I had to wait for a fighter to fight them with, a kid who was not only good but loyal. If he was good but not loyal, it wouldn't help me. I couldn't expose myself, because they were going to get to my fighter, pay him off or do something to get him to leave me."

I can't recall another trainer speaking of a fighter in that manner, as a means to *his* end, a mere agent of his grand scheme. I'm not diminishing the great good acts D'Amato performed—for kids like Brian and others in even more dire circumstances, and for writers, too. While Mailer was regarded, quite self-consciously, as *the* literary heavyweight (a term that, unlike the sport, warrants banishment)—he who wrested the lineal title from Papa Hemingway—not all his work ages gracefully. But his boxing stuff continues to nourish me. Most prescient, I think, is his notion of the fighter's ego or in the case of Muhammad Ali—*Ego!* Any fighter needs an unhealthy dose just to do the job—all but naked before an audience, a gallery of witnesses anticipating some form of submission, a metaphorical death, either his or yours. But the heavyweight champion of the world—or, as the character came to be known in Tyson's time, Baddest Man on the Planet—necessitates an exponential multiple of that self-conceit. Yet there was D'Amato waiting, pining perhaps, for a heavyweight champion whose ego would be subservient to his.

8

The perfect boy walked up those steps to the Gramercy in 1949. He was fourteen, a student at nearby P.S. 614, and possessed of three extraordinary traits: physical ability, a great need to please, and an aberrant disdain for himself.

Floyd Patterson grew up in a series of cold-water Bed-Stuy railroad flats. They were a family of eleven. His mother was a maid, his father a laborer. Floyd would rub his exhausted father's feet when he got home from work. Though he suffered from terrible nightmares, Floyd shared a bed with his two older brothers. Floyd would often study a photograph of the three of them, focusing on his own image.

"I don't like that boy," he told his mother.

Eventually, Floyd carved an X over his face and two more over his body. His mother didn't know what was wrong with him, nor could the doctors figure it out. He would sleepwalk at night and seek darkness come day. A chronic truant, Floyd would sneak into movie houses or cellars or, just past the platform in the High Street subway station, a kind of tool closet. "There was a metal ladder to get up into it, and once you were in you locked the door behind you and there was total blackness," Patterson would recall. "It became my cave, my hideaway—a safe hole in the

Floyd Patterson at the Gramercy Gym, 1954

wall away from the bitterness of the world. I'd spread papers on the floor and I'd go to sleep and find peace."

He was nine.

Floyd wasn't violent, but he stole, mostly food and candy. Once, a plainclothes cop hit him over the head with a wooden crate, trying to elicit his confession for stealing sodas. Floyd became enraged and started swinging wildly at the cop. Upon arriving at the station house, his mother assured the officer that Floyd didn't do it, else he wouldn't be crying.

At eleven, Patterson was sent to Wiltwyck School for Boys, an Episcopal charity for wayward juveniles on the former Whitney estate in Esopus, New York. Wiltwyck had social workers and psychiatrists and teachers who taught him to read and write and gave him his first measure of confidence. He even met Eleanor Roosevelt.

Seventeen years later, Mrs. Roosevelt penned a tribute to the heavyweight champion of the world. It was occasioned by the publication of his autobiography, *Victory over Myself*, and the opening of Patterson

House, his way station for kids reacclimating to city life after Wiltwyck. The former First Lady cited Patterson's "intelligent and sympathetic mother," the staff at Wiltwyck, and "a good, kind teacher" at his 600 school.

"These were the things," she wrote, "that saved a human being who has now become the hero for many other small boys of his race."

NOT LONG AFTER THE FORMER FIRST LADY'S ACCOLADES, PATTER-son made the most admirable decision of his professional life, though I'm not sure Eleanor Roosevelt would have approved. He would fight Sonny Liston.

There is no record of Liston's birth, though a man who knew him once famously said, "I think he died the day he was born." By 1962, Liston had already lived several lives, none of them good. He'd been whipped by his father on an Arkansas plantation. He'd been an armed robber and done time in Missouri (no complaint from Sonny about jail, as he got three squares and a Catholic priest introduced him to boxing). Upon his release, he pursued a two-track career: heavyweight fighter and mob leg breaker. He also beat up cops—*humiliated them* would be more accurate. Liston eventually had to relocate to Philadelphia, where he came under the control of Frankie Carbo and Blinky Palermo.

If Patterson was Eleanor Roosevelt's champ, Sonny represented the nation's shadow government, also a syndicate of territories, but this one with its capital in Nevada, largely built from Teamster pension funds. More than the mob, though, Liston personified white America's greatest fear, that great lurking ghoul in the American psyche: the angry Black motherfucker who was coming to get you.

Earlier that year, during Patterson's trip to the Oval Office, President Kennedy urged him not to fight Liston. At a banquet later that evening, one of the liquor importer's other sons, Attorney General Robert Kennedy, reiterated the administration's preference, citing the brothers' crusade against organized crime. Liston might've been the most feared heavyweight in the world, with the biggest fist ever measured, fifteen inches in circumference, but Patterson had an airtight excuse to avoid him. And it wasn't just the Kennedys. It was the Kefauver Committee. It was the NAACP. And the New York State Athletic Commission, which never had a problem with organized crime but suddenly found the resolve to deny Liston a license, citing, as *The New York Times* put it, not merely his criminal record—nine arrests, two convictions—but "his association with persons of unsavory background," a new standard that, if actually applied, would've been the end of boxing everywhere but perhaps Harvard and Yale.

As it happened, Patterson was more enlightened, possessed of a higher character, and more devoted to fair play than could be rightfully expected of anyone in politics or boxing. "I knew if I wanted to sleep comfortably I'd have to take on Liston even though the NAACP and the Kefauver Committee didn't want me to take on the fight," he explained. "Some people said: 'What if you lose and he wins? Then the colored people will suffer.' But maybe if Liston wins, he'll live up to the title. He may make people look up to him."

Somehow, Patterson found the strength to defy them all, voices of an establishment he revered. What's more, he stood up to Cus. Cus D'Amato had done everything he could to sabotage the Liston fight. Now he, too, would have to be defied.

WHAT PATTERSON ACHIEVED UNDER D'AMATO'S DIRECTION REMAINS singular, and woefully underappreciated. Patterson possessed diligence, quickness, reach, and power. Finally, D'Amato had a student gifted enough to help him evangelize the "peekaboo" style he had developed—gloves held tight against the face, elbows tucked to protect the torso, constant head movement. In 1952, Patterson won an Olympic gold medal as a middleweight in Helsinki. By 1956, D'Amato had trained and maneuvered him so deftly that he knocked out the IBC's man—the aging if still capable Archie Moore, an almost 2–1 favorite—to become the youngest-ever heavyweight champion. Patterson was twenty-one and at 182 pounds not too much bigger than he had been at the Olympics.

They'd made history, Cus and Floyd, but there's little to suggest they derived any lasting satisfaction from it. If anything, Patterson's self-doubt seemed to grow now that he held the most famous title in sports. D'Amato, for his part, became ever more consumed by what he called "my enemies," and even more blind to his own hypocrisies.

After Patterson won the title, D'Amato stopped sleeping solely on a cot in the gym and rented a furnished two-room apartment at Fifty-Third and Broadway. Still, he rarely slept there on consecutive nights for fear that his movements were being tracked. He didn't like talking on the phone for fear it was being tapped. He didn't like going out for fear that someone might plant a marijuana cigarette on him and call the cops.

"I must keep my enemies confused," he famously told Talese.

But nobody was more confused than his own fighters. Loath to put them in with IBC opponents, D'Amato—a manager who supervised the training of his fighters through various assistants—kept matching them with nobodies. At least Patterson won his famous title. Cus's other fighters suffered even more, losing precious years in their prime. It was often said that José Torres—Pete Hamill's great friend and also a favorite of Mailer's—should have been the middleweight champion. Certainly, D'Amato kept promising big fights. But Torres wouldn't get his title shot until 1965—and wasn't nearly the fighter he had been—as a light heavyweight, after D'Amato stepped down as his manager. Another D'Amato fighter, Joe Shaw, considered an elite welterweight, never even got his title shot. For all the fighters ruined by the IBC, D'Amato hurt his own, too. The real price of his self-styled crusade was robbing his best fighters of their best years.

D'Amato liked to say he exposed the IBC's monopoly. He helped, no doubt, but what broke the IBC was an antitrust case brought by the Justice Department back in 1955. What's more, D'Amato neglected his own mob connections.

In 1956, shortly after Patterson beat Moore, the *Daily News*'s Gene Ward asked him, quite pointedly, "Did you incur obligations in bringing Patterson up to the title shot?"

"Yes, but obligations of friendship, nothing else," said D'Amato. "I owe a great deal to men like Charley Black, who has stuck with me all the way."

Black's real name was Antonucci. He was a bookmaker and a loan shark and an occasional fight manager. He was also in tight with his cousin, Fat Tony Salerno, a rising power in the Genovese crime family who just happened to bankroll the first Patterson–Johansson fight. It's not clear whether Salerno was trying to move in on D'Amato's protégé, but that very thought would occur to one of Cus's closest friends years later when the now underboss showed up in Catskill to watch Tyson spar: "I think Salerno wanted a small piece of the action. . . . I believe that they came out with some sort of working arrangement. There was no way of stopping Salerno if he wanted to muscle in."

None of this means D'Amato was a gangster, just that he wasn't against gangsters per se so much as the IBC's gangsters. Maybe he thought he needed muscle of his own to go against Carbo. Still, his connection with Charley Black and Salerno was reason enough for the New York State Athletic Commission to revoke the manager's license D'Amato had

D'Amato, wearing a homburg, walking into court with his lawyer, 1960

already allowed to expire. He also defied subpoenas from the Kefauver Committee and the Manhattan district attorney.

THERE WERE IN EXCESS OF SIX HUNDRED CORRESPONDENTS ON HAND at Comiskey Park for Patterson–Liston. They included A. J. Liebling, Red Smith, Jimmy Cannon, Hamill, Schulberg, Talese, Ben Hecht, Mailer, and James Baldwin, who knew little of boxing but more about these particular fighters than any of the aforementioned with the possible exception of Talese, who'd been examining the D'Amato–Patterson dynamic in granular detail for years and, as it happened, did double duty that week as Baldwin's guide.

Americans of every race, creed, and color—all except the gangster class—were united in the belief that Patterson *had to* win. Nevertheless, it fell to Baldwin—a gay Black man writing for a knockoff titty mag, *Nugget*—to unpack the umbrage with which the champ was regarded on press row:

> Never before had any of the sports writers been compelled to deal directly with the fighter instead of with his manager, and all of them seemed baffled by this necessity and many were resentful. I don't know how they got along with D'Amato when he was running the entire show—D'Amato can certainly not be described as either simple or direct—but at least the figure of D'Amato was familiar and operated to protect them from the oddly compelling figure of Floyd Patterson, who is quite probably the least likely fighter in the history of the sport. And I think that part of the resentment he arouses is due to the fact that he brings to what is thought of—quite erroneously—as a simple activity a terrible note of complexity. This is his personal style, a style which strongly suggests that most un-American of attributes, privacy, the will to privacy; and my own guess is that he is still relentlessly, painfully shy—he lives gallantly with his scars, but not all of them have healed—and while he has found a way to master this, he has found

no way to hide it. . . . Patterson, tough and proud and beautiful, is also terribly vulnerable, and looks it.

And of Liston:

While there is a great deal of violence in him, I sensed no cruelty at all. On the contrary, he reminded me of big, Black men I have known who acquired the reputation in order to conceal the fact that they weren't hard. Anyone who cared to could turn them into taffy. . . . He is inarticulate in the way we all are when more has happened to us than we know how to express; and inarticu-late in a particularly Negro way—he has a tale to tell which no one wants to hear. . . .

And what had hurt him most, somewhat to my surprise, was not the general press reaction to him, but the Negro reaction. "Colored people," he said, with great sorrow, "say they don't want their children to look up to me." . . .

"I would never," he said, "go against my brother—we got to learn to stop fighting among our own." . . .

"They said they didn't want me to have the title. They didn't say that about Johansson." "They" were the Negroes. "*They* ought to know why I got some of them bum raps I got."

THE FIGHTERS WENT ABOUT THEIR TASK—EACH OTHER—WITH A SENSE of grim duty. Midweek, the man who'd assembled all that literary talent, publicist Harold Conrad, received a call from the promoter, asking if he knew a makeup artist.

"For what?" asked Conrad, Budd Schulberg's apparent inspiration for Humphrey Bogart's role in *The Harder They Fall*.

"For Patterson."

Conrad called a guy at the local CBS affiliate. The next day, the guy called back. "What the hell's playing with Patterson? He had my man fix him up a beard."

Never did Patterson look like more of a middleweight than on fight night. Liston was twenty-four pounds heavier, with a thirteen-inch reach advantage. He battered Patterson into submission at 2:06 of the first round.

The following morning, at the postfight presser, Mailer occupied the stage, refusing to cede it to the new champion. Instead, he felt compelled to share theories he'd come upon during a night of heroic drinking at the Playboy Club. What had happened, he argued, had less to do with Liston than with the Mafia casting an evil eye on Patterson. Patterson's mistake had been forsaking D'Amato, who understood Sicilian black magic and therefore could ward it off.

Psychically, as Mailer might've put it, he was onto something; the week had revealed a facet, or perhaps several, of the American condition. Eventually, however, and with great care, Chicago mayor Daley's cops removed Mailer from the stage.

By then, Patterson had been stopped at the side of a road in Ohio, where he had been resting. A state trooper put his flashlight beam on him. "If you don't have a license I've got to take you in," said the cop.

Patterson removed his beard and mustache.

"Are you some kind of an actor?" asked the trooper.

"I lost a fight last night," explained Patterson. "Do I have to lose again?"

The trooper let him go, a courtesy rarely afforded even to rich men of his race. Still, Liston would ensure that Patterson indeed lost again. The rematch, nine months later in Las Vegas, lasted only four seconds longer, until 2:10 of the first round.

Esquire would conclude the year famously: with a George Lois cover that featured Liston in a Santa hat. Only an adman like Lois could truly divine America's heart, which is to say, what *sold*, and it wasn't Patterson, not anymore. Three months later, Talese's brilliant Patterson opus—"The Loser"—got only an inside page in the magazine, though it did contain this extraordinary confession from its subject: "I think that within me, within every human being, there is a certain weakness. It is a weakness that exposes itself more when you're alone. And I have figured out that part of the reason I do the things I do, and cannot seem to conquer that one word—myself—is because . . . is because . . . I am a coward." Pause. "I am a coward."

Patterson's acknowledgment affirms again that what fighters fear most is not pain but humiliation. More difficult to understand is D'Amato. It's worth noting here that both of them, Patterson and D'Amato, were scared to death of flying. But it was Patterson who willed himself to become a pilot. If D'Amato's priority was getting young men to be truly honest with themselves, and to deal with their fears, then Patterson should've gone down as his masterpiece. But fear seems more a means to D'Amato's end, *his* ambition, his legacy.

Like Patterson, Tyson has called himself a coward many times. Still, for all their outward similarity—Blackness, Brooklyn, delinquency, and D'Amato—they seem like mirror images refracted through the man who made them fighters. They're opposites, even in the nature of their self-loathing. Patterson's was directed inward, but Tyson, per D'Amato's tutelage, would unleash his onto the world. If the world had changed by 1980, then so had Cus. Teddy Atlas likened the way D'Amato first gazed at Tyson to lovestruck Michael Corleone's first glimpse of Apollonia in *The Godfather.*

There's another way of looking at it, though: At long last, D'Amato had his Sonny Liston.

9

n early 1975, Brian Hamill showed up at the Felt Forum, Madison Square Garden's theater-sized venue, for an early elimination round of the forty-ninth annual New York Golden Gloves. His older brother Johnny had a friend from Staten Island, and the friend's kid brother, a rough-hewn eighteen-year-old named Kevin Rooney, was fighting as a subnovice representing the Staten Island Police Athletic League. Rooney didn't have a lot of pop on his punches. He wasn't much for technique, either. But something about him—a bravura recklessness, perhaps, the true religion of most adolescent males—suggested possibility.

"The way he came flying out of the corner, throwing so many punches," recalls Brian. "He had balls. And I'm thinking, *Wow! This kid could turn into something.*"

A month or so later, on a Friday night, March 21, before a sold-out crowd of 20,042 at the Garden, Rooney beat a West Point cadet to win the 147-pound title. "It was a bitterly fought three-rounder with the cadet coming on strong in the third, but unable to overcome Rooney's big early edge," noted the *Daily News.* "Rooney expects to enter the Marines in the next few months."

Brian had another idea for him, though. Of course, D'Amato, being his ornery self, didn't want to hear it, having convinced himself that Rooney wasn't actually a subnovice.

"Cus, trust me," said Brian. "This was his first year in the Gloves. He's even got a sidekick, a kid named Teddy Atlas. He's a fighter, too."

"Tell you what," D'Amato told Brian. "Because it's you, I'll let them come up for two weeks. If I don't like them after two weeks, I'll call you to tell you I'm getting rid of them."

The weeks passed without a call. Good sign. Brian didn't bother checking in. Calling Cus meant setting aside an hour at the very least. Anything less the old man might consider an act of disloyalty.

OF THE CIRCUMSTANCES FROM WHICH HE CAME, ROONEY WOULD recall leaving home for good and finding work as a hospital orderly after one particularly eventful confrontation: "I had gotten into a fight with my father and I said to myself, 'I gotta get out of this house. I'm gonna kill him or he's gonna kill me, and one of us is gonna end up going to jail.' He was a drinker. He worked as a longshoreman. He had a good job but somehow fucked that up. I guess he was drinking too much. All of a sudden he stopped working. Then one time he started to push my mother around I went after him. We fought and then he hit me right in the solar plexus and I was done. So the next time he pushes my mother around I hit him with a baseball bat. I was seventeen. So that's when . . . I got that job at the hospital. . . .

"Me and Teddy were best friends growing up in Staten Island. We used to play basketball all the time. He lived up in an expensive house. I lived in a working-class neighborhood. The working-class neighborhood was at the bottom and Teddy was at the top of the hill."

In fact, Teddy Atlas was a physician's son who, for reasons not yet clear to himself, insisted on hanging out with, as Rooney called them, a crew of "heroin addicts, pill poppers, and drunks"—not to mention stickup kids, burglars, and apprentice mobsters.

That's not to say Rooney was a master of self-knowledge, either. But

he knew enough to figure out what bus he had boarded, that metaphorical municipal line making several stops at Rikers (Adolescent Reception
and Detention Center, Anna M. Kross Center, the House of Detention
for Men) before last stops at Greenhaven or Attica. Brian's call to D'Amato
had given Rooney a way to pull the cord and get out. What's more, it beat
his other option, sharing a barracks with dozens of would-be Marines on
Parris Island. Rooney would train while earning his room and board
by mowing the lawn and painting the house in which he would live, a
seventeen-room Victorian mansion situated amid ten acres on the banks
of the Hudson River.

ON JULY 29, 1971, CUS D'AMATO FILED FOR BANKRUPTCY, CLAIMING
$500 in assets and $30,276 in liabilities, most of it from a tax lien stem-
ming from the first Patterson–Liston fight. As enemies go, D'Amato
found the IRS relatively easy to confuse. Eschewing all income was easy
for a man who had always lived like a priest. The question, however, is
how a lifelong ascetic who claimed that money was mammon wound up
in the white gabled manor on Hidden Drive in Athens, New York.

The owner of the house was one Camille Ewald, a Ukrainian immigrant whose sister had married D'Amato's brother, Rocco, whom Cus, as
legend has it, cut off for selling Camille a faulty lawn mower. Cus and Camille were said to have been lovers, once upon a time, when she was a
waitress in a New York diner. Or not. The answer depends on whom you
believe: Cus himself, who claimed to shun female affection lest it leave
him vulnerable, or his most dedicated apostles, who insist he was merely
protecting Camille from the mob. More clear was the source of funds for
the mortgage and upkeep of the big white house.

It was all bankrolled by Bill Cayton and Jimmy Jacobs—Tyson's
eventual managers—and owners of the world's most comprehensive library of fight films, Big Fights, Inc. Cayton, a chemical engineer by training, was content to stay behind the scenes. His involvement in the sport
was strictly mercantile. Cayton recognized opportunities. In the late 1940s,
as a young adman with the Vaseline account, he created *Greatest Fights*

of the Century, a program that followed NBC's stalwart *Friday Night Fights*. Not only did Cayton's show sell tons of Vaseline hair tonic and often outrate *Friday Night*'s main event, but it also cost little to produce. Cayton's biggest expense, acquisition fees, had been kept artificially depressed for years thanks to a federal statute that went to the heart not merely of boxing but of a line of American archetypes whose ranks would include fighters like Liston and Tyson. The Sims Act, passed in 1912, forbade interstate traffic in fight films after riots erupted throughout the South following movie-house screenings of Jack Johnson's TKO of the original white hope, James Jeffries. By the time the act was repealed, the fight-film market had apparently become the province of former bootleggers who felt that Cayton offered a fair value for their inventory. Later, Cayton would do business with the bootleggers' descendants when he purchased the library of the IBC.

Jacobs, who'd eventually become Cayton's partner in Big Fights, was an entirely different sort—not merely a front man but the kind of obsessional fabulist you'll inevitably find at the highest echelons of boxing and politics.

He was born in 1930 in Saint Louis. When he was seven, the family relocated to the Fairfax district of Los Angeles. He was eleven when his parents divorced. His older sister, Dorothy, went to live with his father, while Jimmy remained with his mother, whom he'd ever call "Mother" or, when addressing his sister, "my mother."

While she remained the dominant figure in his life, Jacobs seemed on an endless quest for someone paternal—older, wiser, richer. Cayton, twelve years his senior, might have been that for a time, at least in matters of business. Certainly D'Amato would fit the bill. When actual men weren't available, Jacobs would invent them, telling a childhood friend that his father was Buddy Baer, the heavyweight contender who became a Hollywood actor. Later, reporters would aid Jacobs in propagating the myth that his father was a real estate tycoon who staked him his start in business.

In other versions, he owned a chain of department stores in Saint Louis and left Jacobs millions. In fact, though, his father was a liquor salesman, and, as judged by the accumulation of wealth, not a very successful one.

As for Jimmy's actual start in the world, it began with a comic, Batman, more specifically Detective Comics No. 38, an issue that marked the inaugural appearance of Batman's protégé. Maybe there aren't many kids who identify as Robin, but Jacobs set about his Boy Wonder fantasies with a vengeance.

"Everything athletic that Robin did, I tried to do," Jacobs recalled. "He threw a boomerang. I learned how to throw a boomerang. Robin was an excellent tumbler, and so I would run off diving boards to practice double flips. Robin knew jujitsu, so I took lessons. In one issue Robin swam underwater for two minutes. . . . Before long I could swim underwater for two minutes. I didn't want to admit that Robin could do something I couldn't do."

But there were things Jacobs could do even better than Robin—among them collect comic books, of which he was said to have eventually amassed as many as 880,000 in a Los Angeles warehouse. Another was playing handball, which he first mastered at the Hollywood YMCA.

Jacobs was a phenomenal athlete with an almost simian physique: five nine, 175 pounds of solid yet dexterous muscle. Before dropping out of high school, he was an all-city basketball player, also renowned for posting impressive times in the hundred-yard dash. But his passion remained handball. In all, Jacobs won twelve national championships, enjoyed a fourteen-year unbeaten streak in the United States Handball Association, and cemented a reputation as the sport's Babe Ruth. But while handball was a popular urban game, dominated for a time by Jews, Jacobs's tweed caps and curiously mannered speech spoke to his very particular Anglo-patrician affectations. *I daresay, my good man.* That was a Jimmy Jacobs sentence. Artifice compensates or conceals; in the case of Jacobs, it disguised a certain ruthlessness.

Two nights before the first Patterson–Liston bout in Chicago, Norman Mailer and William F. Buckley debated before a crowd of 3,600 at the Medinah Temple. *The New York Times,* framing its account as a title fight between heavyweights of the conservative and hipster persuasions, declared it a draw. The following evening, however, saw Mailer of Harvard embarrassed by a high school dropout.

Mailer made the mistake of arguing with Jacobs about boxing, a passion that ranked in Jacobs's holy trinity beside handball and comic books. The subject was Patterson's flaws and their woeful lack of mention in a documentary Jacobs had produced. "He ran me all over the court," wrote Mailer in his virtuoso account of the fight, "Ten Thousand Words a Minute," first published in *Esquire*'s February 1963 issue. "It was one of those maddening situations where you know you are right"—in fact, Mailer was, Patterson *had* been dropped by suspect competition—"but the other man has the facts, and the religious conviction as well."

It was a remarkable admission from Mailer, whose own ego was Ali-esque. And it's likely Jacobs knew just that and used it against America's most famous living writer. Jacobs debated as he acquired comic books and fight films (his own collection was second only to the deeper-pocketed Cayton's) and played handball. "Jimmy knew his best shots and your greatest weaknesses," Jacobs's eventual protégé, Steve Lott, once said. "Jacobs didn't so much win a game as force the other man to lose," wrote Tyson biographer Monteith Illingworth. "He played to emasculate."

All of which was fine by D'Amato, who took no small satisfaction in warning Mailer: "He's seen so many movies, he knows more about Floyd's fights than I do. He can beat *me* in an argument."

By then—1962—the bicoastal Jacobs was fully enmeshed in Big Fights as an editor, producer, and procurer of rare footage. What's more, Jacobs had found in D'Amato not merely the most influential of his mentors but also, through the 1960s, his New York roommate. One wonders how two confirmed bachelors, thirtysomething and fiftysomething, would pass the time. "We discuss my favorite subject, fear," D'Amato told *Sports Illustrated*. "Jimmy is one of the few people who have a good grasp of fear. Like me, he feels that fear is necessary for the success of an athlete."

Disciples come; disciples go. Sometimes the arrival of one necessitates the departure of another. D'Amato spent years wondering about Patterson's estrangement, trying to find a reason. Decades would pass before Patterson finally explained himself to *Sports Illustrated*'s Michael Leahy: "There was a man close to Cus who had taken money from me—so

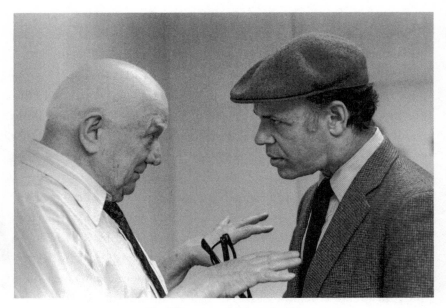

Cus D'Amato and Jimmy Jacobs

close that I knew it wouldn't do any good to tell Cus, that nothing good could come from telling him."

Patterson was referring to Jacobs and the film he had screened for Mailer.

In 1962, Jacobs cut a deal—an oral agreement, actually, struck in D'Amato's presence—for a documentary on Patterson's career. The heavyweight champion was to be paid for on-camera interviews and promised a percentage of the profits for an hour-long retrospective on his career. It aired on syndicated stations across the United States and perhaps foreign markets as well.

Patterson didn't get a penny, though.

"Expenses ate up all the profits, Floyd," Jacobs told him.

Thirty years later, Patterson was still pissed off. So Leahy, the *Sports Illustrated* reporter, went to Cayton. "The memory can play tricks," said Cayton, dismissing Patterson's recollection. "We have signed contracts from 1962, you see."

As it happened, Leahy insisted on just that, seeing for himself.

They weren't contracts, though. They were merely letters of agreement signed only by D'Amato, granting Big Fights, Inc., the rights to Patterson's life story for the sum of one dollar.

While the arrangement proved worthless to Patterson, it might have been valuable to Tyson as a warning, had he known. The same guy who ripped off Patterson—with Cayton as a silent partner—would soon become, after D'Amato, the most important adult in Tyson's life. Jacobs was the man most responsible for spreading—actually, *selling* would be more accurate—the gospel of Cus and Mike. It was all part of D'Amato's grand design. Unfortunately, the old man had no greater grasp of Jacobs's bullshit than of his own. No sooner had Cus entrusted Jacobs with the eventual management and promotion of fourteen-year-old Mike than Jacobs started keeping secrets from the boy.

10

On September 2, 1980, Tyson was released from Tryon to a supervised parole under D'Amato's care. If Lorna Mae had misgivings about her youngest child moving upstate, or her failures as a mother, it didn't keep her from signing the requisite papers. Tyson was fourteen. "My life begins here," he said.

His new world was stocked with the unfamiliar. Starting with the rosebushes. A grandfather clock and a fireplace. Wallpaper. A dining room. A *pantry*. There were bats. And possums. And there were white people, in a constellation revolving around the old man, with white people's hair and freckles and scars and accents.

Cus would pad around the house in a checked flannel bathrobe, eating tuna sandwiches, watching *Barney Miller* and *M*A*S*H*. He commandeered the house phone, snatching it from the cradle on the first ring, barking "hello" with an exuberant growl. He sounded like the trainer in *Rocky*, though it was Burgess Meredith who had tried to sound like D'Amato. His room was on the second floor, directly across from Camille's. The strictest commandment of life in the big white house was a prohibition against entering his quarters. Occasionally, D'Amato would deign to speak to one of the boys through a crack in the door. Upon leaving his room, he'd rig the door with matches, letting him know if anyone

Cus and the Kid, 1981

had tried to gain access in his absence. All the kids knew that he kept a rifle in that room. One morning, Tyson came down for breakfast and saw D'Amato, rifle in tow, crawling across the living room floor, army style.

Dinners were a big deal. Camille cooked; the old man presided. He knew, at a given moment, the pantry's exact inventory. He clocked what everybody ate. There were strict limits. Except for the new heavyweight. The old man loved watching him eat.

"One night I get home and there's no food," says Frankie Mincieli, then hoping to turn pro as a featherweight. "Frickin' Mike ate my spaghetti and meatballs. I'm working two shit jobs—ShopRite and the gas station—to pay my rent there, and Cus says, 'It's okay. He's gonna be heavyweight champ of the world.'"

Mincieli, from South Brooklyn, was Tyson's roommate. "When Mike first got there, his underwear had like seven hundred holes—like mice had been eating them," he says. "But he looked like he just came out of the men's prison."

Aside from Mincieli, whose father used to shine D'Amato's shoes outside the Gramercy Gym, the Catskill regulars included Billy Hamm, age nine. Billy lived mostly with his parents in a trailer but stayed over whenever he could. Then there was Jay Bright, gentle and obese, with a fixation on Muhammad Ali, which is how he met Jimmy Jacobs. Jacobs let him watch Ali's old fights on the Big Fights office projector. Bright had lost his mother first, when he was eleven. His father passed less than a year after that, then his older brother. Jacobs asked D'Amato to take him in. Bright was twelve—385 pounds with a fifty-six-inch waist—when he came to the white house for good. By the time Tyson arrived, Bright was twenty and had shed more than two hundred pounds. Bright messed around in the gym on occasion. But mostly he'd be remembered with merciless derision by Rooney and Atlas for baking quiche and blueberry pies with Camille.

As for Rooney, he was still undefeated as a pro, scourge of the Catholic Youth Center in Scranton, Pennsylvania, where he collected nine of his first fourteen wins. Rooney had recently concluded a stint as a sparring partner for Roberto Durán, who trained at nearby Grossinger's for his first fight with Sugar Ray Leonard. It was a point of great pride at the house how Rooney held his own with the great one known as "Hands of Stone." Still, while the ascending Rooney was known as D'Amato's fighter, it was Atlas who worked Rooney's corner.

To meet Atlas is, inevitably, to wonder about that scar. As he used to tell me, in his own very Cus-like way, the wounds themselves are less frightening than the stories our imaginations invent about them. Still, this one required four hundred stitches to close and must have made an impression on Tyson.

Atlas was another of D'Amato's good works. He was facing armed robbery and gun charges when the old man showed up in a Staten Island courtroom, the final witness on sentencing day, theatrically humble, telling his honor that Teddy, whom he had met through Rooney and trained as a fighter for the Adirondack Golden Gloves, was loyal and brave and could be of help to a great many people if only given the chance. D'Amato began to weep. Then the court officers got a little moist. Finally, the judge released Atlas into D'Amato's custody.

From day one, that was the plan for Tyson, too.

——————

"WHAT THE WHITE DUDE WANT TO DO WITH THE BLACK KID?" TYSON would ask.

At first, everything in his young self impelled him to consider the old man a perv, a degenerate. You didn't have to be a little con to understand no one gives you shit for free. And why did the old man come in his room at night, wake him up to continue with the day's lecture? Was he being groomed?

Still, he eagerly accepted the gifts: the praise, the flowers, even a copy of Nat Fleischer's *The Ring: Record Book and Boxing Encyclopedia*. Starting that first night, while the other boys slept in Elmwood Cottage, Tyson pored through that hefty volume as if deep in Talmudic study, reading, as best he could, memorizing the images, absorbing their stories, descendants of Hebrews and Hibernians, Germans and Negroes, men who'd survived their own Brownsvilles, their own abandoned buildings, only to prosper and conquer and be adored: Benny Leonard, Jack Dempsey, Henry Armstrong, Harry Greb, Jack Johnson.

It was just the beginning of Tyson's indoctrination. He surrendered fully to the stories of those men.

"I got turned out real bad," he would recall.

Turned out. Of all the ways to describe his emerging enthusiasm, the birth of this new life, he uses the most jailhouse verb there is.

Those first few months, Bobby Stewart would drive Tyson to Catskill and he'd stay the weekend. The gym above the police station was roomy, with a mirror for shadowboxing and heavy bags suspended by thick chains. The floorboards were worn dull. The ring was just a single step up, under a bank of fluorescent lights. Behind it was a gallery with chairs and a bench, backed by a wall with fight posters and news clippings, many of them small entries of local kids winning trophies. It's always a wonder how boxing reveres its minor histories. To the side was a small stage, suitable for an elementary school play. It contained yet another heavy bag, a speed bag, and, on either side of the radiator, a mounted mattress wrapped around a girder. Each bore a crude, faded anatomical outline with numbers designating targets: head, liver, ribs, solar plexus, and so on. A concept of the old man's devising, D'Amato called it "the Willie," after Willie Pastrano, whom José Torres beat for his first, long-overdue title in 1965. Back in the day, D'Amato would bark out a series of numbers, and the fighter would respond with a corresponding combination. Now it was Atlas doing most of the barking.

In the months after his release to D'Amato's custody, Atlas began experiencing severe back pain. The old man then decided—actually, *decreed* might be more like it—that Atlas should be a trainer. "If you take a boy and teach him to fight from beginning to end, part of you is in him, too," D'Amato would tell him. "So that when he fights, part of you is in that ring."

It took a while. Atlas retreated to Staten Island, where he'd engage in yet more robberies and bloody brawls. But eventually, he returned to Catskill.

"Suddenly, I discovered he had a real talent for teaching," D'Amato said of Atlas. "This fellow was a born teacher. And he was the type of person that wants to help people, especially kids. And they come to depend on him and rely on him a great deal."

Going back to his days at the Gramercy Gym, D'Amato had always employed trusted lieutenants for the day-to-day training of his fighters. Patterson had Dan Florio. José Torres had Joe Fariello. Across the years, D'Amato's trainers each had their gifts and their vices, typically drinking and gambling. Atlas liked to gamble, too, as I recall, but his real weakness was like a flip of the coin: heads, his aching ego; tails, his violent pride. Still, his deficiencies of temperament paled in comparison with his preternatural gifts as a strategist and a psychologist.

As the decade came to a close, Atlas found himself responsible for an eclectic stable of fighters. Not only was he training his friend, the aspiring pro Rooney, but now he was doing his own good works, mentoring kids who ranged in age from grade school to high school, many of them profoundly damaged.

Certainly the arrangement between D'Amato and Atlas burnished the old man's reputation for spotting and cultivating young talent, be

Teddy Atlas working with Billy Hamm, 1981

they fighters or trainers. For D'Amato, all was as it should be. But for Atlas? His nature was excessive to start. Add to that the ego one needs to be a fighter, not to mention the vanity of an angry young man. You don't just tuck all that away in a cubbyhole.

Still, the potential for conflict between master and apprentice wasn't apparent until Tyson arrived. I'm sure Fariello and Florio bitched about the ratio of man-hours to glory as well. But it soon became clear that this was different, more intense. Time was shorter and the stakes higher. Atlas was still starting out, seen as a kid who worked with boys. But D'Amato, at seventy-two, almost half a century older, was immersed in his last, desperate mission: writing his epitaph. As he told Camille, "This is the one I've been waiting for all my life."

THERE WASN'T MUCH SPARRING AT FIRST. ATLAS WOULD PUT TYSON through his paces, then leave him a captive audience for D'Amato. They could go on for hours, these private tutorials. It began, no surprise, with D'Amato's discourses on fear, followed by lectures on what it meant to be a "a pro." There were countless nights spent in the attic watching old fight films projected onto a hanging sheet, animating legends Tyson first learned of in *The Ring*. He might've been thirteen, but the comparison was always explicit. The endgame in studying legends was to become one yourself.

D'Amato's syllabus included the book Mailer had given him, *Zen in the Art of Archery*. Then there was *Self Mastery Through Conscious Autosuggestion* by Emile Coué, a French psychologist and pharmacist, originally published in 1920. So what if Tyson couldn't get past the first page? Before long, D'Amato had adapted Coué's central affirmation as a mantra for his would-be prodigy. "The best fighter," Tyson would repeat to himself. "Nobody in the world could beat me."

This wasn't a conventional curriculum, nor did it end with now-accepted theories of detachment, visualization, or hypnosis. D'Amato believed in telepathy, claiming that he'd once *willed* Rocky Graziano to a KO victory. He was also a devoted astrologist, believing that Leos like Teddy were born leaders and that heavyweight champions tended to be born under three signs—Capricorn, Taurus, and Virgo. Good thing, then, that Tyson was a Cancer like Dempsey.

It was D'Amato—whose literary tastes ran from the *National Enquirer* (couldn't get enough UFO stories) to Ernest Becker's *The Denial of Death*—who first piqued Tyson's interest in Alexander the Great and Genghis Khan. It was D'Amato who exposed him to Machiavelli and Tolstoy (whether Tyson, still just months removed from Spofford, could actually digest these works is another question). And it was D'Amato, infinitely more captivating than any textbook in American history, who had a talent for personalizing the twentieth century. He admired Che Guevara and mourned the Rosenbergs. Roy Cohn, who not only put the Rosenbergs in the chair but also weaseled his way into the second Patterson–Johansson promotion (perhaps on behalf of his client Fat Tony Salerno), was forever a piece of shit in D'Amato's estimation. Same for the two-bit actor he had just helped elect, Ronald Reagan.

Did Tyson believe in the old man's blatherings? And if so, how much?

Well, there had to be something to them, else why would these big shots keep coming to visit? If he couldn't read Tolstoy yet, Tyson was already fluent in body language. He knew what deference and respect looked like. He saw it in the way Mailer, Hamill, Schulberg, and, more recently, Jack Newfield of *The Village Voice* conducted themselves around the old man. It wasn't just writers, though. On July 11, 1980, two FBI agents arrived in Athens.

"We sat out in D'Amato's yard, at a picnic table," recalled one of the agents, Joseph Spinelli, "and for four hours he presided like a professor of boxing history, offering a lecture on the sport's many ills."

Among those ills was the promoter these feds sought to indict, Don King. They had cause to believe King, a former numbers boss from Cleveland who'd done a stretch for manslaughter, was operating with the blessing and aid of organized crime. King was using option contracts to control fighters the same way the IBC had. King was this generation's Carbo and Blinky and Norris reconstituted as a man with a preacher-like talent for oration. Receiving his guests in the big white house, D'Amato couldn't help but sense how things had shifted. He wasn't a kook or a tax dodge anymore; he was an asset, a gray eminence, and, finally, what he had long hoped to be, the good conscience of this noir epic, boxing.

OF ALL D'AMATO'S BONA FIDES, THOUGH, NONE LIKELY IMPRESSED Tyson more than his ability to get Muhammad Ali on the phone. Ali and D'Amato had a jovial history, appearing together in a 1970 Jimmy Jacobs documentary, *a.k.a. Cassius Clay*, and on *Wide World of Sports* with Howard Cosell. If the boxing world dismissed D'Amato as a has-been, Ali still thought him a sage. In 1974, he sought the old man's advice on how to fight the younger, much-feared, heavily favored George Foreman.

"You must turn his strength into a weakness," said D'Amato. "Your first punch must be one of devastating tenacity, Muhammad."

Devastating tenacity? I want to make sure I have the words right.

"What did I say?" bellows Gene Kilroy, long Ali's right-hand man.

"Cus said 'devastating tenacity.' I was on the line. Those were his exact words. Cus understood Foreman was a bully, like Liston. That's how you beat a bully, by hitting him first, making *him* scared."

Nobody had lasted more than a couple of rounds with Foreman for years. But sure enough, when the opening bell rang in Zaire, Ali made sure to hit him first, a left hook followed by a stiff right hand. Statement made. Ali's eighth-round knockout of Foreman at the "Rumble in the Jungle" ranks among boxing's greatest upsets.

But six years later, on October 3, 1980, D'Amato had Kilroy get Ali on the phone and proceeded to give the Greatest a tongue-lashing in earshot of Tyson. "How did you let that bum beat you, Muhammad?" the old man hollered. "He's a BUM!"

The "bum" in question, Larry Holmes, was the best heavyweight in the world for seven straight years. He was tough, possessed of a devastating jab, and just then entering his prime. Ali was thirty-eight, was fat, and hadn't fought in two years.

Batteries of tests at the Mayo Clinic produced mixed results. But Ali was plainly diminished. His speech was slurry. Still, the Nevada Athletic Commission, prodded by Holmes's promoter, Don King, saw fit to let him fight. Proclamations of Ali's ageless vigor shouldn't have been any more convincing than the jet-black hair dye he'd been using. Tim Witherspoon, one of Ali's sparring partners, feared for his life against Holmes. In the weeks leading up to the fight, Ali took to popping thyroid meds and diet pills like Tic Tacs. Then, with just days to go, he collapsed after his morning run and was hospitalized for dehydration. Still the show went on, a frightful beating that yielded two shameful moments never before seen in Ali's career. In the ninth, the Greatest was heard to yelp with pain. After the tenth, his corner threw in the towel.

Now, whatever Ali told him, Cus wasn't buying. "Don't tell me that. He's a bum," said D'Amato. "Why did you let that bum hit you like that?"

A bum. The old man was still furious.

The night before, D'Amato had taken Tyson and some of the other boys to Albany to watch the fight on closed-circuit television. Now, each *bum*—the ancient fighter's slur—felt like a slap to Tyson, for whom Ali would ever be the superhero of Spofford. Tyson began to weep.

Then D'Amato shifted the conversation, revealing his likely purpose here. "I have this young Black kid with me," he told Ali. "Make sure you tell him to listen to me, Ali, all right? He's almost fifteen and he's going to be champ of the world. He's just a boy, but he's going to be the heavyweight champion of the world. His name is Mike Tyson. Talk to him for me, please, Muhammad. I want you to tell him to listen to me."

Mike took the receiver. "I'm sorry for what happened to you," he said.

The slurring Ali blamed it on the meds.

"Don't worry, champ," Tyson told him. "When I get big, I'm going to get him for you."

Tyson was three months past his fourteenth birthday. He hadn't yet fought an amateur bout. Holmes had already beaten Ken Norton and Earnie Shavers (twice) and wouldn't lose for another five years. Still, this all seemed perfectly rational to D'Amato.

"You have to dismantle that man," he'd tell Tyson. "That's our goal, to dismantle this man and relinquish him from the championship."

For all his supposed grasp of boxing history, especially his scorn of the option contract, D'Amato remained willfully blind to what had really happened. As Holmes's exclusive promoter, King now controlled the heavyweight division, historically boxing's greatest source of profit. What's more, he shorted Ali $1.2 million on the agreed-upon purse. Ali sued, in what seemed like a pretty clear-cut case. But King believed that even the greatest fighters were powerless before stacks of cash. So he dispatched Jeremiah Shabazz, from Ali's inner circle, with a suitcase containing $50,000.

Shabazz was both respected and feared. He'd led Philadelphia's Mosque No. 12, which had strong ties to an infamous criminal syndicate, the Black Mafia. Shabazz would come to despise King and regret delivering, not just the suitcase but also the agreement that came with it.

Don't give him the money until he signs it, King instructed him.

For fifty grand, Ali not only dropped his million-dollar lawsuit but also gave King an option on his next fight.

YOU DON'T SUDDENLY TRANSFORM A KID, THOUGH—CERTAINLY NOT *this* kid—just because you will it so. This wasn't telepathy. Underneath the facade of Tyson's *yes, sir–no, ma'am* manners, there remained an unwashed thief just off the streets. He went through Atlas's wallet—needing money for reefer, he said—just as he'd stolen from Lorna's lovers. He could overhear the nascent conflict through the walls.

"It has to be him," Atlas said of Tyson.

"It's not," D'Amato insisted.

It's Atlas who put it on the record, that which the others would like to ignore: The kid smelled. His feet stank. Body odor announced him before he entered a room. He thought he was being slick, splashing himself with cologne after a workout. "I got angry and told him to take a shower," Atlas recalled.

One day Atlas found Camille crying. "I just told Mike he smelled and to wash," she told him. "He said, 'Fuck you, you piece of shit.'"

Camille implored him not to tell Cus.

Teddy was halfway up the stairs when D'Amato appeared. "Don't do nothing," said the old man. "I'll take care of it."

OF ALL D'AMATO'S DISCIPLES, PERHAPS HIS MOST DEVOUT IS A woman named Nadia Hujtyn. She will defend him, quite ably, by any means necessary—intellectually, psychiatrically, even, if necessary, astrologically.

"Yes, Cus did go by the signs as far as a fighter's basic characteristics," she says. "But there are always exceptions. For instance, Durán is a Gemini, not great for a fighter."

And Tyson?

"Typical Cancer," she says. "They're all about what they feel. The problem is, in boxing, it can't be about what you feel. You have to put all that away."

Hujtyn met Rooney in 1978, during a production of *A Streetcar Named*

Desire at Columbia-Greene Community College. He played Stanley. She played Stella. He suggested coming by to watch him spar. Kevin was funny and charismatic and charming, even if his baggage—the father and the drinking and the gambling—was plain to see. Still, she fell in love—not with Rooney but with the gym itself, the energy of the fighters at their workstations, the Sisyphean beauty of mere mortals training on the Willie, where the goal was a five-punch combination in two fifths of a second.

"As soon as I walked through the door," she recalls, "I knew it was where I wanted to be."

It took a while, but eventually she overcame D'Amato's prejudice against girls in the gym and began to train as a fighter herself. First, she earned D'Amato's grudging acceptance and, later, his respect. Her work ethic was formidable, but she also saw things that guys tended to miss.

"Teddy was always jealous of Kevin," she says. "He thought everybody liked Kevin more."

There is no love lost between her and Atlas. As for Tyson, if men saw him as an angry kid with an overdeveloped musculature, Nadia saw something else. Yes, he was manipulative and immature. But he was also a beaten puppy. He insisted on touching you, constantly. He wasn't fresh, not yet. He was needy.

"He wanted the comfort of physical contact," says Hujtyn. "He was just so desperate for that."

Hujtyn is a longtime trainer herself now, though that's not the kind of remark you're likely to hear from a trainer. "I've been doing this for forty years," she says. "I see what most of these guys are looking for: the father they never had."

Of course. Maybe they want to best the figurative Papa, beat him, or kill him in some symbolic way. Perhaps they just seek his respect. Certainly that was the case with Kevin, whose father was a drunk, and Teddy, who's spoken at length about feeling ignored by his father, and perhaps Nadia, too, as her father died when she was thirteen. Tyson, as well. They all wanted D'Amato as a father figure. But in Tyson's case, that was just the beginning.

"He wanted it *all*," she says. "He wanted a mother, always. He wanted the family he didn't have. He was always trying to get it but never realized it was too late."

She recalls a night not long after he arrived. Tyson was sprawled on the couch, hugging a blanket. He was thirteen, and Nadia still a stranger.

"Would you tuck me in?" he asked.

I find myself anticipating the punch line, that her anecdote won't end nicely.

". . . And?"

"And I tucked him in," she says.

Oh.

"He needed that showing of affection, to know that you cared," she says.

"He always slept on the couch?" I ask.

"Correct," she says. "Do you know why?"

"I have my theory," I say, flashing on Lorna.

"Because he wanted to feel something around him," she says. "I think it was really the structure of the couch. There was a back. There were sides. He was tucked in. He was safe. He was protected."

Tyson and Nadia Hujtyn

11

By the time he got on the phone with Tyson, Ali had long since crossed that vast desert in the American imagination, from heel to hero. If the Holmes fight had aged the man himself, the notion of him remained largely as it had been since he beat Foreman. Ali was a prince. The erstwhile Muslim revolutionary had seduced Middle America. Ali was pretty, and Ali was loved—all that Tyson, his sudden and unlikely fourteen-year-old avenger, could never imagine himself to be.

"I was short and ugly and I had a speech impediment," writes Tyson, dismissing any comparison with Ali.

Rather, Tyson found something kindred—a version of what, in fact, he could become—on the night of July 29, 1980, when ABC's *Wide World of Sports* rebroadcast Roberto Durán's now week-old victory over Sugar Ray Leonard. Leonard had been packaged in a way that belied his true toughness: as an Ali lite, handsome and light-skinned, without the encumbrances of religious or political affiliation. Like Ali, he was trained by Angelo Dundee. Leonard did the shuffle like Ali. He had an Olympic gold medal like Ali. But unlike the Greatest, whose prime some years before granted him only the chance to sell ghetto roach spray, Sugar Ray's likeness could be found on a Wheaties box.

Tyson, still just months removed from Spofford, could no more

envision himself on a Wheaties box than Liston could've imagined playing Santa. It was Durán with whom Tyson instantly identified.

"He was just a street guy," said Tyson. "He'd say stuff to his opponents like 'Suck my fucking dick, you motherfucker.' . . . *Man, this guy is
me*, I thought."

Durán was a *pelao*, a feral urchin from Panama City who knew how
to use a newspaper for a blanket. While still a juvenile, he was sent to a
men's prison for breaking a cop's jaw. On the night of November 23, 1969,
as an eighteen-year-old featherweight who'd just gone 14-0, he won a bet
by knocking down a horse with a single punch. On March 2, 1975, after
watching his convulsing opponent carried off in a stretcher, he did indeed tell the press: "Today I sent him to the hospital. Next time I'll put
him in the morgue." The crowds on the streets of Panama City would
part when Durán took his pet lion for a stroll.

"There was an animal inside me," Durán told his biographer, George
Diaz. "The worst thing you could do with me was be scared, because I'd
smell that fear."

That's what Tyson had homed in on and what his convict self admired. Durán was your nightmare cellmate, the fighter who poked at
your imagination.

I REMEMBER VIVIDLY TEDDY'S SERMONS ON THE PSYCHOLOGY OF
the bully, as most of it wound up in a flimsy first novel. Teddy, I learned,
was like Cus; you had to listen in installments ranging between sixty and
ninety minutes—which I did, devoutly, in a smoke-filled studio on Mer-
cer Street. They were a revelation, at least to my desperately ambitious
thirty-year-old self, explaining everything from Kenny Santiago kicking
my ass outside P.S. 33 to Ali's manner of dispatching bullies—first Liston, then Foreman—with such aplomb. The bully was only as terrifying
as you imagined him to be (by the 3:00 p.m. bell, Kenny seemed pretty
scary to me); but the real fighter—*a pro*, as Teddy would say—had faith
in himself. The bully depended more on his ability to project fear than
on his fists. A pro could detach the bully from his rep. To me, these Teddy

talks comprised a secular theology, a clear and compelling argument that, all things being relatively equal, the better fighter would be the one possessed of a higher character. It was thrilling and, as I'd eventually learn, all taken verbatim from Cus. For all D'Amato's noble precepts, though, there's a central contradiction running through his life's work. He raised his last best hope to be a bully.

AFTER BOBBY STEWART, TYSON'S FIRST REGULAR SPARRING PART-
ner was Lennie Daniels. Daniels was already a grown man, a decade older than Tyson and about to become a state trooper, likely the first Black cop Tyson ever met, which he did in the kitchen at Cus and Camille's.

"I'm trying to be nice, and Tyson's just glaring at me," says Daniels. "Letting me know he's from Brooklyn and I shouldn't be touching him and he wasn't scared to look me in the eye. It was actually kind of hilarious."

D'Amato pulled Lennie aside. "How old you think he is?"

"Seventeen?"

He was thirteen.

"I think he's lying, Cus," said Lennie. "He's saying he's that young just to stay out of state prison."

Daniels was an exceptional and determined athlete, over two hundred pounds, a three-sport star in high school. He was the star running back on Lehigh University's 1977 Division II national championship team and invited to try out for the Cleveland Browns. Still, he ranks his rounds with Tyson among his very proudest moments. In the years to come, he'd watch seasoned professionals leave after a day with Tyson. But in all their rounds, more than a hundred, Lennie never went down.

Not that Tyson didn't try. Even when admonished to take it easy on his sparring partners, he'd sneak in a hard shot. As Atlas recalls in his memoir, "He would damage these guys."

Among them was a heavyweight prospect six years Tyson's senior. Willie Campudoni was a good-looking heavyweight whom José Torres hoped to manage as a pro. It wasn't sparring with Tyson that sent Campudoni back to Spanish Harlem, though. It was merely waiting for those rounds, thinking about them. Tyson would start in on him the night before at dinner. He knew Willie loved Camille's chicken thighs, but always made it a point to snatch the last one. Then he'd remind Willie they'd be going at it tomorrow. "You want to know what happens when he does that to me?" Campudoni told Torres. "I get fucking diarrhea on the spot."

AS DYSTOPIAS GO, THE SOUTH BRONX WAS EVEN MORE ICONIC THAN Brownsville. Not only had it spawned so feared a street fighter as Mitch "Blood" Green of the Black Spades, but successive American presidents visited the neighborhood, Jimmy Carter in 1977 and Ronald Reagan, still a candidate, in August 1980, when he likened the South Bronx to "London after the Blitz." That same year, Tyson arrived in the Bronx for his inaugural bout, an unsanctioned "smoker" at the Apollo Boxing Club on Westchester Avenue.

The stairs leading up to the fight club were strewn with junkies and smelled of piss. The structure shook as 2 and 5 trains rumbled past on the el that ran along the back of the building. Through the sooty windows, you could see sparks off the tracks. The smokers were a party, though: boom boxes spraying the Salsoul Orchestra, plenty of rum and beer, fried plantains, rice, pork, and chicken, men in guayabera shirts waving billfolds to wager on the fates of frightened children.

Matchmaking was done on site, a barter of deceit, as trainers would routinely lie about their kids' ages and experience.

"I'm looking for a hundred and thirty-one pounds."

"I got a hundred and forty pounds. He never fight before."

"Lemme see."

"A slave-market atmosphere," wrote a correspondent for *Inside Sports*.

Presiding over this bedlam was Nelson Cuevas, one of D'Amato's old fighters from the Gramercy. "Nelson would have two pistols on him—a thirty-eight in his waistband and another in his jacket, a twenty-five," recalls Greg Vicenty, a two-time Golden Gloves champ out of the nearby Fort Apache Boxing Club. "And a knife. Nelson would cut you in a heartbeat."

Everybody seems to remember the night Teddy got into a fight and Cuevas broke a trophy over the other guy's head. What stands out to Tyson, though, was his Apollo debut. He was fourteen by then. It took a while to get him a fight, as no one believed that was his age. But eventually Atlas found a guy. He was seventeen or eighteen, Puerto Rican with a prominent Afro, and could more than handle himself. Tyson knew it, too, having seen him in action the week before. By fight night, thinking about Puerto Rican Afro guy had rendered Tyson a nervous wreck. The night of the fight, he slipped out before his name was called.

"I sat on the steps leading up to the elevated line and thought that maybe I should hop on that car, get out at Rockaway Avenue, and walk three blocks to my mom's house," he writes in *Iron Ambition*. "I was scared of getting beat up, I was scared of letting people down, but it all came down to the fact that I didn't want to be humiliated."

Tyson would credit D'Amato's lessons—that even the great ones were frightened—for enabling him to go back in and fight. Others remember differently. Bruce Silverglade, owner of Gleason's Gym, recalls, "Teddy Atlas literally had to coax Mike into leaving the dressing room and getting into the ring."

The first two rounds made for a hell of a fight. In the third, Tyson caught the older kid against the ropes. The coup de grâce was an upper-cut; an arc of sweat rose off the much-remembered Afro and into the crowd, followed by the mouthpiece, which landed six rows back.

A fighter out cold—as the Afro guy was—carries at least a sugges-tion of death. Those moments freeze, as if a study for a painting.

The crowd went wild, of course. Cuevas ordered Tyson to a neutral corner.

Then Tyson, with the Afro guy motionless at his feet, found his inner Durán. He stepped on him.

D'AMATO DIDN'T ATTEND ANY OF TYSON'S FIGHTS UNTIL MAY 27, 1981, at the Catholic Youth Center in Scranton, Pennsylvania. Rooney would raise his record to 14-0 that night, winning by unanimous decision in

Tyson, fifteen, after his first official amateur bout

the co–main event. But amateurs would start the evening, with Tyson facing a seventeen-year-old from nearby Kingston, right across the Susquehanna River. His name was Billy O'Rourke, a senior from Wyoming Valley West High School, and D'Amato made it a point to seek him out before the fight. He was sitting alone on the bleachers.

"Billy? I need to talk to you."

O'Rourke looked up. He didn't know too much about Cus D'Amato, just that he was from New York and looked like Yoda from *Star Wars*. "You're a good-looking boy, nice kid," D'Amato began. "I'm sure you have a good career ahead of you. I just don't want you running into a buzz saw."

Buzz saw?

"Michael is going to be champion of the world," D'Amato said matter-of-factly. *Champeen of the woild*, in the old man's vintage accent. "He's a killer. A monster."

Billy was studying the old man, thinking: *No one does this.*

"He's hurting grown men," D'Amato said grimly. "Everyone's afraid to fight him. I just want you to know so you're ready. You need to be very careful."

Soon Tyson came by. The old man introduced him.

"Hi. Howyadoin," he said softly.

For a killer from Brooklyn, thought Billy, he looked sort of regular. They weighed about the same, two hundred pounds. At six two, though, Billy could see he had about four or five inches on him. And that lisping soprano! *There's no bass in this guy's voice*, he thought. Forty-two years later, I ask Billy O'Rourke, now a retired correctional officer, why the kindly old man was trying to get in his head.

"He wasn't," Billy insists. "He was really trying to warn me."

Had to be frightening, a warning like that. I wonder what Billy was thinking as he left to get his hands wrapped.

"I'm like, *I'm gonna destroy this guy.*"

Tyson was officially 4-0 at the time, not including the smokers at the Apollo. But all his fights had ended pretty much the same, by knockout, most of them in the first round. All he knew of O'Rourke was his ostensible role in this play—the white guy—and, from his immersive studies in boxiana, the presumption against white heavyweights going back more than seventy years to Jack Johnson and the exhortations of yet another popular American writer, who urged former champ Jim Jeffries to come out of retirement and avenge the indignities Jack Johnson had heaped upon the white race. "Jeff, it's up to you," wrote Jack London.

Good thing, then, that London wasn't there for the first round. As it began, Tyson loaded up on a big, wide left hook, gathering great torque from the twist in his torso. Billy saw it coming. He knew exactly what to do and readied his right glove firmly by his chin. Boxing 101: He'd catch the hook on his glove, then shoot back with a hook–right hand–hook combination of his own.

Billy caught the hook, only it wasn't like any other shot he ever caught, before or since: "I blocked the punch, but it went right through my guard. He knocked me up in the frigging air."

Crazy what you remember on the way down. First it was the boxing shoes. Took Billy a moment to realize they were his own. Then the blood. There would be a lot of it that night. Then Tyson caught him with another barrage. He'd need sixteen stitches to close the gash beneath his right eye. But Billy begged the ref not to stop it.

Here, an aside, again, first explained to me by Atlas around 1991, not long after I started writing a sports column in the *New York Post*: Power is an intoxicant, not only for fans but also for fighters themselves, be they fourteen-year-old boys or heavyweight champions like George Foreman. The question, then—a test of the fighter's character, really—is what happens when you come across an opponent who takes your best shot and doesn't—my favorite Atlas word here—*submit*. It depends on the fighter, of course. Is he a bully or a pro? The bully's pulse will quicken. His breath gets short. He starts to think, then doubt himself. Soon enough, he's envisioning his own humiliation. The longer this goes on, the greater the chance he'll find a way to quit.

No doubt this was a test for a kid already touted as a future heavyweight champ. The results, however, remain subject to interpretation or, perhaps, dueling autobiographies. Tyson's account is straightforward enough: an unexpectedly grueling fight between him and "this crazy psycho white boy" who kept getting up. The second round he recalls quite reasonably as "a war." Before the third, Atlas reminded him how he'd spoken of being a great fighter, like the legends they'd studied on film in the attic: "Now is the time. . . . Keep jabbing and move your head." Tyson remembers knocking down O'Rourke twice more. As it ended, though, bloody Billy had him against the ropes and was waling away. If the fans loved it, D'Amato was more measured. "One more round," he told Tyson, "and he would have worn you down."

While Atlas's account makes little mention of D'Amato, it's lengthier and heavy with the kind of savagely inspirational oration for which Teddy would become famous. As in Tyson's recollection, O'Rourke is mere stereotype, almost an abstraction: big, unskilled, tough, white. At the end of the first, after dropping him twice, Tyson returns to the corner and diagnoses himself with a broken hand.

Atlas recalls grabbing the hand in question, squeezing it tight, and giving a speech. It begins with "The only thing broken is you" and ends with the trainer pushing his fighter back into the ring, whereupon Tyson drops O'Rourke twice more. After the second, Tyson returned to the corner and declared, "I can't go on."

"You can't go on?" Atlas recalls saying. "I thought you wanted to be a fighter. I thought you had this dream of being heavyweight champion. Let me tell you something. This is your heavyweight title fight. . . . You bullshit artist. You've been with us all this time, saying you want to be champ, and everything's fine when you're knocking guys out. But now, for the first time, a guy doesn't want to be knocked out, a guy has the balls to get up, and you want to quit? You know what I'd be doing if I was in that other guy's corner? I'd be stopping the fight. That's how beat up this guy is, and you want to quit! Now get up, goddamn it!"

That's a lot to tell a fourteen-year-old between rounds. Nevertheless, Atlas again picked him up off the stool and sent him out once more. When he saw that Tyson was ready to quit again, Atlas got up on the ring apron and admonished him to hang on, which, in an apparent miracle, he managed to do.

"It was a watershed moment for him, a real defining moment," Atlas concludes. "Because if he had quit then, he might never have become Mike Tyson."

They're an interesting exercise in counterpoint, Teddy's and Tyson's accounts. Looking back, though, Billy O'Rourke's seems the most reliable. "I'm not calling anyone a liar," he tells me. "But I was there. I should know. I sparred more than a thousand rounds and had I don't know how many fights. I was wobbled a couple of times. But I was only down once in my entire career."

That was the first round with Tyson at the Catholic Youth Center. What none of them ever cared to know—neither Tyson nor Atlas nor D'Amato—was what kind of athlete Billy O'Rourke actually was. He'd been wrestling since fourth grade and had just knocked out the fourth-ranked heavyweight in the country. He could run eighteen miles in two and a half hours. Triathlons? No problem. Billy O'Rourke didn't have a father, but he did have a coach, like Tyson, who also assured him he'd go to the top. But while Tyson was sparring with Lennie Daniels, Billy was already at Deer Lake, Pennsylvania, where Ali was preparing for Holmes. He'd sparred with Ali. He'd been in with Tim Witherspoon, who in 1984 would win the WBC heavyweight title, and Brownsville's own, Eddie Mustafa Muhammad, who'd just lost his light heavyweight belt to Michael Spinks.

"I've been hit dead square in the face by Ali and Witherspoon," he says. "It didn't really hurt me. But Mike? Mike *hurt* me."

In the second round, as Tyson became visibly tired, O'Rourke faked a jab and shot his right hand. It was maybe two inches from impact when Tyson came back with a hook to the body, followed, with the same hand, by an uppercut. It would become one of Tyson's signature combinations, but O'Rourke remains less awed by the power than by the quickness.

Waiting for the third round, he recalls, "that's when Teddy Atlas and Mike Tyson were having problems, 'cause Mike didn't want to fight no more. He kept saying he hurt his hand. Was it as dramatic as Teddy makes it sound? I didn't see it that way. I just thought Mike was doubting himself a little."

When it was over, Tyson whispered in Billy's ear: "I think you won."

"Did you?" I ask him.

"It was a split decision. A lot of hometown people had me winning the fight. But I was there, Mark. I didn't win that fight."

JESUS CARLOS ESPARZA WAS SIX WHEN HIS MOTHER STRAPPED A shoebox over his shoulder and told him to fill it with olives. The family went where the work was: from Texas to Minnesota, where they chopped weeds to make way for the sugar beet harvest, to California's Central Valley, where they stooped or stretched for whatever was in season: olives, oranges, lemons, peaches, pears, and plums. At thirteen, Esparza's most fervent wish was for a trophy, and he figured boxing would be his best shot. He was a big, strong kid who ran the three miles to the local gym and back every day. By the summer of 1981, with about fifty fights on his résumé, Esparza had qualified for the Junior Olympics. He was

215 pounds, had a decent jab and a good right hand, and prided himself on hitting hard. Though he was sixteen, his coach lied to get him into the fifteen-and-under division. It wasn't much of a favor, though, as he drew Tyson in the first round: Wednesday, June 24, in Colorado Springs, twenty-seven days after Billy O'Rourke.

Esparza arrived in Colorado Springs by Greyhound bus, almost a week before the fight. "There was a recreation area," he recalls, "and all the heavyweights were sizing each other up. But when Mike Tyson walked in we were like, 'Holy shit.' He didn't look like no fourteen-year-old."

Next day, in the mess hall, he heard a coach from New Jersey say only one fighter had ever made it to the second round with Tyson. *Could that even be true?* Esparza wondered.

They all worked out in the same gym. Tyson didn't say much, wouldn't make eye contact. Damn, he was cut up, though. "You lift?" Esparza asked.

"Push-ups," he mumbled.

They took the fighters up Pikes Peak by rail. Esparza remembers the way Tyson's eyes exploded with wonder. They didn't have deer in Brownsville.

Esparza remembers Atlas: "Real skinny. But I'll never forget that scar."

The night of the fight, Tyson was eating a giant hamburger with a mountain of fries and a large soda. It had always been impressed on Esparza never to eat heavily before a fight. He tried to convince himself he had an edge.

By the time the fight began, though, Tyson had become savagely animated, coming out with that frenetic D'Amato dance, gloves at his cheeks, head moving side to side like a pendulum. Wasn't that hard to hit, though. Esparza caught him with a couple jabs. Then a right. Then another.

"I thought they would hurt him," he says. "But they just seemed to piss him off."

Then Tyson hit Esparza, put a jab on his chest. "Knocked me right on my ass," he says. "I remember getting off the canvas, thinking, *What the hell was that?*"

Esparza tried to fight back, but his straight shots didn't seem to have much effect. Tyson kept whaling away. Finally, Esparza found himself against the ropes. He saw it coming: a big, looping right hand. He pivoted to catch it, maybe too much. Or maybe Tyson was long and a little wild. He remembers the blow landing on his back, technically a foul. The ref was on the other side and didn't see it. But Esparza wasn't about to say anything. He couldn't even breathe.

"First time I ever had a fight stopped," he says. "I've never been hit that hard in my life."

I ask him about Atlas's bylined account in *The Daily Mail* (Catskill, New York): "Thor himself couldn't have belted out a more blunderous shot." Atlas had it over in thirty seconds.

"No," says Esparza, "I almost lasted the whole round."

It's the single consolation prize Esparza took from that week in Colorado: At least he lasted longer than the other guys. The next kid was from Texas, maybe 260 pounds. "We were all watching," says Esparza. "He was in cover-up mode the whole time. I remember he was getting the shit kicked out of him, and I remember the sound he made when Tyson kept hitting him."

A high-pitched sound. *Ooh-ooh-ooh-ooh-ooh.* "It lasted forty seconds, I think," says Esparza.

That there was a day off before the final round couldn't have helped Tyson's next opponent, Joe Cortez out of Michigan. Cortez enjoyed a reputation as a knockout artist himself. But Esparza could see him change: "He was trying to act real confident. But you could see he was nervous as hell. Now everybody started telling him, 'Oh, shit, you gotta fight the monster.'"

By now, there was a rumor going around that Tyson was Sonny Liston's nephew. To be sure, he'd already mastered the essential Liston-esque construct. "Anybody I hurt," Tyson recalled of his teenage self, "my life gets better."

Meanwhile, the fighter Cortez beat in the semis was bragging that he *let* the kid from Michigan beat him: "I knew if I won, I'd have to fight that animal Tyson."

Cortez, for his part, would come out swinging, though it wasn't much of a fight. Tyson was wild and wide. But it was over in about eleven seconds: Cortez splayed on the canvas, a doctor and an EMT hovering over him. Esparza will never forget the sight. Still, if he was awed by the Tyson he met in 1981, he thinks better of him now.

"I've worked with kids who had that same rage," says Esparza. "It just grows as they get older."

Esparza went on to get a master's in social work from Fresno State. He's worked in group homes, in women's shelters, on Indian reservations, and with Child Protective Services. I'm not exactly sure what kind of rage he means.

"I give Tyson a lot of credit for talking about being molested as a kid," he says. "I think of some of his interviews over the years and his anger, how he tried to be, you know, really masculine to hide the feelings of what he went through, his past, his memories. It all makes sense, learning his story."

I'm not sure that's much of a comfort to Joe Cortez. As the finals of the Junior Olympics were televised on ESPN, then a fledgling cable

Teddy Atlas, Tyson, and D'Amato after Tyson won his first Junior Olympic title

sports network, they've achieved a peculiar immortality, the first-dated clip in an endless video archive of Tyson the Destroyer. A Google search turns up several versions that refer to him as "an animal." They're without irony, merely intended as flattery, but they obscure what was really happening. For all the wise talk about how a fighter should deal with his fear, this fourteen-year-old boy was internalizing another lesson: how to project his fear, how to use it as a weapon.

"As my career progressed," Tyson would recall, "and people started praising me for being a savage, I knew that being called an animal was the highest praise I could receive."

12

I t was after Tyson turned fifteen later that summer that D'Amato introduced him to Friedrich Nietzsche and hypnosis. While Tyson couldn't
yet get through *Thus Spake Zarathustra*, he was more than able to repeat
whatever his mentor had identified as the philosopher's salient points. If
the Third Reich could tailor the philosopher's notion of an Übermensch
to fit its aims, then so could D'Amato. Hence, hypnosis.

D'Amato's preferred hypnotist, John Halpin, was a former social worker
with an office on Central Park West, where he treated mostly smokers,
overeaters, alcoholics, drunks, drug addicts, and the occasional fighter.
Halpin called his method "benevolent seduction." "I put him in a state
of hypnosis and we get in contact with the subconscious," he once explained of Tyson. "And we address the subject of fear."

If the techniques were Halpin's, the mantra was all D'Amato, his Nietz-
schean vision of the fighter he now needed at seventy-three years old.
"Once I was under," said Tyson, "he'd tell me whatever Cus wanted him
to say. Cus would write out 'suggestions'—commands, really—on a piece
of paper and John would recite them out loud."

What follows is a sampling from Tyson's two autobiographical volumes written with Larry Sloman.

"This is what you were actually born to do."

"Your jab is like a weapon . . . a battering ram."

When Tyson was fully under, D'Amato would take over from Halpin: "You're the best fighter that God has created. You are ferocious. Your intention is to inflict as much pain as possible."

"Your objective is to push his nose into the back of his head. You throw punches with bad intentions."

"You are a scourge from God. The world will know your name from now until the eons of oblivion."

After a while, they got to the point where D'Amato could put him under at home. "Sometimes Cus would wake me up in the middle of the night and do his suggestions," Tyson recalled. "Sometimes he didn't even have to talk, I could feel his words coming through my mind telepathically. I embraced it religiously. Cus was my God. . . .

"I can barely spell my name but I think I'm a fucking Superman."

IN 1988, WHEN I STARTED AT THE *DAILY NEWS*, THERE WAS A PREV-alent notion of D'Amato as a secular saint of New York. Jack Newfield would put him right up there with Jackie Robinson and Bobby Kennedy. I get it. New York is cynical. Newspapers were supposed to be cynical. And during a moment in the city's life when a *Times* literary critic could write earnestly of Donald Trump's "elegant simplicity" while reviewing *The Art of the Deal*, one understands the need to believe in, as you might hear at, say, the Lion's Head, *some-fucking-body*. D'Amato more than fit the bill.

I didn't set out here to diminish D'Amato's legacy. He nourished writers I'll always admire. He changed a lot of lives for the better. If it weren't for D'Amato, says Brian Hamill, "I think I would've done time." Certainly, he helped rescue Atlas from a considerably longer stretch in prison. And if their division of labor favored the old man, it was the old man who recognized what was best in Atlas and gave him a future. "He was like a father," Rooney told boxing historian Peter Heller. "He made me go back to college, get a two-year degree." If D'Amato thought of

Rooney as merely a fighter—as most trainers and managers inevitably look upon their fighters—that wouldn't have happened.

Still, consider Tyson at fifteen: victim and victimizer, habitually incarcerated. "The most insecure young man I've ever met," said Halpin, echoing Bobby Stewart's first impression.

Do you really want to tell that kid he's a scourge from God?

Again, it's Nadia Hujtyn who delivers the most impassioned defense of D'Amato. "The theory is to help the mind work to its greatest potential," she says. "Self-doubt is a large part of what defeats you. You have to do everything you can to erase it. You have to learn to work on a different plane mentally."

In essence, you have to *stop thinking*. Take the Willie bag, for instance, and the way D'Amato drilled fighters to throw five-punch combinations in a fraction of a second. It became pure muscle memory. And that was the point.

"You have to work until it comes unbidden, until it comes without thought," she says. "It's not necessarily the fighter's conscious perception. It's what his brain recognizes in a given moment and causes his body to do."

Then what of that sacred gospel of fear and imagination?

"That's *why* you erase all doubt," she says. "You can't let that be. It's like getting knocked out; think of it as a road. But it's a road that's not open to you. It's a road you cannot go down. Your mind cannot know it even exists as an option."

That's one reason why truly great fighters—like Ali, geniuses of self-belief—tend to fall only from the punch they never see. Tyson, on the other hand, for all his diligence ("It was twenty-four seven," Nadia recalls of those early years. "He ate, drank, slept boxing."), was pathologically insecure. D'Amato knew that full well, yet he persisted with the desperate elation of a mad scientist, trying to create something that was all but impossible. He was trying to create a fighter who didn't fear.

D'Amato himself had seen only two men like that. The first was Jimmy Anest, a deaf fighter from Hackensack whom he trained at the

Gramercy. Silent Jimmy, as he was known, retired in 1948 with a record of 27-26-3. The second was Artie Diamond, who, despite a pedestrian record of 24-9, may well have been D'Amato's favorite fighter.

Diamond was posthumously glorified with a José Torres feature in *Inside Sports*: "The Toughest S.O.B. Who Ever Lived." It ran early in Tyson's second year at Catskill, and by no coincidence does Tyson delightedly re-narrate what's still called "The Artie Diamond Story" in *Iron Ambition*, his memoir of life with Cus. I heard it countless times from Teddy but never really considered the impact it had on Tyson until several years later, in 1997, after his second fight with Evander Holyfield.

Diamond, said to froth and growl on his way to the ring, usually wearing trunks embroidered with a Star of David, retired with great reluctance at D'Amato's insistence in 1952. He'd had fights stopped at the discretionary mercy of referees and ringside physicians but had never been counted out or thrown in the towel. Upon retirement, Diamond resumed his previous vocation: crime. He was soon caught for his role in an armored-car heist, which included shooting a guard in the head and leaving him paralyzed.

On his first day in the prison yard—I've heard versions in Sing Sing, Greenhaven, Auburn, and Attica—Diamond was strolling through the yard smoking a cigar when he heard someone hissing at him.

As Torres, who knew Diamond well, writes: "Artie turned slowly to face"—what else?—"a big, muscle-bound Black man who was showing his teeth as if he had just seen Raquel Welch naked." Meanwhile, an audience had gathered. "With any luck," Torres continues, "they would witness a sexual conquest right there in the yard."

The Black guy then explains that Artie can have all he wants here in prison, once he becomes the guy's wife.

Diamond nods knowingly, leans in close as if to whisper something. Then he bites, clamping down on the Black guy's ear. A howl ensues—"like a wounded beast," per Torres. Then, for the everlasting memory of those in the gallery, that they may swear ad nauseam to what they've seen, Artie Diamond spits out the bloody ear in pieces.

The Artie Diamond Story became a seminal parable for the kids at Catskill: part Grimm, part Aesop, all Cus. Makes sense, as the idea of jail and what the big Black guy represents was central in the minds of so many of them who stayed at the white Victorian mansion. As refracted through the Cusian lens, jail provided the perfect test; physicality was less important than one's ability to control one's fear and imagination. *That* was character. Teddy, in particular, made a point of recounting his Rikers experience in such terrifying detail you couldn't help but wonder if part of him was still locked up.

"Back then, in the dorms, you had to go to the correction officers to ask for toilet paper," he once told me. "I'm in the bathroom and a guy takes mine. Now I know: This is the test."

Atlas wastes no time going into the adjacent stall and delivering a frightful beating. It was an act less of rage than of righteousness, at least that's how it read in my column. "If you don't," said Teddy, "guys will take more than your toilet paper."

After twenty-four hours in the hole, Atlas returned to the dorm, where he spent his nights in a dreamless, fitful state: "You're hearing sounds you don't even want to know what you're hearing. It's the sound of people breaking. You want to put the pillow over your head, but you're scared if you do, you're not going to see the guy when he comes for you."

And he's always coming. *He.* The racial trope isn't mere coincidence, certainly not for most of the kids bunking at Cus and Camille's place in Catskill. *He* is the big Black inmate. He is Liston. He is what you fear. Is he Tyson? I don't know. Certainly, Tyson spent years trying to convince the world—opposing fighters first, then everyone else—that's who he was.

But the hero of the jail fable, in every iteration, is Artie Diamond, who proved himself scarier than the scary guy. And if you're here, in a book of Tyson stories, you can pretty much figure out where this is headed. Desperate and unhypnotized, faced with the prospect of a brutal humiliation at the hands of Evander Holyfield, Tyson made a curiously rational decision. As in most jailhouse altercations, the audience was of paramount concern. The cost of defeat wasn't a mere loss; it was being demystified. If no longer a champion, then what could Tyson salvage? Perhaps a modicum of fear. Yes, he could still be seen as one crazy motherfucker. Tyson went full Artie.

THE INTERVENING DECADES HAVE RENDERED ARTIE DIAMOND AS much of a caricature as the inmate whose ear he bit off. So I'm perplexed by a publicity still, circa 1950, that shows him near the end of his brief but exceptionally violent professional boxing career: puffy eyes, droopy left lid, a nose in the process of flattening. But his face is still as smooth as a teenager's. He couldn't have been much older than twenty, with a look that's less ferocious than forlorn.

The man who gave me the photograph, Fred Islowitz, met Diamond in 1959 at Wallkill Correctional Facility. It was a Saturday morning in a small chapel used by the handful of Jewish inmates. Artie, who'd just arrived from Auburn, was impressed by the way Fred, whose grandfather was Orthodox, read Hebrew from the Torah.

Fred, in turn, was impressed that Artie had been a main-event fighter who, like himself, hailed from the Bronx. Just eighteen, Fred was in for mugging a bodega owner with friends from his gang, the Dragons. He was constantly having to fight other inmates.

"Eventually," says Fred, "they saw I wasn't a punk."

But the testing didn't really stop until Artie showed up. Artie explained that he had been raised in an orphanage and had no family, but he nevertheless began referring to Fred as "my kid brother." Soon, Artie was training him on the bags in the prison gym.

"Just like I became a fighter to please Artie," says Fred, "I think Artie became a fighter to please someone else."

That would be D'Amato.

"Cus. That's all he ever talked about. Cus sent him packages and money every month. I'm sure he felt guilty that Artie got so hurt."

The metamorphosis already underway in the publicity still was complete by the time Artie got to Wallkill. There was a metal plate in his head, the result of his getting piped at another prison. Artie walked on his heels, in a semicrouch, as if stalking prey. His nose had been fully smashed by now, and his growl could be difficult to understand.

"He was already punchy," says Fred, whose recollection inevitably returns to Artie on the bunk in his cell, smoking a stogie, struggling to get through a bestseller, *Cash McCall*, made into a 1960 movie starring James Garner and Natalie Wood. It was not long afterward that D'Amato secured Diamond's release, telling the parole board he had a job waiting for him as José Torres's conditioning coach.

In 1976, Diamond was shot to death while working as a bouncer for a Latin club in the Bronx. His girlfriend, a Puerto Rican woman who lived on 125th Street, called Fred to "get your brother's things." Among them were the old publicity shots.

By then, Fred had become an actor and changed his surname from Islowitz to Dennis. Yet he still has difficulty reconciling his two selves— not their names so much as what they represent, before and after prison. "You take a boy, lock him in his cell, and it's a traumatic experience," he

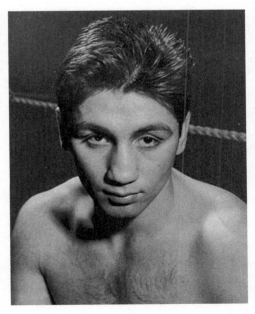

Artie Diamond, c. 1950

says. "I *know* what I'm capable of doing. It's always there, never goes away. And I'm an old man."

As for Artie? "I know Artie did a lot of bad things," he says. "But he wasn't an animal. He was a sensitive, damaged guy."

Nevertheless, it's the animal who lives on in memory. As D'Amato himself told Tyson, "He couldn't have died any other way."

Perhaps there *was* an inevitability to Artie Diamond's death. But it wasn't unlike the many deaths Tyson envisioned for himself.

13

In 1980, Lori Grinker, an aspiring illustrator attending the Parsons School of Design, took a class in photojournalism, the culmination of which was to be a piece of publishable quality. As it happened, that same semester she photographed Jimmy Jacobs's lecture at an Ali symposium at the New School. They got to talking and Jacobs suggested that her story was upstate in Catskill.

So Grinker started spending weekends with Cus, Camille, and the kids. That time, along with the intensely photogenic nature of boxing itself, shaped her ambition. By the end of the course, she had become a professional photographer. Grinker would take pictures of Tyson for the next decade. Of all the Tyson imagery, hers remains the best and most revealing. But the eventual piece born of her class assignment—published in the August 1981 issue of *Inside Sports*—refers to Tyson only once: "a 195-lb, 14-year-old Black heavyweight from Brooklyn who never seems to stop eating mashed potatoes and whose knowledge of boxing lore—names, dates, and details of every championship fight since the turn of the century—exceeds even that of his host."

"Cus kept telling me to photograph him," recalls Grinker, "but it felt too typical. Mike was this big kid who *looked* like a boxer. Nadia was more visually interesting. I started shooting her. Then Billy."

Billy Hamm was adopted and lived in a trailer. But at ten years old and sixty pounds, he photographed like an aggressively muscled version of Dennis the Menace. The piece was titled "Raging Calf."

"Mark my words," D'Amato proclaimed of Hamm, "I predict that someday—and I won't be around 'cause I'm too old—but someday, he'll be champeen of the woild. I know it's a kinda rash thing to say, but I'm not often wrong."

In fact, Billy Hamm never turned pro. He did his first prison bid at seventeen and has been in and out of jails for a good part of his life. Though the piece was framed around Grinker's photographs, it's really a Rip Van Winkle tale about D'Amato, the first most people had heard of him in years. Robert Friedman's text—with an obligatory Mailer reference in the first graf and a mention of Jacobs's largesse—became the template for the great sell to come: D'Amato, now "the Socrates of boxing," who had fought so bravely against the mob and been living "in self-imposed exile for the past decade," was back. He'd found a "chief disciple" in Atlas and an emerging pro in Rooney. Dinners with his young charges gathered at the table had a whiff of blessed ritual to them. And if, at seventy-three, D'Amato's time in this life was short, one of his boys, that future champeen, would grant him immortality.

Really. Who the fuck wouldn't buy that?

SHORTLY AFTER THE PIECE'S PUBLICATION, A GERMAN TELEVISION producer called his U.S.-based documentarian, Michael Marton, to see if there was anything to this story of "the boy boxer." For the next year and a half, Marton and his then-girlfriend, Leslie Parke, embedded themselves in D'Amato's stable. Parke, a young painter with two fine arts degrees from Bennington College, was pressed into service as the sound person. Marton was intense, very much the aspiring auteur, and given at the time to hauntingly animated dreams, reenactments of a hungry, traumatic childhood in postwar Berlin. The way he explained it to Parke, Marton and his mother had been abandoned by his biological father, an aristocratic German officer and dressage champion. Looking back, it seems clear why Marton was so drawn to the fighters in D'Amato's orbit. "They're all looking for the love of a father figure," she says.

They would shoot for countless hours until a story, or something like it, began to emerge. Then they'd shoot some more. The result is a fifty-eight-minute film called *Watch Me Now*, which ostensibly follows a little white kid named Johnny (Billy Hamm had left the gym by then). As it opens, Johnny is aimless, lonely, and contemplating the poster for the just-released *Rocky III*. His mother seems more keen on seducing truckers via the CB radio than she does on Johnny and his siblings. As it ends, Johnny begins training. There's no music, no narration. But there are two indelible scenes, endlessly replayed or cited, that will ever follow and inform the idea of Mike Tyson.

The first is the gathering at dinner. "I learned more about what was required to be a real working artist from Cus than I did from getting my degrees," says Parke, who'd recall the gym on Main Street and those smokers in the Bronx as worthy tableaus for the Ashcan masters. Certainly Cus, Camille, and the kids assembled around the dinner table is itself a painterly composition. There's nothing Ashcan about it, though. It's Norman Rockwell.

Dinner is served: Tyson, D'Amato, and Camille Ewald

But it's not an arrangement that would be so easily allowed today. This was 1982, before the Catholic Church was exposed for harboring generations of pedophiles, before a series of lawsuits bankrupted the Boy Scouts of America, and before the infamous Jerry Sandusky scandal at Penn State.

Certainly the subject of homosexuality wasn't off limits. Nadia Hujtyn recalls D'Amato throwing out an impromptu quiz question: Name the two world champions who were gay. The sexual preference of Emile Griffith, who held titles at both welter- and middleweight, was common knowledge. After all, Griffith had famously put Bennie "Kid" Paret into a fatal coma after Paret called him a *maricón*. But the identity of the other fighter was a stumper.

Finally, Tyson blurted out the name D'Amato was looking for. "Sonny Liston," he said. "Because he was a jail boy."

I've never heard that about Liston, but it says more about the connection a young Tyson already made between incarceration and homosexuality than it does about D'Amato. Nevertheless, the subject of D'Amato's sexuality has long been a source of speculation in boxing circles. The most disquieting anecdote comes via the man who wrote about him most often, Gay Talese, in W. K. Stratton's 2012 biography of Floyd Patterson. "I got the impression that D'Amato had a sexual thing for Patterson—not that Patterson reciprocated," said Talese. "Patterson told me he was lying in bed and D'Amato was lying next to him, slipped perhaps into bed. I don't know. It was training camp, you know. Prizefighters in training camp are intimately open, not sexually, but you are naked, you are free, there is a lot of openness. But this one time in bed, D'Amato had his foot on Patterson's foot, sort of playing with his toes."

"That's consistent with what Floyd told me," says Charles Farrell, a longtime boxing manager and writer who became a friend and business partner of Patterson's. "He mentioned that Cus would be on the bed a lot. He said Cus would watch him when he was asleep and when he was ready to go to sleep. He stayed too long. He stayed too close. It was creepy."

Patterson, he recalls, would concede only that D'Amato was "a very, very strange guy."

While Farrell knows his argument falls well short of actual proof,

Nadia Hujtyn pushes back vehemently on the notion that Cus was anything other than straight. "Cus and Camille were an item for years," she says, noting D'Amato's penchant for leering at her quite attractive mother.

"We were there every day," says Leslie Parke. "We were folding laundry with the kids. If something went down, I think it would have been more obvious. It was hard to keep a secret in that house."

That, too, is perfectly reasonable, but again, less than proof. My own analysis, for what that's worth, is also circumstantial. But I believe it. It *would* have been difficult to keep a secret in that house. And given just a whiff of a pedophile on the premises, Teddy would have killed him.

TYSON WON HIS SECOND CONSECUTIVE JUNIOR OLYMPIC TITLE THAT year. Upon their return to Catskill, he and Atlas were honored as conquering heroes with a banner on Main Street. Tyson had just set a record in the semifinals, knocking his opponent out cold with a single right hand in eight seconds. After the fight, officials asked to inspect his gloves, as there was an allegation that they had been loaded with weighted objects. For Tyson and Atlas, it was more of the same. Days earlier, when tournament physicians concluded their supposedly routine exam by demanding proof of Tyson's age, Atlas produced three copies of his birth certificate and affidavits from teachers at Catskill High School attesting that he was in fact fifteen. In the championship, Tyson squared off against another Texan, Kelton Brown, who was more than a head taller. Again it was televised on ESPN. Just seconds into the fight, Tyson hit Brown with a right hand that lifted him off the ground.

Brown survived. But not for long, as Tyson kept swarming: frenetic, unleashed, his still-nascent career being counted off not in rounds but in mere ticks of the clock.

"The way he would go after a knockout early in the fight, I think that was largely because he didn't want to box," says Parke. "He wanted to be done with it. He didn't want to be vulnerable. He didn't want to get hit. That's my layman's analysis."

"He didn't grasp the idea that it was a battle," Nadia Hujtyn says of Tyson's frenzied charge for a knockout. "It requires emotional maturity."

Nor was that championship—on June 26, 1982—an occasion he'd acquire it. Forty-two seconds into the first round, Brown's corner threw in the towel. Tyson rolled on the mat, unable to contain his joy. But that ecstasy—a release, really—can be truly gauged only by what Marton and Parke captured minutes before.

AS TYSON WAS BEING INTRODUCED, THE ESPN ANNOUNCERS SPOKE of his being a front-runner for the 1984 Olympics. Atlas had already told Marton on camera that Tyson "has the potential to be one of the best fighters ever." D'Amato would tell him that one day, in the not-so-distant future, he'd have to beat women off with a baseball bat, that kids would vie for the privilege of carrying his mother's groceries.

Tyson wasn't sprung from Tryon to compete in the Golden Gloves, or get a GED, or even turn pro. From the outset, expectations were clear: He would take his place among the pantheon of legends his projector brought to life, a heavyweight like Henry Armstrong, ferocious like Jack Dempsey. Before too long, Tyson would be telling his barber to cut his hair like the Manassa Mauler himself.

Just the same, D'Amato cautioned him sometime before the finals: "When you lose, they don't like you anymore. If you're not spectacular, they don't like you anymore."

It's not clear if D'Amato was trying to warn or incentivize him. Tyson didn't have to be reminded of the terms, though. They were already obvious even to an outsider like Parke. "Mike had already won the lottery," she says. "He was living in a mansion and he was being cared for. People were paying his bills and buying him clothes and giving him accolades. But the truth is, he was doing it by being the person that these people wanted him to be."

As the fight draws near, in the locker room, we see Tyson, in a blue satin robe, and Atlas reminding him of the game plan: Be a tiger, be like

Henry Armstrong, move your head and jab. Then Atlas tenderly wraps his hands. "Let's do it," he says.

But the next shot finds them outside in a clearing, vast fields in the background, the sound of traffic. Tyson had left the building, trying to walk off prefight nerves. Atlas followed.

"It took us by surprise," says Parke, who recalls rushing to catch up with a shotgun mic and a thirty-pound tape deck on her back.

She and Marton, who operated the camera, were connected by a cable. Tyson wasn't wired, of course, as he was about to fight. But Atlas wore a mic she had taped to his shirt and a receiver in his pants pocket or taped to the small of his back. They had to hurry. Parke could hear what was happening.

All fighters have fear and self-doubt before a fight. But seeing it raw, unvarnished, and capturing the moment on film is like having a sit-down with a snow leopard.

With Marton shooting again, Atlas puts his arm around an obviously distraught Tyson. Their backs now turn to the camera. Atlas's voice is strong, reassuring, and, above all, clear. "Relax, Michael. Just relax."

Tyson is sniffling and sobbing, his words a whimper but audible through his trainer's mic. "Remember when we first started?" he asks squeakily.

"Just relax," says Atlas, his arm tight against Tyson's neck now. "All it is is another boxing match. You've done it already twenty times. You've done it in the gym with better fighters than you're ever gonna fight here."

"Come a long way, remember?" Tyson says through his tears. "I'm Mike Tyson. Everybody likes me. I'm proud of myself."

Atlas—who just prior to the tournament had been coaching a paraplegic to walk—affirms that Tyson has reason to be proud, that good things are ahead. "Just always remember," he says, "don't let your feelings get the better of you."

Finally, Atlas pats him on the back, turns into a profile shot, and, after studying the landscape, says, "Let's go get ready for a fight."

It's an indelible exchange, endlessly replayed. But no fighter wants to be seen like that. Atlas had to know Marton was rolling. Why not shut it down?

"Teddy desperately wants to be loved and admired," says Parke. "His compassion is almost pathological. He sees someone in need and that's where he goes. That's what feeds him. He wants to fix things. He wants to take care of people because he wants to be in the chorus with God. He wants to be what they're praying to. He's like the archangel Michael."

She likens him to an actor and this, the role he was born to play.

But Tyson isn't playing. The truth has dawned on him, an epiphany, like Aquinas divining faith from reason.

I'm Mike Tyson. Everybody loves me.

As long as you win, sure. As long as you give the people a place to consign their fear. Like a circus. Or a zoo. Or a jail. Give people a safe space to *ooh* and *aah*.

Just don't lose.

He might as well have said, *If I don't win, nobody will love me.*

That's why he was weeping. It was the truth.

14

Upon his release from Tryon, just a couple months past his four-teenth birthday, Tyson was enrolled as an eighth grader in the pre-dominantly white Catskill Junior High School. "He certainly wasn't a normal transfer," says the principal, Lee Bordick, who, prior to the se-mester, had been briefed by a delegation of two: Ernestine Coleman, a social worker with the New York State Division for Youth, and D'Amato himself.

Bordick had warm memories of watching *The Gillette Cavalcade of Sports*, better known as *Friday Night Fights*, with his uncles. He remem-bered Floyd Patterson. He remembered José Torres. And he couldn't help but regard D'Amato with a bit of awe. The principal understood imme-diately the kind of possibility Tyson embodied, but also what the school itself represented to Tyson.

"He had an idea, probably from watching television, what school was like in a regular place in a regular town," says Bordick. "I think it was important to him. He was highly motivated, particularly that first year."

As his new life began, Tyson's days were as circumscribed as those of any child star, divided between school and training. His work ethic was formidable. What's more, it invited the attention of good teachers. Not just Bordick. There was an eighth-grade English teacher, a Mr. Meehan, who worked diligently with him.

Tyson needed remedial training in the basics: reading, writing, arithmetic. Still, Bordick couldn't help but notice: "His verbal skills for that age were very, very keen."

I remind the now-retired principal that he once described Tyson as "shrewd, very verbal, a con artist to some degree."

"*Con artist* was probably a little strong," he says. "Mike was smart. He knew how to bob and weave through life."

But the mores of this strange new world weren't easy to grasp. There was, for instance, just one Black barber in Catskill. "And he didn't even have a shop," says Lennie Daniels. "Just a guy working out of his house."

Then there were the dances, another humiliating ritual for which Tyson hadn't been prepared. "I finally figured out what to do," he once told Nadia Hujtyn. "You don't *ask* them. You just grab them by the hand and pull them out on the dance floor." In other words, don't give them a chance to say no.

Tyson was immediately set apart by virtue of his size, his skin color, and the idea that certain adults had designated him for a kind of fame and fortune beyond the confines of this *regular* world. None of these factors by themselves was likely to ingratiate him to the other kids. "He was charismatic, even as an eighth grader, kind of a rock star," says Bordick. "And some kids resented it."

But the clique that caused him the greatest pain—exponentially more than the pros Cus and Teddy would bribe to spar with him—were Black girls.

"They're saying I'm ugly," he told Lennie Daniels.

"Then they're saying *I'm* ugly, too," Lennie shot back. "'Cause everyone says we look so much alike you must be my little brother."

Mike would laugh. But not for long. "It got worse after he started winning the Junior Olympics and stuff like that," recalls Daniels.

The incident resulting in Tyson's first suspension began with three girls teasing him about his mother, in whose bed he still slept during his occasional visits home. Anticipating the rage to come, they ran into the girls' bathroom. Tyson gave chase, and Bordick was called in to negotiate a cessation of hostilities. The worst possible scenario was already apparent to faculty and students: Nobody in the school could physically subdue Tyson. Bordick understood why he was so furious. Tyson would open up about his Brooklyn friends in jail, or those who had already been murdered. "But his mother," said the principal, "was off limits."

One of the girls took the additional liberty of kicking Tyson as Bordick escorted him from the bathroom. Tyson turned back at her with the same murderous glare that would cause fighters to soil themselves. But that's where it ended. For whatever reason, Bordick never felt endangered, for himself or the girl. He told Tyson to run around the campus until he had calmed down. Then they spoke. Bordick suspended him. All in all, it was a good day, the unlikeliest of all victories for Tyson, one of self-restraint.

Now fast-forward two Septembers. Kevin Rooney has been knocked out in two rounds by the great Alexis Arguello in Atlantic City. The hopes of D'Amato's gym, indeed of Catskill itself, rest entirely on young Mike, winner of consecutive Junior Olympic titles. He's a freshman at Catskill High School. He has friends, among them a Black girl whose locker was next to his. "Cus kept him away from everybody in that big house in the woods, but Mike was a big teddy bear," says Kimberly Heath, recalling that the crowded halls between periods were easier to navigate with Mike leading the way. "He was like my bodyguard."

The two were in the lunchroom. "We were cutting up," says Heath. "It was a good day." She was a few places ahead of Tyson in the cafeteria line, sliding their trays along the metal railing, when the principal, Mr. Stickles, said he'd like to have a word with Tyson alone.

"Mike didn't want to go to the office because he thought he was in trouble for something," Heath says. "So he was like, 'I'm not going nowhere.' He just kept pushing his tray along. 'I'm not going.' And Mr. Stickles is like, 'Mike, please. Just come on.' And I remember him reaching for Mike's arm, not in an aggressive way, but Mike got very huffy. So finally, Mr. Stickles had no choice but to tell him right there.

"And Mike just took his left hand, swept up all the trays, and they went all over and hit the floor.

"Everybody thought Mike was having a fight with the principal, that he was being this bad guy. But he was just a kid in pain. He just found out his mother died. They suspended him, I think. And I may be wrong, but I don't remember seeing Mike in school after that. I don't remember him ever coming back."

AFTER DECADES OF HARD DRINKING, LORNA MAE DIED OF CANCER the first semester of Tyson's freshman year and was buried in a plot she had purchased in Linden, New Jersey. There wasn't enough money for a headstone. She was fifty-five.

Memories around death develop like Polaroid film, the images more certain than the actual dates. I have no doubt, for example, that Kimberly Heath's recollection of Mr. Stickles in the cafeteria is true and that Tyson's rage was tethered to news of his mother's dire condition, though probably not her actual death. Teddy Atlas, for his part, remembers the funeral being the same day as his wedding reception at Schmollinger's Pleasant View Lodge. The wedding was an extravagant affair, certainly by Catskill standards, attended by judges, wiseguys, fighters, writers, and featured a special appearance by the diagnosed paraplegic whom Atlas had by now coached to walk ten paces across the dance floor before collapsing into his arms. "The only one who didn't make it was Tyson," he wrote. "The day before, I drove him to the train station. He was wearing a new warm-up suit I'd bought him with my last fifty bucks."

Again, I'm as sure of Atlas's recollection as of Kimberly Heath's. But his wedding reception was on September 25, 1982. Lorna Mae Tyson didn't die until November. What's more, Tyson recalls his mother's death as a prolonged episode that drew him back into the Brooklyn netherworld.

His last trip home had been after winning that second Junior Olympic title. People had seen him on TV. Erstwhile tormentors were on his jock now. But he could not sway the person he wanted to impress most. He told his mother he was destined for history.

"There's always someone better," said Lorna Mae, citing Joe Louis.

"There is not a man in the world that can beat me, Ma."

She told him to be humble.

He brought his newspaper clippings, the accounts of his fearsome knockouts and gold medals.

"I'll read it later," she said before excusing herself.

They didn't speak the rest of the night.

A MONTH OR SO LATER, AROUND THE TIME OF THE ATLAS NUPTIALS, Tyson returned to Brooklyn. He had been told Lorna Mae was sick, though, in fact, she was already near death. However tough he had been in the streets or the ring, Tyson was no match for the sight of his mother ravaged by cancer. He covered her exposed breast with a bedsheet, then kissed her goodbye.

Each day his sister, Denise, would ask him how his visit with their mother had gone. Tyson would lie, as if he'd been to the hospital, when all he was really doing was drinking, smoking, snorting, and robbing, mostly with Barkim.

"Man, I wish I had some white people that loved me," Barkim told him. "Go back."

He would, after Lorna Mae's death and what he'd recall as a pitiful funeral attended by his ostensible father. "I heard my boy is going to be a prizefighter," said Jimmy Kirkpatrick.

It wasn't an inquiry, as Tyson recalled, so much as a smirk.

Tyson spent the next several days or weeks robbing and getting high. Perhaps that seems irrational, at least from the perspective of *regular* America—that a kid with a legit shot to *make something of himself* would revert to his shittiest self and remain an exile in the wicked land of his birth. But it feels like an acknowledgment, a surrender to something he couldn't yet articulate, but that even his hypnotized mind could not ignore. Tyson would never be one of those kids who got his mama a house. He may have been destined for history, but he'd have to get there without whatever it was that made men like Alexander so fucking great. The condition was permanent now. There could be no corrective. If Achilles had his heel, Tyson had Lorna Mae.

IT WAS DURING THIS APOCALYPTIC SOJOURN THAT TYSON LEARNED that Barkim—the man who had made him his "street son"—had been killed. Then his social worker, Ernestine Coleman, came to take him back to Catskill.

"This was a boy who had more rage than I'd ever seen before, and now he was falling into a deep depression," said Coleman. "The boxing was a positive direction for him. It was either that or the streets, where he would have ended up dead for sure."

Tyson told her he wasn't going anywhere. She told him that she could place him in Brooklyn, but that the cops would have to get involved. He changed his mind.

What Coleman didn't tell him was that she'd been bluffing. Tyson was sixteen, no longer a ward of the state. He didn't need an adult's permission for anything. Looking back, that was the point of a plan D'Amato had already set into motion.

By now, D'Amato had even called Bobby Stewart for his blessing. "Mike was drawing attention in national tournaments and guys like Don King were already taking notice," Stewart told Peter Heller. "Cus told me that 'Jimmy has a lot of money invested in this kid. I'm going to adopt the kid legally.'"

Not long after that conversation, D'Amato showed up at the Town and Country Restaurant, where the county administrator, Bill Hagan, was entertaining friends in a private dining room.

"Bill, I have a problem," he began. "The wiseguys just gave their telephone numbers to Tyson. They're trying to get him. I've got to get guardianship."

Hagan referred D'Amato to his personal attorney, who happened to be sitting at the table.

Before lunch the next day, on the authority of an elected Greene County judge, James Battisti, and apparently without hearing from the prospective ward himself, Tyson had a new father. What brought the case before the court had less to do with actual paternity than with D'Amato's sense of posterity and paranoia.

Really, the *wiseguys* were coming for Tyson?

What wiseguys? Fat Tony? Don King? Or were they ghosts of gangsters past, those vestigial enemies D'Amato was still trying to outwit, the ones who snatched Graziano and came between him and Patterson? If D'Amato had come to think of Tyson as his prophecy, it was still laced with doom.

"He knew Mike was going to leave," says Nadia Hujtyn. "He knew it. And it was too much for him. He was not well. He was elderly."

If D'Amato wasn't wrong, then his fears were premature. Tyson welcomed the new arrangement and asked if he could call Camille his mother.

Of course. He'd recall sitting in the living room, reading, and D'Amato calling out to her, using her pet name: "Look at your Black son, Camillee. He's going to bring pride and glory to this family."

Danny Bucci, another amateur fighter then living at the house, recalls

Thanks, Dad.

a different Tyson upon his return from Brownsville. "He wouldn't even look up after his mother died," says Bucci. "He was so far from home. He was desolate, man. Completely desolate."

There seemed a single, reliable analgesic for his pain. He'd brought it with him from Brooklyn. On Christmas Day, they went up to the attic, Mike and Danny, and snuck out on the widow's walk. It was a beautiful day in late December, the Hudson calm and blue. They could hear Cus growling, wondering where they were. Regular people had already opened their presents. Or maybe they were coming back from church. But this was all the sacrament they needed. Danny had never seen one that big. Mike lit up. They smoked their brains out.

Merry Christmas.

15

D'Amato had two sets of rules: one for Tyson and another for everyone else. Everyone else did chores in exchange for room and board. Tyson was rewarded on the basis of athletic performance and his vast potential and, above all, as a safeguard against D'Amato's great fear, that the kid might leave him before their names were enshrined in boxing history.

It began at the dinner table. While D'Amato clocked what each of the other kids put on his plate, Tyson's appetites were celebrated. He was afforded all-you-can-eat privileges. After that first Junior Olympic title, D'Amato bought Tyson a pigeon coop and gave him the money to fully stock it with birds. There were leather jackets, Adidas sneakers, and gold teeth, two of them, which D'Amato assured him had been all the rage for champions going back to Jack Johnson.

The price of these amateur victories would keep going up, of course. It was never realistic to think that Tyson's rehabilitation would proceed without setbacks, but the State of New York had a right to expect better from its appointed guardian. In Brooklyn, Tyson got by on guile and violence. But in Catskill, for the first time, he was enabled—not only by D'Amato or those with a financial stake in his future but by people who wanted nothing more than to say *I knew him back then*. The mere

Tyson in his pigeon coop, 1985

prospect of fame was an intoxicant. With the financial backing of Big Fights, Inc., and his pull with local officials, D'Amato created a world in which Tyson never seemed to hear the word *no*.

The good behavior he had displayed at the start of eighth grade was temporary, as one might reasonably expect from an angry, hormonal delinquent who's suddenly being told he's a scourge from God. By ninth grade there was talk of Tyson grabbing at girls. There was an incident with a teacher after an altercation on the school bus. He threw an eraser. Later, it was a tantrum, hurling milk cartons in the cafeteria.

"Cus always rushed to straighten out these incidents because he was deathly afraid that the authorities might try to take me away from him," said Tyson.

Tyson had much more power as an enfant terrible in this upstate burg than he'd ever had as a young thug back home. On the street, there were consequences—but not in this supposedly real world. As long as he kept winning, preferably by knockout, Tyson was bulletproof.

His high school experience apparently ended when, as he recalls, "one of my teachers, a real ignorant redneck, started arguing with me and threw a book at me. I got up and smacked the shit out of him in front of all the other students."

Instead of punishing Tyson, D'Amato brought him right back to school. There he demanded an audience with Mr. Stickler, the principal, which he was granted. Then he began grilling the just-beaten teacher in an effort to have Tyson's suspension lifted.

"I had three kids from the class who worked out in the same gym with Mike," Atlas would recall. "They told me it didn't happen, the teacher didn't throw a book. But Cus told Mike, 'Don't worry. If they throw you out, I'll get Jim Jacobs to get you a tutor.'"

In fact, that's about what happened. What's more, the archangel Atlas was becoming a heretic. "I was the fortress of discipline," he said. "I became the guy nobody wanted to hear." The only way to really correct Tyson's behavior was to keep him out of the gym and let him earn his way back. However, that was anathema to Cus, as it could impede his existential race against time or, worse still, drive Tyson to another gym. Hence, each of Teddy's attempted "suspensions" ended with his losing face, showing up at the gym only to see Tyson working one-on-one with D'Amato himself or, probably more hurtful, his old friend Rooney.

In the house, Danny Bucci overheard D'Amato and the young master screaming at each other. "I'm not going to put up with this," said Atlas.

"I'm not going to put up with *you!*" responded Cus. "I *made* you a trainer."

Finally, in early 1983, Atlas came home to find his now very pregnant wife and her sisters in tears. "My wife tells me that Tyson tried to molest her kid sister," Teddy told me. "The girl was eleven years old. Now I know what I have to do. I've let this go too far. I've allowed somebody to take more than the toilet paper."

Teddy, like Tyson, could reduce anything to a jailhouse metaphor. But Tyson had another unwitting gift in speech: a talent for simultaneously portraying himself as both the manipulator and the innocent. "I did something that made Cus get rid of Teddy," he said. "I had known Teddy's sisters-in-law before Teddy even did. We had all gone to school together and were friends. The girls would always be flirtatious with me, but I never had a sexual thing with them. I was hanging out with his twelve-year-old sister-in-law one day and I grabbed her butt. I really didn't mean to do anything evil. I was just playing around and I grabbed her butt and I shouldn't have."

Atlas got a gun, of course, a .38 from a friend at a local disco. Then he waited for Tyson to show up at the gym, pulled him into a nook alongside the building, and put the gun to his head. From his memoir *Atlas: From the Streets to the Ring*:

> "You piece of fucking shit. You think you're gonna do that to my
> family? After the way I've treated you? I will fucking kill you!
> That's my family! My family! You understand, you fucking piece
> of shit?" I was looking at him, staring straight into his eyes. If he
> didn't show me that he knew how serious I was, then I was going
> to kill him. "Make no mistake. If you ever put your hands on my
> family again, you'll be dead. There'll be no talking. No warning.
> You'll never know. You'll just be dead."

That was a little different from the speech he told me for a family newspaper, but the upshot was much the same: *I'm not bluffing.* Which, of course, he was. And that was a problem, as something in Tyson's expression still suggested a smirk, at least to Atlas. He put the gun against Tyson's ear but kept the barrel pointed into the night. Then he fired. At first, Tyson thought his ear had been shot off. Per Atlas, he began to convulse.

"When he got up he had this look almost like he wanted to apologize," Teddy told me in 1994. "I'm not proud of it. But he was making me less than a person, less than whole. And I couldn't allow that."

In Atlas's version, he watches Tyson "stagger away."

In Tyson's version, "Teddy ran."

Either way, the archangel had been cast out.

In the aftermath, Tyson vowed revenge. Not a great idea. I'm sure

Teddy would've been armed and waiting. D'Amato must've surmised the same, as he called Bobby Stewart and asked if he could take Tyson for a few days, through the weekend. "I think he might've said Tyson was bored," recalls Stewart, who apparently left it at that. "But he didn't say anything about the incident. If I knew what happened, I'd have taken Tyson to the police station myself, if nothing else than just to scare the hell out of him. He stayed at my place the first night, then I took him to Tryon and brought him back maybe Sunday or Monday."

I wonder what Tyson told him.

"He didn't say nothing about it. He seemed fine. I didn't know anything until later on. I was surprised that Cus would do that, though."

Surprised that D'Amato would keep the truth from him? If Stewart is without avarice, he's also without guile. Then again, like a lot of people with an interest in Tyson, he admits he was happy not to know, wanting his Pollyanna notion of "Cus and the Kid" to remain blissfully intact.

Still, the mere mention of Atlas pisses him off: "I'd like to slap him. He made it like I was doing Cus's dirty work for him, like I was trying to get Mike away from the cops. My father was a cop for Chrissakes. *He* would've arrested me if I did that. . . . Teddy Atlas is a great trainer and all, but he puts himself ahead of the fighters. He's a selfish guy."

However one sees Atlas, selfish or selfless, the narrative threads of Tyson's life don't fully part until Teddy puts the revolver to his head. In Tyson's telling, he's not especially charitable to himself. Teddy's, the piece-of-shit version, is manna to Tyson's detractors. But in retrospect, though, the storytellers seem more alike, and their stories more ambiguous than they once did.

Each of them, Tyson and Teddy, understood the nature of male power through the prism of jail. They're narcissists, not unlike their mentor, who recognized their gifts, how they could be of use to them—and to him. Neither was immediately cured in Catskill, as both Teddy and Tyson would go back to robbing and violence when they returned home to the city. But D'Amato saved both from lengthier incarceration, gave them each a vocation and a future, though none of it came free and clear.

NOT LONG AFTER THE CONFRONTATION, ATLAS RECEIVED A VISIT from Don Shanager: "Cus said he'll give you five percent for life of all Tyson's future earnings if you just go away."

"They were going to pay me off the way they paid everyone else off," wrote Atlas, who, predictably, tells Shanager to fuck off, that he doesn't want D'Amato's money. In fact, though, money had become an issue between them. For all the hours the twenty-six-year-old Atlas put in at the gym, his father, a Staten Island doctor, was still paying his rent in Catskill. What seems lost—not merely on Atlas but on everyone in this mix with the exception of Stewart—was that Tyson had neither his own money nor any agency over his affairs yet. He was sixteen and had just lost his mother. Still, there was D'Amato offering pieces of his future. Kind of like the mob guys used to do.

16

On February 12, 1983, Tyson knocked a guy cold at 2:35 of the third round in a Golden Gloves bout at the Springfield, Massachusetts, Boys Club. His name was Jimmy Johnson, and like many of Tyson's opponents by now, he was a full-grown man. "His wife, carrying his newborn baby, and his two other little kids ran into the ring, crying," Tyson remembered. "I told Cus that and he laughed. 'What? The babies and the mother were crying? Boo-hoo-hoo.' He was so happy."

Beyond the remark's obvious sadism, D'Amato was teaching Tyson to be pitiless. D'Amato wanted Tyson talked about, feared, his cruelties legendary. Fighters are great gossips. First impressions become reputations, and it's the reputation for which an opponent inevitably prepares.

Amateur boxing is supposed to be a more polite, less violent version of the pro game. But Tyson observed few, if any, of its niceties. Per D'Amato's instructions, he wouldn't even wear headgear unless ordered to by tournament officials. "He had a reputation," recalls Jerry Goff, who fought him later that year at the Ohio State Fair. "You could tell that Mike didn't really respect me at all."

At nineteen, three years older than Tyson, Goff was an elite talent out of Saucier, Mississippi, already seasoned against international competition. He was tall and fluid and knew how to work his jab, which he did to great effect, clearly beating Tyson for a round and a half. Near the end of the second, however, he dropped his hands and Tyson hit him with an almost perfect right hand on the chin. The lasting image of the fight is Goff flat on his back. But there was another sequence, just prior, that remains with Goff, and likely every other fighter and coach who was there.

"I had him really frustrated, and if you'll notice in the middle of the second round when we're clinching, he takes his thumb and sticks it right in my eye—twice!" says Goff, referring to the YouTube clip. "I had never experienced anything like that before. That was real old-school stuff fighters used to do. And the way he did it—on the opposite side of the ref! Cus D'Amato had to be teaching him."

There's no animus in Goff's recollection: "We became super good friends, me and Mike. He'd see me at tournaments, sitting by myself all the way up in the bleachers, and he'd come and grab me and hug me and give me a kiss on the cheek. Then, in eighty-four, we went to Finland for the USA Boxing team. He'd knock on my door and we'd go walking the streets for hours. To this day, people I know run into Mike and ask, 'You remember Jerry Goff?' And he says, 'Of course I do. My man from Mississippi.'"

D'Amato succeeded in crafting Tyson's image to frighten the competition. But he never could make him pitiless. Whatever pathologies Tyson had acquired, for all his jailhouse bluster, his great, enduring empathy is for fellow fighters. If they weren't quite a family, then perhaps a fraternal society.

Among them was Kilbert Pierce, who fought Tyson just months before Goff at a union hall in Dorchester, Massachusetts. Tyson knocked him down in the first and pushed him down in the second. But by the third, Pierce found a rhythm with his jab. "Who the fuck is this kid?" an agitated D'Amato began to scream. "I want to know who the fuck he is!"

"I won that third round," says Pierce. "But it was my first loss, and I took it pretty hard. I was in the locker room, all dejected, and Mike comes in and sits down beside me, puts his head on my shoulder and his arm around me, says, 'You did great tonight. You're going to be a great fighter.'"

They met again in Albuquerque, New Mexico, in March 1983 for the Golden Gloves National Championship but were no longer in the same division. Tyson was now a super heavyweight. Pierce and his younger brother had adjoining rooms with their parents at the hotel. But each morning there'd be a knock at the door. Before long Tyson had ingratiated himself into Pierce's family life, the scourge from God once again doing his Eddie Haskell bit. "My parents really took a liking to him," says Pierce. "He'd be in the room every day, just chilling."

The tournament began with Tyson knocking out his first three opponents on consecutive days. One of them, the nation's sixth-ranked super heavyweight, remained on the canvas for three haunting minutes. His next opponent, second-ranked Warren Thompson, was the defending national champion out of Baltimore. Thompson was twenty-six, a full decade older than Tyson. Pierce remembers seeing him reading a newspaper over his breakfast.

"Watch this," said Tyson, who proceeded to sit down right across from Thompson.

"I'm going to fucking kill you," says Tyson. "You understand? Fucking kill you."

Thompson, who was coming off a spectacular first-round knockout, put down his paper and turned to Pierce: "Hey, man, get your boy."

"*My* boy? Look at him. I can't do nothing with him."

The following night, Thompson would need every bit of his experience and man strength just to last the three rounds with Tyson. "Wherever Mike hit you, you felt it," he says. "It wasn't just the power; he was so fast. He'd dig around your side with a right hand, then jump pivot, come up with an uppercut. He knew what he was doing."

By the end, as the ref raised Tyson's hand, Thompson had a pretty good idea what he now looked like: "My eye partway closed, nose busted, mouth swolled up."

It was then that Tyson embraced him. "I thought you beat me," he lisped. "You're my man. I love you."

As it happened, Tyson lost by decision in the finals to Craig Payne out of Detroit. "Craig kept holding Mike," says Thompson. "He knew how to work in the clinches, put his hand inside your elbow, and pivot so he'd be safe."

"Mike beat the guy and everyone knew it," said Rooney, Atlas's replacement in Tyson's corner. "The crowd booed when they announced the result."

Rooney was emerging as a voluble mouthpiece for the Catskill party line, but even the more objective *Albuquerque Journal* conceded the Payne fight was a "controversial decision." In fact, Tyson was never a darling of the amateur boxing establishment. The quirky old D'Amato and his surly protégé Rooney were seen as arrogant, holding themselves above rules and conventions that bound other fighters and coaches. But so what? Any apprenticeship involved losing; Tyson was receiving a champion's education—learning to deal with haters as well. Besides, he'd already been beaten—just like all the other kids.

The first time was a smoker against a local favorite in Rhode Island. Tyson was fifteen; the other guy was twenty-one and would soon turn pro. "Heard you fought great," D'Amato told him upon his return to Catskill, even offering to give him the day off from school.

His second loss was on December 10, 1982, against Al "Chico" Evans out of Chicago. "He looked at me like he was gonna kill me," recalls Evans. "But he was short. And his arms were short. I was six four."

It was Tyson's first official fight without an age limit, and Evans was eleven years his senior. There seems little debate that Tyson had his way the first two rounds. In the third, though, Evans caught him. "With a hook," he says of the punch that dropped the prodigy for the first time. Tyson got up, then Evans caught him again . . . or did he? Tyson says he slipped, but the referee—citing a two-knockdown limit in the amateurs— declared it a TKO.

"I remember the next morning, they had a buffet-style breakfast, and you could see Al Evans took a beating," says Herb Cox, a heavyweight out of Hartford. "His face was so swollen he could barely get his glasses on. Tyson didn't have a mark on him."

Of course, the truth of whatever happened didn't matter as much as how it was talked about. It wasn't the loss that D'Amato feared; it was demystification. And to this point no one had come close to puncturing the notion of Tyson the Destroyer. There was no internet. You couldn't pull up a clip on your phone. There was nothing to go viral; rather, Tyson's reputation was based on word of mouth. And it was the fighters themselves who became his most enthusiastic propagandists.

Buddy McGirt, a future two-division world champion, remembers Tyson sparring at Grossinger's Hotel and Resort in June of '83. Watching along with McGirt were the reigning light heavyweight champ, Michael Spinks, and three other pros, all heavyweights—James "Quick" Tillis; Eddie Taylor out of Detroit, better known as "Young Joe Louis"; and Jeff Sims, from Belle Glade, Florida, a little older than the rest, as he'd already done time on a chain gang for manslaughter. Tyson, still just sixteen, was in against a pro himself, the formidably muscled Frank Bruno, then 16-0 and considered the best British heavyweight in decades.

"You could *hear* the way Tyson's punches were landing, how much they were hurting Bruno," recalls McGirt. "We were watching a kid have his way with a man. Then my manager turns to me, says, 'We could be watching the next great heavyweight.'"

That night, with Tyson still fresh in their minds, the fighters retired to play spades.

"That boy's a killer," Young Joe Louis said of Tyson.

"I'll kick the shit out of him," said Quick Tillis.

Sims laughed in his face. "He'd fuck you up," he said. "He'd fuck all y'all up."

An uncomfortably silent moment passed. Fighters might talk about being killers, but Sims actually was. Then, in unison, everyone busted out laughing and went back to the card game.

"You know why?" asks McGirt. "Because it was true."

Tyson at sixteen could have beaten them all.

LATER THAT SUMMER, DAVE YONKO RAN INTO A GROUP OF FELLOW fighters at a convenience store in Colorado Springs. They were there for the nationals, the U.S. Amateur Championships. Yonko was looking for a Slurpee. Instead, he got Pernell Whitaker—future Olympic gold med-alist and Hall of Famer—telling him how hard Tyson hit and how Yonko was going to get knocked out in the semifinals.

Yonko had his own reputation for knocking guys out. He'd more than held his own with pros at the Hoover Street Gym in South Central Los Angeles. Also, at 240 pounds, he was a lot bigger than Tyson. Still, what Whitaker said stayed with him.

"It intimidated me hearing all that," he admits. "I was kind of nervous."

The next night, Tyson hit him harder than he'd ever been hit.

It was happening just like Whitaker had said it would. "I'd never been knocked down before," says Yonko. "I'd never even been dazed. So I started to panic."

The ref saw it in his eyes and waved off the fight.

The notion of Tyson the Destroyer was gathering great momentum now. As best I can tell, there was but a single dissenter. He, too, was an amateur, and had been in attendance the night Tyson fought Al Evans. He just refused to see it like everyone else.

"I saw him get hit on the chin and fall on his face," he said of Tyson.

And no one was going to tell him any different. Then again, nobody really listened. The kid wasn't even a heavyweight, just a spindly mama's boy from Atlanta, Evander Holyfield.

17

Sparring with Tyson was a peculiar proposition. On one hand, D'Amato and Rooney were always complaining about sparring partners being in short supply, that Jacobs and Cayton had to bribe pros—up to a thousand dollars a week, same as Ali was paying—just to give Tyson rounds, and still those same pros frequently left before the agreed-upon term. On the other, they wanted Tyson to spar as he fought, intending to send a message even as he sent his sparring partners home.

"I get my sparring at tournaments," Tyson said with a whiff of the arrogance for which he'd become known.

There were exceptions, of course. One of them arrived in Catskill at D'Amato's invitation early in the spring of 1984. Lennox Lewis came from Kitchener, Ontario, by way of London's East End. His mother, Violet, grew up in Jamaica, but had her heart broken in England, where she got by, barely, as a nurse's aide. Lennox's father didn't tell her he was married until she became pregnant. "I think he was the only man I ever really, really cared for," she would say decades later. "The sadness is still there."

Instead of aborting the pregnancy, as most of her friends advised, Violet doubled up on her hospital shifts to pay for the baby. All the love she had for the father she'd now bestow upon Lennox. And it still wasn't quite enough for her, her son from a previous relationship, and the new baby. When Lennox was four, Violet left for Chicago. The plan was to get a job and an apartment, then send for Lennox. Chicago didn't work out, though. Then it was Ontario, where she was hired at a Styrofoam factory.

"She went ahead to secure a new life for us, the way it is for a lot of immigrant families," Lewis tells me. "But I felt abandoned. Your mom is your calming force, the one who tells you everything is all right. But when you don't have anyone to tell you that, you grow up fast." He was left with an aunt, but his anger became too much to handle. His initial expulsion, in grade school, came after he punched through a glass window in the principal's office. What followed was a series of "boardinghouses," as he calls them, the first of which was for juvenile delinquents. "It's like going to jail," Lewis recalls. "All of a sudden you got to get hard, too."

How old? I ask.

"Seven or eight," he says, quickly recalling the most frightening kid in the home. "She was fifteen. She had stabbed her boyfriend. She would talk kind of threatening, like 'Yo, where the fuck you going?' I remember she was telling me basically 'You're nothing' and kept pushing me from behind, and then I just turned around and—POW!—I punched her right in the face. Then I ran away and locked myself in the bathroom."

Lewis was twelve when his mother finally sent for him. "She gave me a kiss that went on so long I didn't think it was ever going to stop," he said. "We hadn't met for years, but as soon as I saw her I felt that something that had been missing was suddenly there again."

In short and predictable order, the angry Black kid with a Cockney accent, made angrier by the locals who teased him in school, found himself at the Waterloo Regional Police Boxing Association, run by the prominently mustachioed Arnie Boehm. Boehm is occasionally compared to D'Amato.

"He told me I'd be a champion long before I knew it," says Lewis.

Certainly Boehm became a father figure to Lewis, the greatest talent ever to walk into his gym. But boxing was merely Boehm's abiding passion, not a holy calling. Boehm had a job—as a lineman with a local power company—and five children of his own. "He was one of these guys that would have fifteen kids in his car and we'd travel three hours to a tournament," Lewis once said. Unlike D'Amato, though, he'd never trained pros and never would.

In many respects, Lennox and Arnie were perfect for Mike and Cus to measure themselves against. Lewis, ten months Tyson's senior, was long and fluid where Tyson was short, coiled, and frenetic. And while Lewis didn't have Tyson's fearsome reputation in the States, he was more accomplished in international circles, having won a Junior World Championship (eighteen and under) in Santo Domingo the previous November. What's more, they each had the same summer plans, destination Los Angeles, site of the 1984 Olympics.

It was D'Amato who called Boehm to broach the idea of their sparring, after introducing himself.

Boehm asked, "*The* Cus D'Amato?"

"Tyson was a nice guy to me," recalls Lewis. "He took me up to his room, where there was a bedsheet hanging, and he put some film into the projector and we started watching."

Which fights? Which fighters? I wonder.

"The dirty ones," he says. "The guys who knew how to do headbutts and throw elbows—those specific guys. Mike was showing me what they would do. And I was like, *Wow, this guy is so educated on these old fighters.* I couldn't believe he had access to all this stuff."

He also had pigeons. Mike could even call long distance—he kept calling Montreal, where he said he had a girl—without worrying about the phone bill. They went to a dance, Mike and Lennox. They ran and worked out together. Finally, on the third day, D'Amato asked if the sparring might begin.

Boehm was concerned, as Lewis had a cold. But Lewis insisted on getting in with his new friend. "They're joking and the best of pals," Boehm recalled, as the coaches laced on their gloves. "Cus rings the bell and Tyson comes tearing across the ring like a raging tiger."

"He was a different person with gloves on," Lewis recalls. "He blitzed me."

Lewis returned to his corner with a bloody nose after that first round. "We don't have to spar today," Boehm told him.

"No," said Lewis, "I know what to do now."

Knowing and doing are different, of course. But with each successive round, Lewis took a little less of a beating. "The first day was rough," he says. "I remember Arnie saying, 'You're in his house. He's protecting his territory.' Then we watched fights of Muhammad Ali and Joe Frazier. 'This is how you have to fight him,' said Arnie, 'like Ali.'

"So the second day was better. Tyson did the same thing, but I was more prepared."

It wasn't until day three, though, that Lewis sent a message of his own: "He's still coming at me, but now I'm moving, boxing him at distance."

And Tyson wasn't too happy about it. Speaking to Lewis's biographer, Ken Gorman, Boehm would recall Tyson's calling him a "chicken." Lewis doesn't have that recollection: "Because I wasn't the chicken. I would've remembered it if Tyson had been rude to me."

What he does remember is Tyson putting his hands down, sticking his face out, and daring Lewis to hit him, a request that was promptly granted.

"Two uppercuts," says Lewis.

It was then that D'Amato began to bellow: "Mike, don't you do that! You're going to fight him someday!"

Yet another flurry left Tyson with a bloody mouth. "I worked out the puzzle," says Lewis, an avid chess player. "Mike's aim is to get inside. My aim is to keep him out. But when he does come in, I have to make him pay. Most boxers came to Catskill, sparred one day, and left the next. I wasn't looking to leave."

IN APRIL, AN ABC SPORTS CREW ARRIVED IN CATSKILL TO INTER-view D'Amato and Tyson in anticipation not merely of the Olympics but of the trials and the box-offs, which themselves would be televised on *Wide World of Sports*. It was a dress rehearsal for the pieces to come:

D'Amato in a suit, Tyson a stylish white Kangol. Still, their moods evoked an even starker contrast.

"I don't trust anybody," says Tyson, suspicious and unsmiling. "I don't like people to know me at all. . . . Nobody's really friendly with Mike Tyson except Cus D'Amato."

But the old man, seventy-six and shaking off a case of pneumonia, is nevertheless vital, animated, and in fine spirits. After all, he's framing this as a story about mortality—his own. "If he weren't here, I probably wouldn't be alive," he says, glancing at Tyson, who's sitting uncomfortably still. "But I have a reason with Mike here. He gives me the motivation. I will stay alive, and I will watch him become a success. I will not leave until that happens."

The interview—an hour and seventeen minutes of raw footage with the two side by side—was conducted by a producer known for his boxing acumen, Alex Wallau. About twenty-two minutes in, Wallau asks why Tyson, who'd been fighting at super heavyweight—201 pounds and over—was electing to fight at heavyweight for the Olympics. In other words, why would a kid who'd been fighting at around 210 and knocking out super heavyweights for more than a year now suddenly starve himself to make 201 pounds? Was it strategy? Were they trying to avoid anyone? Perhaps the great Cuban, Teófilo Stevenson?

No, it was Bob Surkein, long a fixture on the amateur boxing scene. Apparently Surkein had wanted Tyson to compete in the Junior World Championships, that same tournament Lewis won in Santo Domingo. It was not an unreasonable ask, given the heat and the expectations around Tyson. D'Amato had also wanted Tyson competing as a super heavyweight, his best weight, to prove he could beat anyone, including Stevenson, and had been willing to let Tyson go. But a month before the tournament, the U.S. invaded the tiny island of Grenada. "Then I remember reading in Jack Anderson's column that Castro had said he was sending out a squad of terrorists, and I felt maybe they might do a thing like that there," said D'Amato. "So I refused to let him go. This infuriated Bob Surkein. And he tried to bully me and intimidate me. . . .

"He said that if I didn't go down there that [Tyson] would never box

Tyson and Henry Tillman square off before the Olympic trials.

as a super heavyweight. . . . This guy is a kind of vicious man. . . . I don't allow people to intimidate me."

D'Amato goes on for several more minutes, uninterrupted, about the stranglehold Surkein and his minions had over the U.S. Amateur Boxing Federation. There's no doubt Surkein was angry about Tyson's pulling out of the Junior World Championships, nor that he had a strong dislike for D'Amato. But if Surkein was such a master of the dark arts, it would have been just as easy to handicap Tyson's chances at heavyweight as at super heavyweight. Either way, what was accomplished by D'Amato's self-righteousness and his now-public feud? It certainly didn't help Tyson. All that seemed clear was that the D'Amato of 1984 sounded very much like the D'Amato of 1964, railing about his enemies at the expense of his fighter.

Tyson arrived in Fort Worth on June 4 for the Olympic boxing trials. "It doesn't really matter who I fight," he said. "I plan on knocking everyone out." It wasn't the typical amateur's modesty, though it was unmistakably great copy. Tyson wasn't an enthusiastic interviewee. In fact, he was palpably disdainful of the "A" storyline, that inevitable comparison with Floyd Patterson. But no one had seen this combination of sullenness and esoterica before.

"My idols are Jack Dempsey, Henry Armstrong, and Panama Al Brown," he said, before excusing himself for having to mention that Panama Al, in addition to being one the greatest-ever bantamweights, was also a dancer with Josephine Baker's Paris revue and the longtime lover of Jean Cocteau.

Actually, the whole Catskill crew was media catnip, such was the brazenness with which they announced themselves. "He'd beat Holmes in three rounds," Rooney said of Tyson's chances against the reigning heavyweight champ, who by now had run his record to 42-0.

"They call him the Tan Terror," D'Amato said of his protégé, trying out a nickname that mercifully didn't stick. "He's the most destructive puncher in the country."

By now, the battle lines had been drawn. D'Amato wasted little time confronting the Olympic team coach, Pat Nappi, in full view of the press. The *Los Angeles Times*, quoting an unidentified member of the U.S. Amateur Boxing Federation, called Cus "a cranky old man." Then there was Surkein himself, a retired army major, weighing in on Tyson to dump on D'Amato the creator himself: "He's been taught all the pro rules. Twice disqualified for fouls." In fact, just once. "He was fighting super heavyweights and didn't belong." Why? He was knocking most of them out. "Whether he can overcome those stinking pro tactics Cus has taught him, we don't know."

TYSON'S FIRST TELEVISED BOUT, IN THE SEMIFINALS, PAIRED HIM with the world's highest-ranked American heavyweight. Henry Milligan was a former defensive back at Princeton. He'd turned down a professional baseball contract to box. As a fighter, his natural athleticism manifested itself in pure punching power. He'd already knocked out Al Evans and knocked down Henry Tillman, the tournament's presumptive favorite.

Milligan believed he'd put Tyson down, too. He was a twenty-five-year-old man; Tyson was a kid, just days from his eighteenth birthday, and still relatively obscure in open amateur circles.

As it happened, though, Tyson knocked out Milligan in the second—following two standing eight counts—with a right uppercut. "That's it! Fight's over!" hollered Howard Cosell, among D'Amato's steadfast allies from the 1960s. "All of the power I told you about. Trained by Cus D'Amato! D'Amato says, 'This young man is my reason for still living.'"

Tyson kissed Rooney first, then his opponent. None of that stands out to Milligan. What he recalls most clearly was, earlier in their fight, hitting Tyson cleanly with punches that had dropped the best amateurs in the world. "He never blinked," says Milligan. "He had a great chin. And that was the really scary part—the fact that I couldn't hurt him. I'm just thinking, *Well, you're shit out of luck now.*"

GOING INTO THE FINAL ROUND, TYSON WAS WELL ESTABLISHED AS the A-side. The crowd was with him, awed by his power. Cosell was with him, verbosely narrating a prefight feature on his old friend Cus and the boy he had saved. From any network's perspective, Tyson had the most precious commodities in boxing—violent power and a backstory. His opponent, Henry Tillman, had a story, too, though no one much cared. He was twenty when he went away for armed robbery and started boxing at the Youth Training School in Chino, California. Now here he was, but just a guy as far as the audience was concerned. If there was delight when Tyson knocked him through the ropes in that first round, there couldn't have been too much surprise.

"Mike Tyson," wrote Galyn Wilkins of the *Fort Worth Star-Telegram*, "fights like something in a dark alley."

That wasn't a compliment, but it spoke to a disquieting truth—what fans really want to see. There were 4,105 in attendance that day at the Tarrant County Convention Center, and most of them booed when, at the end of three rounds, Tillman won a unanimous decision.

It's difficult to disagree with them after watching the fight on You-

Tube. Tyson is the physically dominant fighter, though the idea of him as a crude slugger neglects his obvious dedication to the craft of boxing. He knew more than the dirty stuff. At five ten, facing a six-three opponent, he knew how to get inside. He knew how to go to the body; I wonder if the judges even bothered to count the body shots. Still, per the amateur rules, a mere jab counted as much as the body shot that felled Tillman in the first round or the right hands that stunned him in the third. That said, at least the judges didn't lack for a clear and consistent rationale, nor did Tillman's victory lack merit.

He had an excellent jab. What's more, he had the courage and composure to get off the canvas and use it well. "They had me watch some film on Tyson," Tillman tells me. "I knew I had to keep moving. I knew I couldn't stand there and trade with him. Mike Tyson had that reputation of being a young killer. Everybody feared him."

And you? I ask.

"I'm from South Central," he says. "I was raised up in juvenile hall, too."

As it ended, Tillman found himself in the peculiar position of consoling Tyson. Still, whatever Tillman's virtues as a sportsman, they were lost on Tyson's stewards, who wasted no time lighting into Surkein and his officials. "There's more scandal in this outfit than there ever was in the pro game," yelled D'Amato, waving a towel for emphasis.

"What happened to us here was political," said Rooney. "They don't want us around. . . . They want us out."

In fact, the federation quickly designated Tyson a "most worthy opponent," meaning he would have yet another chance to make the team at the Olympic box-offs—an additional championship round in which ostensibly amateur athletes would beat the fuck out of each other yet again for the glory of sport and the benefit of the federation and ABC.

ON JUNE 29, THE DAY BEFORE HE TURNED EIGHTEEN, TYSON OPENED the box-offs by quickly knocking out the other "most worthy" heavyweight, Olian Alexander. That set up a rematch with Tillman the following week at Caesars Palace in Las Vegas.

For all the anticipation, it wasn't much of a fight, though. Even Co-sell, an epic hype man, felt obligated to note midway through the second round that it was "hardly setting a high mark in excitement." There would be no knockdown this time. Tyson, wearing star-spangled shorts as if to appease the patriots on hand, didn't go to the body as he had in the first fight. Nor did he cut off the ring, as promised. He did connect with a few good shots in the final round, but not enough to really hurt Tillman, who stayed true to his plan to poke and move and won on de-cision, 4–1.

The postfight was more eventful. "Mike was robbed," said Rooney. "That's my official statement."

D'Amato unleashed a stream of invective and tried to punch an of-ficial. Tyson, moved by such a demonstration of loyalty, followed with a tantrum of his own. At some point, he even complained that Tillman was "trying to stick his thumbs in my eye." Then he walked past the Sports Pavilion and the TV trailers until he came to a salt cedar tree growing against a fence. From Earl Gustkey of the *Los Angeles Times*: "With his

Tyson and Henry Tillman in the box-offs at Caesars Palace

gloves off but his hands still taped, he pounded the tree with his fists, howling in fury. It went on for a minute or two, tears streaming down his face, until D'Amato wrapped him in a fatherly embrace and led him away."

Atlas had been right: There was no one to set an example for Tyson, to give him even a shred of humility or accountability. There was no sense of fidelity to anything so mundane as the rules. Rules were for the other fighters. It had always been this way; Rooney was just louder than D'Amato. Al Evans didn't knock down Tyson; it was a slip. Or the ref. Or the judges. It was Castro's terrorists. Or Bob Surkein, the reincarnation of enemies past. Cus and Rooney were ever ready to proclaim, "We was robbed!" After all, it was less precarious than telling the kid he'd have to improve at cutting off the ring. For D'Amato and Rooney, faulting Tyson, or telling him that word he never heard—*no*—would have been to drive him into the hands of rival managers or promoters. That wasn't coaching, though. And as far as his guardian was concerned, it wasn't parenting. It was enabling.

So they sent him to Houston, where the Olympic team would be training, with explicit sparring instructions to hurt his rivals. "Maybe Mike can knock Tillman out," said Rooney. "If he does, maybe Mike will still get a shot at the Games. . . . We told Mike that if he gets the chance for a knockout, to go for it."

Under amateur rules, any fighter who suffered a knockout, even in training, would be prohibited from competition for thirty days, thus, in the case of Tillman or even super heavyweight Tyrell Biggs, knocking them out of the Olympics. As the alternate, Tyson would get their spot. That wouldn't happen, though, as the Olympic coach, Pat Nappi, got wind of the plan and sent him home—though not before a ferocious if short-lived session with Evander Holyfield.

There are several versions. In one, after Tyson has knocked out all his usual sparring partners, Holyfield, a light heavyweight, volunteered for the job. In another, Holyfield was offended by the suggestion that Tyson—who had him by about twenty-five pounds—use only one hand. Either way, the session quickly devolved into something more desperately violent than sparring should be, and Nappi cut it short.

"This guy's got an ego," Nappi told Holyfield. "He'll try to hurt you."

Holyfield recalled differently: "He hit me with one right hand and near knocked me across the ring, but every time he stopped punching, I'd get my combinations off on him. I know I threw more punches at him than anybody else."

Still, whatever happened in the ring that day seems of less import than the fight that *didn't* happen. They were playing pool. Tyson had just lost. Holyfield had the next game, and the cue stick firmly in his grasp. He had seen Tyson take the cue stick from other fighters, most of whom were terrified of him.

"I'm playing," said Tyson.

"You ain't taking this stick from me," said Holyfield.

Tyson began to pace. Holyfield had seen this before: *Means he's mad.*

"Look here, Tyson, you ain't taking this stick. You might as well stop being mad."

Then Tyson started to laugh, the bully playing off his defeat. It would all be forgotten soon enough—though not by Holyfield, who, in a matter of weeks, would be controversially disqualified in the Olympic semifinals *after* knocking out his opponent. In all, nine Americans—including Henry Tillman—won gold medals that summer in Los Angeles. By then, however, Tyson was no longer anyone's ward but an eighteen-year-old negotiating with D'Amato for his Cadillac.

18

n October 1984, in anticipation of Tyson's professional debut, CBS News sent a crew to Catskill. "I fought very hard to do that one," recalls the correspondent, Robert Lipsyte. "It wasn't the kind of piece we usually did."

CBS Sunday Morning, as hosted by Charles Kuralt, had a distinct sensibility. Beginning with its theme music, a baroque trumpet fanfare, the show had a way of announcing subjects that possessed a certain dignity and merit that weren't often found in the vast wasteland of American television. The resulting piece, "Making Fire Out of Fear," aired on December 2, remains the fullest and most seductive telling of "Cus and the Kid."

Looking back, a vantage point that rarely makes journalism seem grander, it neglects all that was hidden from Lipsyte's view. There's no mention of the Cadillac Seville purchased to appease Tyson after he'd lost in the Olympic trials, his debauched nights in Albany, his forays into Brooklyn, where he would still, on occasion, rob and pillage, or the nastiness with which D'Amato would now regularly refer to his charge.

There were always those, a distinct minority, who found Cus and the Kid less charming than advertised. The author Thomas Hauser met them both the previous year, at the behest of Jacobs and Cayton, while researching his book *The Black Lights*, a study of the way boxing actually works, with heroism and exploitation acting in concert. "I spent a weekend in Catskill with Cus and Mike," he recalls. "Jim and Bill had explained to me how Cus had rescued him from the reformatory and how he was going to be the greatest heavyweight champion of all time—but more than that, how Cus had turned him into a model citizen. They made it sound like he'd get a PhD in literature from Harvard and go on to a career in academia. That may be an exaggeration—but not by much. Instead, I found an angry, hostile young man who was surly, rude, and disrespectful to Cus. By the end of the weekend, I didn't like him."

D'Amato, for his part, seems to have grown tired of Tyson, at least in stretches. "If Jimmy and Bill didn't have so much money invested in this kid," he told a couple of friends during the box-offs in Vegas, "I'd get rid of the son of a bitch right now." There was another instance—also reported in Peter Heller's 1989 biography, *Bad Intentions*—in which D'Amato referred to Tyson as "a n——r."

Lipsyte wasn't looking for dirt, nor did he have any cause to be. He was traveling around the country, working at a grueling pace, delivering a story a week for the broadcast. D'Amato and Tyson presented a rare opportunity, he recalls, "as much of a sentimental journey for myself as a piece."

Lipsyte grew up in Queens. His father was an educator who not only ran the 600 schools but also dropped on young Bob, then a copyboy at the *Times*, his first scoop. HEAVYWEIGHT CHAMPION IS HERO IN HIS OWN SCHOOL ran on June 25, 1960, marking Patterson's return to his alma mater, P.S. 614, after winning the title back from Ingemar Johansson.

Five years later, Lipsyte found himself in Las Vegas covering Patterson's beating and eventual humiliation at the hands of Muhammad Ali. The days leading up to the fight changed his professional life. D'Amato, who no longer had any official role in the Patterson camp, had been given "some walking-around money by the promotion," as Lipsyte recalls, presumably to talk up the fight.

"He was just kind of *there*," says Lipsyte. "I guess I felt sorry for him. We'd go out to dinner, then back to the hotel, sit around the pool, and he'd talk about the gym he owned on Fourteenth Street, how he slept there with the guard dog and how he'd be waiting for the Kid"—the paradigmatic pupil, that noble boy willing to face his fears—"to walk up those stairs, alone at night."

Lipsyte was twenty-seven and mesmerized by D'Amato—as was I at twenty-seven, when Teddy started telling me his version of Cus's stories as well as his own. It goes to the least appreciated facet of D'Amato's genius—and later of Atlas's. Whatever they were saying, they made you feel chosen, as if they were letting you in on a secret. When Lipsyte returned to the newsroom, there was a letter waiting for him. It was from an editor at Harper & Row, asking if he'd consider writing a novel with boxing as its "milieu." The resulting book, *The Contender*, was published in 1967. It's considered a young adult classic and has never been out of print.

It featured a kid from Harlem and a trainer, Donatelli, modeled after D'Amato. Lipsyte brought him a copy of the book. D'Amato was upstate by then, probably in Rhinebeck. "He was on the porch, just rocking," says Lipsyte. "Like he was waiting to die."

Fast-forward seventeen years. Lipsyte doesn't remember how he heard about Tyson or, rather, what he now calls "this creationist myth" of Tyson. Possibly the Olympic trials, but likely before. Whatever the case, Lipsyte knew it was time for another audience with D'Amato. "It suddenly hit me, at least metaphorically, who Tyson was," says Lipsyte. "He was the boy who came up the stairs in my novel."

It's difficult for any reporter, exempting the true sociopath, to be objective about his or her sources. Each scoop incurs a debt. But the greatest obligations are to sources who themselves are stories. The lives they gift you, which you appropriate or steal outright, aren't mere scoops but tend to be something grander, the kind of material that can make you, well, more than a reporter.

So it wasn't by accident that D'Amato had accrued so many credits and such goodwill among the now-regular pilgrims to Catskill. As boxing trainers go, D'Amato was a veritable patron of the arts. Was there a more willing subject for Talese as he learned to master the magazine piece? And there he is in Mailer's "Ten Thousand Words a Minute." Then there's Lipsyte's Donatelli and Hamill's Gus Caputo, the trainer in his boxing novel, *Flesh and Blood*.

It's Caputo who drives Hamill's fighter protagonist, Bobby Fallon, home from prison, where he has kept his honor intact—no coincidence, in Artie Diamond style—by savagely biting the nose of a big Black predatory con called Elizabeth Taylor. It's Caputo who gives Fallon a biography of Robert E. Lee and puts him on a diet of old fight films while extolling Ho Chi Minh's virtues as a strategist.

"Cus understood this strange affinity that writers and fighters have, or at least that writers have for fighters," says Lipsyte. "And he played it."

It wasn't just writers: Lori Grinker's photographs were gaining traction and Michael Marton's documentary had been released the year before. But it was the writers who still had influence in this predigital world. And it was the writers—Mailer, Newfield, and Hamill—who implored

José Torres at the Garden, 1958

Mario Cuomo to appoint José Torres the chairman of the New York State Athletic Commission.

New York's was still the most influential of the state commissions that regulated boxing. Now two of its three commissioners were D'Amato's former champions: Patterson, with whom he'd had a rapprochement, and Torres. Torres was not only the new chairman but also a perennial darling of the Gramercy school of literature, most of whom—the aforementioned, plus Schulberg—were on hand to celebrate his appointment during a well-attended presser at 2 World Trade Center.

It was the best kind of politics in that it *felt* righteous. "The Lost Hero," Hamill's 1966 *Saturday Evening Post* piece, recalls both the bartender at Toots Shor's who once balked at serving Torres, eyeing him as if he were another too-dark penniless immigrant, and the old Puerto Rican guy with a snowy mustache who wept with joy the night Torres knocked out Frankie "Kid" Anselm at the St. Nick's Arena. Now Torres was a boss, his appointment being celebrated by the bandleader Tito Puente, City Council president Paul O'Dwyer, and FBI agent Joe Spinelli, whose inquiry into boxing corruption had begun with a visit to the oracle of Athens four years prior. Of course, this being boxing, the much-alleged grand corrupter himself was there as well, front and center. "At last," Don King said of Torres, who'd spoken of unionizing fighters to protect them from their paymasters, "one of our own is in a position to guide us."

If the new chairman was a reformer, then D'Amato—the erstwhile crank who "never took a penny from my money," said Torres—had now become the sport's good conscience. Finally, he had his revenge on the body that had once tried to take his managerial license. So honored was D'Amato that he overcame his fear of heights and took the elevator to the governor's office on the fifty-seventh floor of 2 World Trade Center. Of course, he brought Tyson with him to hobnob with all the big shots. At seventy-six, D'Amato was having a moment, his last but also his grandest. He was ascendant.

Lipsyte's piece aired that Sunday. Tyson was charming, animated, thoughtful—exactly unlike the character he had played during the

Olympic selection process. "There's that pleaser aspect to Mike," says Lipsyte. "He's always had that."

And in this context, what could please more than an adolescent male, a fighter of all things, confessing to his fear. "I used to always think for some reason that I was a coward," Tyson tells Lipsyte. "I was afraid because of the way I felt."

The original cowardly boy in this construct was Floyd Patterson—and Lipsyte's affection for him throughout the piece is palpable. "Cus loves him a great deal," allows Tyson. "That's all Cus talks about . . . what Floyd did."

"In a strange sort of way, you are Floyd Patterson's younger brother," says Lipsyte. "You understand that?"

"Far off, no way," Tyson responds, firmly but still graciously. "There's no way I could be compared to Floyd Patterson. Only reason is that we're both Black and from Brooklyn and both met Cus at the same age. But other than that, to me I don't think there's no comparison."

In fact, belying his apparent affability, Tyson despised Patterson. "I was jealous of Patterson," he'd say years later. "Cus loved him so much. He never told me he loved me. . . . I was respectful to Patterson only because of Cus. I never said two words to him when I met him in person, though."

Still, it's more than that. Tyson had a lot to learn—of himself and of the world. One thing he did know, however, is that he'd never be like Floyd. Nobody would ever cast Mike Tyson as the Good Negro.

But the real star of the piece, of course, is D'Amato. "More than a manager of champions," in Lipsyte's voice track, "he's a saver of souls."

Given the chance, I'd have written the same line—gladly and proudly. This was the man, after all, who gave Lipsyte Mr. Donatelli and *The Contender.* "I was still grateful in the way that writers are grateful to their subjects," Lipsyte tells me. "I didn't buy everything *totally.* I saw him as something of a flimflam man. But I could not resist that story."

Resist? For fuck's sake, why? The sportswriter spends his life listening to professional killjoys, grown men ever tamping down expectations: *one game at a time, he's still young, a lot can go wrong, no sure things.* But

Lipsyte wasn't a sportswriter anymore. And here was D'Amato, on network television, betting on immortality, Tyson's and, by extension, his own: "He may go down as one of the greatest fighters of all time."

But the truly arresting line—the real confessional, as it were—is D'Amato's recollection of seeing Tyson punch for the first time. "I got excited, just like a young fella," he says. "Like a guy who's no longer capable of any sexual involvement and then, all of a sudden, becomes sexually interested again after he hadn't been that way for twenty years. . . . I get excited all over again."

Sexual potency was, if nothing else, an extraordinary choice of metaphor. It wouldn't have gotten on television today, certainly not network television. But, again, it was a different world. "In eighty-four," says Lipsyte, "I don't think we would have been quite as plugged into the homoeroticism of boxing. Obviously, it's there. . . . In both their cases there were always rumors of homosexuality."

"He was an egomaniac," says Lipsyte. "But above all, he was a teacher. He was endlessly didactic. He was not complete without a student. And Mike was a sponge. Mike absorbed all the stories, all the one-liners, all the bullshit. But in many ways, Tyson was his most brilliant student. Tyson made him complete."

That was the story: Poor Black kid saves old white man, frees him from shame and regret and renders them both immortal in the process.

Lipsyte wasn't the only one who couldn't resist the story, though he did a great service by codifying it for the rest of us.

Us, meaning reporters. Among my favorite passages is Mailer's description of the press headquarters—the cavernous "media workroom" in my day—for the first Patterson–Liston fight: "All the trash, all the garbage, all the slop and a little of the wealth go out each day and night into the belly of that old American goat, our newspapers. . . . So great guilt clings to reporters. They know they help to keep America slightly insane."

The goat has evolved, of course. But he gets only hungrier. So there's only one seduction here, one grooming to which I would swear. That would be the press, the media, whatever you're apt to call that insatiable beast.

Getting ready, early 1985

From 1979 through 1984, a period corresponding with his tenure as associate editor, then editor in chief of *Ring* magazine, Randy Gordon would meet Jimmy Jacobs every Wednesday for breakfast at the Cosmic Diner on Eighth Avenue. Without fail, Jacobs left a quarter as a tip, and he castigated Gordon on those occasions when he slipped the waitress a dollar.

That said, they got along well, two fight nerds. Jacobs was a reliable source of information and, after Gordon left the magazine, of income. By then, Jacobs had been talking about Tyson for at least a couple of years, telling Gordon how he'd be the heavyweight champion of the world before he was twenty-one, younger even than Patterson. That autumn, Jacobs proposed a deal: Use all your contacts. Every sparring partner procured for Tyson is a hundred dollars in your pocket. The fighters get fifty dollars a round and a bonus if they return for a second day.

"That was great money back then," says Gordon. "But everybody would bail out after a day or two. They'd call me up: 'You sonofabitch, who'd you put me in with?'"

Gordon received another kind of bonus—full run of Big Fights's extensive library and screening room, where one day in late 1984 he ran into Tyson. Gordon remembered when Tyson was still obscure on the amateur circuit, when other fighters just called him "the Monster." But as he found him that day, ensconced in the screening room, his mien suggested the most dedicated of scholars.

The room was a sanctum of boxiana: neatly stacked reels, shelves with year after year of *Ring* record books, and, as he came upon Tyson, lit as dimly as a confessional. The projector would hum and click as Tyson immersed himself in a generational study of heavyweight champions, beginning with Jack Johnson and Tommy Burns in Sydney, Australia, December 26, 1908. Then it was Jess Willard's turn with Johnson, the historical personage Tyson would have most liked to meet. Next it was Dempsey, with whom Tyson clearly wanted to identify—not merely for his ferocity but for his having survived among the hobos while riding the rails as a mere boy.

"Do you know he slept in boxcars?" Tyson asked Gordon.

Through most of the fights, Tyson would bob and weave on the couch, moving in time with the images on the screen. It was clear that he had meticulous command of each sequence in the action. When it came to Dempsey, he stood, his silhouette against the screen, fighting from a crouch, a bend in his knees, stalking, as if he were Dempsey himself.

Then they were on to Joe Louis. "Did you see that?" asked Tyson, referring to the nuances of Louis's right hand. "No one ever threw punches with that kind of precision."

They went through reel after reel: Jersey Joe Walcott and Ezzard Charles, Marciano, whose chin Tyson admired, and Floyd Patterson. "He was just too small," Tyson said of the fights with Liston. "Cus told him, but he wouldn't listen."

Of all the fighters, or ghosts of fighters past, it was Liston, even more than Dempsey, who ramped up Tyson's senses. They watched Liston's two knockouts of Cleveland Williams, the first in 1959, TKO 2, then the following year, TKO 3. Williams—"Big Cat," as he was known, with size, athleticism, and devastating power—might be the best heavyweight never to win the title. But he was helpless before Liston.

"Do you mind if I play it again?" Tyson asked when the reel was done.

Gordon couldn't help but notice the practiced dexterity with which Tyson handled the reels and the projector. They watched the second fight again. At one point, in the darkened room, Gordon heard "a kind of grunt" from Tyson. At the end of the fight, when one can't help but be struck by the valiant idiocy of Williams for having risen to his feet a second time, Tyson got up and turned on the lights. Gordon could see his eyes welling with tears. He looked as if he'd been weeping.

"What's the matter, Mike?"

"I could never beat him."

Tyson was eighteen, with fewer than thirty amateur fights and nursing an injury to a ligament in his left hand. His pro debut was still months away. "I'm fighting each of these guys as I watch them," he explained. "And I really see myself beating them all."

Except Liston, who had died under mysterious circumstances in 1970.

As the kid was in real distress, Gordon tried to comfort him: "The fact is, you're never going to have to fight him."

"But I *do* fight him," Tyson sniffled.

Gordon didn't understand.

"Up here," said Tyson, touching his temple with an index finger. "All the time."

"Do you ever beat him?" asked Gordon.

"Never," said Tyson, his voice breaking. "I could never beat him."

19

No one would confuse Hector Mercedes with Sonny Liston, though he, too, has his place in boxing history, albeit a footnote. Mercedes was listed at 199¾ pounds for Tyson's pro debut, almost 40 pounds heavier than he'd been two years prior when he lost his own pro debut, as a middleweight, by TKO, to somebody named Bob Sokol in Portsmouth, New Hampshire.

Mercedes was an opponent. The professional loser is a vocation unto itself in boxing. He's there to lose credibly, or spectacularly, and, when possible, to teach the prospect something about ringcraft even as he grooms the kid for stardom. Mercedes was born in Puerto Rico and boxed out of Lowell, Massachusetts. Judging from the prefight story in the Albany *Times Union*, he understood his end of the bargain. "I'm going to try to ruin his reputation," Mercedes said of Tyson, the reporter giving him credit for his "good command of English."

The date was March 6, 1985. The venue was the Empire State Plaza Convention Center in Albany, an odd concrete bowl better known as "the Egg." The promoters were a couple, Bob and Lorraine Miller, small-timers who did local shows—then again, that was the point. Tyson had already gotten more coverage and created more buzz than any fighter not to medal at the Olympics, and even some who had. Now, after years of

bankrolling both Cus and the Kid, Jacobs and Cayton would begin mon-
etizing the fable. This had long been an article of faith among them, that
D'Amato would grant Jacobs and Cayton stewardship over his ward's
professional endeavors. Together, they'd manage Tyson's career both in
and out of the ring. Boxing managers usually found themselves at the
mercy of promoters, who set the price and paid the fighters. But Jacobs
and Cayton sought promoters who served at *their* pleasure. They might
dangle Tyson as a potential prize to a given promoter but had no intention of entering into any long-term agreement, certainly not the "option
contracts" D'Amato so dreaded with boxing's most powerful promoters,
Bob Arum and Don King, who ruled the heavyweight division. Jacobs
and Cayton didn't want partners, much less bosses. Their strategy was
meticulous and they valued control above all else.

Mostly, that meant control over Tyson. The previous September, he
had signed an exclusive deal with Reel Sports—whose sole owner was
Cayton—to have Cayton serve as his "exclusive personal manager." Unlike
a boxing manager, his personal-services manager would be responsible for
all nonboxing income—that is, commercial appearances, endorsements,
film, and television. While most personal-services managers received commissions of between 10 and 15 percent, Cayton cut himself a bigger slice,
a full third over the staggering term of seven years. Of course, Tyson had
no lawyer, only D'Amato, who sought to clarify his standing in the agreement by adding under his signature: "Advisor to Michael Tyson, who
shall have final approval of all decisions involving Michael Tyson."

Weeks later, Tyson had signed another deal, making Jimmy Jacobs
his boxing manager at the then-customary (though still larcenous) rate
of 33⅓ percent. Also filed that day with the New York State Athletic
Commission was a form granting Cayton 50 percent of Jacobs's managerial cut and an application for Tyson's boxing license. Though D'Amato
would never work Tyson's corner—"If I die, I don't want you to look up
and see my face missing," he told him—the application identifies him as
Tyson's trainer. He's also listed as one of the eighteen-year-old's three references. The others include Jacobs's protégé, Steve Lott, a thirty-four-
year-old former handball champ working for Big Fights, and Pete Hamill,

whose name replaced the crossed-out entry for José Torres, as it was Tor-res who officially signed off on all these arrangements for his old friends.

If Tyson didn't understand the implication of all he'd signed, then neither did the Millers, who gave away their video rights to his fights (crudely filmed by Lorraine's brother) to Jacobs and Cayton. The Millers' ignorance of the master plan was evident from the start, when D'Amato asked Lorraine to redo the original fight poster. Figuring this was just another local show, she had Rooney—who was fighting an opponent of his own in the main event—in the customarily featured place. Though Tyson would appear in just the second of six bouts, D'Amato wanted him front and center. "I want people walking on the other side of the street to be able to see Mike Tyson's face," he told her.

Hence, while Tyson was identified as the "uncrowned Olympic champion," Mercedes's name didn't appear on the eventual poster. After watching their fight on YouTube, I'd like to say he warranted a mention, though I'm not sure I can. More notable, even with the videographer's limited recording capability, are the distinct thuds of Tyson's body blows. They're a worthy homage to Dempsey himself, as was Tyson's haircut—

D'Amato wrapping Tyson's hands for his pro debut

conspicuously shorn in a bowl-like circumference at least an inch above his ears. At 1:47 of the first round, his flanks under relentless attack, Mercedes crumples in a corner. Before the referee can count to five, Mercedes indicates he's had enough.

Tyson fought about every three weeks through the end of 1985, raising his record to 15-0, all by stoppage. The pace, like his haircut, was meant to evoke a hungrier, ostensibly more virtuous time in America. But the plan was more than mere nostalgia. "There was a shared sentiment on Tyson's management team," recalls matchmaker Bruce Trampler. "They came into our office and it started like this: 'Every day this kid has the potential to get in trouble. So we want to keep him busy.'"

The erstwhile mugger was now a celebrity in Brownsville. And what do celebrities want, even more than women? Street cred, of course. Something about street life remained addictive to Tyson, even if, or perhaps *because,* it had grown considerably more lethal in the years since he went upstate. The introduction of crack cocaine had transformed the stickup kids of yore into full-on gangsters. As a capitalist construct, it was near perfect. Misery produces great demand for illicit palliatives. On the supply side, there were few barriers to market. You didn't need a union card. You didn't need an old Italian man to put you on the books. Anyone with a 9-millimeter and a microwave, a little imagination, and a set of balls could now try his hand at becoming a boss. You could be Don Corleone or Tony Montana—until you weren't. That life appealed to something near Tyson's core. He would typically return to Brooklyn after fights. An old friend tells a story of riding in a project elevator with him: A third guy gets in the elevator. Tyson yokes him around the neck, goes through his pockets, comes up with eighty dollars, more than enough for the radio he has somehow convinced himself he needs. That should've been the end of it. Instead, though, Tyson starts banging the vic's head into the elevator wall.

IT'S NICE, OR PERHAPS CONVENIENT, TO THINK OF BOXING AS A SPORT.
At the nub of its attraction, though, what informs every second of the

audience's anticipation is a moment of violent resolution, something that would otherwise be illegal. People, mostly guys, want to see people fight. Maybe it's a kind of narcotic as well. Certainly, if boxing were outlawed—as the American Medical Association famously argued it should be in 1983—illegal fights and illicit venues would rise up as quickly as speakeasies and bootleg gin did in the 1920s.

Point is, what happened in that elevator—artless and brutal and damnable—wasn't unrelated to what drew fans to Tyson. He knew the game much better than those who came to see him fight. But they weren't there for tutorials in "the sweet science." That required a trained eye, not to mention patience. No, they came for the quick, apocalyptic finale, a guilty pleasure if ever there was one, the possibility of seeing something less than civilized. There was a palpable sense of violence—of threat—to everything Tyson did. His fights were short plays told in rounds, not acts: Tyson and his new cellmate.

If boxing is unpredictable, opponents are not. Only four of the first sixteen made it past the second round with Tyson. The one who went longest, Don Halpin out of Lowell, Massachusetts, was punished for his bravery, smashed with a gratuitous right hand as his head bounded off the bottom rope, his ass already firmly planted on the canvas. Another ref might've disqualified Tyson. But the refs—especially local guys in local venues—knew better than to trifle with the house. Besides, who would know? I'm sure the ref wasn't alone in that thought as Halpin, with his now-ruined nose, remained on the canvas for several uncomfortable minutes. It's not like the fight was on network TV or that channel on your cable box, ESPN.

In fact, Tyson did have four ESPN fights that first year, but ESPN had an exclusive deal with promoter Bob Arum's company, Top Rank. Arum and Don King were boxing's nuclear superpowers, though D'Amato claimed to hate Arum even more and had a beef with Arum's matchmaker, Teddy Brenner, going back to 1954. Of course, being declared an enemy of Cus wasn't a novel distinction in boxing, where enemies did business all the time. But now there was talk that Brenner was less than enamored with Tyson.

But that's not the reason he didn't sign with Top Rank. "Tyson was good for the ESPN audience," says Bruce Trampler, the aforementioned matchmaker who apprenticed under Brenner in those years. "But the true story is that they wanted to be the promoters."

They being D'Amato, Jacobs, and Cayton, of course. The bigger the promoter, the more control they would have to relinquish. So they stayed with small promoters they could control—like the Millers and, later, Jeff Levine, who ran an outfit called the Houston Boxing Association. "They weren't going to sign a long-term deal with anybody," says Levine's matchmaker, Ron Katz. "They just wanted somebody to provide them with a certain number of dates and do what they were told to do."

Matchmakers aren't necessarily the smartest people in boxing, but they're the smartest people *about* boxing. Pairing a prospect with the right opponent is less a science than an art. While Tyson already had a backstory, the fights themselves were to build him into an attraction. That's where the matchmaker came in. Katz had never seen a fighter like Tyson before, what with the lisp and the way he'd ask Katz's wife to take him for ice cream on the boardwalk after his fights in Atlantic City. It was like watching some bizarro science experiment, as if the kid had a switch that toggled between two channels, one with theme music from *Leave It to Beaver*, the other with Grandmaster Flash. But the talent was unique, too.

"Cus taught him well," Katz says. "Tyson was more than just a puncher. When you're a pupil, like he was, twenty-four seven, it's like someone put an electrical brainwashing thing on your head. After a while your mind does what that thing tells it to do."

Tyson knew angles, leverage, and, of course, dirty tricks. He studied his opponents. What's more, his jab had in fact evolved into the battering ram D'Amato had envisioned when he first had Tyson put under hypnosis. Not only did it move like a piston, but Tyson knew how to use it to get inside a larger man's defenses. Heavyweights were evolving, getting bigger and longer each year. Tyson, however, remained biometrically distinct.

I'm reminded of Brian Hamill's first glimpse of Tyson. He walked into the gym, saw a kid in street clothes, and asked: "Where's the heavy-weight?"

"You'll see," said D'Amato. "He expands."

In fact, he did—in a way that's almost beyond calibration. The spar-ring session that followed, recalls Hamill, ended with his "watching a fifteen-year-old kid beating the shit out of a grown man, a pro."

"He wasn't a big guy, but he was huge, if that makes any sense," the Schenectady *Daily Gazette*'s Bill Buell would recall of Tyson.

He could take out guys with a single straight right hand, and often did in that first year. But that wasn't his forte. Rather, it was the unique coil and torque from which he summoned his blows. They came from below, physically and perhaps, in a way, metaphorically. D'Amato fa-mously taught fighters to throw punches with "bad intentions." Tyson's were murderous. If there's been a more destructive right uppercut in the history of the division, it's news to me. At his best, or even close to it, Tyson was as vicious a body puncher as the heavyweights have ever seen. But his greatest weapon—his genius, you could argue—wasn't a punch or even a skill. Fans look at the fighter, but a matchmaker considers the opponent, *his* guy, as it were. Katz signed twelve Tyson opponents start-ing in July 1985—and almost every one had the same thing in common.

"They were shitting in their pants," says Katz. "I can't tell you how many times I literally had to push guys out of the dressing room. Tyson had an intimidation factor that you see in—what?—one in ten thousand fighters? Maybe."

"Where are you gonna make this kind of money for going this short?" Katz recalls pleading with a fighter named Michael Johnson, September 5, 1985, at the Atlantis Hotel in Atlantic City. "Just get out there, do what you can, and don't get hurt."

The fight was over in thirty-nine seconds. But the ring walk, the in-troductions, all the time it took for Johnson to anticipate the beating he would take, must have seemed an eternity. Waiting for that first bell, he looks like a condemned man. When he finally rose from the canvas, minutes after the second knockdown, he was missing a front tooth.

Tyson's next fight, against the "always tough" Donnie Long, as the former fringe contender was described on ESPN, was billed as his "toughest test yet." As it happened, Long went down three times before the ref called it off at 1:28 of the first round.

"It was no comp," Tyson said in a postfight interview that touched on all the rising contenders who had come to measure him for themselves from ringside: Jesse Ferguson, James Broad, Marvis Frazier. "All of you come get some. Mike Tyson is out here. He's waiting for you."

Tyson's first main event was on November 1, 1985, at the Latham Coliseum, just outside Albany, where he had been spending an increasing amount of time. It was also his first sellout, about 3,400 tickets sold, from twenty-dollar "Golden Ringside" seats to twelve-dollar general admission. The crowd, recalls one correspondent, was "chaotic" and "well lubricated." Judging from news footage, that seems a polite way of describing drunken white guys. I have nothing much against drunken white guys, having spent much time among their ranks as both participant and observer. But to watch snatches of the video is to *feel* them: guys who hung around the OTB or the VFW. There are some college kids, too. And small-time wiseguys. Their grandchildren will watch *The Hangover* and inquire as to the funny man with the face tattoo. But it's unlikely millennials could understand the improbable beauty of that night, what a former skell from Brooklyn has done in a country that five days later would give Ronald Reagan forty-nine of fifty states. Tyson has pierced something here—part of it racial, part ethnic—a barrier that divides most of American culture. They fucking love him.

"I had known nothing like it in sports before and have experienced nothing like it since, a full-body paralysis of expectation," writes Tim Layden, looking back on his first fight for the Schenectady *Daily Gazette* after a quarter century at *Sports Illustrated*. "From the moment Tyson stepped between the ropes, you could not look away, you could not speak, you could not move."

Just a week had passed since Tyson's last fight, a thirty-seven-second knockout in Atlantic City. Tonight's opponent, for what it's worth, is pretty big, a cop, in fact, back home in Trinidad. His name is Sterling Benjamin. He lasts fifty-eight seconds. Tyson is now 11-0.

"He have a sledgehammer, mon," Benjamin tells a local reporter. "It's the hardest I've ever been hit."

As it ends, Tyson offers his gloved hands through the ropes, palms up, to the delighted crowd. It's a gladiator's salute.

In three days, Cus D'Amato will be dead.

20

Their final conversation, at Mount Sinai Hospital in New York City, began with D'Amato having a last bowl of ice cream. For more than a year now, breathing had been becoming increasingly difficult for the old man. Now, at seventy-seven, he was dying of interstitial pneumonia. Tyson threatened to quit fighting, swore to always take care of Camille Ewald, and witnessed, for the first time, Cus moved to tears. Later that day, Jacobs took Tyson to the bank to deposit a check for $120,000. He wept in front of the tellers, with whom he usually liked to flirt. When it became clear D'Amato would not make it through the night, Tyson took a subway to Brooklyn. He was on a stoop in Brownsville when someone told him that news of the passing was on the radio.

"I know," he said.

Pallbearers for the funeral at St. Patrick's Cemetery in Catskill included Floyd Patterson, José Torres, Jay Bright, Jimmy Jacobs, Kevin Rooney, and Tyson. "Mike didn't want me to photograph him—didn't like it at all," recalls Lori Grinker. "But Jim explained how important it was to photograph the funeral. Jim talked him into it."

The day afterward, Tyson returned to the cemetery and performed his own ritual, dousing the grave with champagne. That was November 8. On November 13, in Houston, he knocked out six-foot-six Eddie Rich-

D'Amato's pallbearers included, *from left*— Jay Bright, Jimmy
Jacobs, Floyd Patterson, Tyson, and Kevin Rooney.

ardson at 1:17 of the first round. On the twenty-second, back at the
Latham Coliseum after a memorial service for D'Amato, he knocked out
Conroy Nelson, who managed to survive thirty seconds into the second
round with a broken nose before spitting out his mouthpiece.

I'm not sure if Jacobs's schedule was cruel, therapeutic, or both. Tyson
was still nineteen. He'd lost the closest thing he had to a father. But the
apparent ease with which Tyson maintained the pace—knocking out
professionals, albeit opponents, in just a round or two, is anything but
easy—obscured the least appreciated component of his makeup as a
fighter. At nineteen, grief and turmoil seemed second nature to him. Perhaps they constituted his natural state. He was, like Durán, a violent fighter.
But it's difficult to think of another boxer for whom rage and technique
were so indivisible. It was something to behold: the heel and the baby
face wound so tightly together, the thug who'd taken a sacred vow. Only
with the greatest solemnity did he address the TV announcer in Houston after relieving Conroy Nelson of an incisor: "We have to go on."

D'Amato's memorial service was held at the Gramercy Gym. "Jimmy

Unleashing a long left to Conroy Nelson's body

asked if I would sit next to Mike," recalls the author Thomas Hauser. "I was honored. But then he came back and asked if I could move so Tyson could sit next to someone who could be of more use to them. I think it was a newspaper columnist." While the fable of Cus and the Kid had now entered its eulogy phase, the memorial itself, described in the *Daily News*, was a distinctly literary affair. Budd Schulberg compared D'Amato to "Diogenes holding up his lamp—a strange maverick in the boxing world, looking for an honest man."

"His influence on boxing style was greater than Ernest Hemingway's impact on young American writers," said Mailer, a blatant falsehood.

"I always thought there was something kind of feminine about Cus," said Talese. "He was kind of grandmotherly in that he always cared about his fighters after their careers were over."

The truly great tribute, Pete Hamill's "Up the Stairs with Cus D'Amato," had appeared that morning in *The Village Voice*. It wasn't much different from the others, just richer, wiser, more personal, the end of something. But really what distinguished D'Amato's obituary was the narrative itself. His death had legs; his dream—producing a heavyweight champion even younger than Patterson—could live on.

"I can't call it a dream," Tyson told the *Daily News*'s Bill Gallo. "I see it happening like I know tomorrow's going to come."

How could you not root for that?

When has so vicious a fighter been rendered so sympathetic?

IF MAILER WAS WRONG ABOUT D'AMATO'S STYLISTIC IMPACT (BY MY count, there have been just three peekaboo champions), he'd been right about Jacobs, going back to Jacobs's Patterson film in 1963. He was a hack documentarian but relentless as a flack. And now he put it all to use. This was his moment.

Unlike America's great Olympic class of 1984—whose nine boxing gold medalists were christened on ABC—Tyson's career didn't unfold on network television. However spectacular Tyson's knockouts were, local cable was far from a guarantee that they'd be seen. Even ESPN, the country's largest cable network, was in only about 40 percent of American households. So using what was still a novel technology—the VCR—Jacobs and his boy wonder, Steve Lott, cut a highlight reel and sent it all over the country: to sports editors, boxing writers, news directors, network types, but most of all, to he who was still king in every affiliate's market, your local sports anchor giving scores and highlights.

"He has to fill three and a half minutes on your local newscast every single night, regardless of whether anything is actually happening locally or nationally," says Jim Lampley, a former KCBS sports anchor then working for ABC Sports. "But if Jimmy sends a tape—I think it was about a minute and a half—that can be used at any time by any sports director around the country, then at some time they will use it. He'll lead to a piece of tape: 'Hey, lemme show you something interesting: Young heavyweight just coming up. But he's got twelve or fifteen or seventeen knockouts in a row already. Take a look at *this*.' That's how most people met Mike Tyson."

"The best marketing job ever done on a fighter," said the British promoter Mickey Duff.

Seth Abraham, president of HBO Sports, recalls playing the tape in
his office with Bob Greenway, his director of programming, as they were
already immersed in negotiations with Jacobs and Cayton: "We kept trying to increase the brightness on the television. It was so poorly lit in
those little arenas upstate. But the impact—all those one-round knockouts strung together—was staggering."

The price would be staggering, too, at least by prevailing media-rights
standards, though by then Abraham was prepared for it. Greenway had
come to him the previous spring, already apprised of simultaneous negotiations Jacobs and Cayton were holding with the USA Network for
smaller fights and with ABC Sports. He thought Tyson would make great
sense for HBO. So did Abraham's acclaimed boxing commentator, Larry
Merchant. "Jimmy had created such a buzz and the heavyweight division
was so thin," recalls Merchant, a former columnist at the *New York Post*.
"So I went to Seth. I said, 'We've never done this. Let's follow this kid and
see where he takes us.'"

Like Merchant and Newfield and a slew of Tyson's early proponents
and patrons, Abraham was a Jew from Brooklyn, part of a generation
well versed in Irving Shulman's novel of teen depravity in Brownsville. I
recall some years later—'88 or '89, at a dinner at the Supreme Macaroni
Company on Ninth Avenue in Manhattan—Newfield explaining the pull
of Tyson's story with outstretched arms, *ta-da*: "It's the Amboy Dukes!"
The reference confused me briefly—I thought they played the Jersey
Shore—but Jack's larger point was impossible, even for me, to miss. He
was longing for the mythical Brooklyn. Hamill was, too, of course. Even
if that Brooklyn never really existed, it was worth convincing yourself it
had: an idealized, melting-potted workingman's Athens. It had its own
angel—Jackie Robinson, saint of courage and racial tolerance—and a ca-
thedral in Ebbets Field.

As it happened, Abraham grew up around the corner from Ebbets
Field. He earned a baseball scholarship to the University of Toledo, then
a master's in journalism from Boston University. By 1985, he had built

HBO into the premier outlet for championship-level boxing. But meeting Tyson, as he had late the previous spring, watching him work out in Catskill, took him back to the point of origin.

"It reminded me of the first time I ever saw Jackie Robinson," he says. "I couldn't take my eyes off him."

I remember Seth playing ball Saturday mornings at the McBurney YMCA. Though genteel in speech, he had very sharp elbows. On the High Holidays, I'd see him sitting in temple with his wife and daughter, a boutonniere in his lapel. Point is, I remember Seth fondly, and respect him. But Tyson wasn't anything like Jackie Robinson. Jackie Robinson was merely a sentiment that Seth—like Newfield and the rest of that Brooklyn tribe—wanted so desperately to see in young Tyson. Jimmy Jacobs had baited the hook very well.

Still, Seth doubles down—not as a nostalgist but as a ruthless television executive concerned with supply and demand of the medium's true and precious fuel. "Some athletes, very, very few, have a perpetual arc light on them—whether they're working or not," he begins. "Think of that famous photograph with Joe Namath at the Super Bowl, sitting by the pool, and all the reporters gathered around him. Namath had it. Johnny Unitas—great quarterback—did not. Jackie Robinson had it. Babe Ruth and Willie Mays had it. Hank Aaron did not. And of course, Ali. No one could match that shine."

Least of all the guy tasked with succeeding him. Larry Holmes was a great and courageous champion. But he was resented less for the beating he'd reluctantly put on Ali than for his own lack of charisma. Holmes was merely a fighter, neither heel nor hero, and a lightning rod for exactly nothing. To a TV executive, Holmes was death. Worse still, the heavyweight division itself had fractured. In September 1985, the undersized Michael Spinks beat Holmes for the IBF belt. Meanwhile, Tony Tubbs and Pinklon Thomas—each controlled by Don King—held the WBA and WBC belts, respectively. For the first time in the American Century, people couldn't name *the* heavyweight champion.

In Tyson, TV executives saw a potential solution. Television was even more voracious than that old American goat, the newspapers. Television eats story incessantly. But Tyson had so many stories: Brooklyn, Cus, the pigeons, the palpable savagery with which he fought. What's more, he had this great capacity to surprise.

Abraham recalls Tyson visiting his office. He had a well-stocked bookshelf, full of histories and biographies, some gifted to him by his fellow history buff Don King. In the midst of these fat volumes were a series of slimmer ones. They did not have dust jackets, just a distinct burnt-orange binding, no discernible letters on the spine.

"Oh my God," said Tyson. "Is that *Black Dynamite*?"

A first edition, in fact. *Black Dynamite: The Story of the Negro in the Prize Ring from 1782 to 1938* was a five-volume history written by *The Ring* editor Nat Fleischer and published by C. J. O'Brien in 1938.

"How do you know that?" asked Abraham.

"Are you kidding?" said Tyson. "I've always wanted it. But they're so old."

"Mike, take one or two for yourself."

"I couldn't. They're too valuable."

"My wife is a librarian. I'll replace them."

Tyson gingerly selected two volumes. "Are you sure?"

"Of course. My gift to you."

Tyson sat back down, stroked the covers gently, then cradled each in a hand, looking at them in wonderment.

"Like they were newborns," says Abraham. "That always stayed with me. It struck me how many Mike Tysons there actually are. It made for great journalism. And great television."

TELEVISION IS VISUAL, OCCASIONALLY AESTHETIC, BUT MOSTLY COM-mercial. Rarely, though, have commerce and journalism come together so harmoniously as they did for the Selling of Mike Tyson. He fought twice that December of 1985: his New York City debut against a 250-pound journeyman named Sammy Scaff at Madison Square Garden's Felt Forum, and an opponent named Mark Young back at the Latham Coliseum. Both were first-round knockouts televised on the USA Network, and they generated nearly identical responses when Tyson was asked of his future plans: *You'll have to ask my managers.*

More notable was Tyson's new look: making his gladiator's procession to the ring with no robe, no socks, just black shorts. The idea, again, was to evoke the sepia-toned glories of Marciano or, before him, Dempsey, as if Tyson himself stepped out of an old fight film. Steve Lott, an assistant in Tyson's corner and his roommate whenever he stayed in Manhattan, thought to put a small American flag on his trunks.

"I felt the flag would have a subliminal effect on the press," said Lott. "They'd find it more difficult to write negatively about Mike."

You wonder, then, as the press could not have written more glowingly about Tyson: What did Lott know that the rest of us did not? Athletes could lie about not reading their newspaper clippings, but broadcast executives read them like tea leaves. *The New York Times*'s Phil Berger did a two-page spread (with a Grinker photo on the jump page) in anticipation of Tyson's Garden debut: "Tyson, at Age 19, Rushes to Fulfill D'Amato Vision." Newfield got four open pages in the *Voice*, along with four Grinker shots, calling Tyson "D'Amato's Unfinished Masterpiece" and noting that author and subject attended the same elementary school in Bedford-Stuyvesant. Then there were segments on *Good Morning America* and the *CBS Evening News with Dan Rather* and an almost-six-minute interview with Bryant Gumbel on *Today*. Finally, when you anatomize Tyson's incipient fame, there's that cherry, still regarded as the most valuable coin of the predigital realm, a *Sports Illustrated* cover.

This one, by the excellent Bill Nack, had a headline, KID DYNAMITE, that spoke to the arrival of "the most electrifying heavyweight prospect in years." By the time it hit the stands the first week of January 1986, Tyson had a four-fight deal with ABC, whose VP of program acquisition, Bob Iger, seemed to have gotten the memo: "Nothing seems to electrify the boxing world more than the talents of a young heavyweight with a big knockout punch."

Certainly not the Olympians ABC had signed with such fanfare after the Los Angeles Games. The contract of one gold medalist, Meldrick Taylor, had already been allowed to lapse. And while Iger would readily admit that the '84 team had failed to produce a star like Sugar Ray Leonard, boxing ratings were down on each of the networks. Some of it probably owed to the cry to banish the sport. If signing the palpably violent Tyson would only antagonize the American Medical Association, then perhaps, at some level, that was the point. Tyson represented a change in strategy, in the nature of the attraction, but also a new way of doing business. By now, HBO had also locked up its deal with Tyson, due to begin sometime after he debuted on ABC. While networks often insisted on "exclusivity" with certain fighters, Jacobs and Cayton insisted on nonexclusivity when dealing with the networks. It made them want the kid only more.

ON MAY 18, 1956, WHEN HE WAS SEVEN, HIS FATHER ALREADY DEAD of cancer for a year or so, Jim Lampley attended a party with his mother, Peggy, in their hometown of Henderson, North Carolina. It was an adult gathering, and Mrs. Lampley had no one to mind her boy, so she instructed him to sit on a couch in the den and watch *Friday Night Fights*.

"This is what your father would've wanted," she told him.

There was a little transistor television on a TV dining tray. To Lampley, it cast a kind of blue-gray magic over the combatants, Sugar Ray Robinson and Bobo Olson. That was the first fight he saw, and it was not, in a particular way, unrelated to the first fight he called. That was on February 16, 1986, Tyson's ABC debut against Jesse Ferguson, who was 14-1 with ten knockouts, most of those owing to Ferguson's formidable left hook. It was a Saturday afternoon, *Wide World of Sports*. But the venue itself, configured to accommodate a sellout crowd of 7,600, looked and felt like something out of time. The Houston Field House, on the campus of Rensselaer Polytechnic Institute in Troy, New York, was built in 1949 and was primarily a college and minor-league hockey rink. The fans were locals, but for a smattering of big-city sportswriters and broadcast executives. They sat amid steel girders. Smoke hung in the air. It could've been a Friday night long ago.

That had to be the first Tyson fight I ever saw as well. I was twenty-three, in graduate school, and my limited exposure to boxing had been acquired while beer-buzzed or high, or both, during closed-circuit fights at the Ritz or, once, up in the blue seats for Marvin Hagler–Mustafa Hamsho at the Garden. Sitting up in the blues, I couldn't get any sense of what Hagler was actually doing. But even buffered through the lens of analog television, Tyson seemed a revelation. If writers and artists seek to distill art from boxing's savagery, Tyson distilled the violence itself, liberating the sport's guilty pleasure from the sweet science. That's not to say Tyson was unskilled or without craft—just that I wouldn't have been able to discern it then. What you couldn't ignore, though, was the fight's distinct sociology. Bernie Goetz, Eleanor Bumpurs, and Michael Stewart were still in the news. In the city, the story was race and crime. But all these yokels upstate were cheering for a brother from Brooklyn? What stayed with me, though, was the particular sound and ferocity of the body shots Tyson put on Ferguson. I was another casual fan. And like the rest of them, I wanted more.

It's nice to know, after watching the fight on YouTube, that I remember it properly—though not as well as Lampley, who met Tyson at the usual "fighter meetings" with broadcasters the day before the bout. "He'd been carefully schooled," says Lampley. "He knew we were network broadcasters and to be nice to us. All the street roughness seemed to be smoothed off when we spoke. He was shy, very capable of expressing himself, but still very much under the control of Jacobs and Cayton. He never went anywhere without Steve Lott at his elbow."

Ferguson wasn't a bum, certainly not at that point of his career. But four decades later, those body shots still sound as if the audio has been enhanced. What finally dropped Ferguson, in the fifth round, would become recognizable as Tyson's signature combination: a right hand to the body, followed by a right uppercut.

"It exploded Ferguson's nose," says Lampley. "There was blood all over the place."

In the sixth round, the referee disqualified Ferguson for doing all that he could at that point, which was holding on for dear life. The DQ would have ended Tyson's knockout streak at seventeen, had it not been for the chairman of the New York State Athletic Commission, José Torres.

"We called it a disqualification on the air. "What is it officially?" Lampley asked him.

"The referee chose to call it a TKO because he warned Ferguson four times to fight. He also noticed Ferguson was incoherent."

Incoherent but had the presence of mind to hold? The interview concluded with Lampley bringing in Tyson. That had to be a first: a state athletic commissioner welcoming a fighter with a kiss on the cheek.

"They have a plan in their mind to beat me: jab, potshot, and grab me," said Tyson. "But eventually I'ma catch them."

"You could see it coming," Lampley says four decades later. "The public was going to fall in love with him: the blood, the instantaneous destruction of the opponent, and then—balancing the ledger—that *voice*. He was like this semiformed little kid, but he's capable of saying things that are profound about the sport. And he doesn't even realize he's doing it. He had a unique education from Cus, and he was smart enough to retain things and repeat them back in an interesting way."

Among the profundities that afternoon yielded was Tyson's quote describing the uppercut that ruined Ferguson's face: "I was trying to catch him at the tip of the nose and push the bone into the brain."

It was another Cusism, drilled into his subconscious. But given the AMA's well-known call for the abolition of boxing, it was considered a problem. Jacobs and Cayton blamed the press agent, of course. His name was Mike Cohen, and they promptly abolished him by firing. In actuality, though, they should've given Cohen a raise.

Lampley, still at ringside when he heard the quote, understood exactly how it would play: *Oh, my God*, he thought. *This isn't gold. This is platinum.*

21

Back in the summer of 1984, after the Olympic trials, Tyson competed in the Empire State Games, where, in the course of winning another amateur title, he befriended a basketball player from the Albany region, Chris Holloway. Some weeks later, Holloway's younger brother, Rory, came downstairs for breakfast and found a stray. "I see this big freaking guy just sleeping on the floor in his underwear," says Rory. "I guess him and Chris had been hanging out the night before. So his head pops up and I say, 'Who the hell is you?'"

"I'm Mike Tyson," he lisped.

Holloway had heard the name, vaguely knew the rep.

"Where you going?" asked Tyson.

"You know, run some errands, play some ball."

"You got a car?"

Technically, yes. It was an old Lincoln Holloway had resuscitated after his father had left it propped up on cinder blocks, intending to salvage the parts.

"Oh, man," said Tyson, "I'm gonna hang out with you."

So it began.

"The thing that made me and Mike so close is we were complete opposites," says Holloway. "But we understood each other. I mean, Mike is like the best, the *only* friend I ever really had in my life."

Rory was laid-back, while Mike tended toward chaos and grandiosity. Mike was verbal, manipulative, funny. Rory never had a street fight and didn't smoke or drink. Still, at first, it was Rory who had the higher social standing, having been, in the not-so-distant past, the starting quarterback and star point guard at Albany High School. He'd been written up in the papers, even mentioned on the local news. Rory's plan—play some junior college ball, get his grades up, then go Division I—hadn't exactly panned out. But unlike Mike, he says, "I had a car. I had money. I was working."

He had two jobs, in fact, the first of them at the family business, Holloway's Grocery, a little market and then a soul food restaurant, whose pantry he would often raid on Mike's behalf. The second was as a counselor at the Berkshire Farm Center, under the state's Division for Youth Services. It was primarily a group home for foster kids, some hard cases, but not the kind that got sent to Tryon. "I actually loved that job," says Holloway, recalling how he played ball with the kids. "I learned to listen. I learned how to be vulnerable. I learned how to make those kids feel like they was wanted. Like, 'Hey, man, you ain't by yourself. You got somebody.'"

Looking back, Holloway's knack for making himself amenable to adolescent males was not unhelpful in his relationship with Tyson. But the real attraction for Tyson, that which kept him a regular guest in the Holloway household, was his mother.

"She treated Mike just like me or my brothers, like one of her own," says Holloway. "Like, when he'd get all upset—'Everybody's messing with me, Ma'—he called her 'Ma'—she used to rub his head. She loved Mike. She babied him.

"And after we opened up the soul food place, soon as Mike walked in, my mother would put a big pile of wings in front of him. Mike would sit at the counter, just him and my mother. But say the guys come in and Mike started cursing? All she had to do was look at him."

Tyson would hang his head. *I'm sorry, Ma.*

As for Tyson's own mother, recalls Holloway, "Mike didn't talk about her too much."

Nor his father. "Not at first," he says. "But later on he would say things like 'Yo, my father was a pimp. A pimp and a preacher.'"

For all of Jimmy Kirkpatrick's supposed skill with women, though, it wasn't a gift that Tyson inherited. "I mean, we were two broke guys driving around in a raggedy-ass car," says Holloway.

After the Lincoln died, they rented something car-like from a guy named Gino. While it had a tape deck from which Tyson would blare Run-D.M.C. and UTFO's "Roxanne, Roxanne," the heater didn't work, and there was a hole in the driver's-side floorboard. During snowstorms, a slushy blizzard would come up through the open gap.

"Don't worry," said Tyson, "when I'm champ—"

"Better hurry your ass up," said Holloway. "Cause we 'bout to freeze."

Still, Tyson loved cruising Albany. "Compared to Catskill—which is like one red light in the whole town—Albany was the closest thing to Brooklyn," says Holloway. "I would always drive, because Mike couldn't. And he would *try* to talk to girls. But mostly Mike would play the 'shy guy.' Like, 'Yo, Ro, tell that girl this, tell this girl that.' We did some double-dating. He tried to make it seem he was this humble guy. He was anything *but* that. But that's the role he played."

It would change as Tyson acquired more buzz and more money. Being on TV helped. So did the Cadillac Cus got him (and Rory mostly drove). Quite suddenly, torn slips of paper with phone numbers began appearing under the windshield wipers. "His name started vibrating through the neighborhood and the girls started giving him some play," says Holloway, whom Tyson shouted out following his knockout of Donnie Long on ESPN.

"My dearest friend Rory Holloway back in Albany, New York," he said.

Whatever Tyson thought of Holloway, though, it was not an enthusiasm shared by his handlers. Holloway recalls driving home one morning after an especially eventful night. Mike wanted to go home and sleep.

But Holloway insisted that he head straight to the gym in Catskill. They began to argue. "Why you so worried about the gym and *those* sons of bitches?" Tyson asked. "Those motherfuckers don't like you anyway."

"Cus and them didn't want Mike around no Black people—period," Holloway tells me now. "They didn't want Mike to have nothing to do with Brooklyn or anything that looked like Brooklyn. And I guess, to them, I look like Brooklyn."

Did they dislike Holloway because he was Black? Or, more likely, because he was beyond their control? Those needn't be mutually exclusive answers. What's inarguable, however, was the void created by the death of D'Amato. Without the guardian-Svengali, who really had custody of Tyson's body and soul? For now, it was Jacobs. "Cus told me that if anything happened to him I should depend on Jimmy," said Tyson, who came to think of his manager as family. If D'Amato was a father figure to Tyson, then Jacobs was somewhere between an uncle and a brother.

It was a role Jacobs loved to play, referring to Tyson as "my guy" or, on occasion, deaf to his own condescension, "my little guy." In private, though, Jacobs was different. "Michael is a thug, and he'll always be a thug," Jacobs confided in Bob Gutkowski, then president of Madison Square Garden Television. "I can protect him with the local police. But once he discovers women, I won't be able to protect him anymore."

Of course, he already had. And while Tyson may have played the "shy guy" around Holloway, the greater part of him remained the feral outcast who had to drag eighth-grade girls onto the dance floor. He'd merely become more aggressive.

Kenny Adams, an Olympic coach, remembers walking down a street with Tyson during the Los Angeles Games.

"Hey, bitch," Tyson catcalled a woman passing by. "Hey, bitch, come here."

"Hey, Mike! You don't *do* that," Adams admonished him. "You have to apologize."

Mike did.

Unfortunately, there was nobody like Kenny Adams in Tyson's orbit. He wasn't taught; he was enabled. The dynamic had been established years earlier after he grabbed at Atlas's sister-in-law. Now Jacobs was no better than D'Amato. Tyson's handlers would do whatever was necessary—typically deny, blame, bribe—to diminish the incidents' severity or make them disappear altogether. Besides, most women said nothing—even Lori Grinker, who recalls a shoot in Catskill, a winter's day with Tyson not long after he turned pro.

"He wanted me to let him feel my breast," she says.

Tyson became angry when Grinker pushed his hand away, throwing her light meter in the snow. Still, she let it slide. "It was a one-time thing," says Grinker, "and he was mostly very respectful."

"Did he apologize?" I ask.

"Probably not," she says.

Tyson had no talent for rejection, ever. Four days after the Ferguson fight, he apparently got very fresh coming on to a department store sales-clerk. She didn't appreciate it and told him so. What happened next was cause for a front-page scoop in *The Knickerbocker News*, March 1, 1986:

AREA MALL KOs TYSON

FIGHTER OUSTED FOR "LEWD" REMARKS

It was a short story—just twelve paragraphs—but the kind a young reporter tends to remember. "My editors were very excited," recalls Pamela Newkirk, then covering the suburb of Guilderland. "But no one wanted to go on the record." In due course, though, she got confirmation from the mall manager, Kenneth Beckman, who explained that on February 20, four days after the Ferguson fight, Tyson "went into Filene's"—a local department store at the Crossgates Mall—"and caused a disturbance and security asked him to leave. He then caused a similar problem at the cinema." A security guard went on to tell Newkirk that Tyson "made lewd and obscene comments to female customers and was throwing clothes around" at Filene's. Tyson, with a crew of friends at the time, including Holloway, apparently left before the cops were called. Still, it was Tyson's first dose of bad press and carried the implicit suggestion that the

Capital Region's now-favorite son had been less than fully rehabilitated and, at least by inference, that the great D'Amato might not have entirely succeeded in his existential errand.

Jacobs, who professed to be unaware of the incident, refused to even raise it with Tyson, lest the matter distract him. "Mike is in training," he told Newkirk.

The day after her scoop, a reporter from the Albany *Times Union* showed up at Filene's department store. The manager confirmed the story with an apprehensive nod but refused to give her name or comment further for fear of getting fired.

Reading it now, the rest of the *Times Union* piece feels like every other denial still to come from the Tyson camp: from Rooney's vociferous denial ("didn't happen") to the oft-repeated assertion that things had been blown out of proportion due to Tyson's fame (such was Holloway's recollection). If that didn't work, there were the local cops. "The Albany police commissioner was valuable in taking care of Mike Tyson in many ways," Cayton would recall years later. "Steps were taken with the help of police to put lids on things."

Looking back, the entire mall episode—minor as it might've seemed at the time—formed a template for things to come. If Tyson was culpable in the creation of his own caricature—that angry Black man from whom no woman was safe—then so, in part, were the monkish D'Amato; the Boy Wonder Jacobs and his reserved-to-the-point-of-arrogance partner, Cayton; the hard-drinking Rooney; and the ever-present Steve Lott—all the great ladies' men in charge of his life.

THE FALLOUT JACOBS AND CAYTON FEARED AFTER THE FERGUSON fight—mostly from the "I was trying to push the bone into his brain" comment—never materialized. In fact, the remark elicited a round of hearty guffaws in the postfight press scrum gathered around Tyson. The single known objection was logged by Ernestine Coleman, Tyson's former social worker, who read about it in the newspaper. "I was very angry," she said. "I wrote Mike a letter and I asked him to be a man, not an animal."

It was Coleman who had arranged Tyson's release from Tryon and his placement with D'Amato and who had taken it upon herself to retrieve him from Brownsville when he was depressed and mired in self-pity following the death of this mother. Hers was the voice so conspicuously absent from Tyson's life—a Black woman interested in the person, not the pugilist. Just the same, her concern was lost amid an uncomfortable, rarely mentioned truth.

Among the greatest flatteries any athlete can receive—from a fellow athlete, especially—is to be called an "animal" or a "beast." It's said without irony and intended mostly as metaphor. But the other sports—even violent ones like football and hockey—are merely metaphors for what boxing actually is. Boxing is combat. Its very animalism—what would be illegal on the street—is what people come to see. Even the great pure boxer, that defensive wizard so glorified in sweet-science lore, celebrated in that same way Middle America dutifully claims to revere jazz, requires *a fuckin' animal*, as it were, to prove his prowess, else it just looks like he's shadowboxing.

Tyson knew all this at his core. It was a lesson begun in Brownsville. But D'Amato drilled it into his subconscious. And what a glory it must have been for a boy with no family: to find his place in such a historic fraternity, whose lineage ran from Dempsey to Durán, LaMotta to Liston, a barbarian tribe whose ties ran even deeper than race. Tyson loved all fighters but the animals most of all. Among the animals, he was kin.

His handlers weren't unaware of this dynamic. They had a keen understanding of the sport's history and knew exactly where they intended for him to sit at the table of immortals. They *wanted* an animal. But their sensibilities were antiquated, of an age that still insisted on the artifice of respectability. They didn't understand what his pre- and postfight comments would become, or how to monetize them, the windfall that would come of his malaprops and grandiosities, those born of anger and others curiously innocent. Jimmy and Bill still wanted a polite beast.

After the Ferguson fight and the Crossgates Mall, though, Tyson wasn't trending in a polite direction. Some of it might have owed to his boozing, much of which he did in and around Albany, where he felt protected.

"We partied after the Ferguson fight," he would recall. "I was drinking heavily at that time . . . a full-blown alcoholic."

His facility for drinking, likely inherited from his mother, was astonishing. "He'd take the hardest liquor and just turn it up," said Holloway. "He'd put the cup down, and it was empty, like a little kid trying to do big-boy things."

Jacobs and Cayton, meanwhile, just wanted to keep the wheels on Tyson's bus until it could arrive at its destination. "I had to watch him constantly, remind him how to behave after a fight, and rehearse what he should say," said Lott, who by now had become Tyson's full-time babysitter.

Soon after the Crossgates incident, Jacobs and Cayton convened an off-the-record meeting with those they deemed the most influential boxing writers in New York. The site was a Midtown steakhouse, which recalls the first tenet I learned upon leaving the city desk for sports: "If it ain't catered, it ain't journalism." Guests included Phil Berger of the *Times*, Mike Katz and Bill Gallo of the *Daily News*, and Ed Schuyler of the Associated Press. Those uninvited—the wild cards whom Jacobs felt less likely to control, Wally Matthews of *Newsday* and Mike Marley of the *Post*—would ever refer to it as "the Bootlickers' Ball."

"Jimmy was very conscious of making Mike likable . . . so that if he got into trouble we'd all say, 'Oh, well, he's just a kid,'" said Schuyler. "There was a desperation about it all. Like, *Let's get this guy a title before he gets into serious trouble.*"

22

The mall incident would be quickly forgotten or referred to, mostly in the local press, as "unsubstantiated." But it initiated a curiously fallow stretch for a fighter still deemed a prospect. Perhaps the partying had taken its toll. More likely, Jimmy Jacobs had outdone himself—engendering expectations that weren't merely unforgiving but truly had no precedent.

On March 10, at the Nassau Coliseum, Tyson knocked out a journeyman named Steve Zouski in the third round. Though Zouski had never before been down, it was regarded as an underwhelming showing—even by Tyson himself. "I didn't like my performance," he told Randy Gordon, who'd been hired by Jacobs to call an otherwise untelevised fight recorded for the Big Fights video archive. "I have a lot of personal problems that I'm just getting over."

The way Jacobs and Cayton spun it, Tyson was just another nineteen-year-old having "girlfriend problems." In fact, though, while he was already running around with any number of women, he had no *girlfriend* per se. Rather, his despondence reflected a wholesale change in urban life, something as yet unnoticed by Middle or white America—the introduction of crack cocaine. The body count in places like Brownsville and East New York made the days of Murder, Inc., seem tame. Tyson's old friends included both shooters and victims, and victims who'd been shooters themselves. Still, Tyson was periodically, perhaps inexorably, drawn back to the streets. Per *Sports Illustrated*, Rooney became "frantic" when Tyson went to visit his sister, Denise, without telling him.

Then there was a persistent ear infection that kept him on intravenous antibiotics in Mount Sinai Hospital for the better part of a week. Almost two months would pass before Tyson's next fight, the longest inactive period in his still-very-young career. His opponent was James "Quick" Tillis, a rugged, experienced Oklahoman and easily the best fighter Tyson had yet faced. Now the Glens Falls Civic Center was packed with a crowd of 7,600, all apparently rooting for Tyson to extend his knockout streak to twenty. ABC made the fight part of its *Wide World of Sports* package on Kentucky Derby day.

Joe Cortez, a Golden Gloves champion from Spanish Harlem, was already refereeing his fourth Tyson fight. He remembered Tyson as a kid at Nelson Cuevas's smokers in the Bronx. This wasn't expected to go any longer than those. "When I'm giving them their instructions," says Cortez, "I look in their eyes."

For fear. Always for fear. Cortez was pretty sure he saw it in "the Fighting Cowboy," as Tillis had taken to calling himself. Perhaps he did.

"He can hurt you with either hand early in a fight," ABC's Alex Wallau said of Tillis. "But he's always faded and tired badly."

In other words, it was only a matter of time.

Tillis turned pro back in 1978 and won his first twenty fights. Now he was twenty-eight, with a record of 31-8. He'd already been knocked out by three of that era's champions, Tim Witherspoon, Pinklon Thomas, and Greg Page, none of whom had close to Tyson's power. Tillis had been around long enough to know how this was supposed to go.

Opponents may well have the loneliest job in the world, not unlike the bull in a bullfight. But the bull doesn't know it's his day to die; the opponent does, at least metaphorically. Quick Tillis knew that all these happy people in upstate New York, not to mention all these TV guys with their cameras, were united in expectation: to watch him stagger, fold, and fall, to see how well, or how badly, he would die.

Though prizefighting is a cynical, dispiriting game, a fighter's greatest virtue is the ability to remain undiscouraged. Tillis found something in himself that afternoon. He boxed, something most fighters found too psychologically strenuous to do when confined to the same ring as Tyson. And for most of the ten-round distance, he gave as good as he got. Tyson, for his part, showed there was a formidable chin attached to his twenty-inch neck. Though he won by unanimous decision, if he hadn't knocked down Tillis in the fourth, the fight would've ended a draw.

There had been a smattering of boos in the latter rounds—no surprise, as the audience had been denied that felled and bleeding bull so implicitly promised. But the heckling spoke to an ignorance of what was really happening. Tyson himself would always recall what Tillis taught him: "He gave me such a body beating that I couldn't even walk after the fight. . . . I found out what fighting was really about that night. Several times during the fight I wanted to go down so bad just to get some relief, but I kept grabbing and holding him, trying to get my breath back."

Nevertheless, Tyson's knockout streak was over. "Simply marvelous," bullshitted Jimmy Jacobs. "Now he knows he can go the distance."

James "Quick" Tillis educating the young pro

"When it was over," recalls Joe Cortez, "I said to myself, *Tyson's gonna have some trouble with guys who are tall and decent punchers who can box him from the outside.*"

As it happened, Tillis fought another fifteen years, until he was forty-three, with a record of 42-22-1. The finale came Friday, the thirteenth of April, 2001, when Tillis was knocked out in the ninth round in his opponent's hometown of Saint Joseph, Missouri. Cortez reffed that one, too. At some point, both Cortez and Tillis moved to Nevada, where they run into each other from time to time at boxing functions. Every conversation seems the same:

"Hey, Joe, I gave him a tough fight. You *know* that, right?"

"Yes, James."

"I'm the first one," he says.

"You are," says Cortez.

"Couldn't knock me out."

"Yes, James. You should be proud."

IT IS NOT UNUSUAL FOR THE PROSPECTS I COVER TO WORK HARDER on their Instagram feeds than they do in the gym. Then there are heavyweight champions who find excuses not to fight for less than eight figures. In every division, a tough fight—win or lose—now seems an excuse for a mental health sabbatical and a year's worth of tomato cans. Yes, I know what I sound like. And perhaps I am. I recall cranky old men complaining that the game wasn't what it used to be. Now I'm one of them. Boxing is never what it was or, perhaps, only what it seemed to have been. But I do know, as judged by the standards of any era, that it's to Tyson's everlasting credit that he fought Mitch "Blood" Green only seventeen days after going the distance with Tillis.

"Seventeen days?" says a manager friend of mine, Keith Connolly. "I can't get a kid back in the gym after seventeen days."

The Green fight would mark Tyson's HBO debut, his first time headlining at Madison Square Garden, and his first encounter with Green's promoter, Don King, about whom he'd be amply warned. "The individual who controls the heavyweight title controls boxing," Jacobs would lecture the Garden's Gutkowski, envisioning a not-so-distant future with Tyson as the undisputed champion. "I don't want to give that away to anyone."

Anyone included Bob Arum, whose promotion of Marvin Hagler and Ray Leonard was crucial to the ascendance of HBO Sports; Butch Lewis, who controlled Michael Spinks, recognized as both the IBF and "linear" champion for beating Larry Holmes; and King, who controlled just about anyone else of note in the division. "The very last thing Jimmy wanted was for Mike to get involved with King," says Gutkowski. "He was more worried about King than anyone."

Toward that end, Gutkowski—who had already cut a groundbreaking deal with George Steinbrenner to broadcast the Yankees on the MSG Network—had begun discussions with Jacobs about the Garden's parent company, Paramount, coming aboard as Tyson's promoter. Paramount would act as a bank, while granting Jacobs the autonomy he needed to continue orchestrating Tyson's career. Paramount would also buy or lease the entire Big Fights library, a windfall to entice Cayton. But the real impetus for these discussions would be keeping Tyson from King's grasp. Then again, as Tyson himself assured Gutkowski in private, there was nothing to worry about: "King is a prick. Fuck him. I'll never be involved with him."

If Tyson was mimicking what he'd heard from Jacobs, he'd also, at nineteen, perfected his knack for telling the grown-ups—particularly New Yorkers of a certain vintage, like Gutkowski—exactly what they wanted to hear. While the Garden fancied itself "the Mecca of Boxing," it could no longer compete with the casinos of Las Vegas or Atlantic City. In fact, there hadn't been a heavyweight main event there since 1981, when Gerry Cooney knocked out Ken Norton in fifty-four seconds. But Tyson's impassioned recitation of the Garden's past glories inflamed Gutkowski's sense of possibility. "Mike knew the entire history, just about every fight, and told me what an honor it was to fight at the Garden," he recalls.

But back to Mitch Green, who had his own local pedigree, having won his fourth consecutive New York Golden Gloves title when Tyson was still in Tryon. Now the World Boxing Council—King's preferred sanctioning body—had Green ranked seventh, ahead of Tyson at number eight. Still, what made Green intriguing was his standing on the street. At six five, with an abundant, Jheri-curled mane and a ubiquitous toothpick dangling from his mouth, Green looked as if he'd just stepped from the set of *The Warriors* or *Escape from New York*. Unlike movie legends, though, Blood's could be vouched for.

"He belonged to the 17th Division, the meanest squad in the Black Spades," recalls Greg Vicenty, a two-time Golden Gloves champion from the South Bronx. "Whenever the gangs had a one-on-one situation, they'd bring in Blood. They'd meet under a bridge or in a dead factory on Bruckner Boulevard. They'd agree on who was gonna fight—you're talking a bunch of crazy Black guys and a bunch of crazy Puerto Ricans, a lot of them ex–Vietnam vets—then everybody made a circle and started screaming. I was a kid. I would sneak out of the house. We'd be watching from outside a fence, and they would just beat the shit out of each other until somebody didn't walk.

"I never saw Mitch lose. He was so big you couldn't hurt him. He'd just come in with that giant Afro, take off his vest, and smash you into the pavement. Everybody knew him. He was a beast."

Green still saw himself as he'd been in those rumbles. What's more, he saw Tyson as he'd been, too. In Green's view, the pecking order still held. While he remained the indomitable standard-bearer of the Black Spades, Tyson might well have been among the urchins watching awestruck from behind the fence. Green could feel it. He could smell it, Tyson's shadow self, that bruised boy rummaging through an abandoned building. If nothing else, it made for an interesting promotion. Unlike any of the previous opponents, Green was genuinely and demonstratively unafraid of Tyson, whom he called "this ugly little kid."

HALF A CENTURY REMOVED FROM GREEN'S STREET-FIGHTING HEY-day, I reach him by phone in Jamaica, Queens, where he still lives with his mother. I wonder what he remembers about Spofford.

"Judge remanded me for another ten days," he says. "I was a little hostile, I guess."

"How old?"

"When I was thirteen. Kids was older than me, but I was bigger."

"You fight when you got there?"

"I didn't have to. I got my respect."

"What was it with Tyson?"

"I *asked* for Tyson. The way he talked, the way he acted, way he looked— soft. Little motherfucker like that? Shit, I knew he been picked on."

PERHAPS THAT WAS ON TYSON'S MIND WHILE HE TRAINED FOR Green at D'Amato's old Gramercy Gym. José Torres's older brother, Andresito, watched the workouts closely and reported back that Tyson seemed "unnaturally scared." Just the same, amid the cast of uninspiring and nondescript heavyweights, Tyson was just now beginning to comprehend his true power in the business of boxing. The week of the fight he did *Good Morning America*, *Entertainment Tonight*, and *The David Letterman Show*.

A crowd of five hundred or so packed the lobby of the New York Penta in anticipation of his public workout. "We want Tyson!" they chanted.

"There's no fighter in the world as famous as I am," he told *Newsday*'s Wally Matthews.

Still, it was Green who stole the show at the weigh-in, which was going along smoothly until he learned that Tyson's purse under his new three-fight HBO deal would be $250,000. Green was making $30,000.

"I ain't no bum or no opponent for this boy," he said. "No way he deserves ten times as much money as me."

Green was 16-1-1 as a pro. He trained sporadically and complained chronically, mostly about his purses, the biggest of which had been $10,000, earned the previous year in a close decision loss to Trevor Berbick, now one of King's champions.

"I want my money," screamed Green, who said he'd been promised

Mama's boy: Mitch "Blood" Green heeding his mother's advice
during the weigh-in at Madison Square Garden

a purse roughly equal to Tyson's. That was highly likely, as boxing
promotions—King's especially—were often conceived around a fighter's
susceptibility to flattery, false promises, and phony inference.

"They just want to send me out to get knocked off," wailed Green,
threatening not to fight, saying he hadn't even signed a contract for the
bout. Interesting, then, that José Torres had thought to bring with him
that very item—the signed contract—from the Athletic Commission.

"That's not my son's signature," said Green's mother, Charlene.

True. Green's name had been signed by Carl King, his titular manager, whose single qualification for the job was being Don's adopted son.
Actually, most King fighters were then managed by Carl. Technically, the
arrangement was not illegal, just an outrageous conflict of interest, the
price of doing business with King, and a form of extortion worthy of a
Budd Schulberg script. Still, it was Schulberg's buddy, Torres—the ostensible reformer, appointed to defend the proletarian fighter—who rushed
to King's defense, saying it was perfectly fine for a manager to sign for
his fighter.

"If Mitch does not fight, he will never fight again in the United States," Torres told Mrs. Green. "The New York Commission will not only take his license away, it will write letters to every commission urging them to do the same."

Green, who by then had already shoved Carl King, then carried on some more. But he was out of moves.

That night, King called Gutkowski. King played a role to the public's great delight: the bombastic ghetto Barnum with gravity-defying hair. It was a clown suit he wore as camouflage. Underneath, though, the true man was preternaturally bright and a straight gangster. It was that guy, the authentic King, who rang Gutkowski, telling him not to lose any sleep over Green. "That fucking nigger will be there," he said.

MY MANAGER FRIEND, CONNOLLY, ATTENDED THE FIGHT WITH HIS father, who had come into possession of a press pass from *The Irish Times*. They started in Green's locker room, where the former gang leader was chewing on his toothpick and still blathering about the Kings. More noteworthy, in Connolly's estimation, were the two statuesque, immodestly clad women nodding in time to everything he said.

I imagine them as wrestling valets.

"More like strippers," says Connolly.

In the other dressing quarters, Tyson had just emerged from a shower to a room packed shoulder to shoulder with reporters and hangers-on. Tyson made Green's girls seem chaste, as he wore only a towel around his neck. He was now ready to be interviewed, a session that would be less memorable for whatever he said than for the unmistakable if off-the-record messaging.

"I was only thirteen," says Connolly. "I mean, I didn't even know they make them that big. Then somebody pokes his head in and says, 'Yo! Don King and Dick Young'"—of the *Post*, famously irascible dean of the New York sporting press—"'are about to fight.' All of a sudden, Tyson got *so* happy. He threw on his clothes, then we all ran out to see what was going on."

That's an accurate anecdotal approximation of what it feels like covering a fight: the unintended comedies; the manner in which it transforms everyone, even the innocents, into voyeurs; the humidity; and the adrenalized pack with whom you run from skirmish to skirmish as if chased by bulls. King was six four, a *big* six four. Young, now the star of Rupert Murdoch's *Post*, was what one might term regular sized. "But he wouldn't back down," says Connolly. "I remember that."

The exact source of their beef was unknown, though Young took some obvious delight in Green's again trying to shake down the promoter, threatening not to come out for the main event. "I want the whole thirty thousand dollars or I won't fight," Green told Torres, who then delivered the message to the promoter.

"Give him all the money, José," said King.

"That's not right," said Torres. "What about the manager's share?"

"Give him that, too," said King, referring to his son's $10,000 cut.

With that, Green went out and lost nine of the ten scheduled rounds. He was a lot bigger than Tyson—six five, 225 pounds, to Tyson at maybe five ten and 215—with a good fast jab but only a slapping right hand. Much to the crowd's dismay, Tyson didn't even knock him down—

Green, on fight night, taking his beating

though he did succeed in sending Green's mouthpiece flying three times, once with a section of his bridgework as well.

Still, one can argue Green notched a kind of victory that night, and not merely by defying the widespread expectation of his early demise and going the distance. The unlikely triumph was in beating the Kings— *père et fils*—out of ten grand. King had killed men for less.

The following year, cops pulled over a thirty-year-old Black male at the intersection of 124th Street and Seventh Avenue in Harlem. He had been driving while watching television, a small set mounted on the dashboard of his Lincoln Continental. His license had been suspended fifty-four times. Also found was an unknown quantity of pills and a bag of "angel dust." It was the first, or maybe just the first known, of Green's habitual arrests for possession of PCP.

It's tempting, then, to write him off as a dust head, just another New Yorker who spoke in manic tongues. So I wasn't surprised when, toward the end of our conversation, Green became agitated after I told him I had another call coming in.

"They telling you to get off the phone with me, right?"

"Who's telling me, Mitch?"

"The government. I got the fucking government on my phone."

Of course.

Really, though, what's the difference between a madman and a seer? Call him crazy if you must. Just understand, as it pertains to Don King, Mitch "Blood" Green was a lonely prophet.

23

As mere eighty-six-year-olds, epic antagonists who had arrived, somewhat improbably, at a gentler time in their lives, Don King and Bob Arum agreed to sit with me for a joint interview in 2018, occasioned by their last copromotion. The taping was intended as light fare—*Hey, look at boxing's grumpy old men*—promoting a 140-pound title fight between Arum's guy, Jose Ramirez, and King's fighter, Amir Imam, at the Garden's Hulu Theater. And for the most part it remained a cordial yuk-fest, though King, still a man of prodigious appetites, threatened to walk when he saw the bare place setting where he was to sit.

"Doughnuts," he said. "There should be a plate of doughnuts, at least."

The interview would not commence until a PA returned with a box of doughnuts. Then the two promoters agreed that the secret to a long life was doing what you loved, even if, I was left to assume, the day-to-day of one's passion included betrayal, bribery, and litigation. Perhaps more to the point, they also agreed on the advantage of dealing with fighters in cash.

"That was a disadvantage to me as somebody out of Harvard Law School," said Arum. "I wasn't in the numbers business. You could offer a fighter five million, or you could give him five hundred thousand in cash, and he would grab the cash."

Every time.

"Anybody would," said King.

I remind King that a mere fifty grand in cash not only got Ali to drop his lawsuit but also gave King an option on his final fight, what eventually proved to be a grotesque beating at the hands of Trevor Berbick in the Bahamas.

"I used to have drawers full of money," explained King, recalling from decades prior his initial seduction of Ali. "I let Ali come to my house and said, 'Whatever you can pick up out of there is yours.'" Per King's rules, the bounty was limited to a single fistful of dollars, whatever Ali could grab with one hand, though not underhanded in a scooping motion. "He'd see all that money and his eyes would get bigger than his stomach. One time he got thirty-five thousand. One time he got twenty-five thousand. But most of the time, like, ten or fifteen thousand."

Arum can't contain his mirth at King's description of an otherwise majestic Ali inevitably grabbing more than his hand could hold and spilling the stacks of cash.

"There's nothing illegal about it," says Arum.

Still, it's odd seeing Arum come to the defense of his former nemesis, especially as it was King who usurped him as Ali's promoter. In the mid- to late eighties, during one of the periodic federal investigations targeting King, Arum received a call from an assistant U.S. Attorney in the Southern District of New York. The prosecutor explained that death threats had been overheard in surveillance and he was now obliged to apprise Arum of the possibility of "imminent bodily harm."

Arum figured it had to be King and called a mob lawyer in New Jersey. The attorney then flew to Florida, sat down with the appropriate parties, and promptly forwarded the Mafia's message to Arum. "If I step off the street and a bus hits me," he recalled, "Don King doesn't live for thirty minutes."

Within the hour, Arum got a call from King himself: "Har-har-har. I would never do any harm to you."

King listens intently, wearing his usual: a spangled, bejeweled denim jacket, a badge declaring his allegiance to Donald Trump, a prominent

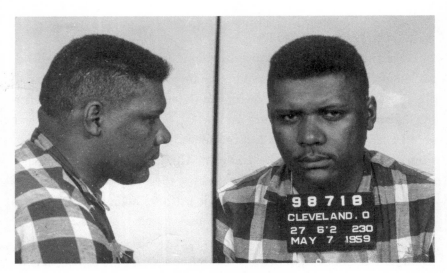

Don King, age twenty-seven

crucifix dangling from his neck, and those flags he likes to wave, among them the colors of America, Israel, and Mexico. It's as if he were kin to the Joker, the Riddler, and the Penguin. Behold, the aging archvillain.

The basis for humor isn't costume, though. Humor derives mainly from what's plausible.

"Would you ever," I ask King, "take a contract out on him?"

I'm playing for the easy laugh, of course, and waiting for the *har-har-har*. This time, though, King fails to see the humor.

"What for?" he says plainly. "If I wanted to do something to him, I'd do it myself."

KING WAS BORN AUGUST 20, 1931, ON THE EAST SIDE OF CLEVELAND, the fifth of seven siblings born to Clarence and Hattie King. His father died at his place of employment, the Jones & Laughlin steel mill, the day the Japanese bombed Pearl Harbor.

"Consumed by molten steel," said King.

Whether due to grief or in spite of it, the boy exhibited a fervent, Al-geresque industriousness. He worked all through high school, shining shoes and busing tables at local country clubs, and upon graduation took 3:00-to-11:00-p.m. shift at Midland Steel. Then there was a midnight shift as a sweeper at the government-owned defense contractor Tapco on Euclid Avenue, and a side gig running numbers for extra cash. King's plan had been to make enough to cover tuition at Kent State, where he hoped to eventually study law, but he found himself seduced by the feel of the cash in the numbers game and, at nineteen, he went into business for himself.

"What's your limit, son?" prospective customers would ask.

"The sky is my limit," he'd say.

When it came to paying out, young King would tell the winner to meet him at, say, the Trophy Lounge, where he'd arrive at least half an hour late. Just when the winner had begun to sweat, he'd make a grand entrance: holding a brown paper bag with about ten pounds of street-worn bills. "I'd just dump all the money out on the bar," King would recall to the late Red Smith. "All the bartenders would be laughing and the barmaids be pouring the drinks."

Then the precocious hustler would buy a round for the bar, explaining to the now-grateful winner that he'd been paying off bets all over town. "Tell the people where you got it from," he'd bellow. "When you bet with DK, you got to get paid. I'm like Fort Knox."

They called him the Kid. He was a star on the street, what with a piece of the Corner Tavern, where B. B. King and Lloyd Price played regularly. By his mid-twenties, King had established more than a mere numbers operation. He was one of the "Big Five," a cartel composed of Cleveland's most prominent numbers bosses.

King logged fifteen arrests between 1951 and October 1956, most of them minor traffic or gambling violations, nothing that stuck and nothing violent. It was clear, however, that King was fully prepared for the rough stuff endemic to his profession. On December 2, 1954, King scored his first known kill in a shoot-out with three men sent from Detroit to rob one of his gambling spots. As it ended, a stickup man named Hillary Brown lay dead. King used a Russian-made revolver.

"He shot up the house," King recalled of his brief encounter with

Brown. "I had on a camel-hair coat. Bullet went right through the camel-hair coat but didn't touch me. I tell you it's divine providence."

Perhaps just as divine was the county prosecutor ruling Brown's death a "justifiable homicide." Even as King's rap sheet grew, so did his standing in the community. By now, he had taken a common-law wife, Luevenia Henderson, and adopted her son, Eric. Whatever late hours he kept, whatever his nocturnal vices, he'd found that balance amid the competing impulses so familiar to hustlers of a certain generation: the sacred and the profane, street life and family life. A two-part profile by Christopher Evans in *The Plain Dealer Sunday Magazine* notes that the wunderkind numbers boss enjoyed "a reputation for never missing a Sunday morning church service no matter how late he was out on Saturday night."

THE ANNALS OF AMERICAN ORGANIZED CRIME FEATURE SEVERAL figures renowned for their facility with numbers. Meyer Lansky and Abbadabba Berman, Dutch Schultz's accountant, come readily to mind. But King had it, too, that gift of mathematical dexterity.

There were two kinds of numbers games in Cleveland, "policy" and "clearinghouse." Policy was a straight lottery, a numbered ball that was drawn and witnessed. Policy operators exploited the bettor's highest hopes with infinitesimal odds and were eventually replaced by the same state governments that could not shut them down.

Clearinghouse was based on a series of digits found in *The Wall Street Journal*, the last number in each column for the market's daily composite of advances, declines, and unchanged stock prices. But King developed a system called "the Count" or "the Rundown." As explained in the *Plain Dealer* profile: "He would call a stockbroker in New York to get the listings just before the market closed. He would then work up combinations based on those figures and bet them"—using his brigade of runners—"with other policy houses. It was almost foolproof, and Don would hit big and regularly, always driving a fancy car, dressed like a player with a .38 in his belt and a big cigar in his mouth."

Hence, among the Big Five, it was the upstart King who quickly established himself as *primus inter pares*. It was more than his mind for business, though, as evidenced on the night of May 20, 1957, when a bomb blew his front porch into splinters.

The gangsters of Cleveland had long been partial to bombings. But this one came from the most feared man in town. At 3:40 a.m., King called the vice squad sergeant at home. "Shondor Birns did this," he said.

Birns, Cleveland's "Public Enemy No. 1," was born in Hungary and grew up on the East Side, the son of a butcher. His mother burned to death in 1920, after an illegal pot still she was tending blew up in the family apartment. Shondor grew up to be an avid whoremonger, with nondescript features but always well dressed—even in prison, he maintained a locker full of silk shirts, suede shoes, and perfumed soap. Among the endeavors that kept Birns in the finest haberdashery was protection, a service for which policy and clearinghouse operators would gladly pay, even if they didn't need it. Most of them, anyway. Though the Big Five had agreed to pay Birns a thousand dollars a week for the privilege of not being firebombed, King came to see it differently and ceased payment. Now, his porch still aflame, King informed the vice squad sergeant, Carl Delau, that he'd testify against Birns in open court.

As the trial drew near, King was ambushed outside the garage at his home. He took twenty-five to thirty pellets of number 5 bird shot to his ears, the back of his head, and his torso and spent the night under police guard at St. Luke's Hospital.

Birns didn't turn up for a couple of days. "I knew the police wanted to talk with me," he explained. "But it was a Jewish holiday."

Just weeks later, still undaunted, King and Luevenia testified against Birns. They apparently convinced all but a single member of the jury. That would be the one Birns reportedly bought for eight grand.

Fast-forward: April 20, 1966, 12:30 p.m.

Officers Robert Tonne and John Horvath of the Cleveland PD's "Green Beret" tactical squad—each of them in plain clothes—were on routine patrol at the corner of Cedar Avenue and East One Hundredth Street when they came upon a crime in progress outside the Manhattan Tap Room. As Tonne phrased it in his incident report: "A colored male

King making himself at home in the local cop shop

was laying on the northerly sidewalk and another colored was kicking him in the face and head."

The man doing the stomping was amply framed, about six three. He was also brandishing a .357 Magnum with which he had pistol-whipped the prone man, identified as Samuel Garrett, thirty-four, a frequently hospitalized, tubercular drug abuser getting by on a single remaining kidney.

"How much do I owe you?" Garrett kept repeating. "How much?"

By now, a crowd had gathered in front of the Tap Room. "Donald, don't kick him no more," an onlooker called out. "He's hurt."

The cops—"rollers," they were called back then—approached with service revolvers drawn and yelled for King to drop his gun, which he did in the manner of a seasoned felon: turning slowly and tossing the blood-stained .357 onto the trunk of the nearest parked car. As Tonne went to retrieve the gun, he saw King deliver the coup de grâce, one last kick to Garrett's already ruined head. Garrett's left eardrum was ruptured, his jaw broken, his skull fractured.

Tonne would later recall, for Jack Newfield's investigative biography *Only in America*, bending down to surmise Garrett's condition—bleeding from the ear and mouth. "Don," he moaned, "I'll pay you the money."

Then Garrett lost consciousness.

The cop recalled thinking it was odd that the perp, of whom he had no recollection, already knew *his* name. "Tonne," he said. "You don't have to cuff me. I'm Donald King."

IT WASN'T UNTIL HE READ FREUD THAT KING COULD UNDERSTAND what had happened that day with Sam Garrett. "I was transferring guilt," said King, who famously characterized the fatal beating as "frustrations of the ghetto expressing themselves."

In fact, though, King had long since left Cleveland's East Side for tony Shaker Heights after a tip that yet another bomb had been planted in his automobile. "The car was parked in the garage," said a friend of King's. "Don never moved the car. He moved his family . . . but left the car in the garage."

By the time of Garrett's death, newspapers referred to King as the "notorious clearing house operator." Still, the title itself obscured yet another of his gifts for unfettered commerce. To King, enemies were fungible. No offense was so grievous or personal, no adversary so odious, as to prohibit a rapprochement for the sake of additional profit. For example, not only had King made peace with Shondor Birns, but they'd become partners. By late '66, though, with Birns facing legal issues—taxes, bribery, witness tampering—King stood to become *the* numbers man in Cleveland.

His base of operations remained the Corner Tavern, where he was ostensibly the manager—but he had a new Cadillac convertible and a trusted assistant. Her name was then Henrietta Renwick, widow of the late John Renwick, another Cleveland numbers boss. Following a raid by IRS agents, the *Cleveland Plain Dealer* identified her as "the chief clerical employee of King's operation." In fact, she was already more than that and, even when offered immunity, "Henri," as King called her, took the Fifth.

In the years to come, King would cross a variety of boundaries with the women in his life. But they all stood up for him. Some would testify on his behalf, as Leuvenia did against Birns. Another would go to jail for him. Others would function in his orbit as both executives and mistresses. But for all the pimp-like loyalty King extracted from his women, whatever his faithless proclivities, Henri would always remain the love of his life. Not only did he adopt her son, Carl, but they even shared a lawyer, James R. Willis, with whom King surrendered to police at 9:00 a.m. on April 26, 1966, the morning after Garrett finally expired.

King knew his victim. "When Sam Garrett come home from the penitentiary, he come to me for a favor," said King, who put him to work laying off bets and sent him to a dentist. "He knew I had helped him every way there is."

Perhaps, as King argued, his very largesse was the source of the fatal ghetto transference. Whatever the case, prior to the killing, one of King's side bets had hit—he was playing 3-4-7 that day—and Garrett didn't pay. They got to arguing. Then, per King, Garrett attacked him as he was trying to flee in his Caddy. That's when King reached for the unregistered gun, which just happened to be lying on the front seat because, as he told the cops, he was on his way "to buy some new grips for it and have it registered" that very day. Again, King argued divine providence, as it was the gun, he said, "that really saved me."

Even before consulting with his estimable counsel, King framed the incident as self-defense. Unfortunately, the knife he suspected Garrett had in his pocket was never found. Garrett was unarmed. He weighed 134 pounds; King went 240. Still, cops would hear that King bragged of spending $30,000 to bribe witnesses and even bet $5,000 while in Houston for the Ali–Ernie Terrell fight that he'd never serve a day. But while the civilian witnesses against him had either become forgetful or disappeared, the cops—especially Tonne, who turned down King's repeated enticements before trial—proved especially convincing. After deliberating just four hours on the judge's instructions, the jury found King guilty of second-degree murder.

Though the charge called for life in prison, Judge Hugh Corrigan allowed King to remain free on $5,000 bail pending Willis's motion for a new trial. Five months later, on a Friday afternoon in July, Corrigan reversed his own ruling at trial and reduced the jury's conviction to manslaughter. Then he left for a two-week vacation in Michigan, where he was unavailable for comment.

"The judge was a stinking bastard," said Captain Carl Delau of the homicide division, who was just a sergeant back when King, a sometime informant of his, called him at home the night of the Birns bombing.

Some years later, while researching his King book, Newfield received an FBI memo curiously absent from the judge's file. It's dated 1965, from the special agent in charge of the Cleveland office to J. Edgar Hoover, noting a mobster informant's allegation that Judge Corrigan had already granted an illicit "favor" for $6,000. Apparently, a local Mafia figure was looking to gauge Corrigan's amenability to future favors and was told the guy to see was Shondor Birns: "Corrigan will probably grant him whatever he asks." The capo in question was James "Jack White" Licavoli, future boss of the Cleveland Mafia. It was Cleveland that controlled the Teamsters and their Central States Pension Fund and, by extension, held great sway in Las Vegas. The main artery of criminality in postwar America ran right through Cleveland. And if it fed Jack White, then so too did it nourish Don King. No surprise, then, that Licavoli was also a client of James R. Willis. He did good work, as evidenced by the sentence he got King—one to twenty years, of which he'd do only four at Marion.

FATHER FREDERICK FUREY, MARION'S LONGTIME PRISON CHAPLAIN, had two favorite clerks—Birns and King, whom he called "a genius."

"Donald had no use for the Black Muslims or militants," said Furey, a former Golden Glover from Boston. "He probably had a couple of hundred thousand dollars when he came to jail and, like Shondor, he wasn't unwilling to use it."

The difference is, no matter how many times Birns went away, he would always remain Birns, until the night of Holy Saturday 1975, when his torso was cleaved in half and blown through the roof of his

Continental Mark IV. King, on the other hand, was transformed in prison. He likened it to a religious conversion—Daniel in the lion's den, Jonah in the belly of the whale. If that pleased Father Furey, it was merely King's natural aptitude for telling people what they wanted to hear. More likely, King's transfiguration was closer to what he told Norman Mailer, which, I have no doubt, was exactly what Mailer wanted to hear.

"I had to put in the years," he said, "had to learn how to rechannel myself, and be able to meditate in a room full of violent men. No easy task. It was sheer hell just to go to the hole. You could wake up in the middle of the night and have to take a leak. What a sight in the urinals. Prisoners sucking guards. Guards going down on prisoners. One man taking another's ass. Hell, man, you got to get your head in order. . . .

"I decided to study," said King. "I got myself a list. Got my education in prison. Read Freud. He almost blew my mind. Breast, penis, anus. Powerful stuff. Then Masters and Johnson, Kinsey, and . . ." He hesitated. "Knee's itch. I read a lot of him."

Nietzsche.

"Who else did you read?" asked Mailer.

"Kant—*The Critique of Pure Reason*. That helped my head. And I read Sartre—fascinating!—and then the guy who wrote the book on Hitler, Shirer. I read him. And Marx, I read Karl Marx, cold motherfucker, Marx. I learned a lot from him."

To others, King cited Socrates, Plato, Frederick Douglass, Shakespeare, Kahlil Gibran, Victor Hugo, Marcus Aurelius, and Voltaire. Such a carefully curated syllabus would, of course, become media catnip. To be sure, King read them all voraciously, but he consumed even the most esoteric texts as if they were vocational manuals. They honed his powers to profit, convince, entice, and control.

The great books didn't set King straight so much as provoke his ambition. Genius? Yes, a uniquely American sort. King had that which defined the robber barons of every industry, from railroading to bootlegging to Hollywood: a larcenous imagination. And by the time he left the Marion Correctional Institution, on September 30, 1971, at the age of forty, it was unbound.

TITANS OF BUSINESS, ILLICIT AND OTHERWISE, TEND TO WORK IN the shadows. But promoters, by necessity, are different. Dismissing them as measly Barnums, vulgarians, and clowns, is itself an ignorance. The circus is a theater. Boxing—like all combat sports, really—is theater of a particular kind. It's a drama ripe for tragedy, of course, but with comedic potential at the margins, in and around a ring strewn with bit players: cut men, trainers, state bureaucrats, and ring-card girls.

Drama requires conflict. Boxing *is* conflict—ritualized, stage-managed, stripped down to its naked essentials.

But the ringed construct itself begs for a master of ceremonies, a grand barker, the salesman writ large. No surprise, then, that the great promoters have a deep need to be front and center: Tex Rickard, Arum, Dana White, and, as gifted as any, he who primed Donald Trump for political glory, Vince McMahon. Promoter is that most star-spangled of occupations, requiring indefatigable narcissism. And King would prove the greatest of all.

What made him unique wasn't merely his ego or his verbal relentlessness. He had impeccable timing. His parole came amid a time of Black Consciousness and blaxploitation, and King used them both, creating a character more deliberately than any Batman villain, drawing from the church and the street, words and numbers, the preacher and the pimp.

The day after his release from Marion, King was joined by Lloyd Price—the seminal rock and roller who had introduced him to Ali back in the sixties—at King's burgeoning forty-acre estate in Ashtabula County. It's said that Price discovered Little Richard. Perhaps it might also be said that Price midwifed King's persona.

"Make me big, Lloyd," King told him.

Price then delivered Ali, who agreed to box in a King-inspired exhibition to "save" Forest City Hospital, an institution run by Black physicians. Never mind that all the Black fighters not named Ali were stiffed. Or that King made out better than the hospital, which would close its doors before too long. King had found his calling. The rest of his transformation was cosmetic.

"He needed a distinctive look if he was going to become a star," recalled Price. "He needed an image, like Daddy Grace"—Charles "Sweet Daddy" Grace, founder and first bishop of the United House of Prayer for All People—"or Reverend Ike, who was his hero in those days. I told him all stars have some unique gimmick that fans can recognize them by—a hat, a uniform, a way of dressing.

"As I was saying that, Don was absent-mindedly pulling on his hair, which was his habit when he was thinking. I stopped and said, 'That's it! That's the look right there!'

"So he started combing his hair straight up and it did look distinctive. I told Don he should have a crown to go with the name King, and his straight-up hair looked like his crown."

Some years later, after his hair had become an internationally recognized symbol of his brand, an emblem evoking chuckles at his grand deceits, King would recall differently: "My hair was kinky and nappy and curly, like any other Black's. But then one night I went to bed with my wife, Henrietta, and she shook me because my head was rumbling and moving and my hair was just popping up—ping, ping, ping, ping! Each hair. All them curls was straightening out and going up. Henrietta couldn't believe what was going on, so she woke me up and said, 'Look at yourself in the mirror.'"

Hosanna!

"360 degrees of light," he told *Playboy* in 1988. "Like an aura from God."

The same divine providence that had struck down Hillary Brown and left a loaded .357 on the front seat of his Caddy. It remained with him. How else to explain that perpetual ability to defy the odds?

Actually, it was a revelation about the odds themselves. That was the real lesson in all his prison readings, what separated the tycoon from the mere hustler: Don't go for short money, never play the short game. I'm reminded of something Abraham told me: "Don worked like a grand master plays chess. They don't play move by move. They see the whole board. From the first pawn, they've got a plan. Don always played the long game."

By the time of that *Playboy* interview, King had survived a debt to the Cleveland mob, a phony ratings scandal in a tournament he'd promoted for ABC, federal income tax charges (for which his trusted assistant and sometime mistress, Constance Harper, went to jail), and lawsuits by three of his champions. One of them, Tim Witherspoon, would always recall the day when King pulled up at the gym he maintained for his fighters in Orwell, Ohio, near the Ashtabula compound.

It was probably late 1984, maybe '85. Most of King's heavyweights were there, at least a half-dozen top contenders. It's worth noting here that fighters bound by managerial or promotional affiliations are referred to as a "stable"—no, not unlike a pimp's stable. Certainly, the metaphor wasn't lost on King. "My philosophy is that all fighters are two-dollar whores," he once said. And now, in true pimp fashion, King let them know he wasn't at all pleased with their lazy asses.

"Y'all better get in shape," he said. "This young boy ain't playing."

The fighters looked at each other. *Who?*

"Kid's name is Tyson. Mike Tyson."

The long game was now Tyson.

24

By 1986, Tyson and Holloway had an apartment in Albany, paid for by Tyson via accountants hired for him by Cayton and Jacobs. With all the sly, inspired wit of suddenly desirable teenage boys, they christened it "the Bone Center." Passing through, as if hourly-rate tenants, were the willing women D'Amato had promised Tyson. Without the cranky old man, Tyson's sense of martial asceticism gave way to excess. The Lancaster Street flat soon achieved some measure of bacchanalian legend, as it was not unusual for the aspiring champion and his wingman to host three or five or seven women at a time. Some were recruited from Sal DiCarlo's strip joint on Central Avenue (which Mike and Rory convinced DiCarlo would be more profitable reconstituted as a "gentlemen's club" than the honky-tonk bar he'd been running); others were eager civilians. If Tyson had a preference, or at least a type with whom he was clearly most comfortable, it was your average—Holloway's words—"hood rat."

"I was always attracted to street girls," Tyson himself would recall. "That was from my mother."

The dime-store psychologist would say it was all tethered to the Oedipal gene—eros, the want of love, the will to conquer. Emotionally, Tyson was both foal and stallion ("Stallion," incidentally, being the nickname

Who knew Johnny Tocco's had a ladies' room? 1986

Holloway had given him). His inability to reconcile these two overpowering desires—to fuck and be mothered—would remain unexplained to him for years. After all, none of his fraternal or paternal surrogates—Cus, Jimmy, Kevin, or Steve Lott—were exactly equipped to deal with psychosexual nuance. It wasn't a shrink who eventually figured it out. It was a pimp. Some years later, Tyson had an audience with Iceberg Slim, whose book *Pimp* contained more applicable wisdom than anything Tyson would read on Alexander the Great. Holloway would never forget: first, how Tyson sought out Slim like a cure at Lourdes, then, the diagnosis itself.

"You got a lot of pain, son," Slim told him. "You got women issues. Something happened with your mother."

In the meantime, Tyson went through women much as he fought—as if intent on proving his legend, reaching a level of carnality and orgiastic achievement worthy of comparison with any of the great champions. "He just had these inhuman testosterone levels," said Holloway, who once recalled with great enthusiasm—as Tyson issued intermittent confirmations while watching a *Super Ninja* VCR tape—his friend's conquest of twenty-four women during an eight-hour stay outside Philadelphia. It was not a romantic encounter, as many of them were pros. One woman apparently fainted in the process.

More typical, perhaps, was Tyson's encounter during a Run-D.M.C. concert. It was July 1986 at Madison Square Garden, where executives wanted to make sure Tyson felt cared for and happy. A young assistant in the boxing department, Carl Moretti, was dispatched to check on him.

Tyson had been comped in the front row. But Moretti couldn't find him. He asked the ushers, but they didn't know. He kept looking, urgently, then panicked, thinking of how much trouble he'd be in if he couldn't find Tyson. Finally, a security guard pointed to a stairwell off to the side of the stage. There Moretti found Tyson standing over his momentary interest, *in flagrante delicto*.

Moretti rushed to the house phone. "What's taking you so long?" he was asked. "You found him yet?"

"I found him."

"He okay?"

"Yeah, he's good."

DON KING AND SETH ABRAHAM SHARED A BIRTHDAY, AUGUST 20, and a love of Chinese food. They dined regularly at the Canton, tucked away on a side street in Chinatown. A frequent topic of conversation was the biographies they periodically gifted each other, typically thick volumes on statesmen or political figures like Churchill, FDR, and Frederick Douglass.

"Agitate, agitate, agitate," King liked to say, repeating Douglass's famous exhortation. "That's me."

If King wanted to believe that his many ploys—frequently backed by the Reverend Al Sharpton—were less about profit than about empowerment, or that profit itself was a worthy political aim for a Black man in America, Abraham would not have argued. It was enough that King came to the table without his persona, and that their dialogue remained an engaging subtext to their real business.

"We spent so much time together—in hotels and airplanes, promoting, marketing, and advertising—that it was kind of like a marriage," says Abraham.

As in a marriage, they weren't always in perfect alignment. Abraham understood that his friend, the charming history buff who traveled with all those hefty hardcovers in his briefcase, could also, if the need arose, conduct himself in less-than-savory ways. Still, he felt protected. "I was Don's bank," says Abraham. "It was my name that appeared on all those checks. So Don never wanted to lie to me outright. That was a red line to him. Instead, he'd just go 'har-har-har.'"

Again like partners in a marriage, they had their signals, their secrets, and their roles. King had the fighters, particularly the heavyweights. Abraham had the money, lots of it. By the mid-eighties, CBS, ABC, and NBC could no longer compete with him; the only HBO department head *expected* to exceed his annual budget. While the networks remained locked into an ad-based programming grid, casinos gladly paid promoters site fees to fill their hotels and stock the gaming tables with high rollers on weekends. What's more, live sports drove cable subscription rates. So fuck *The Love Boat* and *Fantasy Island*; Abraham and King were tasked with seducing another demographic, the treasured eighteen-to-forty-nine-year-old male.

It all worked—their boundaries, their mutual enthusiasms, the nuanced phrasing—but never better than the night King pitched Abraham a title fight between Trevor Berbick and Pinklon Thomas. Abraham rejected it out of hand. After all, who *cared* about Berbick and Thomas? Instead, he proposed a tournament that would end by crowning the first undisputed heavyweight champion since 1978.

What would you need? Abraham asked.

Twenty million, King shot back.

No problem.

"The World Series of Boxing," as Abraham liked to call it, would satisfy his own corporate mandate, the creation and commodification of stars for its target demographic, not unlike, say, the role Tony Soprano would play for HBO a decade hence. It would satisfy King, who had long controlled every heavyweight of consequence but IBF champion Michael Spinks. Finally, it would address their shared interest, that which they each coveted more with each passing day: Tyson. Jacobs and Cayton had plotted meticulously to keep him contractually unencumbered and un-beholden to anyone but them. But the tournament created a kind of in-evitability. They could lead Tyson on any number of paths to the titles. But eventually they all went through Don King and HBO.

THE HEAVYWEIGHT DIVISION HAD BECOME A BIFURCATED PROPOSI-tion: In one grouping were mostly Black fighters whom the press and the public did not care to individuate. "Greedy, overweight, suspicious, and shamefully devoid of talent," as one sportswriter put it. In the other was Tyson, already being cast as the division's "savior."

"When Tyson comes in," Abraham told *The Washington Post*, "we'll start hitting home runs."

In the meantime, after successive opponents took him the distance, Tyson resumed his biweekly assault on the division's journeymen: Reggie Gross at the Garden; William Hosea at the RPI field house in Troy, and at the Stevensville Hotel in Swan Lake, New York; Lorenzo Boyd, who, unlike the previous two, managed to survive until the second round. Fif-teen days later, Tyson was back in Glens Falls for an ABC *Wide World of Sports* card against the WBC's ninth-ranked Marvis Frazier.

Frazier had had a distinguished amateur career, beating two future heavyweight champions, Tim Witherspoon and James "Bonecrusher" Smith, and winning the National Golden Gloves. As a still-inexperienced pro, he was knocked out in the first round by Larry Holmes, then 44-0 and at the height of his considerable powers. But he'd come back nicely, notching consecutive wins over Quick Tillis and another over Bonecrusher. But the real reason people took notice of Marvis Frazier was his father.

Joe Frazier won the "Fight of the Century," on March 8, 1971, at Madison Square Garden, famously dropping Ali in the fifteenth round. Less well known but no less germane was Frazier's history with King. Frazier was actually the first reigning champion to whom King ingratiated himself. In January 1972, King traveled to Jamaica as part of Frazier's entourage for his defense against George Foreman. He rode to Kingston's National Stadium in Frazier's limo, then took his front-row seat by Frazier's corner. But each time Frazier went down—six times in just two rounds—King moved closer to Foreman's corner. By fight's end, as Howard Cosell was interviewing the new champion in the ring, there was an exultant King, shouting over Cosell: "I got him. He's my man." King rode back from the stadium in Foreman's limo that night.

"I came with the champion," King liked to say, "and I left with the champion."

Two years later, in Manila, King would promote the finale of the Ali–Frazier trilogy. Though Ali closed Frazier's eye, forcing his corner to throw in the towel, the fight ennobled both men, as the winner himself would famously remember it as the "closest thing to dyin' I know."

Now Frazier was training his son. It made for wonderful television. But the same forces of will and ego that took Ali to the limits of mortality blinded Joe Frazier to his son's limitations. It's not that Marvis was a bad fighter, just that he fought with the same earnest bob and weave as his old man—and that made him a perfect mark for Tyson.

In fact, it was José Torres who urged Jacobs to have Tyson fight Marvis Frazier in the first place. "He has an incredible name," Torres told him, "but he's also made to order for our style."

Our style, said the chairman of the New York State Athletic Commission.

Meanwhile, matchmaker Ron Katz made an equally impassioned plea to the elder Frazier, whom he had known since the seventies. "Marvis has absolutely no chance," Katz told him. "He's not you, Joe."

"You'll see," said Frazier, who tried his best to antagonize Tyson during the lead-up. "Trust me. You'll see."

By fight night, as he gave the fighters their instructions, Joe Cortez saw past the younger Frazier's scowl to his eyes: "Marvis was already intimidated. And I can see Mike wants to go right through him."

It lasted thirty seconds and remains the quickest knockout in a career already full of them. Tyson quickly jabbed Frazier into a corner.

Then the first in a series of three right uppercuts, traveling in a comic-book arc, clipped Frazier on the chin, causing him to slump. The second knocked him out cold. The third kept him upright just long enough to be hit with a vicious left.

"Get up, son," exhorted the elder Frazier. "Be a man, son!"

Cortez counted to three before waving it off. The moments that followed capture the split in Tyson: first his scowling exhortation of the crowd, sending already-gleeful fans into full bloodlust, then kissing and consoling Frazier. Watching it back, though, the image most difficult to unsee is the fold of Frazier's body as Cortez starts to count: propped up on the bottom rope, his head, neck, and upper torso angled like a limp wrist, though not as limp as his lower half. Frazier is sitting on his left foot, his right splayed outward at a ninety-degree angle to the rest of him.

Later, in the dressing room, Jacobs asked for Tyson's gloves. "I want them for the Boxing Hall of Fame," he explained.

Tyson had just turned twenty.

"I use the fear," Tyson said immediately after the fight, "to reflect it on my opponent."

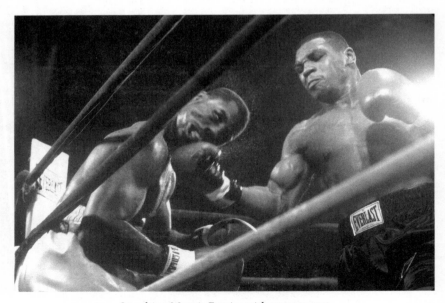

Smashing Marvis Frazier with an uppercut

Going back to the amateurs, Tyson had preyed on his opponents' self-doubt—in locker rooms, press conferences, and weigh-ins. It's how D'Amato trained him, honing his intuition to sense and exploit trepidation and anxiety in those physically close to him. But now the television itself had become a powerful instrument in projecting Tyson's menace, piercing the psyches of future opponents, among them Jose Ribalta, who had already lost a majority decision to Marvis Frazier.

By August 16, the day Ribalta weighed in at the Trump Plaza Hotel in Atlantic City, he was 211 pounds—11 fewer than when he'd left Miami a couple of days prior. "He was very, very, very scared," recalls his then-twenty-eight-year-old manager, Luis DeCubas. "He's thinking to himself, *If Marvis went the distance with me, then this guy is going to blow me out.*"

Boxing doesn't work like that. At six five, with a graceful jab and a nine-inch reach advantage, Ribalta was actually better suited to fight Tyson than Frazier had been. But that was physical. What ailed Ribalta was not. DeCubas now remembered what his own mentor, Chris Dundee (brother of Ali's trainer, Angelo), had told him: "You're not a manager. You're a psychiatrist."

"I had to do *something*," says DeCubas, who brought Ribalta to a *santero*, a Santeria priest, before the fight. The *santero* lit a cigar, blew the smoke on his assortment of seashells, then cast them on the ground. He repeated the ritual three or four times. "Don't worry," he assured Ribalta. "You'll have a great night."

In the second round, Tyson dropped Ribalta with his signature combination—right to the body, followed by a lightning-strike right uppercut that literally lifted the taller man off his feet. To see Ribalta fall in a heap is to figure he's done.

But he got up at the count of two.

Tyson would knock him down twice more—in the eighth and the tenth, just before referee Rudy Battle stopped the fight. By then, however, Ribalta had made his point, as evidenced by the fans who had been chanting his name. With a fluent left hand and a frighteningly robust chin, the spindly fighter wasn't interested in merely surviving but in fighting.

Tyson was now 26-0. The WBA's eighth-ranked heavyweight had

just made for his twenty-fourth knockout victim. Still, judging from the postfight interview, he had failed.

"He did well and I commend him," Tyson said of Ribalta, whom he'd later deem the strongest and best-chinned fighter he ever faced. "I had a bad night."

Tyson was less charitable to the chirpy upstart manager Luis De-Cubas, whom he grabbed by the neck after the press conference. "Call me all those names you been calling me now," said Tyson.

"It was the beginning of a beautiful friendship," says DeCubas.

Over the years, Tyson wondered what kept Ribalta up from the second round on, and why he'd fought so bravely. Decades passed before DeCubas told him of the *santero*. They got a laugh out of it.

DeCubas is the son of a physician who got out of Cuba in 1965. He's not the kind of guy who puts much faith in seashells and cigar smoke. But that wasn't the point. "*Jose* believed it," he says. "That's all that mattered."

JACOBS AND CAYTON HELD TYSON OUT OF THE TOURNAMENT FOR as long as possible, spending a good part of 1986 negotiating with MSG-Paramount for financial backing and with Larry Holmes—ostensibly free of King now—for a closed-circuit fight. But Cayton balked at the Paramount deal, and Holmes kept raising his price and adding conditions (refusing, for example, to fight in Vegas, where he'd lost by decision to Spinks), telltale signs that he really didn't want Tyson, especially with no title at stake.

HBO had all the titles now. By designating King and his rival, Butch Lewis, as a single promotional entity for the tournament—"Dynamic Duo," they called themselves—HBO effectively had rights to both King's stable and Lewis's champion, Michael Spinks, who was scheduled to defend his IBF belt on September 6 at the Las Vegas Hilton, less than three weeks after Tyson–Ribalta.

With nowhere else to go, Jacobs and Cayton accepted an offer Abraham carefully framed as a deal with the network, not a promoter. First they'd shoehorn Tyson onto the Spinks undercard, then a title shot against one of King's fighters, likely Trevor Berbick, later that year. "The series involved three title fights and, in all fairness to HBO [which put up the $20 million for the tournament], we agreed that if we should win the tournament they would have two options," said Cayton. "So we thought we were involved with King for five fights and no obligation beyond that."

The impact was immediate. While Spinks's consecutive decisions over Holmes earned him both the IBF title and recognition as the division's "lineal" champion, he wasn't a great draw. Being matched against an obscure Norwegian, Steffen Tangstad, didn't help either. But word of Tyson's inclusion on the undercard quickly propelled the Hilton's live gate from an embarrassing $217,000 to $1.1 million.

As for the card itself, Spinks finished Tangstad fifty-eight seconds into the fourth round—an eternity compared with Tyson and Alfonzo Ratliff, a six-five former cruiserweight champ. Ratliff, another King fighter managed by his stepson, Carl, for a mere 50 percent of his purse, ran around the ring until Tyson finally caught him. The ref called it off at 1:41 of the second. "He has no choice but to fight for the title now," Jacobs said of Tyson.

It was already scheduled: November 22, Las Vegas Hilton. Tyson would be twenty, five months younger than Floyd Patterson when he became the youngest heavyweight champion in history.

25

Not long before the Berbick fight, Jack Nicholson ran into Brian Hamill at the trendy restaurant Columbus on the Upper West Side. "I tell everyone how you introduced me to Mike Tyson," he said. "You *knew*."

They'd met the summer before—ringside at the Garden, the night Lonnie Smith knocked out Billy Costello. "I don't know, Brian," Nicholson drawled after Tyson stepped away. "He looks a little small to be the heavyweight champ."

"You'll see," said Hamill. "He expands."

As expansions go, Tyson's had been unprecedented. Case in point: his sudden standing in places like Columbus, owned by a sometime actor, Paulie Herman, along with Robert De Niro, Mikhail Baryshnikov, and Regis Philbin, each of whom had small pieces. Tyson arrived there with more than an introduction from Brian and Pete Hamill; he was that most rarefied of prospects, who stood to become the first *interesting* heavyweight champion in years, a figure who could reduce celebrities to mere hangers-on, straining for a chance to watch up close as he became his generation's Ali or Dempsey. What's more, though barely twenty, Tyson already had a unique mix of street cred and literary cachet. Word was the novelist Joyce Carol Oates was working on a profile in anticipation of his upcoming title shot. Fabulous people were already jockeying for a spot, a vantage point from which to say, "I knew him when . . ."

"Enjoy this now," Pete Hamill told him one night, as they stopped for an ice cream cone on Columbus Avenue. "Because soon you're not going to be able to do this anymore."

It was one thing to entertain Norman Mailer at D'Amato's behest up in Catskill. But this was different. This was suddenly finding himself chatting with Raul Julia at Liza Minnelli's apartment. And it didn't matter where you were; fame was currency redeemable as sex. Fancy as the Columbus girls might've been, *the next heavyweight champ* found that they clung to their virtue no more or less than the average hood rat. He'd take them downstairs to the bathrooms, right there on the floor, after which they'd reemerge in states of obvious dishevelment.

"Yo, Mike," Paulie Herman would scold him. "They're all coming up dirty."

YOU COULD CHART TYSON'S ASCENT IN THE GOSSIP PAGES, MUCH of it orchestrated by Jacobs and Cayton—feeding the flacks who suckled the columnists who dropped his name in all the right places—among them Page Six, Liz Smith, Cindy Adams. There he is at a "KO Crack" appearance along with Hector Camacho and Julio César Chávez, three eventual drug addicts. There's a photo op at Shea Stadium with yet more cokeheads-to-be, Darryl Strawberry and Dwight "Dr. K" Gooden. Then there's a shot with Rickey Henderson at Yankee Stadium. He bowls to raise money for Big Brothers with Cher, Matthew Broderick, and Emmanuel Lewis, then shares a table with a rapt Robert Duvall at Columbus. He's spotted strolling through the Gucci store with his Walkman. "The heavyweight champ of the future," writes Liz Smith. "He's 20 and has expensive tastes." And if, on the morning of August 2, 1986, you absolutely needed to know what he ordered for breakfast at the Stage Deli? Page Six reported it was three omelets loaded with cheese, pastrami, and salami, four large glasses of orange juice, six bialys, five glasses of water, and a sandwich to go: turkey, pastrami, roast beef, Swiss, coleslaw, and Russian dressing. The bill came to thirty-six dollars. No word on the tip.

And don't forget the talk shows: *Letterman*, *Joan Rivers*, *Dick Cavett*, and, likely the most revealing exchange of all, *Nightlife* with David Brenner on October 6, 1986. Tyson was six weeks out from his title fight with Berbick. Jake LaMotta, Brenner's other guest, was promoting the second volume of his autobiography, *Raging Bull II*.

LaMotta's life had swerved from one boxing archetype to another: a violent city kid introduced to the fistic arts while in juvenile lockup, the animalistic champion, and now a Borscht Belt–style comedian. "Theresa and I are very compatible," said LaMotta, referring to his sixth wife. "Every night when we go to bed, we both get headaches at the same time."

Amid the shtick, though, was a moment of prescience. LaMotta told Tyson he'd be a great champion, "a bigger and stronger Marciano." It's an interesting comparison, as Black athletes are usually compared to Black athletes and white athletes to white ones. What's more, Marciano remained a sacred symbol among Italian Americans. LaMotta might've been a piece of shit, but he wasn't bound by the prevalent racial coding. In the broad phyla of fighters—from slick-fighting "Sugars" to pug-like "Rockys"— Jake and Mike weren't merely the latter but Rockys of a very specific type. It wasn't boxing that made them kindred; it was their shadow selves.

"Keep yourself busy and make believe you're in jail for a couple years," LaMotta advised him. "Stay away from all the garbage out there."

"Why does it have to be garbage, though?" asked Tyson.

"Unfortunately, guys like you and I, we attract garbage."

NOT EVERYTHING IN TYSON'S LIFE WAS SCHEDULED, SCRIPTED, OR even predictable—like his friendship with actor Anthony Michael Hall, who had already appeared in *Sixteen Candles*, *The Breakfast Club*, and *Weird Science*. "I met Mike Tyson at one of his fights and he told me he admired my movies," Hall remembered. "You just don't picture Mike Tyson watching John Hughes movies for fun."

Actually, their friendship makes sense, as each was a teen star prone to excess. Hall was on the cusp of his first flameout—at eighteen, the youngest-ever cast member of *Saturday Night Live* and already drinking on the set. But he looked up to Tyson and one night brought him to the Museum of Natural History, where *The Pick-Up Artist* was shooting. Hall wanted Tyson to meet the star, his friend Robert Downey Jr. But the more consequential introduction was to James Toback, the movie's director.

Toback was forty-one. He had grown up on Central Park West, attending Fieldston and then Harvard, where he seems to have majored in literature and acid. He had written a great screenplay for *The Gambler*, starring James Caan as a degenerate bettor with an English professorship (much as Toback himself had been), and later would write an even better one, *Bugsy*, for his pals Warren Beatty and Annette Bening.

In between, it was his great good fortune to meet Tyson. If there's a tell regarding Toback's enduring fascination with Tyson in particular, and Black virility in general, it was his debut as an author. I'm the last guy who should be criticizing the preening work of one's younger self, but *Jim: The Author's Self-Centered Memoir on the Great Jim Brown*, published in 1971 by Doubleday and later reissued under the personal imprint of Brett Ratner, is as spectacularly bad as its title. The intended highlight, as best I can tell, is an orgy scene in which author and Great come together literally, metaphorically, and, of course, spiritually while double-teaming the same woman (again, as best I can tell, as the passage is written in an opaque, affected stream of consciousness).

Toback's connection with Brown had been solidified with an extended stay at Brown's Hollywood Hills home. But his bond with Tyson was instant. "A profound communion which we felt from the minute we started talking," he would recall.

They wandered around Central Park until 5:00 a.m., Toback regaling Tyson with tales of his frightful college acid trip, saturnalia with Big Jim, his audience with Dempsey when Dempsey had his bar across the street from the *old* Garden, parsing the difference between dread and fear. They spoke, too, of madness, a topic about which Tyson seemed especially inquisitive.

"I don't think anybody had ever asked me, 'What do you mean when you say you experienced madness?'" Toback told *LA Weekly*. "And as I tried to answer the question, I realized how unusual it was and how significant it was that he seemed so eager for me to explain it to him. I ultimately ended by saying that the only way to know it is to experience it—everything else is just going to sound like words."

By dawn's light, Toback had a feeling their communion would bear fruit: "What we were going to do with the friendship was never articulated, though as far as I was concerned it was almost certainly going to take the shape of my using him cinematically."

Toback would go on to cast Tyson in three of his own movies, including the feature-length documentary *Tyson*, with Tyson reciting Oscar Wilde's "The Ballad of Reading Gaol." So I called him. I had questions, most of them having to do with the heady new world Tyson had entered. Unfortunately, a lifetime of gambling debts had caught up with

Courting Beverly Johnson

Toback. What's more, he'd been unable to work in Hollywood since 2018 when the *Los Angeles Times* reported that 395 women had accused him of sexual assault or harassment going back to 1978, accusations that he denies. Also, he was working on his memoir, and though it would be full of juicy Tyson stories, he said he would share them with me—for a cash price. I passed.

Rather, what turned out to be a truly valuable memoir for establishing the rules of engagement for Tyson's new life in Manhattan was Beverly Johnson's. Paulie Herman introduced them, telling Johnson that Tyson, then preparing to fight Berbick, was the next heavyweight champion. Johnson was from Buffalo, the first Black woman to appear on the cover of American *Vogue*, and almost fifteen years Tyson's senior. She found him to be endearingly naive in the world of celebrities—exactly unlike the last man she had dated, albeit briefly, Eddie Murphy. Murphy had his bodyguards remove Mick Jagger from the bathroom at Mr. Chow's that he might piss alone. But Tyson was sincere and persistently flattering. He called often, their conversations long and full of laughter.

The shy-guy bit was working. Still, it wasn't enough.

And why should it have been? Love was never unconditional. D'Amato's certainly wasn't. Beverly Johnson merely made it explicit. Here was the deal, kid, the cosmic truth of your new world: "If you win," she said, "I'll give you some."

26

During the lead-up to the Berbick fight, Tyson was asked if he believed in life after death. He was sure he did not: "I believe when someone dies, he dies—that's it." Certainly nothing in his Brooklyn boyhood suggested much that was divine or paranormal, ever after, or evermore.

Still, Joyce Carol Oates, now on her cover assignment for *Life*, saw him as a kind of fairy-tale figure. "Those legendary tales of abandoned children so particularly cherished by the European imagination," she wrote. "These children, invariably boys, are 'natural' and 'wild'; not precisely mute but lacking a language; wholly innocent of the rudiments of human social relations. They are homeless, parentless, nameless, 'redeemable' only by way of the devotion of a teacher-father—not unlike Tyson's Cus D'Amato."

The problem was, Tyson had neither a system of belief nor a fairy godmother to facilitate communication with his deceased teacher-father. Instead, as the fight approached, he found himself talking to John Halpin, the hypnotist who now traveled with the team and sat ringside. It wasn't unusual for them to speak twice a day.

"I'd hypnotize him and feed him the same lines," said Halpin. The same lines as D'Amato, he meant: the gospel of bad intentions, the anatomy of

Kevin Rooney adjusting Tyson's headgear at Tocco's
while getting ready for Trevor Berbick

hurt, Tyson's destiny as a scourge from God. They'd become a dead man's
mantra, a way to summon his spirit, the essence of incantation.

Once training camp moved to Las Vegas, Tyson stayed in the gated
community of Spanish Oaks, a few miles off the Strip, at the home of
Dr. Bruce Handelman, a handball-playing anesthesiologist and friend
of Jimmy Jacobs. Also there were Rooney and Tyson's highly stressed,
eager-to-please aide-de-camp, Steve Lott. Tyson spent his days there
watching cartoons and kung fu movies, the VHS tapes strewn about
his room, telling Lott when and what to order out or when to boil
more pasta.

Tyson trained at Johnny Tocco's Ringside Gym, a proper boxing
establishment, which is to say dilapidated, odiferous, and insistently
nostalgic, with an entire wall of photographs devoted to Tocco's old pal
Sonny Liston. Tyson had seven regular sparring partners, and their sessions remained merciless, all-out affairs, even during the week of the

fight. That wouldn't happen today. Nor would reporters be invited to watch, as Tim Layden, then of the Albany *Times Union*, was. He recalled sparring coming to a hasty halt with just four days to go. Tyson had a welt over his eye.

"I'm fine," he said.

In fact, they're never fine. They're fighters. I once heard a heavyweight champion, a guy who commands north of $30 million a bout, proclaim himself "the highest-paid male escort in the world." It wasn't without basis. Nor is it inappropriate to compare fighters to hookers and strippers in the sense—an almost Marxist sense, really—that all they actually have to sell are their physical selves, a steeply depreciating capital asset that's inevitably consumed in the course of their working lives. What's more, fighters and hookers share many a common fate, as Tyson learned just days before his welting. He was funneling through a car wash with Steve Lott when he pulled down his pants for his factotum to inspect.

"Look at this," said Tyson, pointing to the telltale signs of gonorrhea on his underwear.

He was promptly given antibiotic injections, along with a disclaimer. "The doctor said it would make me weak," he told José Torres. "I say he's full of shit 'cause I want that title so bad."

IT WAS SAID, AT LEAST BY SOME, THAT BERBICK—WHOM HBO FILMED preaching to inmates at the Southern Nevada Correctional Center— would be immune to Tyson's bullying tactics. At thirty-two, after a full decade as a pro, the WBC champion was a man of varied experience. He'd worked on cruise ships and at the American naval base in Guantánamo Bay, Cuba, where he was said to have beaten the Marine champion. He fought for his native Jamaica in the '76 Olympics and was ordained a minister at the Moments of Miracles church in Las Vegas.

But even as astutely cynical a student of human nature as Don King couldn't decide if Berbick was devout, cunning, or full-on crazy. When

King had been grimly preparing for his federal tax trial, Berbick sought him out. "Every morning at six thirty there'd be a knock at my hotel door and there stood Trevor carrying a cross and a Bible," said King. "He told me the Lord was at my side and every morning he read the ninety-first psalm."

As the Tyson fight came into focus, though, Berbick started threatening to leave the HBO tournament for an easier, more lucrative fight with Gerry Cooney—who, like most white hopes, remained commercially viable long after he'd been demystified in the ring. King would have easily won in court. But a lawsuit would've cost him his moment with Tyson. Again, this was about the long game.

So King bumped Berbick's purse from $1.6 to $2.1 million. Soon the fighter would be complaining he got only a third of that, anyway. In the meantime, let "the Fighting Preacher," as he called himself, do his nutty best to sell this fight.

Berbick had some mystifyingly bad performances on his résumé, the most recent being a loss to a cruiserweight named S. T. Gordon back in 1983. "Someone put something in my food and tampered with the air coming from my air-conditioner," he told Tom Archdeacon of *The Miami News*. "I met this guy in Miami and he confessed to me. He told me he got paid to do it.

"So I've learned. Now, I'm clever."

So clever, in fact, that, as champion, he chose to wear the black trunks, exploiting a Nevada rule that obliged opposing fighters to wear different colors. "This is 'Judgment Day,'" said Berbick, referring to the fight's billing, "and I'm the judge. The judge always wears black. . . . We're going to take away his mystique."

"Remember that mystique that Sonny Liston had? Tyson is trying to get that," explained Angelo Dundee, who'd be in Berbick's corner. "Tyson may have petrified some of those other guys, but not Berbick."

By now, Dundee was less a working trainer than a mouthpiece, a hired gun trading on his rep as Ali's chief second. It was tempting to dismiss both Dundee and Berbick as guys reciting lines from a wrestling promo. Still, despite Berbick's lackluster losses to journeymen, the bigger the fight, the better he fought. He had taken a prime Larry Holmes the full fifteen-round distance. Eight months later, he retired Ali, or what was left of him after King had fed him to Holmes. More to the point was Berbick's knack for beating heavy favorites: knocking out Big John Tate, earning a unanimous decision against a 19-0 Greg Page, knocking out David Bey, and beating Mitch Green. Even with late money coming in on him, Berbick was still a 3½–1 underdog against Tyson. Then again, he'd been as low as 7–1 in his last fight against Pinklon Thomas, the WBC champion and considered by many to be the front-runner when the unification tournament began. Berbick took Thomas's title by unanimous decision. Now he was easily Tyson's most formidable opponent, with the deepest résumé.

Meanwhile, the real questions, at least for those not inclined to be spoon-fed by Jimmy Jacobs, revolved around Tyson: his maturity, his resilience under new levels of scrutiny and pressure, but mostly his vulnerabilities, both stylistic and psychiatric. Was a twenty-year-old with five amateur losses really invincible? "He's not as tough or as hard as people think he is," Atlas told *Newsday*'s Wally Matthews. "He is capable of weakening, but so far, he has always overcome his self-doubts."

The most interesting prefight piece was by the *Daily News*'s Mike Katz, who caught up with Tyson's rarely mentioned brother. "I had to make him fight on occasion," said Rodney Tyson, referring to the pre-Spofford version of his brother.

Now twenty-five, Rodney hadn't seen his brother in two years and must've been quite jet-lagged, as he had flown in from Japan, where he was stationed as a petty officer in the navy. But the siblings' stories were fascinating juxtaposed against each other. Rodney graduated from Brooklyn Tech, one of New York's elite academic high schools. Then he attended St. Francis College and Old Dominion University before enlisting to receive training as a pharmacist. As it happened, Rodney's athletic career ended at Tech, where he played tight end on the football team. You wondered where, when, and how their lives had turned out so differently.

In a classroom or a dayroom? A corner or the vacant lot? Was it nature or nurture?

TYSON WOKE ABOUT 5:30 A.M. ON THE MORNING OF THE FIGHT, ATE a bowl of cereal and some leftovers from the night before, then went back to bed. At 1:00 p.m., he had some pasta. A few hours later, Lott ordered him a steak.

At 5:30 p.m., as Lott was packing for the arena, Tyson woke from a nap. "Steve," he yelled, "I'm hungry. Make me some dinner."

More pasta. Washed down with orange juice. Lott was worried they'd be late but figured it was better for Jacobs to be miffed at him than not to give Tyson what he wanted.

At 7:20, the challenger entered the ring. He wore his customary black shorts, for which Jacobs and Cayton gladly paid the Nevada State Athletic Commission a $5,000 fine. The ref was Mills Lane, a former fighter and the district attorney in Reno. Lane was looked on favorably by the Tyson camp, as he demanded that fighters fight. "He understood, like most good referees, that the boxing fan paid to be entertained," wrote José Torres, who as a New York State athletic commissioner had no official standing here but still managed to get himself photographed as much as anyone not named Tyson or Don King.

The arena was packed. The $1,000-a-ticket VIP section included Jack Nicholson, Kirk Douglas, Eddie Murphy, and Muhammad Ali, who urged Tyson to avenge his loss to Berbick. "Kick his ass for me," he told Tyson.

Lou Rawls, who had appeared with Ali at King's inaugural boxing event, the ill-fated scheme to save Forest City in Cleveland, sang the national anthem. Berbick, wearing his black satin judge's robe, came to the ring with Carl King in tow. As Lane convened the fighters to touch gloves, Berbick wouldn't look Tyson in the eye.

As the fight began, the champion seemed stiff but insistent. "I was trying to prove I could take his best shot," said Berbick, who merely proved he could not.

There was an audible thump to Tyson's punches. Toward the end of the first round, Tyson slipped Berbick's jab and came back with a four-punch combination—right-left, right-left—that sent Berbick sprawling across the ring.

Back in the corner, Dundee was heard to yell, "Where's the fucking sponge?" before admonishing Berbick for fighting the wrong fight. Indeed. But the truth was, whatever style he chose wouldn't have made much difference.

Berbick went down shortly after the second round began. On unsteady legs, he assured Mills Lane he was okay to continue. He survived until, with forty-five seconds remaining in the round, Tyson began his signature combination, sinking a right hand behind Berbick's left elbow into the kidney. The uppercut missed this time. But the third punch, an impossibly short hook to the temple, did not.

"I wanted to bust his eardrum," Tyson clarified later.

Berbick seemed to wait a moment before toppling backward.

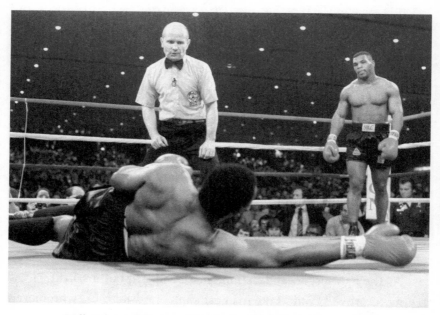

Mills Lane and Tyson appraising the fallen Berbick's condition

He tried to raise himself immediately again, as if trying to prove something, but found himself tumbling into the ropes on the other side of the ring. He bounced off the bottom rope, which sent him reeling back, cartoon-like, toward the spot where he had first fallen. He dropped again. And rose again, a moment that seemed to call for animated tweeting birds. Finally, Mills Lane cradled Berbick in his arms and called off the fight at 2:35 of the second round.

Any more, said Lane, "would have been criminal."

Tyson was exultant, then thought to comfort Berbick, just as he'd seen Dempsey check on Firpo. While George Bellows immortalized Dempsey–Firpo on canvas, Berbick–Tyson would live on video. By now, the HBO crew was already replaying the finale in slow motion, a clip that would eventually become more accessible and enduring than anything composed of paint or prose. The bandy-legged progression of Berbick's fall—three falls, actually—suggested the way vaudeville clowns used to play drunks. It was an unforgettable humiliation, a reminder of the new champion's wrath, but most important, a visual calling card that would last in perpetuity. The sequence crystallized a notion of Mike Tyson.

As Joyce Carol Oates would write, "A terrible beauty is born."

But even the clip obscured what Tyson had actually accomplished. Floyd Patterson had been five weeks shy of his twenty-second birthday when he won the title in 1956. Tyson was twenty, plus five months. Unlike Patterson, Cus had died on Tyson. His mother died on him, too. Tyson was still just six years removed from juvenile lockup. As title runs go, there would never be another like this. Berbick was Tyson's sixteenth fight in just a year.

"Every punch I threw was with bad intentions to a vital area," he told Larry Merchant. "I'm the youngest champion in the history of the sport. My record will last for immortality."

Quite suddenly, Tyson the agnostic believed in heaven. "I would like to dedicate my fight to my great guardian Cus D'Amato," he said. "I'm sure he's up there talking to all the great fighters saying his boy did it."

In his close to the broadcast, Merchant called Tyson "a young champion

Don King, in his glory, hoisting the new champ

who can revitalize the game." Then he evoked John Lardner's famous description of Dempsey. "He is a pure fighter," he said of Tyson. "He is the pure flame."

Before the night was over, Merchant ran into Ali in the casino. If Tyson had avenged Ali's loss to Berbick, he'd also elevated himself onto a kind of Olympus, a realm of godlike egos and resentments. Ali leaned in close and whispered amusedly, "Let's see how long he can keep it up."

The great still images of that night belong to Lori Grinker. She captured an exultant King hoisting Tyson aloft, his right arm raised, with Torres looking on, so eager to be close. Then there was Tyson's delighted call to Camille back in Catskill, his "white mother," on the push-button phone, the belt on his lap. Finally, from the balcony of Cayton's suite on the twenty-ninth floor of the Las Vegas Hilton, Tyson poses bare-chested with the belt around his waist, his expression unmistakably beatific. In the background was the city itself, before it was supersized, made corporate and ordinary. It was the most American city of all, suckled on every outlawed Protestant vice, in full nocturnal bloom, dotted with ambered globules of colored light.

"I didn't take that belt off that whole night," Tyson recalled. "I wore it around the lobby of the hotel. I wore it to the after-party, and I wore it when I went out drinking later with Jay Bright, my roommate at Cus's house; Bobby Stewart's son; and Matthew Hilton, the fighter. We went to a dive bar in Vegas called The Landmark, across the street from the Hilton. Nobody was in there, but we just sat and drank all night. I was drinking vodka straight and I got truly smashed. At the end of the night, Matthew passed out and I went around to different girls' houses, showing them my championship belt. I didn't have sex with them, I just hung out with them for a while, and then I'd leave and call another girl and go over to her house and hang out."

After his own rambunctious evening, Wally Matthews returned to the Hilton around 4:00 a.m. Tyson was there in the lobby, the belt around his waist. "He was lonely, isolated, wasn't sure what to do with himself," said Matthews.

Forever man: celebrating with his new belt

If so, he'd have time to figure it out. That night—his best night in the ring, Tyson would ever insist—didn't fulfill his ambition so much as inflame it. The full rush had engulfed Tyson just moments after winning the title, as if his voice and Cus's were now one.

"I want to live forever," he said.

27

Nineteen hours after winning the belt, Tyson showed up at Beverly Johnson's apartment on East Eighty-Ninth Street, where he was welcomed with the favor now due a man in his position. "Mike was young and still learning how to please a woman," she recalls, "but I very much enjoyed it anyway." Johnson's account of their monthslong affair seems predictable enough: the precocious champion and an older lover, a worldly celebrity grown otherwise disillusioned with men. He is, by turns, passionate and playful, guzzling too much champagne, crooning off-key, grossing her out with a display of the food in his mouth. What's striking, though, at least in a relationship whose term limits seemed clearly defined, was his insistence on flying with Johnson and her seven-year-old daughter to her hometown of Buffalo to meet the family.

Johnson had no expectations regarding Tyson's fidelity, what with the legions of women throwing themselves at him. "I just wanted to have a good time with a man who seemed to enjoy being with me," she writes. "That said, there were moments when I felt more like his mother."

In due course, Tyson was soliciting her opinion on his other lovers, including one whom Johnson once overheard demanding that Robert De Niro, her boyfriend at the time, buy her a building. Naomi Campbell, for whom the term *supermodel* seems to have been invented, was of Jamaican ancestry by way of South London. She met Tyson at a party in a lavishly appointed Fifth Avenue apartment. She gave him her number; he remembers calling her the next day. Rory Holloway remembers a different encounter.

"I was there to keep Mike out of trouble, doing my usual babysitting job," he said. "I'm stuck holding their drinks 'cause Mike says he's got to use the restroom. Next thing I know Naomi's following him in there."

Holloway takes a position by the door, telling guests that the lavatory is occupied. Minutes pass. Finally, concerned, he opens the door slightly: "She's up on the toilet, heels and long legs spread, skirt hiked up, and Mike's pumping away."

The relationship that followed, by any account, was carnal, incendiary, and, in retrospect at least, entertaining. Campbell once scaled the outside wall of the Las Vegas Hilton—Spider-Man style—from balcony to balcony, many stories above the Strip, where Tyson was ensconced with one or several lovers. More remarkable, at least in Holloway's recollection, was the evening he and Tyson emerged from Bentley's Discotheque, 25 East Fortieth Street, to find Campbell, about the height of a small NBA player, digging into the hood of his new Rolls-Royce with her high heels.

"I can't take this," Tyson confided in his friend.

What did he do after she scratched up the Rolls? I wonder.

"Nothing," says Holloway. "She got in the car. He took her home. He says to me one time, 'Ro, I think I met my match. Naomi scares me.'"

THE CULTURE OF MANHATTAN IS ABOUT STATUS AND THE WAY IT'S refracted through the media, which in that moment reflected the primacy of newspapers and magazines. When Tyson first arrived in *the city*, he was still a former mugger from Brooklyn. In another life he could've easily been among the kids Bernie Goetz shot on a downtown number 2 train headed to New Lots Avenue. No one at Elaine's, Oren and Aretsky's, or even, say, Indochine, would've given a flying fuck—apart, perhaps, from mild applause—if he'd wound up dead, in prison, or testifying with a colostomy bag. But the championship belts—the one he now had and those still to be claimed—seemed to alter Tyson less than they did the world around him.

His augmented status was epitomized by an illustration leading a feature on celebrity restaurants in *New York* magazine: caricatures seated around a table at Columbus, among them Madonna, De Niro, Baryshnikov, Jackie Mason, and Eddie Murphy. At the center, though, depicted sumo sized in a suit and tie, is the moment's unmistakable kingpin, Tyson.

"Being with Mike was a come-up for most of them," Holloway says of Tyson's celebrity love interests, including, in the months to come, the former Miss America Suzette Charles. "They needed Mike to take their careers to the next level."

That's not to say Tyson ignored the adoring hordes of nonfamous women. Before long, he had harems in every city he visited. Occasionally, he'd wear the championship belt to bed. "I really believed that every woman who approached me wanted to have sex with me," Tyson recalled.

There was, as best I can tell, a single notable exception. She, too, was from Brooklyn, diagnosed with a speech impediment as a child and now on the cusp of stardom. She had just left *Soul Train*, where she worked as a dancer, to try her hand as a choreographer. They ran into each other regularly at house parties and the emerging hip-hop clubs, among them the Roxy, the World, the Latin Quarter, and the Fun House. Where they first met is murky. More memorable was the savoir faire with which he tried to pick her up: "Damn, Wosie. You got a biscuit booty. Love to pour gravy all over that shit."

The line, or its equivalent, had no doubt worked countless times on a bevy of supermodels, beauty queens, and actresses looking for a come-up. This one was different, though.

"Mike, shut up," she told him.

Rosie Perez was born in Bushwick, out of wedlock, to a merchant seaman and a schizophrenic mother who carried a pistol. For years, she had great difficulty understanding who her actual parents were. The seaman, she was told, was her uncle, while his sister, whom she called Tia, did most of the mothering. At three, Rosie was sent to Saint Joseph's Catholic Home for Children in Peekskill, New York. There she was regularly beaten by a woman she calls Sister Renata, but managed to avoid being sent to the local psych hospital, from which children would return drugged and stuporous after shock treatment. During her home visits, Rosie was beaten by her mother, who in turn was being beaten by her husband, who, among other things, resented that Rosie wasn't his biological child. When a half brother tried to sexually assault her, her mother accused her of lying and smacked her around some more.

As she moved through the child welfare system—from St. Joseph's to an assortment of group and foster residences—Rosie suffered from what would now be called PTSD. "I had a lot of bad nightmares," she recalled, "of Sister Renata trying to kill me, of the Home, of my half-brother trying to molest me, and of my mother punching me or at times trying to kill me too. I would wake up in the middle of the night breathing heavily."

And still, by her early twenties, she was studying biology at Los Angeles City College, dancing on *Soul Train*, and choreographing routines for the likes of Bobby Brown and an act called the Boys.

If anyone could've used a come-up, it was Rosie Perez, who likened herself to a dented can discounted and left to collect dust on a bodega shelf.

Still: *Mike, shut up.*

"When you grow up with childhood trauma, you don't get to be a child," she says. "I saw that in Mike. I saw the abused kid, really just a good kid who got damaged. I saw the dented can. You know how people say, 'Game recognizes game'? Well, damage recognizes damage."

Still, it would be a mistake, cautions Perez, to consider their journeys as parallel. "The Home was the frying pan," she says. "But Spofford is the fire. If a kid was sent there, we would be racked with dread for that person."

As for the young champion whose advances she shot down, Perez recalls: "He kind of slumped over. And he goes, 'Okay, sorry.'" Quite suddenly, ghetto Alexander had been reduced to a sheepish, penitent kid.

"My heart just cracked," she says. "I was like, 'Oh, honey.' And I remember turning to smile at him and I just kind of *mushed* him"—as one would a soft-mouthed puppy—"and he mushed me back. But I almost fell 'cause he's so damn strong."

Tyson never hit on her again.

"That's when I fell in love with him," she says.

28

After Tyson's victory over Berbick, the HBO tournament felt less like a playoff than a star vehicle organized around the ascendant young champion. "Everything was Tyson, Tyson, Tyson. Bow down to Tyson," said Butch Lewis, the tournament's titular "copromoter" with Don King. "In September"—two months before the Berbick fight—"King said to me, 'Butch, we got to get Tyson away from Jacobs and Cayton.' 'Don,' I said, 'I'm not in the business of stealing anybody's guy.' So King takes it on himself and I'm on the outs."

Though the parties had by now signed a deal memo allowing for Tyson to enter the tournament, the actual contract was still being negotiated—mostly, it seems, by King. "He'd tell me that Jacobs and Cayton had problems with the contract, then he's telling them that I don't like the contract," said Lewis. "King's saying that they don't want me at the negotiating table. Jacobs would be asking me why I'm causing so much trouble, and I wasn't. It's King working his magic, playing one big con game. King was romancing them to get inside so he can steal Tyson."

Abraham has another take on Lewis, who promoted Michael Spinks but was nevertheless best known for going shirtless with a formal collar and tux on fight night. "It was part of an act, just like Don's hair," says Abraham, who considered Lewis as Machiavellian as King. "The truth is Butch was incredibly concerned about Tyson. He was already figuring out a way to get Spinks out of the tournament so he wouldn't have to face him."

Though undersized for a heavyweight, and his second win over Holmes still the subject of debate, Spinks was the tournament's only other *name*: an Olympic gold medalist who held the IBF title. Even more valuable was his recognition as the "linear" champion, the man who had beat the Man—again, the terribly unappreciated Holmes. Now, as next up in the tournament, Spinks was due to defend his belt against the IBF's number one contender, Tony Tucker.

Lewis didn't really want Spinks fighting Tucker, who was better than he got credit for, but was even less enamored with the prospect of Spinks having to fight Tyson next if he won. Spinks—always a dutiful and courageous champion—wasn't keen on it, either. "I wasn't real interested in fighting Mike," he tells me now. "He was very, very strong. I just wasn't too excited about getting in the ring with him at all."

So Lewis pulled Spinks from the tournament to fight the perennial white hope, Gerry Cooney, just as Berbick had threatened to do. HBO sued, obtaining a temporary restraining order.

"Buy a shirt," an infuriated Abraham advised Lewis. "I want to be able to take the shirt off your back."

In due course, the IBF stripped Spinks of his title. It seemed like a refreshingly novel move from one of boxing's notoriously corrupt sanctioning bodies—actually enforcing its own rules. But it had the unintended consequence of liberating Spinks from his HBO contract, which hinged on his standing as a belt holder. He was now free to fight Cooney.

"I'll have twenty thousand seats," bragged the undaunted Lewis. "Closed circuit all over the world."

Better still, his guy wouldn't have to fight Tyson. Though Spinks weighed in twenty-nine pounds lighter than his challenger and found himself an 8–5 underdog, he stopped Cooney in the fifth. What's more, his winnings were said to exceed $7 million, more than thirteen times what he would have made fighting Tony Tucker on HBO.

IN THE AFTERMATH OF BERBICK–TYSON, WITH LEWIS ALREADY plotting his exit from the tournament, Don King effectively became its sole promoter. The next bout, on December 12 at Madison Square Garden, was a WBA-ordered rematch between its champion, Tim Witherspoon, and the man he had beaten for the title, Tony Tubbs. But with eight days to go, the aptly named, habitually overweight Tubbs pulled out with what was described as an injured shoulder.

King offered another diagnosis. "Extortion," he called it. If so, it was Tubbs's response to a usurious arrangement with his promoter, entitling Carl King to 50 percent of his earnings. His previous fight, Tubbs complained, had netted him only $1,750 of a $75,000 purse.

No matter. King the Elder already had an ingenuous replacement in mind. James "Bonecrusher" Smith was already training to fight Mitch Green. True, Witherspoon had already beaten Smith. King couldn't do anything about that. But the fact that Bonecrusher was suing King made for a win-win.

"Bonecrusher, I want to settle this lawsuit with you," King began. "I'm gonna give you that world title fight and I'm gonna give you a lot of money."

"That's awesome," said Bonecrusher, whose eagerness belied the degree in business administration he'd received from Shaw University.

King went on to explain that Smith would be fighting Witherspoon again, but this time for the title at Madison Square Garden and televised on HBO.

"Don," Smith recalled saying, "you mean to tell me you are going to give me a whole seven days' notice to fight a guy that's had plenty of time to train for me and he beat me from pillar to post?"

"Yeah," said King. "Take it or leave it!"

Bonecrusher took it, of course. As part of the deal, though, he also took on a new manager. Carl King would again represent both champion and challenger in a title fight promoted by the man he called his father.

Witherspoon, meanwhile, was coming off an eleventh-round knockout of an apparent British sensation, Frank Bruno, in front of forty thousand fans at Wembley Stadium. Though his purse was reported at $900,000, his actual contract called for a $400,000 payment plus $100,000 in training expenses, all paid through Carl King's Monarch Boxing, a company that just happened to have the same address—32 East Sixty-Ninth Street—as Don King Productions. After Monarch took its customary 50 percent and deducted various fees for humanitarian organizations like the WBA and the IRS, the newly minted world champion received a check for $90,094.77.

Little wonder, then, that by the time Witherspoon arrived in New York for his title defense he was depressed, discouraged, and threatening to pull out of the fight. He had already signed two contracts: one to fight Tubbs and another, anticipating his victory, to fight Tyson in March for a million dollars. But now Carl King took the liberty of signing his name to a third: an amended contract in which he crossed out Tubbs's name and wrote in Smith's.

Witherspoon argued, quite reasonably, that he'd trained for Tubbs, not Smith, and hadn't even seen the contract he'd supposedly signed. The New York State Athletic Commission argued differently. Actually, it wasn't an argument so much as another threat delivered by Chairman José Torres. First, Torres maintained that under commission rules a manager had the unilateral right to sign for his fighter, even if that fighter claimed not to know—a perfectly reasonable position from a guy whose own manager, D'Amato, kept him from a title shot through the prime years of his career. Then Torres told Witherspoon that withdrawing from the fight meant—guess what?—*that he'd never fight again*. Not only would he be suspended but the Panama-based WBA would strip him of his title.

Witherspoon's attorney responded that it would take months to strip the champion. "I'm telling you," Torres shot back, "after New York suspends Timmy, it would not take one and a half months or one and a half weeks or one and a half days for the WBA to strip him. It would take one and a half seconds and you can go to Panama and try to get it back."

The cantankerous prefight presser at the Garden featured a 105-minute monologue by King, railing against his ingrate fighters while misquoting or misreferencing Einstein, Freud, and Shakespeare. The highlight, however, was an encore appearance by Mitch Green, whom King had now screwed out of yet another payday with Bonecrusher. With that signature toothpick dangling from his mouth and a female admirer trying to hold him back, Green made another run at King on the dais. The promoter managed to shield himself, as the *Times* noted, by standing "behind burly colleagues," among them the Reverend Al Sharpton.

"I'll break your neck!" yelled Green.

All the reporters got the break-your-neck threat in their stories. But only the AP captured the truly prescient remark Green directed at King: "You're taking from everybody and nobody is saying anything."

IF YOU'RE ASKING WHAT THIS HAS TO DO WITH TYSON, THE ANSWER is pretty much everything. While Tyson had an encyclopedic knowledge of boxing history, he was blind to its present tense.

The game was changing. HBO's subscriber base grew at a rate worth $5 million a month through 1986, a phenomenon that would cause Abraham to call Tyson "a walking billboard" for the network. Even when he wasn't fighting, he was the story.

"The only one out there who sells tickets is Mike Tyson," said King.

There were seventeen thousand empty seats at Madison Square Garden the night Tim Witherspoon fought Bonecrusher Smith for the heavyweight title. Witherspoon came in fat and demoralized and was knocked out in the first round by a guy he had beaten with ease just eighteen months prior.

"I knew his mind couldn't be on the fight," said Bonecrusher, the new WBA champion. "He couldn't be thinking about me."

Witherspoon lost his belt, an incisor, and a payday with Tyson. Nor would his indignities cease. His $400,000 purse would net him only $129,000, most of which went to the IRS, with another $30,000 going to pay his trainer. Then José Torres suspended him for traces of marijuana showing up in his system. In fact, it was a botched test, with a mishandled sample that Torres tried to walk back as "a clerical error." But it brought to light his conduct as commissioner.

Torres had long since made himself a target, what with the way he openly rooted for Tyson, jumping into the ring to kiss him amid the victory celebration. But now he'd strong-armed Witherspoon just as he'd strong-armed Mitch Green, telling them their careers would end if they didn't fall into line—for Don fucking King of all people! Worse still was his willfully blind eye to Carl King managing opposing fighters. "A conflict of interest," Torres conceded, "but the rule is rarely enforced."

It's worth noting how chummy the King and Tyson camps were quickly becoming. Certainly, the cocksure Jacobs now thought he had an ally in King, who seemed so eager to serve up his deep inventory of heavyweights for the privilege of serving as Tyson's promoter. "The team is Cayton, Jacobs, King and HBO," he'd declare soon enough. "It's a team that works brilliantly together."

It was even more brilliant with Torres using his agency to provide cover. The effect of his strong-arm threats—first Green, then Witherspoon— was the same, intended to keep the Tyson train moving on schedule. The winner of Witherspoon–Bonecrusher (like the ill-fated Witherspoon–Tubbs) had already been penciled in as Tyson's next opponent. That Torres valued his standing in the Tyson camp more than his duties as a civil servant or his obligations to the long-suffering fighters may not have distinguished him in the long, inglorious history of hacks who ran the state commissions. But it was a special betrayal of the supposedly D'Amatoesque ideals and the celebration (at least among boxing's literati) that had attended his hiring back in '84.

Newfield once told me, sadly, that "José was in over his head" as chairman. Competence wasn't the only issue, though. It's still plain to see in the YouTube clips: the unmistakable desperation with which Torres hovers around Tyson. It wasn't just the money, though he needed it, I'm told. There was something else at work. Torres had learned to gladhand and bullshit, life skills that serve ex-fighters well in retirement. But he could never reclaim, as Hamill once wrote, "that brilliant boy he was that night a long time ago in St. Nick's." Torres wasn't what he should have been. And he knew it. His fidelity to Cus cost him his prime.

Now Torres wanted a piece, not merely of the pie but of the glory.

Torres liked to be seen with Tyson.

Torres had given his best years to Cus. He had remained the devout apostle. Shouldn't there be some payback?

Something about Tyson had compromised Torres, turning a good man into a venal one. To me, it says less about Torres than about Tyson, not the man but the snowballing phenomenon of him. The corruption of Torres—like Jacobs and Cayton greasing the local cops or D'Amato casting off Teddy—was merely a harbinger of things to come. Quite suddenly, Tyson had become a prize unlike any the game had ever seen. So valuable, arousing such greed, such ambition, that he had the unwitting effect of tainting, or further corrupting, everyone and everything around him, including, ultimately, himself.

IN ADDITION TO HIS DAYS AS AN UNDERGRADUATE, BONECRUSHER Smith—a son of sharecroppers in Magnolia, North Carolina—had been a file clerk in the army, a car salesman, and a prison guard, a job so profoundly depressing it made him consider fighting for a living. An accidental pro who didn't step in a ring until he was twenty-three, Smith anticipated what would become of the American heavyweight, who is frequently built like something out of a comic book (Smith went six four, 235) but came to the sport only after washing out at something else, typically football or basketball, which Smith played through college. What Smith did to Witherspoon wasn't an accident; he was heavy-handed. Still, the prior occupation that seems to have helped him most as a fighter was car salesman. Bonecrusher, then almost thirty-four years old, was a pretty good bullshit artist. "Larry Merchant said it was the biggest upset in boxing history when I knocked out Witherspoon," he said. "What will he say when I knock out Tyson?"

Bonecrusher Smith was fourteen pounds heavier than Tyson, with a spectacular eleven-inch reach advantage. His signature victories—against Witherspoon and Mike Weaver—were both first-round knockouts. He had boasted about testing Tyson's chin. But when his moment arrived, he chose discretion over destruction. Smith had seen all that valor had done for Berbick. He knew why Butch Lewis had pulled Spinks from the tournament. So he held, hugged, and held some more.

Smith was cut over the left eye in the second, a round that saw Mills Lane deduct a point from him for excessive holding. Unfortunately, it did nothing to dissuade Smith.

A big man fighting scared is not a pretty sight. The Hilton had built and packed a 13,600-seat arena in anticipation of Tyson's title fights. But now the fans had begun to boo.

Lane, who deducted another point from Smith in the eighth, would have been well within his rights to disqualify Smith. That might've been more merciful. Instead, it just went on and on. And on. It remains the most dreadful of Tyson's fights.

"The only interesting thing," noted Merchant, "is to watch Tyson and see how he tries to deal with this."

Not well. Smith's wasn't a novel strategy, but something about all the grabbing and clutching broke Tyson's rhythm and concentration. He seemed deaf to Rooney's instructions. He stopped jabbing, didn't bother attacking Smith's body, and abandoned his uppercut. He merely continued to punch upward at a man at least six inches taller.

"He didn't want to fight," Tyson said afterward.

For the first time, Tyson had failed to impress or to grow. But he'd also won every round on each of the judges' cards. More important, he had both the WBC and the WBA belts. For the first time since 1978, there was one heavyweight champion.

The following week, Tyson traveled by Concorde to London. His ostensible mission was to scout Frank Bruno, who was fighting at Wembley Arena. Tyson had his photo taken with bobbies. He entertained the press at the Grosvenor House, talking up Bruno and calling Bonecrusher "a disgrace to boxing." Still, the precocious champion found time to enjoy himself.

He'd recall being in bed with a British woman, an episode of *Soul Train* playing in the background. It had first aired December 20, 1986, featuring Al Jarreau and Vesta Williams. And her.

"Who's that girl?" he asked.

29

Her name was Robin Givens, then best known for her role in an ABC sitcom, *Head of the Class*. It was about a group of gifted students and their teacher, played by Howard Hesseman, at a fictitious Manhattan high school. Tyson, who dropped out of his own high school while living with D'Amato, developed a fixation on the show and Givens's character, Darlene Merriman. "Darlene," wrote a *People* correspondent, is "the snobbiest kid in Howard Hesseman's class of brilliant misfits—a gorgeous high school senior who plays Trivial Pursuit in French."

Givens and her sister, Stephanie, a professional tennis player, were raised by a fiercely driven woman, the former Ruth Newby of Lexington, Kentucky. Like Lorna Mae, Ruth grew up in both the South and New York, to wit, Seymour Avenue in the Bronx, where she lived with her mother. And like Lorna Mae, Ruth also found herself a single mother. But men didn't leave Ruth; she left them.

At sixteen, while visiting her father, a bricklayer, back in Kentucky, Ruth met Reuben Givens at a local bowling alley. As a junior in basketball-crazed Lexington, Givens—a slender five-foot-ten guard with a deft ball-handling touch—was named first team All-City, the first Black student to lead the county in scoring. Though denied the coveted scorer's trophy when a local merchant suddenly withdrew its sponsorship, Reuben's

Robin Givens, 1987

prospects still seemed bright. After all, his family owned the town's second-biggest waste-management company, Dave Givens Garbage & Sanitation. Ruth decided to stay in Lexington for her senior year. ,

They were married the day they graduated, June 6, 1964. Five months later, Robin was born.

By then, Reuben had played a stint with a Pittsburgh Pirates farm team in Buffalo. Just as he had failed to impress the big-league club, it soon became clear he would fail as a husband, too. "I told her I didn't want to live up to her standards," he said of Ruth. "I was not sophisticated in the sense that she wanted to be."

They tried to save the marriage back in Lexington, where Ruth became pregnant with Stephanie. But before too long, mother and daughters were all living back in the Bronx. In 1969, Ruth boarded a flight to Juárez, Mexico, had the stewardess bring her a glass of champagne, and toasted the dissolution of her marriage.

Ruth had a thing about drinking well, or at least affluently. She taught Robin how to make daiquiris and drink martinis, as those were rich-people drinks. One gets the sense that Ruth—now raising two kids on her own—didn't merely aspire to wealth but thought of it in a way that was emancipatory, or even divine. Though she was raised Catholic and managed to send her daughters to a Montessori grade school, Ruth consulted a spiritualist when it came to Reuben's delinquent child support payments. When that didn't work, she dressed the girls in their Sunday best and brought them to see Don King's favorite preacher, Reverend Ike.

Mom's been possessed, thought Robin, even as Ruth put her last twenty-dollar bill on the collection plate.

The next day, Ruth was informed that she had an interview with Electronic Data Systems. She got the job. "For years," recalled Robin, "neither Stephanie nor I left the house before Mom had pinned one of Reverend Ike's prayer cloths to our panties."

In 1979, Ruth married Franklin Roper. It lasted a year. She divorced Roper but kept his surname. Mostly what Ruth did was work. She was, by turns, a ticket agent for TWA, a travel agent, a headhunter, and by 1982, the owner of R. L. Roper Associates, a computer consulting firm bankrolled, at least in part, by Yankees outfielder Dave Winfield. She would eventually sue Winfield, claiming that the Yankees all-star outfielder gave her a sexually transmitted disease in 1985.

The case was settled and sealed. It wasn't unusual, however, for Ms. Roper to wind up in court, mostly as a civil defendant: skipping out on lease payments or stiffing tenants on their security deposits for a property Ruth owned in Freeport, Long Island.

Even the plaintiffs understood she was a formidable woman, though. As one, a former business associate, recalled: "She worked till eleven o'clock at night. On Saturdays, she was always there. Eighteen hours a day . . . Her choice was poverty or survival. It was not easy for a Black woman raising two kids by herself. . . . Basically she's a very sensitive woman. But if you hurt her, she'll reach out and smack you. . . . When Ruth put the gavel down, those children would never disobey her. In her family, she's the rule."

And her greatest rule of all? Marry well. Robin was first up. "I have to get her a rich husband," she said.

ROBIN WAS BRIGHT AND BEGUILING, ENDOWED WITH HER MOTHER'S drive and her father's elegant bone structure. Still barely in her teens and recently graduated from New Rochelle Academy, she dated Master Gee of the Sugar Hill Gang. While attending Sarah Lawrence, where she matriculated as a precocious fifteen-year-old, she fell in love—"my first serious romance," she called it—with Eddie Murphy. Though their relationship stalled when he went off to shoot *48 Hrs.*, one has to admire her dauntless opening line: "Do you want my autograph?" She was barely sixteen.

Robin graduated from Sarah Lawrence, class of '84, at nineteen. By the time Tyson saw her on *Soul Train*, she'd been living in a Los Angeles one-bedroom for the better part of a year. A relationship with Michael Jordan, whose photograph was taped to her dressing-room mirror, was at its end. "Both distance and the demands of our careers were the problem," she told *People*.

Her big break came after guest starring on *The Cosby Show*, an episode that would air in early March 1986. To that point, Ruth had insisted that her brainy daughter would become a doctor. But Cosby himself was apparently so taken with Robin's performance that he invited both mother and daughter to join him for dinner at his Upper East Side brownstone. There he argued on the ingenue's behalf, that she might follow her heart, forsaking medicine for a career in the arts. He even offered to pay for medical school if she didn't get an acting job in six months.

"Bill's confidence in Robin's chances ultimately convinced me we should give Hollywood a try," said Ruth.

In a matter of weeks, mother and daughter were staying at Cosby's place outside LA. Cosby had gotten Robin an agent. The agent got her a reading. And within hours she was cast as a high-class call girl (is there any other kind in a network movie of the week?) in *Beverly Hills Madam*.

This story of Cosby's largesse was better when he was still America's favorite dad, not the serial sexual predator who's been accused, sued, and prosecuted on behalf of more than fifty women going back decades.

Then again, Robin's story was also better in its original incarnation, most succinctly expressed in a legend above her full-cover photo on the June 29, 1987, issue of *Jet*: "Robin Givens Leaves Harvard Med School for Hollywood."

By then, it had been taken as gospel in countless local newspapers and national publications that Robin had done at least a year at Harvard Medical School before Cosby's offer caused her to drop out. It was a fiction that continued unabated for another couple of years, until Betty Liu Ebron of the *Daily News* thought to actually call the school.

"She never applied, let alone went here," Ebron was told.

I understand the machinery at work here—flackery as mythology in the predigital age. The first reference I find to Givens and Harvard went out on the Knight Ridder wire just as the pilot for *Head of the Class* wrapped: "This time last year, Givens was an undergrad at Harvard."

A couple of months later, Robin told Vernon Scott of UPI: "After a year at Harvard, I suddenly didn't care about school anymore." Then, when a New York paper asked about her time in Cambridge, she said: "I was Black and I was a woman. But I showed them you can be equal and as intelligent." And there was this to a Gannett correspondent, when asked about dropping out of med school: "I called him"—Cosby—"from Boston one day and said 'I'm convinced. I'm ready.'"

In her 2007 memoir, *Grace Will Lead Me Home*, Givens writes that she applied to Harvard's Graduate School of Arts and Sciences to appease her mother and stayed only a month or so before getting the Cosby audition. "It took everything in me to last the short time that I did," she writes.

Note she'd never actually *said* she'd been enrolled in the medical school. But she didn't discourage the notion, either. In fact, it was part of her official ABC biography along with her years at the American Academy of Dramatic Arts ("She only attended five sessions," said its director) and her career at Ford Models.

"Can't find any trace of her," Eileen Ford told *Newsday*. "She's pretty enough, but she's too short."

I know full well that reporters actually *want* to believe in fairy tales.

"Cus and the Kid," after all, was better when the old man was a dejected mob buster and Tyson his Nietzsche-reading ward. I get the context as well; Givens wasn't the first actor to stand back as press agents and reporters whipped mere puffery up into something more grandiose and deceitful. What's more, it couldn't have been easy for Robin, trying to reconcile her own emerging vision of herself with the one prescribed for her by Ruth. She was young, the driven daughter of a driven mother who was single, ferociously self-made, and, yes, Black. On the other hand, Robin *was* talented. She *was* beautiful. And she was certainly bright enough to know better.

Going through the news clippings (one of them with Robin referring to her "parents" and the writer spectacularly misidentifying her dad as a gynecologist), I hit on something Ruth's erstwhile partner said when she asked him to bankroll her company in 1982: "She was making a good living, but she wanted to make more." If this really were a fairy tale, there's its core: *more*, the American disease. A hot young actress is desirable, but a hot young actress who went to Harvard Med School is infinitely more. That was part of the appeal here, for everyone from the ABC execs to Eddie Murphy. "He was so completely hurt," Robin said of Murphy. "He used to call me 'Doc' and make me bring my books on dates. I think he wanted me to be a doctor more than my mom did."

Certainly, in the months to come, Tyson would brag with pride and delight of his girl from Harvard. And what was wrong with that? He wanted to believe in her tale, just as people wanted to believe in his.

As for Robin, she sees herself among a line of single, abused women going back to her grandmother. Her 2007 memoir recalls visiting her father back in Kentucky. She was ten. He was furious as he ordered her to drop her pants and took off his belt. Robin began to cry, then lost control of her bladder. Unmoved, Reuben Givens continued excoriating her. But just as he was about to strike with the belt, Robin was rescued by the kindly grandfather she would come to associate with Cosby.

It's a haunting passage but, like so much of Robin's account, leaves me wondering. It's not just the med-school story or what was to come. It's not her dating history, per se. There's something unsettling in her patrons, starting with Cosby. There is a notable entry in the acknowledgments to *Grace Will Lead Me Home*. The tribute to the man who owned the publishing house comes after salutations to Jesus and her mother but before her salute to Oprah: "Harvey Weinstein, your friendship brought me here. . . . You made me feel safe enough to say yes, I can share my life's journey. . . . Thank you, Harvey, it has without a doubt been the most healing experience of my life."

WHATEVER TYSON SAW ON *SOUL TRAIN*, HOWEVER FLEETING, IGNITED his obsession. And why not? "Cus always told me that anything I ever saw on TV I could have," he'd recall. "And that included women."

"What's wrong with you?" asked Holloway, watching Tyson obsess over *Head of the Class* in their Albany apartment.

"I gotta have her," said Tyson, who implored Holloway to enlist the help of his friend John Horne, a fledgling comedian in Hollywood. Horne apparently came up with the number for Roper Associates, which an undaunted Tyson began calling frequently.

Eventually, Robin suggested lunch at Le Dome. It was on. Holloway recalls Mike bathing assiduously and practicing his lines each day for a week or so prior. Then they flew to LA and checked in to the Beverly Wilshire, where he left an assortment of suits strewn all over his suite before settling on the blue Armani.

Robin was sipping champagne when Mike and Rory finally arrived, at least an hour late. She wore a black velvet Betsey Johnson dress. "I felt a strong sexual vibe from her, some sort of chemistry," recalled Tyson.

Still, their meeting seems less a first date than a very public summit. Le Dome, where Robin first met her agent from William Morris, had been described that year in the *Los Angeles Times* as "a Sunset Strip powerhaven." But there they were: Mike, Rory, Robin, Robin's sister, Ruth, likely Ruth's assistant, and at least one publicist.

Tyson began by apologizing to Ruth: "I was so nervous about meeting your daughter, I couldn't decide what to wear."

In the years to come, Robin and Ruth would become famously known as a "package deal." But while Ruth had reservations about Tyson, he was blind to them. In fact, given the number of mothers Tyson had already puppied up to, I'd venture an educated guess that he fell so hard in love not *despite* Ruth's constant presence but because of it. As eager as he was to get into Robin's pants, so was he eager to call someone "Ma."

SOME WEEKS LATER, FOLLOWING THE DELIVERY OF HIS NEW ROLLS-Royce, Tyson showed up for a press conference at the Waldorf-Astoria. The champ wore all white, but for the V-neck trim on his Gucci tennis sweater. More striking, however, was the fetching Robin on his arm.

When Tyson entered the HBO tournament, it was hoped that this date—April 22—would occasion the announcement of a grand finale: Tyson, with his WBC and WBA belts, against Spinks, who held the IBF and "lineal" titles, to produce a single, undisputed champion. But Spinks's departure had forced the network and King to scramble. Now Tony Tucker, the number one–ranked contender formerly designated as Spinks's mandatory opponent, would fight number two–ranked Buster Douglas for the IBF title. Meanwhile, at the top of the card, the real attraction, Tyson, would fight Pinklon Thomas.

Prior to being upset by Berbick, Thomas had been considered a front-runner to win the tournament. Now, as King's best available heavyweight, he'd become a placeholder, a guy to keep Tyson busy until he could fight to unify all three belts later that summer.

Tyson–Thomas was also Tyson's first fight with King as his exclusive promoter. Unlike those of King's other fighters, who typically signed blank contracts after accepting Carl King as their manager, Tyson's deal was a testament to his burgeoning economic might. It called for a million dollars up front, $100,000 in training expenses, two thirds of the net, and the right to inspect all of King's contracts and financial records. In addition, the Tyson camp would receive thirty round-trip first-class tickets to the site, a total of four hotel suites and thirty double rooms, plus meals and 130 tickets to the fight, including 20 in the first three rows, 40 in the first seven, and 50 in the first twelve.

Though one couldn't tell from the coverage, Pinklon Thomas wasn't a bum. He was six three, a seasoned former champion with an excellent jab, and tough enough to have kicked a teenage heroin habit back in Pontiac, Michigan. He didn't seem scared of Tyson, what with the way he needled him at the presser. "You got a squeaky little voice," Thomas told him. "Is your name Mike Tyson or Michael Jackson?"

But by the time *Sports Illustrated*'s Ralph Wiley caught up with him on fight week, Thomas was upset, muttering to himself about something Tyson had said. "He told me to suck his dick!"

That was jailhouse talk, of course, and would become standard at Tyson's press events. Wiley figured the remark was Tyson's way of ensuring that Thomas, unlike Bonecrusher Smith, would actually fight Tyson—which he did.

It wasn't the best of strategies. Two of the three judges scored the opening round as if there'd been a knockdown, 10–8 for Tyson, even though Thomas managed to remain upright. Thomas recovered, using his stiff jab well and getting Tyson to lunge and miss wide. After the fourth, Merchant had it tied two rounds apiece. In fact, you could see eventual problems for Tyson—along with his own rather formidable chin, off which Thomas's jabs seemed to just bounce—but only if you were so predisposed, or a natural contrarian. Everyone else got what they were looking for: a fearsome Tyson onslaught that began with his right hook–right uppercut, then, moments later, a frightening sixteen-punch barrage that put Thomas down, then out, for the first time in his career.

"Might have been the most vicious knockout of my career," Tyson himself would recall. "It was like hitting the heavy bag."

Tyson retains a deep admiration for Thomas's attempt to rise. But in the moment, the ever-smug Jacobs saw only the bottom line. "People pay to see Mike knock someone out," he pronounced.

That's why the price kept going up. In fact, Jacobs and Cayton were already close to finalizing a shockingly lucrative new contract with HBO. Earlier that evening, Tucker had knocked out Buster Douglas to win the IBF title. Now the date and the deal for Tyson–Tucker were set. After beating Tucker, Tyson would become the first fully undisputed heavyweight

Tyson hurting Pinklon Thomas

champion of the three-belt era. In the next year or so, it was thought he'd embark on his world tour—first England, then perhaps Italy, then Japan, where Cayton and Jacobs were working on a deal reportedly worth $10 million for the live gate and Japanese television rights.

All was proceeding as scheduled, every detail foreseen and accounted for—except, perhaps, for the fighter's own heart. Earlier on that evening's broadcast, HBO aired a prefight package featuring Tyson at the Young Adult Institute, a group home for the mentally disabled in Manhattan. It was the most timeless and cynical kind of piece: Star athlete parachutes in, shares a tender moment with the disadvantaged, and burnishes his reputation. "But Tyson seemed to know it," recalls a friend of mine, not a boxing guy, who found himself covering the event for *Newsday*. "It was clear to me he had empathy for the kids." That's what I thought, too, watching the piece—the ease with which Mr. Suck My Dick could swerve into actual empathy. What's more, there's the *Head of the Class* T-shirt on which he'd written in marker: "Mike T. + Robin G." with an arrow through a crudely drawn heart. Just the day before, Dick Young had informed readers of the *New York Post* as to the twenty-year-old champion's dead-set intentions regarding the "knockout" who dropped out of "Harvard pre-med."

"He wants to marry her."

30

Going back several fights, Tyson had developed alopecia, a condition that manifested itself with a bald spot on the right side of his scalp about an inch above the hairline. He attributed it to stress—not just the pressure of being heavyweight champion but also the unforgiving pace of his training schedule and the gladiator-like sparring. What's more, Tyson's courtship with Robin was a turbulent one: passionate, tempestuous, full of fits and starts. He'd push; she'd pull. There was also an incident that summer at the Greek Theatre in Los Angeles: Tyson tried to kiss a parking lot attendant, then smacked around the guy who came to her defense. Jacobs and Cayton took care of it, of course—for a total of $105,000 and an admonition, for anyone who cared to listen, that "the little guy" was now a target for gold-digging litigants everywhere.

What followed was a difficult camp, training for his final unification bout with IBF champ Tony Tucker. Robin showed up. They fought. Tyson informed Steve Lott he was retiring, then flew to Albany to hang out with Rory Holloway.

That he was AWOL for the better part of a week led to a spate of columns by Don King's go-to reporter (and eventual publicist), Mike Marley of the *New York Post*. There were questions as to whether Rooney could handle the now-twenty-one-year-old champ. Jacobs and Cayton

From left: Bill Cayton, Tyson, Steve Lott, and Jacobs

even had a sit-down with the venerable trainer Eddie Futch in Las Vegas. They denied it, of course. But Marley only came back harder, writing on "the summer of Tyson's discontent" and opining that Rooney and Lott had him under a kind of house arrest in Vegas. "They even grab his mail," said Marley's source, whom I'd bet was King.

It was a grievance that Robin had already seized on. "These people"—Jacobs, Cayton, and their underlings—"don't understand Mike," she told Torres. "They will never know how to deal with him."

By August 1, 1987, as Tyson entered the ring for the Tucker fight, the once-nickel-sized bald spot was more like a silver dollar. Not that anyone mentioned it. HBO was determined to present the Tyson camp only in the most flattering light. First came a prefight feature on the now-embattled Rooney, or as Merchant called him, "D'Amato's keenest disciple." Rooney was shown at home with his two small children, working with inmates at the Greene Correctional Facility in Coxsackie, New York, and, of course, ever ready with a "dese, dem, and dose" tribute to D'Amato. His gambling and drinking weren't part of the script, and neither was his former friend Teddy Atlas.

Then, quite abruptly—like hearing ad copy before you know what's being sold—a Father George Clements came on camera attesting to Tyson's good works. Clements, a friend of Jacobs going back to his days in Chicago, was a Catholic priest whose South Side parish church had burned down the year before. But just two weeks before the Tucker fight, Tyson and King miraculously appeared at a ground-breaking ceremony for his new house of worship and presented him with a $20,000 check.

"I have no doubt in my mind," Clements told HBO viewers, "that with the help of the heavyweight champion of this planet, that church will go up."

Fourteen minutes later, after the baroque trumpets (thank you, Don) heralding Tyson's arrival but still just seconds into the opening round, the young champ took a left uppercut that lifted him clean off his feet.

Tucker was a 10–1 underdog, an ancillary presence going into the fight. If he seemed nondescript, then it was a judgment rendered largely by the same people (not merely fans, but those in the press box as well) who failed to individuate just about every Black champion and challenger going back to Larry Holmes, as if they were all versions of the same bum. In fact, what was most typical about Tucker was the way in which he'd been divvied up, with chunks of his purse going to promoters Cedric Kushner, Jeff Levine, and Josephine Abercrombie and managers Dennis Rappaport, Alan Kornberg, and Emanuel Steward, not to mention his own father, who had auctioned off these aforementioned shares of his progeny. Percentages aside, though, Tucker was a real talent, well schooled, with a fine pedigree. He'd won an assortment of national and international titles while Tyson was still at Spofford. Now, at twenty-nine, he was at his physical peak. Six-five, 221 pounds, with a thirteen-inch reach advantage over Tyson, Tucker was the kind of athlete who in later years would have forsaken dim, fetid gyms for an athletic dorm in the SEC or the Big Ten. Undefeated in thirty-four fights, Tucker had never even been knocked down. So perhaps it shouldn't have been such a shocker that he lifted Tyson airborne.

Still more shocking was the manner in which Tyson took it—without so much as flinching. The chin that absorbed the blow remains Tyson's most undermentioned virtue. The uppercut wasn't the last clean shot he took, either. It was easy to see why Michael Spinks—now sitting with Butch Lewis in the uppermost row, UU, of the Hilton Center, pretending to be inconspicuous—had avoided him for the easier money against Cooney.

Tucker had an assured left hook he could throw moving backward and an excellent straight right hand whose proficiency waned through the bout, as he'd hurt it the week before in sparring. But Tucker knew how to tie up an opponent without looking like a cowardly lion. It was a good fight, belying the notion that Tyson's opponents were either heartless huggers or petrified victims. Eventually, though, Tyson's power, relentlessness, and dauntless chin proved too much for Tucker, who suffered his first loss by unanimous decision.

TYSON NOW HAD ALL THREE BELTS, THE UNDISPUTED HEAVY-weight champion. Barely twenty-one, he was not merely king of the division but, as Cus and Jimmy had envisioned, king of all boxing. Such an occasion called for a coronation, or as King put it, "a throneization." Hence the baroque trumpets—a band of six, played by grown men in feathered caps, velvet pantaloons, and sequined tunics—now heard again to summon all Tyson's subjects, loyal and otherwise.

In addition to the trumpeters was a delegation of Beefeaters, one of whom was the otherwise no-shtick ring announcer Chuck Hull—an offense that, wrote the *Daily News*'s Mike Katz, "no amount of gin could blot." Hull, a pit boss by day, had vowed never to "prostitute his craft" like the new, attention-seeking generation of "Let's get ready to rumble" announcers. Nevertheless, there he was reading from a script that began, "Hear ye! Hear ye!"

Tyson, to his obvious chagrin, was seated in a red velvet throne and presented with what King called an assortment of "baubles, rubies, and fabulous doodads." They included a chinchilla robe from Lenobel Furriers of Las Vegas and a studded necklace and scepter, courtesy of Felix the Jeweler. A crown from the same set was placed atop his head by Muhammad Ali.

More astounding, and an even greater testament to King's powers of persuasion, were the "knights" the new champion had vanquished, among them "Sir Bonecrusher" and "Sir Pinky," otherwise known as Pinklon Thomas. The heads of the notoriously feudal, tribute-demanding sanctioning bodies were all there, as were a bevy of HBO executives who received statuettes, leading Eddie Murphy to wonder why in a room full of Black fighters, only the white guys got trophies.

There was a children's choir from Chicago and a female gospel singer from Cleveland. The Reverend Al Green sang "Our Precious Lord." The Reverend Charles Williams, leader of the annual Indiana Black Expo, blessed the meal. Then the Reverend Al Sharpton—newly famous from his protest marches in Howard Beach, New York—presented Tyson with his championship belts, while Robin Givens, his ostensible queen, was seen beaming as the photographers snapped away.

The single victory for modesty that night was notched by "Sir Seth" Abraham, who declined to wear the robe King had selected for him.

"Is it real sable?" he asked.

"Of course not," said King.

But consider the force of ego, the power required of King to create such an assemblage. What must it have taken to hold the assorted dignitaries hostage for almost two hours *after* a title fight? Bad taste? Vegas was founded on bad taste. This wasn't about the entertainment or the blessings. It was about the real king. If Tyson were a Tudor and Seth Abraham the Bank of England, then Don King was a version of Cardinal Wolsey. He wasn't the jester; he was the *power*. And if this was Don King's tribute to Olde Las Vegas, it was also his message to her founding fathers, many of whom, just like Don, came by way of Cleveland, members of a Hebraic criminal aristocracy.

It was now supposed, given the rapidity and relative ease with which Tyson seized custody of all three belts, that his reign would last beyond even the foreseeable future. His next opponent, Olympic gold medalist

Al Sharpton presenting Tyson with one of his
championship belts during the "coronation"

Tyrell Biggs, was already on the books for that fall. But while Biggs's mobility and jab were often cited as the tools necessary to beat Tyson, no one really expected that much of the erstwhile Olympian, who had already endured at least one cocaine rehab. Beyond that? George Foreman, retired for a decade, had just embarked on what seemed a circus-like comeback. Cruiserweight champion Evander Holyfield was talking about eventually moving up, though his chances as an undersized heavyweight seemed fanciful and owed mostly to the success of Michael Spinks. Spinks was seen as the only truly interesting fight for Tyson.

The real question, then, was for Tyson himself. What would his long reign signify? How would he compare with his predecessors? The question had less to do with his actual self than with his persona. Dempsey, who had ridden the rails as a boy, came to personify the Roaring Twenties. Joe Louis was pressed into service as a shining example of American democracy on the eve of World War II. Just the same, there was a reason that the photograph of Marciano ruining Joe Walcott's jaw had assumed a place of such reverence, along with the Christ heads and centerfolds, in

Italian social clubs and barbershops across America. Finally, there was Ali, whose mythic self had evolved into several incarnations, each one bigger than the last.

Garry Wills once called Ali "catnip to the intellectuals." And it felt like Joyce Carol Oates began in a similar vein with Tyson in *Life*. Her note on Tyson as "a psychic outlaw" feels like warmed-over Mailer, while her notion of Tyson as perhaps "the first heavyweight boxer in America to transcend issues of race" seems hopeful but naive. Still, she made explicit what had been hiding in plain sight: "He is trained, managed and surrounded, to an unusual degree, by white men." That these white men had given Tyson, quite intentionally, a kind of *Good Housekeeping* seal of approval led to another of Oates's keener observations, in a subsequent piece that year for the *Voice*: "For all his reserve, his odd, even eerie combination of shyness and aggression, his is a wonderfully *marketable* image."

Consider that Ali in 1979—not yet retired but a beloved global icon—managed to get an endorsement for d-CON roach spray. But Tyson at a mere twenty-one—in addition to being HBO's "walking billboard"—already had deals with Diet Pepsi, Eastman Kodak, and the Japanese brewer Suntory, as well as a groundbreaking agreement (negotiated, like the others, by Cayton) with Nintendo for *Mike Tyson's Punch-Out!!*, a video game that would sell more than two million copies in its first year. Cayton even thought to trademark Tyson's very Rocky-like nickname, "Iron Mike."

Perhaps, then, Tyson's true meaning had to do with his value as a commercial touchstone. But playing the pitchman—at least as his handlers had scripted the role for him—required some image scrubbing. "To overcome the stigma attached to Mike's juvenile delinquent past," recalled Cayton, "we arranged for Mike to make a commercial on behalf of the New York City Police Department and an anti-drug commercial for the Federal Bureau of Investigation. Mike also did a commercial for the Internal Revenue Service and for United Cerebral Palsy. Each commercial was designed to foster the image of Mike as civic-minded and law-abiding."

And, in a very particular way, whiter. "In the way he's been handled," noted *The Ring*'s Jack Obermayer, "it's almost like he's a 'white hope' in a Black man's skin." Of course, the selling of Tyson began with the fairy tale of "Cus and the Kid." He had lived, essentially, in an all-Black world until D'Amato and his minions "saved" him, in part by segregating him. He then attended mostly white schools and learned his craft in a mostly white gym above a small-town police station. His trainers were white, as were his patrons and even his cornermen, cut man Matt Baranski, and bucket man Lott, who'd now remind Tyson, per Jacobs's instructions, to remove his blingier pieces of jewelry before being interviewed on camera.

Tyson, like Patterson before him, had been taught obedience in matters of commerce but had begun to bridle at the way he was being monetized. All those "Just Say No"–style PSAs made him feel like "a fake fucking Uncle Tom nigga" and "a trained monkey," he says in *Undisputed Truth*.

Nobody transcends race, not in America. But Tyson's racial predicament—or his cultural one, depending how you parse it—was distinct, and connected or perhaps conflated with his old neighborhood. "Jimmy and Bill were intent on stripping away all the Brownsville from me," he writes in that same passage. "But Brownsville was who I was. . . . Everyone knew I was a criminal. I had come from a detention home. Now all of a sudden I was a good guy?"

Something in Tyson would always romanticize the street and judge himself more harshly than his contemporaries who hadn't had the benefit of an old man to save and rehabilitate them. Whatever Tyson had accomplished, he still wondered how it would play back home. That he no longer had a Brooklyn address didn't mean he'd ever left. Or ever would.

"To be honest," says Lennie Daniels, one of his early sparring partners and among the very few Black men he met in Catskill, "I don't know if he ever was happy being away from it."

That summer, Lori Grinker finally prevailed on him to do a shoot back in Brownsville. They left from Steve Lott's apartment in Midtown. Tyson wore all white but for the geometric print on his T-shirt and his

With a new Rolls in the old neighborhood, 1987

gold watches—a thin Cartier on his left wrist, a Rolex on his right. Grinker's photographs of that day seem straightforward enough: Tyson at the barbershop; Tyson signing autographs for the admiring children gathered around his blue Rolls-Royce; Tyson in sunglasses, resplendent in his white ensemble, sitting on the hood of the car, set against a pocked and weedy lot, greeting old friends like supplicants. More remarkable, in Grinker's recollection, was an encounter on the drive out. Halfway across the bridge—either Williamsburg or Manhattan, she doesn't recall—a woman pulled up alongside the Rolls and handed Tyson a slip of paper. It was her daughter's phone number. Nothing unusual in that—except for the question it provoked. "People who see me in this car, what do they think?" Tyson asked Grinker. "That I'm a drug dealer?"

The streets of Tyson's childhood had become only meaner and more deadly in his absence. The introduction of crack cocaine in the mid-eighties changed the culture of crime. Crackheads re-upped more frequently than heroin junkies. On the supply side, all those stickup kids from Spofford were bosses now. Or they were dead. Crack democratized the gangster life. You didn't need a French Connection or a made man willing to sell you kilos on consignment. You didn't need some weathered Sicilian to "open the books" or get you a union card. There weren't many freer markets than the one for crack. All you needed was some cocaine, baking soda, a 9-millimeter automatic pistol or an Uzi, and enough balls to hold your corner. This was a new kind of Murder, Inc., and everyone seemed to be in the line of fire—not merely bystanders, innocent and otherwise, but also witnesses, potential witnesses, protected witnesses, even cops. I remember stories of teenage gangsters who had prepaid for their funerals, that they might go out with the proper pomp and respect, like something out of a vintage mob movie. Perhaps the stories were only apocryphal. But they had the ring of truth, or rather, in places like Brownsville and East New York, the ring of cinematic reality. By now, Pacino's *Scarface* had become a kind of documentary, a how-to primer on being a gangster. In the Seventy-Fifth Precinct, mothers put their children to bed in bathtubs, fearing stray shots that came through the windows after dark.

ON JUST SUCH A NIGHT IN THE SUMMER OF '87, THE BLUE ROLLS made an encore appearance in the neighborhood, rolling up Sutter Avenue from Brownsville to East New York, past the beleaguered Seventy-Fifth Precinct toward the Cypress Hills projects. It had to be around 10:00 p.m.

Brian Gibbs, known as "Glaze," remembers standing outside his mother's apartment at 1266 Sutter and being dressed for work: jeans, a baseball jersey (likely the Cardinals) over his Kevlar vest, and a 9-millimeter Taurus in his waistband. He had recently been released after thirteen months in Rikers and the Brooklyn House of Detention, the case against him—the murder of a woman Gibbs suspected of robbing one of his drug spots—having fallen apart after he bribed a witness $25,000 not to testify. Now he was clearing $40,000 a day as the boss of his own crew, "M and M," short for "money and murder." Beyond that, though, what made Glaze Gibbs one of most feared men in New York was his position as "security chief" for two guys he'd met in prison, Fat Cat Nichols and Pappy Mason.

Glaze was just starting to make his rounds when he saw the blue Rolls coming slowly, deliberately, almost trolling its way up Sutter. The windows were down, Uzis dangling from the passenger side.

It wasn't a prudent or professional move. Rather, it was someone who *wanted* to be seen. Just as Gibbs asked himself, *Who the fuck is this?*, a murmur swept through Cypress.

Yo, that's Mike Tyson's car! That's Mike Tyson!

"Tyson wanted people to know he was around," says Gibbs. "He wanted to make a statement."

Tyson wasn't a gangster, but he loved hanging out with those who were, some of them old friends. What's more, he was conspicuously generous to them. There were two ways, Gibbs was told, that Tyson would help out a Brooklyn guy with the proper rep. First, in jail, he'd break off some cash and have it put in your commissary account. Second, in death. Tyson paid for a lot of funerals in those years, many of them at the Lawrence H. Woodward Funeral Home, 1 Troy Avenue, Bedford-Stuyvesant, which turned out to be as frequently surveilled by cops as Midnight Rose's had been half a century earlier. Tyson even went so far as to bankroll one old friend's crack operation: "Five thousand here, twenty thousand there, just so that he didn't have to work for someone else. I wasn't a partner and I never wanted any return from my investment."

"He wanted to be like us," Gibbs says of Tyson. "Mike wanted to be *down*."

And he was. The era had its own signposts, its own distorted frame of reference: the glorification of gangster pictures, Mafia tropes, and automatic weapons. More important, though, was its soundtrack. Tyson was in Spofford when he first heard "Rapper's Delight." Hip-hop quickly evolved from mere braggadocio to a reflection of life on the streets. He was sequestered in Catskill when Grandmaster Flash released "The Message," a percussive allegory about a stickup kid turned jailhouse punk and found hanged to death in his cell. "Those was our people—all the criminals and thieves," Tyson would recall of the genre's early years. "We all listened to hip-hop: the moneymakers . . . the killers the robbers. All the fucking street urchins. We all listened."

By 1987, the vernacular and imagery had changed again. Boogie Down Productions released *Criminal Minded*, a seminal hip-hop album that featured KRS-One and Scott La Rock (who'd die by gunfire just weeks after the Tyson–Tucker fight) with an arsenal on the cover. References to Uzis and 9-millimeters became common, including the inaugural hit from Public Enemy, eponymously titled "Public Enemy No. 1": "I'll show you my gun, my Uzi weighs a ton / Because I'm Public Enemy number one."

Gibbs remembers the cut fondly. It was a Friday night on D block, eighth floor of the Brooklyn House. "Yo, Glaze," inmates started yelling, "did you hear that?" Walter "King Tut" Johnson—also from Cypress, famous for robbing at gunpoint three hundred members of his own mother's church—had called in to WBLS during *Mr. Magic's Rap Attack* and dedicated the song to Gibbs. Coincidentally or not, the single also contained hip-hop's first lyrical reference—as best I can tell—to Tyson: "I can go solo, like a Tyson bolo."

Never mind that neither Chuck D nor anyone else had ever seen Tyson throw a bolo punch. Tyson had now entered the zeitgeist in a way that hadn't been scripted by a white man. For a couple of years, Tyson had been promised as a successor to Dempsey, Joe Louis, and Rocky Marciano. Surrounded by white ethnics in his camp, he was seen as *safe*. But Public Enemy—whose logo featured a man posing B-boy style in the crosshairs of a rifle scope—was not. "Here's a rap group that doesn't aim to—or have a chance of—crossing over," Daniel Brogan wrote in the *Chicago Tribune*. "They're raw and confrontational, just the sort of thing that frightens programmers of every ilk."

Or would it? Hip-hop would change the market itself. Hip-hop *wanted* a Sonny Liston. Whatever Tyson looked like to network executives or that guy with a VFW cap in the Latham Coliseum, he was something else entirely refracted through the prism of hip-hop.

"The moment was right for Tyson just like it was right for Dempsey," says Larry Merchant. "Dempsey didn't become *the* Jack Dempsey of story and song until after World War I. Then a heavyweight champion suddenly materializes from our Wild West, with that rip-roaring style, fighting in places like Montana. There's a metaphor in there somewhere. But the same way all the dots connected for Dempsey, they connected for Tyson with Black inner-city culture. The street guys adopted him. They *got* Mike Tyson."

America was at the cusp of a bull market for bad guys. Merchant didn't comprehend this so fully at the time—nor did anyone at HBO. Ditto Jacobs and Cayton. "They wanted me to be a hero," recalls Tyson, "but I wanted to be a villain."

There was only one man who had any real feel for what Tyson actually wanted, or how it would play.

"Don King," says Merchant. "King sensed Tyson could be bigger than big."

31

By the time he fought Tyson, Tyrell Biggs, former darling of America's amateur boxing establishment, was 15-0. He was also a recovering drug addict under the care of a psychiatrist. Though Biggs credits the doctor with helping to keep him basically sober since December 28, 1984, his own promotional team would deride him as "crazy." While they were frustrated his pro career had been less than consistent, it's worth noting Biggs didn't lack for toughness. In 1986, he won a unanimous decision over Jeff Sims after boxing eight of the ten rounds with a broken collarbone. On the Tyson–Bonecrusher Smith undercard, he knocked out David Bey despite a gash over his left eye that required thirty-two stitches to close.

Yet all that paled in comparison to the damage Tyson wanted to inflict on him. "I want to give him a good lesson," said Tyson. "I want to hurt him real bad."

In fact, this would be the second time Tyson tried to hurt Biggs, still the only American super heavyweight to win an Olympic gold medal. The first had been in Texas, per D'Amato's instructions, a two-round sparring session during the lead-up to the '84 Games. "I was seventeen years old and Biggs was a big-shot amateur," said Tyson, recalling the rib protector Biggs wore on his sore flanks. "I hit him there every chance I could."

The intervening three and a half years had done nothing to ameliorate Tyson's resentment. "I hate Tyrell Biggs," he told the *Times*'s Phil Berger. His explanations were numerous but all stemmed from jealousy. Biggs was six five, handsome, glib, good with the ladies, and, at his best, a stylish heavyweight in the Ali mold. His mere presence still reminded Tyson of all he was not. "I remember Pernell"—Olympic gold medalist and Hall of Famer Pernell Whitaker—"and a couple of the other guys teasing him about not making the team," says Biggs. "Tyson was pissed off."

Tyson said Biggs teased him, too, while waiting for a flight headed to Los Angeles for the Olympics. A woman wished them both good luck in their upcoming fights.

"She must mean good luck on the flight," said Biggs, as Tyson was just an alternate.

"That one thing stuck to my mind a long time," said Tyson.

Now, if he needed the fuel of any additional resentment, all Tyson had to do was peruse the New York papers, where the archcontrarians of the boxing beat had suddenly fallen in love with the notion that Biggs had the tools required to beat him: height, mobility, and an accurate jab. Even worse, Tyson had inspired a new breed of expert whose ignorance was commensurate only with their celebrity. "I've watched Tyrell a long time," said Donald Trump. "He can box and he can punch and I give him a shot."

Trump, the former owner of the recently defunct New Jersey Generals, whose epically bad decisions and arrogance in testimony during a lawsuit against the NFL had proved fatal for the United States Football League, had set his sights on boxing, having paid a then-stunning $3.5 million to host Spinks–Cooney. "I have a very distinct advantage," declared the forty-one-year-old developer. "Money."

Trump had also built a walkway that led directly from the Trump Plaza casino to the Atlantic City Convention Hall. Not only did it ensure access to a sixteen-thousand-seat arena Trump didn't have to build, but it hermetically sealed his high rollers off from any whiff of the dilapidated boardwalk below, where the assortment of convicts, cripples, and grotesques gave one the feel of being trapped inside a Diane Arbus photograph. Tyson–Biggs—acquired for the relative bargain price of $2.1 million—was Trump putting boxing on notice. Not only would the sport have to accommodate another monumental narcissist but Trump's dealings with King and HBO also earned him the right of first refusal for the bout everyone always seemed to be talking about: Tyson–Spinks.

"If I want the fight," said Trump, "nobody else will get it."

TYSON–BIGGS WAS THE LAST HEAVYWEIGHT CHAMPIONSHIP SCHED-uled for fifteen rounds, though it wouldn't last that long. Biggs boxed well in the first, moving and pumping his jab. "About as perfect a round as he could have to start this fight," noted Larry Merchant. Nevertheless, as Tyson had warned him—in a quote that's improved greatly over time—"everybody has plans until they get hit for the first time."

In the second round, Tyson started catching Biggs with quick looping shots, hooks, and right hands, busting up Biggs's lip. In the third, Tyson opened a large, leaky cut over Biggs's left eye.

"It wasn't his power," Biggs tells me. "I underestimated Tyson's speed."

Also underestimated was Tyson's sense of malice. Even on YouTube all these years later, Tyson's body shots still sound like effects dubbed into a kung fu movie. The way Biggs began to wilt was all too real. For all his Olympic pedigree, Biggs's courage was now greater than his vaunted technique. Tyson knew he was ready to go but sought only to prolong the agony. "I wanted to make him pay," he said. "I could have taken him out in the third round, but I wanted him to remember this for a long time."

TIME OUT.

I have an old friend, Lou DiBella, who met Tyson entirely by chance, earlier that same year at a hospital in Albany. His brother had been airlifted there in critical condition after a skiing accident. "He was in a coma," says DiBella. "No one knew if he was going to live. And as I get off the elevator in ICU, I see Mike Tyson walking out of his room."

After greeting his mother, DiBella said, "Mom, that was Mike Tyson."

"I know," she said.

On a chair lay a well-worn *Sports Illustrated* with Tyson on the cover. It had been autographed by the fighter himself for DiBella's comatose brother with best wishes to get well.

"He saw me crying," Mama DiBella explained. "Then he came in here and he put his arm around me."

"Your son will be okay," he told her.

As it happened, Camille Ewald had been on the same floor of the hospital. The magazine had been left there by someone who took it from the waiting room. DiBella was then a young lawyer just out of Harvard. In a couple years, he'd be working for Seth Abraham at HBO Sports. "I was really critical of Tyson later on for being violent and fucked up," DiBella says. "But I always knew there's this yin and yang with him: this sensitive, decent soul fighting with an angry, depressed, kind of unstable person."

TIME IN.

The same guy who volunteered to comfort a stranger's weeping mother hit Biggs with everything but a shank. That would include, as Mike Katz cataloged in the *Daily News*, "his elbow, his head, his shoulder, low blows, hitting after the bell and what Biggs said was the toughest punch in the fight, a left hook on the break in the third round."

This very deliberate beating would endure as a message for future opponents: *Fear me*. It was intended for anyone who had seen or could imagine Tyson as he had been—teased, humiliated, had, punked. By the sixth round, you had the feeling that the combatants were confined no longer to a ring but to a kind of metaphorical cell.

As the seventh began, and Biggs tried to clinch, Tyson hit him with a left elbow. Biggs's legs were gone. He was swollen and bloody, swaying like a human punching bag. At last, with twenty-eight seconds left in the round, Biggs dropped from a left hand. Though actually knocked through the ropes, he rose at the count of nine.

"How do you feel?" asked the ref, Tony Orlando. "Okay?"

As Orlando excused himself, Tyson wound up like a pitcher and clobbered Biggs with a right hand. Then a left. Then a flurry to the body. Finally, Biggs tumbled backward from another left, his head resting against the ring post as the ref waved it off.

What happened next might be better remembered than the fight. It was another of Tyson's postfight specials, a viral moment before there was a term for it. "What broke him down?" asked Merchant.

"I was hitting him with body punches," said Tyson, "and I heard him—actually, he was crying in there. Making woman gestures, like"—here Tyson faked a high-pitched sob—"I knew that he was breaking down."

"You're saying that Biggs was crying when you hit him?" asked Merchant.

"Yes. Yes."

"When did that happen?"

"In perhaps the fourth round on," said Tyson, adding that he had been channeling Roberto Durán.

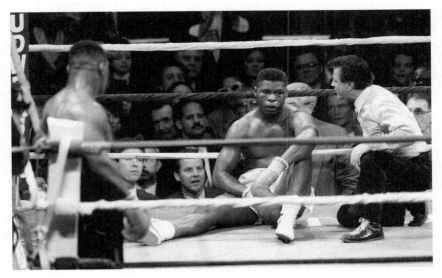

Tyrell Biggs, broken down

Thirty-six years later, Biggs seems remarkably good-natured about it. He doesn't remember teasing Tyson at the airport. I ask if he was there at the Olympic Training Center when Tyson and Holyfield had their short-lived sparring session. He doesn't remember that, either. But he does remember the girls. They were two sisters, living together in Los Angeles some years after the fight. Biggs was seeing one, Tyson the other. "It was one of those things," he says. "I'd be leaving my girl's house when Mike was just getting there for her sister." Beat. I could tell this one hurt. "But I got a funny feeling he messed with my girl, too."

NOT LONG AFTER I STARTED AT THE *DAILY NEWS*, JACK NEWFIELD invited me to dinner at the Supreme Macaroni Company, on Ninth Avenue in Manhattan, where he'd hold court with colleagues, friends, and sources, who were often one and the same. It was heady conversation, reinforcing my notion that New York was really the only city in the world. The line I remember best, though, and, again, could have been uttered only in that city, was Newfield's: "Tyson does the same thing as Norman." Meaning Mailer. "He confuses the violent with the erotic."

Mailer was a nice Jewish boy playing tough guy. Tyson wasn't playing. The line between the violent and the erotic, victory and humiliation, domination and submission, runs through the main artery of his story. Perhaps it *is* the main artery.

The signs were always there: his predatory come-on to Atlas's wife's sister; the breast grabbing; telling Pinklon Thomas to suck his dick; and incidents from the Crossgates Mall in Guilderland, New York, to the Greek Theater in Los Angeles. That no one had yet caught on owed much to Jacobs and Cayton, who peddled one kind of Tyson story while suppressing another. In the meantime, though, a kid brainwashed to believe he was a marauding conqueror had come into possession of all three heavyweight belts and was conducting himself as if he were untouchable.

A couple months after the Biggs fight, Tyson taped an HBO promo at Gleason's Gym in Brooklyn. Arlene Schulman, a veteran boxing writer and photographer, recalls approaching him after the shoot, as the crew broke down equipment on the far side of the ring. When she explained that she was writing a piece for *El Diario / La Prensa*, New York's Spanish-language daily, Tyson began gyrating suggestively, addressing her in nasty street-corner Spanish.

Schulman had grown up in the Linden projects in East New York and lived in Washington Heights. She'd heard it all before and wasn't impressed. "But then he reached out and grabbed my breast," says Schulman, who immediately backhanded Tyson in the chest, closed her notebook, and walked off—bewildered, angry, and confused.

"I was humiliated," recalls Schulman. "I mean, there was no #MeToo. There was just me. Who would believe me? He had this whole machine behind him."

Before leaving, she mentioned what had happened to a boxing writer from one of the other New York papers. "He's the heavyweight champion of the world," he told her. "He can do anything he wants."

A GOOD MANY OF TYSON'S WANTS WERE TIED UP WITH ROBIN GIVens, or at least the idea of her. But even as their romance proceeded apace, she had already aroused a visceral dislike in those who knew Tyson best and longest.

Kimberly Heath, Tyson's friend from junior high, ran into the couple on Main Street the first time he brought her to Catskill: "We go into the store and Mike holds the door for me and she gives me this *look*. Like, if looks could kill? And I say, 'Mike, what's her problem?' And he's like, 'Just ignore her.' She could have smiled and introduced herself. I wasn't a threat to her. But the way she was on TV is the same way she was in person: fake."

Lennie Daniels, the state trooper, even checked her out: "When Robin was talking all this nonsense about going to Harvard, I knew somebody who was affiliated with the university. I talked to Mike about it until I had a headache. But I could see him getting a little bit mad at me. So finally I just said, 'Mike, I'm your friend. If you want me to lie to you, I'll lie to you.'"

More to the point were the lies Tyson told himself. Robin made him feel like the man he wanted to be. With her, he saw himself as he wanted the world to see him. Why would Tyson want to know she hadn't gone to Harvard Medical School? Why would he want anyone to disabuse him of his notion of Robin Givens? He was in love.

But for Mike Tyson, what was love?

There was a *Raging Bull* element to the courtship—fits of jealousy, rage, and violence. Steve Lott would recall a night at his Midtown apartment, which Tyson used as a crash pad, early in the courtship. Lott had been sleeping when the doorman arrived around 4:00 a.m., having been alerted to a disturbance by a neighbor.

"Steve," said Tyson, "everything is okay. Get back into your room and close the door."

As usual, Lott did exactly what Tyson told him. But later, when Torres asked Tyson about the best punch he ever threw, he cited that night. It was a backhand slap, said Tyson: "She really offended me and I went bam"—backhand slap—"and she flew backward, hitting every wall in the apartment. . . . The bitch wanted to call the cops from my own fucking telephone. Was she fucking crazy or something?"

32

Giachetti isn't thinking about throwing in towels and neither am I. Larry Holmes does too have a shot against Mike Tyson. A small one, perhaps, but it's there, and if Giachetti tells me, I believe him.

"I really think we're gonna knock the kid out," he said.

MICHAEL KATZ, "HOLMES COULD TURN
ROCKY ON TYSON," *DAILY NEWS*, JANUARY 4, 1988

Richie Giachetti trained Tyson's next opponent, Holmes. There were any number of reasons to make the fight. First, as Jimmy Jacobs said just after Tyson beat Biggs: "Ninety percent of the world thought that Larry Holmes beat Michael Spinks the last time they fought." Second, a Holmes fight would antagonize Butch Lewis, who had full control of Spinks. Third, from the very beginning, D'Amato had ordained it: raising his charge to avenge Ali's loss to Holmes. Finally, though Holmes was now thirty-eight—the same age Ali had been when they fought—his reign had lasted more than seven years since valiantly winning the title in the fifteenth round against Ken Norton. Per long-standing custom, the young champion found himself matched against the best of the preceding era. Just as Marciano knocked out an over-the-hill Joe Louis and Holmes pounded on Ali, so, too, would Tyson now presumably dispatch Holmes. And if these fights put the deposed king in neurological peril, so what? The audience loved them—for underneath all the metaphors of succession was something very close to a ritualized beating. Tyson was an almost 8–1 favorite. Still, I'm more taken with Katz's faith in Giachetti here.

Katz was an occasionally subversive and dependably irascible correspondent (arrested for battery and disorderly conduct after a drunk got in his way on deadline at Witherspoon–Greg Page back in '84). In the coming years, he would scream at me often and teach me a lot. Little surprise, then, that I would make the same mistakes he had. A boxing adage holds that one should never fall in love with a fighter. But Katz fell for trainers, as I would, just harder, for Teddy Atlas. It wasn't a baseless affection. This is, after all, a story largely set into motion by writers who fell in love with a trainer in D'Amato. Katz's favorites included Eddie Futch and Georgie Benton, then working with Evander Holyfield. They were great trainers. Giachetti was not. But he's more than a guy at the intersection of Holmes and Tyson. And he's more than Tyson's future trainer. It's the storylines emanating from Giachetti—and how they all led back to Tyson–Holmes—that speak to King's continued ascent despite so many years in the crosshairs of the FBI. Even more remarkable than the assortment of fighters and flunkies in King's stable was how they kept coming back to him, ever more dependent. If King had learned anything in prison, it was *not* to seek vengeance against those who'd betrayed or disappointed you but to use them even more.

Giachetti, from Cleveland by way of Uniontown, Pennsylvania, had been with King since 1972 and the ill-fated attempt to save Cleveland's Forest City Hospital. "I gave him credibility with white people," Giachetti once bragged.

If so, it was a certain kind of white people. By the time he met King, Giachetti had been, by turns, a Golden Gloves champ, stock car enthusiast, and soldier in the labor movement. "I was sort of an enforcer for Babe Triscaro's truck drivers," he once recalled, citing a boss in Cleveland's most successful criminal enterprise, the Teamsters.

Giachetti had thick, blunt features and an ample belly, a physique that had seen action in some of Cleveland's most esteemed establishments—including the Theatrical Grill, where he once took on a bunch of off-duty cops. He'd been shot, knifed, and ice-picked. A broken bottle had left a ridged, crescent-shaped scar under his left eye. The cut took seventy-eight stitches to close.

By the mid-seventies, Giachetti had three primary assets: a body shop, a gym, and an insistent belief in a young heavyweight named Larry Holmes. "I treated him like a brother," Giachetti told the *Plain Dealer*'s Dan Coughlin. "Not a Black brother, either. Like a relative."

Holmes often stayed at Giachetti's house. They roomed together on the road. Giachetti even lent him money. By the time Holmes became champion, though, Giachetti was also taping their phone calls, many of them regarding Holmes's belief that King was ripping him off. Giachetti was sympathetic. King was ripping him off, too—installing him as Holmes's manager only to have him kick back half his share. But Giachetti wasn't just taping King's calls. He was also talking to the feds, to wit, Special Agent Joe Spinelli.

On January 21, 1981, six months after Spinelli's sit-down with D'Amato in Catskill, Giachetti produced six tapes for Spinelli's investigation, code-named "Crown Royal." That March, Giachetti appeared before a federal grand jury probe of King in Manhattan. Two days later, Holmes testified under subpoena. He didn't say much. He was scared to death. "King's got a lot of bad friends," a teary-eyed champ told Spinelli. "I have a family. . . . He can hurt me."

After the story broke, it was Giachetti who claimed King put a hit on *him*. "The mob guys have come to see me," he told the *Post*'s Mike Marley. "My lawyer was told by a federal prosecutor that there is a contract out on me."

King dismissed it as "absolute paranoia from a diabolical and sinister mind." That's not to say the promoter lacked the contacts to do the job. As Spinelli's investigation wore on, it became clear that King was as connected in New York as he was in Cleveland. Through the fall of '82, he was seen several times dining in Manhattan with a fast-rising Gambino gangster named John Gotti and Matty "the Horse" Ianniello, a power in the Genovese family. Then there was Victor Quintana, a South American drug dealer looking to launder his illicit millions in a boxing promotion, and Michael Franzese, the ambitious Colombo capo Quintana had enlisted in his venture.

On January 12, 1983, King met with them at his Sixty-Ninth Street offices. Franzese pitched himself as a silent partner in a copromotion with King and Quintana initially financed by Quintana's drug money. "I made him understand that my family was very interested in seeing this deal go forward," Franzese later explained to a Senate subcommittee.

King was in. "It was agreed that the copromotion would go forward," said Franzese, the so-called Yuppie Don, who had an abiding interest in the music and movie businesses.

Also present that day was the man who'd arranged the meeting on Franzese's behalf—a charismatic twenty-nine-year-old preacher from Brownsville, the Reverend Al Sharpton. Sharpton, a kind of surrogate son to James Brown, had known King since 1974, when Brown performed in Zaire for the Ali–Foreman fight. "He often boasted of having a close relationship with King," said Franzese, explaining why he reached out to Sharpton. "I knew Sharpton and was aware that he was associated with people in the Genovese family, in particular with a family soldier, Danny Pagano."

Sharpton has said he knew Pagano only as a record label executive and that any proceeds he received from the promotion were to go to his National Youth Movement. Unfortunately, such charity wasn't forthcoming, as Quintana never produced the money.

In fact, his surname wasn't *Quintana*. Nor was he a South American drug dealer. He was an FBI agent acting the part in an elaborate sting operation. Money didn't change hands because, in the months after Korean lightweight Duk-koo Kim died of injuries suffered in a nationally televised title bout with Ray "Boom Boom" Mancini, the Justice Department decided against bankrolling a boxing promotion. "What if some fighter got killed," Spinelli's supervisor told him, "and it came out that the FBI was involved in the promotion?"

But the decision in Washington wasn't the only problem. Holmes's fear of testifying against King didn't help the cause. Nor did Giachetti, who promised more than he delivered, then bragged about having "double-crossed" the FBI.

Still the investigation limped on, and as it did, Spinelli came to think his last chance at getting the promoter was through the garrulous Sharpton. Sharpton had amused the agents monitoring the surveillance tapes: talking tough, passing himself off as an organized crime buff, opining on King's roots with the "Jewish Mafia of Cleveland." Sharpton even warned an informant not to deal with King unless he had some real muscle behind him. "Don will steal from the blind," he said.

Eventually, "Quintana" broached the prospect of a drug deal. "Let me see what I can do," said the reverend, whose National Youth Movement held periodic antidrug rallies. "I know some people."

Whatever Sharpton's intention, Spinelli knew the remark wasn't evidence. But because the conversation was secretly videotaped, he made a bluff play anyway. On June 30, 1983, Spinelli and another agent burst into the apartment the FBI had rented as "Quintana's" cover and confronted Sharpton. "He was scared," recalls Spinelli. "First, he got taken by surprise. Second, he knew what he was doing was wrong."

So began Sharpton's peculiar career as an FBI informant. He taped at least several conversations with Holmes—who contradicted his grand jury testimony—and with King, who by now was enraged that Holmes had finally left his promotional umbrella. King tasked Sharpton with spreading stories in Black publications to depict Holmes as an ingrate Uncle Tom. But again, though Sharpton's recordings were typically interesting and often entertaining, they were of no use in a prosecution.

It was enough to wonder whether Sharpton, like Giachetti, was double-crossing Spinelli to remain in King's good graces. "Sharpton played the same game," says Spinelli.

"The rev was a great bullshitter," said John Pritchard, Spinelli's former partner. "I have to say he probably conned the FBI in terms of the boxing investigation."

That's not to say Sharpton's cooperation was of no value. But he was much more effective—and courageous—after going to work for Pritchard at the FBI's Genovese squad. Sharpton's intel and tape recordings figured in several successful mob prosecutions. He also provided information on Black political figures, mostly elected officials or his more established rivals in Brooklyn. But all that remained secret until 1988, when, just two days before the Tyson–Holmes fight, a blockbuster scoop began in large-point type on the front page of *Newsday*:

> For the last five years, the Rev. Al Sharpton Jr., one of the city's most vocal and visible Black activists, has been secretly supplying law enforcement agencies with information on boxing promoter Don King, reputed organized crime figures, and Black leaders and elected officials, according to sources.

Sharpton has long denied ratting on King or fellow Black leaders. He's attributed his work for the FBI to his antidrug stance and cast the periodic timing of stories depicting him as a government snitch as part of a long-standing effort "clearly designed to discredit me."

Indeed, on the eve of Tyson–Holmes, Sharpton was a different figure than he had been back in 1983. He'd led the protests in Howard Beach and had begun advocating for Tawana Brawley, a Black teenager claiming four white men had raped her. What's more, he was a frequent presence around Tyson and tighter than ever with King: attending press conferences, giving away Thanksgiving turkeys in Brooklyn, celebrating with Donald Trump at his book party for *The Art of the Deal*. Sharpton even helped King organize a benefit for Father Clements's South Side church during which Tyson sparred in an exhibition.

Whatever damage the *Newsday* story caused Sharpton, it did nothing to diminish his standing with King. Come fight night, their bond remained firm, King in his tux and the voluble clergyman in a yellow tie and matching pocket square, side by side.

"I don't believe that about Sharpton," King told reporters, willfully oblivious to already-published transcripts of certain government recordings. "They try to get any Black leader."

So *what* if Sharpton talked to the feds? So had Richie Giachetti.

And where would Giachetti be on fight night?

Exactly where King wanted him to be.

Same as Holmes.

"They'd bitch and moan about King being the worst guy in the world, and where do they end up?" asks Spinelli. "Right back where they started."

Spinelli would always remember his audience with D'Amato in Catskill, as if the old man had tasked him with a sacred mission. In the end, though, Crown Royal became just another boxing noir: valiant but doomed. The final frame could well have been the former federal agent, his long quest failed, sitting down to watch Tyson–Holmes.

"I had this sickening feeling," says Spinelli.

It wasn't just Giachetti and Holmes. It was King's inexorable progression, inching ever closer to D'Amato's living legacy.

Tyson–Holmes—dubbed "Heavyweight History"—wouldn't go down as a great fight. But it was a great promotion, and one that *only* King could have pulled off. I'm less struck, though, by the considerable heat it generated than by the assemblage of characters who had returned to

Only in the eighties: Trump, Sharpton, and King celebrating *The Art of the Deal*

King's fold—including his erstwhile enemies, others who'd sworn never to do business with him, even those who had spoken to the FBI about their dealings with King. They couldn't quit him. For one reason or another, they all needed him. Even Jacobs and Cayton were doing his bidding now, insisting King had to be the sole promoter of a Tyson–Spinks fight. "Don King promotes Mike Tyson fights," said Jacobs. "It's as simple as that."

Jacobs and Cayton had been chasing a Holmes fight for years. That only King could finally close the deal was an extraordinary coup. Holmes didn't merely resent the way King had ripped him off (about $10 million over his career, he'd estimate later that year) but the way his own promoter had unabashedly—indeed, gleefully—pimped bigotry itself to make his fight with Cooney. "Let's put it on the table," King said back in 1981. "I'm selling racism." Holmes despised King. But he still couldn't turn him down.

Holmes would recall a conversation I'll summarize only slightly, beginning with the resolute knock at his door one night in Easton, Pennsylvania.

Thrilled to be wearing an NYPD cap for the Tyson–Holmes presser

"Har! Har! Har!"

"What's up?"

"I want you to fight."

"I'm retired, Don. For two years. You know that."

"Yeah, man, but I got the fight for you," said King. "And I know you can beat this guy."

"Don, I ain't gonna fight," said Holmes, who nevertheless asked, as any fighter would, "Who you want me to fight, anyway?"

"Mike Tyson."

"Ah, shit."

"I'm gonna give you three and a half million dollars."

In fact, the price was $3.1 million, from which King would award himself a $300,000 "finder's fee."

The selling of Tyson–Holmes got off to a promising start when Tyson—wearing a visored NYPD cap at the press conference—refused to shake his opponent's hand. "I don't like Larry Holmes," he said.

Holmes had been harping on Tyson's being a dirty fighter since the Biggs bout. But Tyson's beef with Holmes began long before that. He still vividly recalled D'Amato's directive to his fourteen-year-old self: "You have to dismantle that man."

So much of what D'Amato envisioned had already come to pass— not just the titles or the hordes of women he now had to fend off but wealth of a sort that previous heavyweight champions couldn't have fathomed. The Holmes bout was the first in Tyson's new, record-breaking HBO deal that would pay him a total of $26.5 million for the next seven fights. Holmes's envy was palpable—and personal in a way other opponents hadn't dared to be with Tyson. Mike Marley caught up with Holmes at his bar in Easton, where the ex-champ had been drinking beer just two and a half weeks out from the fight. "In four or five years, he will be out of the picture," said Holmes. "He will be in jail. . . . He's just that type of person. I can recognize that because I was raised on the streets."

Holmes mentioned Tony Ayala, a once-promising fighter then serv- ing thirty-five years for rape. "Mike Tyson is the same type."

———

BY FIGHT NIGHT, THE ATLANTIC CITY CONVENTION CENTER WAS
sold out with a record gate. There was a particular kind of buzz, as if the
fight had been conceived with Page Six in mind. Jack Nicholson sat next
to Cheryl Tiegs. Then there were the celebrity couples: John McEnroe
and Tatum O'Neal, and Don Johnson with Barbra Streisand, who paid
their respects to Tyson in his dressing room. As did Kirk Douglas. Also
in attendance were at least four Tyson girlfriends, including Robin Givens, who couldn't have been too happy about a gossip item identifying
Suzette Charles as his date for the fight.

"What about Givens?" the reporter asked.

"He's still dating her also," said Cayton. "He's a young man, and he's
not ready for marriage yet."

At the epicenter of all this, the crowd nourishing his already infamous ego, was Trump. At forty-one, he seems more pale and stringy
than you might remember. He had insisted, despite HBO's reluctance, on
being in the ring for the final introductions with Muhammad Ali. Evidently, Trump's thirst for prime television exposure was greater than his
now-famous aversion to the wounded, as Ali was clearly diminished, the
bills for the beatings he had endured now well past due. Ali wore thick,
dark glasses. His gait was halting, the kiss he blew to the loving crowd
weak and constrained. He greeted his old sparring partner, Holmes, but
then made a point of whispering to Tyson: "Get him."

Giachetti had promised vintage Holmes. Understanding that Tyson's
greatest asset was his ability to instill fear in opponents, Giachetti argued
that the fighter who'd walked through fire to beat Norton and Shavers,
and made a prime Cooney look so easy, had the ideal makeup for Tyson.
"The way you beat Tyson is to take his heart away from him," said Giachetti. "He's never had anybody do that. He's always been the superboy,
the intimidator. . . . If he starts that dirty stuff with Larry, Larry will take
him right into the trenches. It will be open warfare, World War III. Nobody is going to get away with that stuff with Larry."

Nevertheless, as the fight began, referee Joe Cortez saw something in

Holmes not unlike what he had seen in Marvis Frazier. "Larry looked intimidated," recalls Cortez.

Good thing, then, that he hadn't seen Tyson put his gloved fist through the wall in his dressing room. The hole it left was fairly approximated at ten by twelve inches. One could now see through it to a billboard across Pacific Avenue: 6 HOURS/PARK FREE/ATLANTIS/CASINO HOTEL.

Holmes spent the first two rounds mostly in retreat. Holmes seemed spindlier, more knock-kneed than in his prime. That's not to say he didn't have a plan, though. His reach a full foot longer than Tyson's, he used his left, not to throw his once-vaunted jab so much as a stiff-armed shield, trying to keep Tyson at bay and at range for a straight right hand.

It wasn't a bad strategy, as Holmes threw the right with conviction. But Tyson would just dip and slip past, penetrating Holmes's perimeter and forcing him to hold. Even when Holmes finally caught him in the third—a right hand that might've taken out a lesser fighter—Tyson just shrugged it off.

They were fighting at two different speeds, thirty-eight and twenty-one years old. But there was an equally disparate gap in strength. While Tyson was coiled and twitchy, he, too, had a plan, bequeathed to him by D'Amato: "He had given me a blueprint—hit him with the right, behind my jab."

"Let's go now," Giachetti told Holmes before the fourth round. "Come on."

As if on cue, Holmes came out jabbing and moving, much to the crowd's delight. But the youthful display was short-lived. Just past the round's midpoint, Tyson landed D'Amato's jab-right combination— *thump-THUMP!*—on Holmes's chin, toppling the big man.

The second knockdown came with a left hand. Holmes rose again, after crashing into the ropes, at the count of four. Again Tyson swarmed. Holmes retreated until he ran out of territory, his back now against the ropes. A delegation of humanitarians at ringside were already screaming to stop the fight.

"That should be it," said Merchant.

Joe Cortez stopping the Holmes fight

Still, Holmes took more right hands, as if his head were on a swivel. Finally, he fell: face up, eyes closed, arms perfectly splayed as if poised for a crucifixion. Cortez knelt to remove his mouthpiece, then waved it off.

"Larry Holmes was a legendary fighter," Tyson told Merchant. "If he was at his best, I couldn't stand a chance."

Holmes had been a great fighter. But the line itself belonged to a ghost, another champion who lived in Tyson's mind but whom he'd never fight. "I was quoting Fritzie Zivic, the great champion, who said that after he beat Henry Armstrong," Tyson said.

Moments later, Cayton came on camera to give an update on the ongoing negotiations for a Tyson–Spinks fight. The sticking point, said Cayton, was Spinks's promoter, whom he and Jacobs had come to loathe every bit as much as King did. "Butch Lewis cannot be the promoter or the copromoter of a Mike Tyson fight," he said. "That is the only problem we have. . . . Very good. Happy to talk to you, Larry."

Happy to talk to you, Larry. It's easy to see why Jacobs was the Tyson team's usual front man. There was a stilted quality to Cayton. The broadcast then cut to the loser's locker room, where Ray Leonard was asking

Holmes about his game plan. The real question, however, was, where was Jimmy Jacobs?

IT SEEMS THAT TYSON HAD MORE OF AN INKLING THAN THE REST OF the world. A week or so before the fight, he sat for an interview to air on *The Sweet Science*, a boxing show hosted by Bruce Beck and Randy Gordon on the Madison Square Garden Network. Both Gordon and Beck, a longtime New York sports anchor, remember it the same way.

"Randy," Tyson whispered, "did you hear that Jimmy Jacobs is dying?"

Gordon, like a lot of people around the Tyson camp, knew that Jacobs hadn't been well. Or maybe he'd heard Jimmy was in Texas getting a procedure. But dying? "No, Mike."

"They're doing a blood transfusion," said Tyson, his voice breaking, trying to hold back the tears. "He's not going to make it."

33

The first sign Jimmy Jacobs had chronic lymphocytic lymphoma (CLL) came in 1975, when a blood test indicated abnormally high levels of lymphocytes, a type of white blood cell. By 1980, when he met Tyson, it was clear that Jacobs was in the initial stage of the disease. The median survival rate was then six to nine years.

Through 1985, a period that covered the Olympic trials and Tyson's professional debut, he received periodic chemotherapy and radiation treatments. By April 1986, however—per a professor at the Georgetown University School of Medicine who reviewed Jacobs's medical records—he had entered stage 4 in the cancer's inevitable progression. Median life expectancy was approximately nineteen months. In 1987, Jacobs received radiation treatments to his neck, groin, and spleen. At one point, his eye began to bleed. That Jacobs's condition remained largely secret was a testament to the ferocity of his will.

On January 4, 1988, two and a half weeks before the Holmes fight, Jacobs and Cayton met to finalize Tyson's new HBO deal at Abraham's office, where the champion's handlers began by insisting on haggling over standard legal fees. Finally, an exasperated Abraham produced a nickel and proposed a coin flip. It was heads, just as Jacobs had called, meaning HBO would pay. For a lucky guy, he didn't look the part: sal-low, jaundiced, and perspiring profusely. "I knew something was wrong," says Abraham. "I remember thinking I wouldn't be surprised if it was liver cancer."

What made it sadder was the triumph of the deal itself, then the largest-ever contract involving any individual athlete. It called for seven fights, expected to run approximately fourteen months, to March 1989, with a total payout of $26.5 million. By comparison, Patrick Ewing, the NBA's highest-paid player, had an annual salary of $2.75 million. What's more, the new deal didn't even include Tyson's purse in the event of a Spinks fight—a potentiality already forecast to exceed the Yankees' league-leading $19 million payroll—or the additional $3.1 million HBO had now agreed to pay him merely for the right to rebroadcast it a week later.

The Tyson–Spinks matchup loomed as another "fight of the century," a kind of holy grail for the sporting public, and for someone in Jacobs's dire straits it would be a resounding final victory. But the opposing camps seemed further apart now than they had been back in '86 when Tyson entered the unification tournament.

Spinks's exit from the HBO competition, while exceedingly profitable for the fighter and his promoter, had enraged Jacobs and Cayton to the point where they couldn't negotiate effectively with Butch Lewis. Then there were Lewis and King, whose mutual contempt went back to 1982, when Lewis sued King for $50 million (of which he'd eventually collect $200,000) for stealing a future heavyweight champion, Greg Page, from his stable. Still, it was Lewis's healthy mistrust of King and his larcenous arithmetic that had shaped the negotiation. Knowing how King could carve up a fighter's purse, Lewis cared less for the back end or closed-circuit revenues than the guaranteed up-front money.

The hondling began with Jacobs and Cayton making an offer of between $4 million and $5 million for Spinks, recalls Rock Newman, then acting as Lewis's consigliere and spokesman. Later, Jacobs upped the guarantee to $8 million and demanded that Lewis sign immediately, or else negotiations would break off and not resume for another year. Jacobs made a great show of circling the date on the calendar. Lewis laughed in his face and walked out of the room.

Fuck that, said Lewis. Jacobs would be back before too long.

"We had the secret sauce," says Newman.

Lewis understood from the beginning that neither Jacobs nor Cayton wanted anything to do with him. He also knew King would do everything in his power to kill the deal. So early in the negotiation, Lewis made a move that went to the true heart of the boxing business: money, street rep, ego.

There was a guy they called "Willie D," a friend of Rory Holloway's or John Horne's from Albany. And Willie D knew where Tyson was at any given moment. "Every move Tyson made," says Newman. "He knew what city Tyson would be in, what club he was going to, when he was going to pick up some girl. *Everything.*"

Lewis put Willie D on the payroll.

"I probably talked to him eighty percent of the time," says Newman. "And every single time he wanted the same thing: more money. Over eight or nine months, we probably paid him seventy-five thousand dollars. You know: four grand here, five grand there, eight there. It was a serious campaign to put pressure on Tyson. Willie would call and we'd have ten people waiting outside the club when he showed."

Spinks gon' knock your ass out!

You scared!

Bitch!

And of course, boxing's oldest, fail-safe slander: *Faggot!*

"I'm talking no less than ten times a month," says Newman. "And it wasn't just guys, we had girls showing up, too. And Tyson was getting calls at home—didn't matter how many times he changed his number. I'm telling you, Tyson was getting worn out."

On January 7, Jacobs checked in to Mount Sinai, where his spleen and a lymph node were removed. On January 18, not long after Tyson's interview with Randy Gordon, he went with Lott and Rooney to visit Jacobs at his Fortieth Street apartment. They stayed only about ten minutes, as Jacobs was in obvious pain, exhausted, and alarmingly thin, having lost twenty pounds in the hospital. Nevertheless, just four days later, Jacobs willed himself to the Holmes fight, sitting with his wife, Loraine, and his physician.

It was an act of great determination. By now, tests of the removed tissue revealed that he had entered the final phase of the cancer. Under the best of circumstances, he likely had less than four months to live. Even a practiced denialist like Jacobs had to know it was well past time to get his affairs in order.

But closing the Spinks deal wasn't his only priority. Earlier that month, he'd received a call prompting him to summon Torres to his office. "Miss Roper tells me her daughter is three and a half months pregnant . . . by Mike," Jacobs explained. "She says we must take appropriate action or else."

Torres endorsed the prospect of marriage. "Cus would have loved her," he said.

If the notion of wedlock morality seems antiquated, then so were Jacobs, Cayton, and the tinseled artifice they'd strewn around Tyson. More to the point, though, were the morals clauses in the endorsement deals Cayton had delivered, including a million-dollar Pepsi campaign that was soon to close.

There was still another matter, one of even greater urgency. Jacobs leaned in, grabbing Torres by the elbow. Torres couldn't help but notice a certain ghastliness in his appearance. "Bill and I made a serious mistake," he said, referring to their manager-assignee contracts with the State Athletic Commission. "If anything happens to us . . . our boxers could all wind up in the wrong hands, including Mike."

Including Mike? Jacobs spoke as if an archvillain were lurking, ready to snatch the wards of Boys Town. But really, Tyson was all they had. Their only other fighter of consequence, Edwin Rosario, had recently been pounded into submission by Don King's guy, Julio César Chávez, and would never be the same.

"We must amend the existing contract in order to protect our boys," continued Jacobs, as quoted by Torres.

In fact, Jacobs was only protecting his interests, and Cayton's. "I realized that he must have been sick," Torres recalled of that meeting and

Jacobs's subsequent anxiety over the amended contracts. "He was calling me up all the time, pushing me." The bigger picture, however, never seems to have dawned on Torres. Jacobs had tasked the chairman of the New York State Athletic Commission as if he were his personal assistant. Still, Torres took the assignment without any apparent regard for the responsibilities of his office or the fighter he was supposedly protecting.

A COUPLE DAYS AFTER THE HOLMES FIGHT, NEWS BROKE THAT LEWIS had turned down a $10.8 million guarantee for Spinks, a figure exceeding the combined sum of all the purses across his entire career. This time it was Cayton who delivered the ultimatum: "If you walk out that door don't come back."

Again Lewis walked.

"Even I thought he was crazy," said Newman. "Me *and* the lawyers. We told him to sign it. But to Butch's credit, he hung the fuck in."

Meanwhile, Cayton vowed he would no longer negotiate with Lewis. Maybe he was just playing bad cop. But a more likely explanation is how little Cayton actually knew of his own client, the undisputed heavyweight champion of the world, who, by now, had become the single fiercest advocate for the Spinks fight.

"I still didn't get the respect I deserved from the people in the street," Tyson said of that period. "I'd be walking around in New York or LA . . . and guys would come up to me. 'Spinks is going to knock you out, nigga.'"

AS CAYTON CONTINUED TO POSTURE AND RAIL AGAINST LEWIS, Jacobs called a friend, Shelly Finkel, a shrewd dealmaker and manager whose stable included the stars of America's great 1984 Olympic team: Pernell Whitaker, Mark Breland, Evander Holyfield, and Tyrell Biggs. "It just has to get done," Jacobs told him. "Otherwise, we got problems with Mike."

With *Mike*?

"Mike is adamant. He wants it so bad he won't accept anything else."

This was the biggest deal of Jacobs's life, and likely his last. But to have a chance at closing it, he went against his very nature—not merely delegating but asking Finkel to negotiate what he and Cayton now admittedly could not. Nor would King be of any value here, such was his fervor to minimize Lewis. Finally, Jacobs explained, whatever Spinks got, Tyson's number would have to be "substantially more."

"Can you do it?" Jacobs asked.

"I will talk to Butch," said Finkel.

"What do you want in return?"

"I want to do the closed-circuit," said Finkel.

Done.

FINKEL, NO SURPRISE, HAILED FROM THAT MYTHICAL BROOKLYN, NEAR the border of Crown Heights and Bed-Stuy. His father died of a heart attack when Finkel was thirteen, leaving the family tight for money. Upon graduating from Brooklyn Tech, Finkel started selling copy machines. Then he tried a computer dating service. In 1966, while a night student at Hofstra, he got a job managing a club called Action House. Everyone gigged there: Cream, the Rascals, even the Doors, whose lead singer prevailed on Finkel to let him drink for free. That night, Jim Morrison got so drunk he fell off the stage.

Apart from the bacchanalia, though, the rock scene was bound by a set of economic strictures not unlike boxing in the fifties. The revelation came to Finkel after he signed the Vagrants away from their usual venue in Brooklyn.

"Don't do that again," his partner told him. "We'll have a bomb in our club."

Finkel's partner happened to be under Paul Vario, a Lucchese family capo, who, it turned out, very much wanted to meet Finkel. Finkel politely declined Vario's offer to run his Brooklyn disco, preferring instead to manage acts like Vanilla Fudge and Mountain, a group from Long Island who became famous for the hit "Mississippi Queen." He also went on to promote Summer Jam, a concert featuring the Grateful Dead, the Allman Brothers, and the Band, which drew a mere 600,000 to Watkins Glen, New York.

But it's clear what Vario saw in the mild-mannered Finkel: a good earner who had a way with talent and was exceedingly resourceful for a "clean" guy. In all, rock and roll served Finkel well for his eventual career in boxing, whose big-fight closed-circuit business was divided into territories—again, not unlike organized crime. Finkel's first experience with a closed-circuit deal was in 1980, when promoter Bob Arum offered him the New England territory for Leonard–Durán I.

Shortly thereafter, Arum called back, telling Finkel he'd made a mistake and that Leonard's lawyer had already given New England to a guy named Dan Doyle.

"Bob, do me a favor," said Finkel, "stall for one day."

Using his concert connections, Finkel called every arena in the territory—the Boston Garden, New Haven Coliseum, and Hartford Civic Center among them—and booked June 20, the night of the fight. "I tell them I'm doing Joe Cocker here, I'm doing Ten Years After *there*, I'm doing Jethro Tull *here*," recalls Finkel. "I blocked every hall in New England."

Then he heard from Doyle, who eventually went away for embezzlement.

You're out of luck, Finkel told him.

"What do you want?" asked Doyle.

"I'll split it with you," said Finkel. "We'll copromote."

The Leonard–Durán closed-circuit established Finkel in boxing. Now, eight years later, he was fully incentivized by the prospect of selling Tyson–Spinks. It wasn't just the blockbuster closed-circuit that enticed him but the potential for a new money stream from the cable companies' nascent "pay-per-view" business.

On February 4, 1988—less than two weeks after Jacobs enlisted Finkel's help—*The New York Times*, belying her Gray Lady reputation, ran a bulletin-style box on the front page, right below news of a secret deal between the Reagan White House and Panamanian general Manuel

Noriega. The Tyson and Spinks camps, it said, had finally reached an agreement in principle for a June fight that "could produce the biggest revenues in boxing history."

Tyson was, of course, greatly pleased with the chance to quiet his critics. Lewis, who just the week before had said *he* was walking away from the deal due to his differences with King, was very happy to accept a record guarantee of $13.5 million, plus the ceremonial but deeply satisfying title of copromoter. HBO and its corporate parent, Time, Inc., had finally landed a "fight of the century" for closed-circuit and rebroadcast. Cayton, too, was happy, as much as his staid disposition would allow him to be. And Jacobs, despite the calamitous state of his health, was greatly gratified to be making history. "I told him unequivocally that Mike would make over twenty million dollars," said Finkel.

Only one party didn't share in the joy. Normally, the promoter negotiates everything from the fighters' purses to the broadcast rights. In this case, however, the promoter seemed an afterthought. While Tyson–Spinks was the biggest promotion since Ali and Frazier in '71, the promoter himself would be given no upside—just a flat fee of $3 million, from which he'd pay the undercard fighters. It would come to less than his archrival, the so-called copromoter, would make.

"Don King was not happy," says Finkel.

34

The 1988 NBA All-Star Weekend at the old Chicago Stadium is regarded as an iconic event, fully consecrating a new kind of star named Michael Jordan. Jordan, who played for the crowd's home team, the Chicago Bulls, won the first of his several All-Star MVPs and won the dunk contest on his final attempt, taking flight just inches inside the foul line. The resulting image would come to represent the idea of an athlete as a brand, though I can't imagine Tyson sharing in the crowd's enthusiasm for Robin's ex-beau.

What Tyson didn't understand, or perhaps what his insecurities blinded him to, was Givens's own narcissism and how it truly endeared her to him. By both their accounts, the relationship was dysfunctional, violent, and sexual. Just the same, though, Tyson did for Robin what she did for him, allowing her to play the role of Robin Givens just as *she* envisioned her to be. Suddenly, she was on *The Tonight Show*, with Joan Rivers asking about the ring Tyson had given her. *People* declared her "a break-out star." That hadn't happened when she was dating Eddie Murphy or Michael Jordan. Jordan may have been ascendant, but the heavyweight champion of the world dwelled in that mythical place Cus had promised.

Givens would recall their first dinner at Nicky Blair's, another celebreteria on Sunset Boulevard in Hollywood. Sylvester Stallone walked in. The room began to hum. "Watch this," Tyson whispered. "I'm star to the stars."

On cue, Stallone came by to pay his respects. Tyson was polite but a bit standoffish—quite deliberately, it turned out. After Stallone left, Tyson told Givens he didn't want anyone interrupting their time together. "Now I was beyond flattered," she said.

There's a hierarchy to fame. Tyson knew it. Givens knew it. And they both worked it—which brings me back to that most celebrity-conscious of institutions, the NBA All-Star Game. Tyson had purchased Robin's outfit for the event the day before on Rodeo Drive, and also her jewelry— a multitiered diamond necklace with matching earrings.

"I had forgotten that I was wearing them until Oprah and I greeted each other," Givens writes. In the coming months, Oprah would cast her in a miniseries she was producing, *The Women of Brewster Place*.

Robin and Mike had already spoken of marriage and agreed it was in their future, though the subject of her pregnancy apparently never came up. By several accounts, including Tyson's, it was Jacobs who had already given him the news. After the game, Tyson directed their limousine driver to an address on the South Side. He had a plan.

When they arrived, Father George Clements, Jacobs's old friend, whose church King and Tyson had helped rebuild, greeted them at the rectory door. "Hello, Robin," he said. "I've heard so much about you."

Clements had marched with Dr. Martin Luther King Jr., harbored fugitive Black Panthers, crusaded against local drug peddlers, and, citing the plight of orphaned Black boys, adopted four sons. The coming decades would bring increasingly familiar, though ultimately unproven, allegations of sexual impropriety against the priest. But Tyson saw Clements— as described to him by Jacobs—as a Cus-like figure. The priest's adoptions, he had told the *Chicago Tribune* some months before, "reminded me of my story."

Now, after ten minutes of premarital counseling—"stressing the permanency of the marriage vows," said Clements—the priest rendered a quick verdict on the couple's prospects. "It's clear you two love each other," he told Robin. "I can feel it and I don't think I've seen Michael happier."

Witnesses included three of Clements's sons, the church secretary, and Holloway's friend John Horne. Now married, at least in the eyes of God, the couple returned to the hotel, where Tyson called Camille. Camille was very happy for them. Then Tyson thought to phone "Ma," as he had taken to calling Ruth Roper. Robin got out of the bath and grabbed the receiver. Her sister picked up.

Just as Ruth got on the line, Tyson grabbed back the receiver. "Ma, we got married!" he exclaimed.

Jimmy called next. Tyson went through the day's events just as he had for Ruth. Then Jimmy asked to speak to Robin. He explained that the marriage wasn't legal as they hadn't gotten a marriage license. Tyson grabbed the receiver and hung up on him.

They went to a nightclub that evening. Tyson ordered champagne. Then he commandeered the stage, the band, and the microphone, delivering what is likely among the worst but most heartfelt renditions of "My Girl."

Tyson and Robin in the back of a limousine, January 1988

Tyson and Robin flew back to New York the next morning, Monday, February 8, 1988. By the time they landed, Ruth had already placed a call to Jacobs. "We either agreed immediately to have them legally married in New York or she was going to have them flown to Las Vegas for the license," said Cayton. "She said Givens was three months pregnant."

Jacobs, who understood that antagonizing Roper now threatened his life's work, instructed Lott to arrange for a civil ceremony the following morning. He also called Torres, pressing him on the documents he'd so urgently requested. Then he spoke to reporters. "I know Mike has been contemplating this for a while," Jacobs lied to his favorite correspondent, Katz. "She's an exquisite girl."

The civil ceremony went off without a hitch the following morning at the Manhattan Municipal Building, near City Hall. Lott, the best man, kissed both groom and bride, who wore dark sunglasses indoors. Robin remembers that the now-legal couple went to her mother's office, where Roper and her assistant were already feverishly arranging a reception for Valentine's Day at the Helmsley Palace. From there, Tyson left for New Jersey, where he was to deliver an antidrug message to an estimated 4,500 students at Elizabeth High School, then speak to inmates at the Union County Juvenile Detention Center. The couple reunited that evening at a press conference primarily for Japanese reporters, as Tyson was next scheduled to fight former WBA champ Tony Tubbs on March 21 at the Tokyo Dome.

Informed that Japanese women were heartbroken that Tyson was no longer available, Robin said, "Women are in love with him everywhere. But now I'm Mrs. Mike Tyson. The game's over."

In fact, it had just begun. The next day, Wednesday, February 10, Torres convened a meeting of the New York State Athletic Commission. Also present were Torres's assistant, commission lawyer Carl DeSantis, and Commissioners James Dupree and Rose Trentman, both of whom voted with their chairman to unanimously approve five resolutions involving the future of Mike Tyson, whose absence, like that of his representatives, might've raised some eyebrows in a more vigilant public body. The order of business, from the meeting's official minutes:

1. A new four-year boxer-manager agreement for Jim Jacobs and Mike Tyson;

2. A contingent boxer-manager agreement in the event that Jacobs is deceased to complete the 4 year term of the first contract;

3. A 50% assignment of the manager's share of the first contract to William Cayton in the event that Jacobs is deceased;

4. A contingent assignment, assigning 50% of the manager's proceeds to Mrs. Lorraine [sic] Jacobs in the event that Jim Jacobs is deceased;

5. A contingent assignment, assigning 50% of the manager's proceeds to Mrs. Doris Cayton in the event that William Cayton is deceased.

In other words, while Jacobs was Tyson's manager of record (in New York State a fighter could have only one), Cayton—with whom he already split everything down the middle—would take over in the event of his death, while Jacobs's widow, Loraine, would be entitled to his 50 percent share. To make everything look kosher, it was agreed that Cayton's wife would get his half if Cayton died first. Of course, the entire proceeding was only slightly less kosher than a bacon milkshake. In actuality, this was a Torres fix: essentially willing an absent, lawyer-less twenty-one-year-old fighter to his dying manager's widow and partner.

Though commission rules required both fighter and manager to be present for such a proceeding, Torres explained that the parties were unavailable, immersed in training for Tubbs. As for the actual agreements, they had been drawn up by DeSantis, the commission lawyer, in accordance with Torres's specifications, exactly as they had been relayed to him by Jacobs. But the commissioners themselves never actually got to see the documents, apparently assuming everything was on the up-and-up.

Perhaps they also assumed, as this was about managing Mike Tyson, that Cayton, who'd been around so damn long, after all, was a licensed manager in New York State. In fact, he was not. He hadn't even applied for the license until Mike and Robin returned from Chicago, then had it approved by Torres the very next day—record time for any municipal bureaucracy, though the commission didn't formally record receiving his fee until a month later, leading eventually to accusations that the document had been backdated. Finally, neither Commissioner Dupree of Syracuse nor Commissioner Trentman from the Bronx—each with a full-time job apart from boxing and compensated on a per diem basis by the commission—had a clue that Jacobs was dying. Had they known, each of them swore in subsequent affidavits, they wouldn't have approved the contracts, which would posthumously grant Jacobs's business partner and widow a third of Tyson's future earnings. After all, as Dupree himself later said, "the role of the commission is to protect the fighter from those kinds of contracts."

On Friday, February 12, Tyson woke up in Camille's house upstate. Between seven and ten inches of snow had blanketed Catskill, canceling school and a special performance by the New York City Opera company at Coxsackie-Athens High School and all but overwhelming the county highway department. The gravel road leading to and from D'Amato's former residence looked undrivable. After breakfast, Tyson called Jacobs to explain that he couldn't make it to New York as planned.

Cayton interrupted. "Sit tight, Mike. I'll take care of this." Then he called the Albany police chief, who arranged for a marked car to drive Tyson to the Big Fights offices in Manhattan.

Tyson was not in a good mood when he arrived. He didn't like sitting in the back of a police car. Still, there was nothing atypical about his impatience to sign the documents. Nor was there anything unusual about the fact that he didn't have a lawyer. He'd been signing documents this way for years, whatever and however Jacobs and Cayton instructed him. "I paid very little attention," he would recall, "because I was young and I trusted them."

Cayton was a remote figure—to everyone, but especially to Tyson. On the other hand, Jacobs, his adoptive father's former roommate, carried D'Amato's imprimatur. Jacobs was like family through Cus. So was Torres, also present that day, having granted Jacobs and Cayton yet another favor by conducting this business in their offices rather than where it should have been done, at the commission, downtown at 270 Broadway.

The contracts were pretty much as described—with one difference. The minutes of the February 8 meeting cited a term of four years. Indeed, Tyson's previous contract with Jacobs was for four years. What's more, the commission's standard boxer-manager contract called for a term "not to exceed four years." But the contract now before Tyson stipulated no term. The years had been left blank—an especially startling omission considering that the chairman of the New York State Athletic Commission was expediting this whole affair. Maybe it was an accident. Or maybe Torres had convinced himself that D'Amato would've wanted it this way, with Tyson indentured to Cayton and Jimmy's widow, Loraine, in perpetuity.

However one feels about the cult of D'Amato as a kind of family, familial relationships are often corrupted by money. And by now, with the Spinks fight looming, Cayton and Jacobs were bragging that Tyson would make $70 million, all in, over the next two years. Using that estimate, each manager's cut alone would be in excess of $11 million, around $29.5 million in 2025 dollars. In other words, everyone with a stake in Tyson had reason to lie. They would all find themselves swearing to the same story—that they'd had *no idea* how sick Jimmy really was, or that he was about to die.

The lawyers would get to all that in due course. For now, though, it's enough to know that no one broached the subject of Jacobs's health that day. It's also worth noting that Torres—the only person to attend both meetings, at the commission offices and at Big Fights—took great pains to dwell on Jacobs's duty-bound respect for both the process and his twenty-one-year-old client.

"You're my manager," he quotes Tyson as saying. "I trust you guys a hundred percent. We don't have to go through all that bullshit."

Still, Jacobs insisted: "It's a matter of law and proper conduct and not of choice that I have to explain the precise contents of these papers."

Though not that he was dying.

The next day, Saturday, February 13, a limousine bearing Tyson, his bride, and Don King, in his full-length mink coat, arrived in Wappingers Falls, ninety miles north of New York City. An excited sixteen-year-old girl ran out to meet them, asked if she could get in, then sat between the newly married couple.

"I've always wanted to sit in a limo," said the starstruck teenager.

Her name was Tawana Brawley. Her story of being sexually assaulted and humiliated by a group of white men—one supposedly with a policeman's badge—would eventually prove fraudulent. It was a fraud during which the Reverend Al Sharpton—the most visible and voluble of Brawley's three "advisers"—perfected his media strategy. Sharpton understood the media better than the media understood itself. And one of the things for which the media had no defense was fame—hence Tyson's visit.

Brawley invited him in. According to *Outrage*, a chronicle of the case by six *New York Times* reporters, "Tawana, wearing her modeling outfit, an alluring black velvet dress cut deep in the back, settled on the sofa next to Tyson and began whispering things in his ear as Givens sat sourly on the hard cushions and sipped something that was too sweet."

"I've always wanted to date you," she told Tyson.

Toward the end of their visit, Tyson removed his solid-gold, diamond-encrusted Rolex and gave it to her. "I want you to wear this and know everybody's with you," he said.

Brawley blushed, then wept. Earlier, she had given him a handwritten note of thanks, which King and Tyson would display for photographers at a subsequent press conference. They would each contribute $50,000 to her care and education.

"She shouldn't feel dirty," Tyson told reporters. "This was something nobody could control."

The Brawley case still feels like a deeply cynical exercise. But something in it resonated deeply with Tyson. Unlike with the corny antidrug PSAs Jimmy and Bill had him do, Tyson *wanted* to be there. In fact, just days before, he'd admonished Sharpton for asking Bill Cosby—who offered a $25,000 reward for information on the case—before him.

"You know Mike should be there," King joined in. "Get on the phone and arrange a meeting, Reverend."

If King, like Sharpton, saw value in the coverage, Tyson saw something else. Tyson wanted to be the one to save the girl found in a trash bag behind her apartment complex. "Lots of children are being abused," Tyson said. "I just want to do something about it."

THE NEXT DAY, VALENTINE'S DAY, RUTH ROPER HELD A WEDDING reception for the newlyweds in the Library Room at the Helmsley Palace. She wore black, strapless and formal, as did her daughter, Tyson's multitiered necklace shimmering below her neck. The groom wore a white formal jacket with a black bow tie, pink boutonniere, and black slacks. You get the sense, reinforced by Lori Grinker's photographs, that every one of these details, the direction and flow of the entire affair, was orchestrated by Roper.

There's a sweet shot of Bobby Stewart, a well-earned cigar in hand, cuffing Tyson with a hug. In that moment, Tyson looks twelve again.

Ruth Roper directing traffic at the wedding reception,
Valentine's Day, 1988, at the Helmsley Palace

There's Tyson with an arm around his sister, Denise, his only blood relative at the reception. She's beaming and bejeweled. The group shot—intended as a family portrait, I guess—is only slightly disjointed, with the diminutive Ruth, a champagne flute in her hand, at its center. She has these darting eyes.

"Ruth was always so suspicious," Grinker recalls. "And always organizing everything."

Meanwhile, Tyson is hugging in-laws clearly less effusive than he. Kevin Rooney, sans jacket by now, in a state of merry dishevelment, holds up a fist for the camera. Absent are Torres, Cayton, and Jacobs.

Torres might've been off completing his task, obtaining the signatures of Doris Cayton and Loraine Jacobs on the contracts that entitled them to their husbands' share of Tyson in the event they became widows. As it happened, both Cayton and Jacobs were hospitalized the next day. Cayton went in for endocarditis, an inflammation of the heart membranes. Jacobs checked into Mount Sinai for a scheduled round of intensive chemotherapy. Cayton told Tyson that Jacobs "was in Texas trying to buy some rare fight films."

35

Paul Antonelli can't swear who confirmed the story that Givens was pregnant, though it was likely Tyson himself. At twenty-four, sports editor for the hometown paper, Catskill's *Daily Mail*, Antonelli had been writing about Mike since they were both in high school. His soon-to-be father-in-law, a physician, had treated all of D'Amato's fighters. He was welcome at Tyson's private workouts, even on sparring days and when Tyson was downright miserable, which was pretty much his normal state during training camp. Tokyo was different, though; Tyson had never seemed happier.

Antonelli made a mental note back in the States, during the presser at HBO. While the Japanese reporters were asking their questions via video monitor, he sat directly behind the conspicuously lovey-dovey newlyweds. Maybe it was the way Tyson touched her tummy. Antonelli can't swear to that. When he got to Tokyo, though—and it was a big deal for the *Daily Mail* to send a reporter to Tokyo—he asked Kevin Rooney. Turned out Rooney had been wondering the same thing: Had Mike knocked her up?

Tyson was a citizen of the world now. Cayton bragged about selling foreign broadcast rights to the Holmes fight for record amounts in up to fifty countries. But only by seeing the phenomenon up close could you actually grasp what was happening to Tyson. Whether it was his appearance at the Tokyo zoo or palling around with Konishiki, the sumo wrestler, "it was like covering the Beatles," says Antonelli. A hundred photographers and cameramen gathered in darkness to accompany Tyson on his first predawn run through Tokyo.

Still, the young sportswriter saw him—idealized him, perhaps—as being rooted in the small towns of upstate New York. "Mike was the kind of guy, if he got a girl pregnant, he'd marry her," says Antonelli, who distinctly remembers Tyson talking about the pregnancy after a workout in Japan. "He was so happy the baby was coming. He couldn't wait to have a family."

Whenever they actually had that conversation, Antonelli managed to get the item into the March 16 edition of the *Daily Mail*: "Tyson learned his newly wedded wife, Robin Givens, is pregnant with the couple's first child. Givens is currently filming 'Head of the Class' in Hollywood."

Robin had been with Tyson in Tokyo, then left to help her mother finalize the selection of the couple's dream house. That very morning, on the front page of the Morristown *Daily Record*, was a story about the couple purchasing an eighteen-thousand-square-foot manor house listed at $4.25 million in Bernardsville, New Jersey, where their neighbors would include Jacqueline Onassis, Malcolm Forbes, John DeLorean, and King Hassan II of Morocco. Still, Givens managed to return to Tokyo in time to steal the show at the prefight presser, remaining after the fighters left to entertain a group of twenty or so English-speaking reporters.

"We're going to start our family in New Jersey," Antonelli quoted her as saying. "We started one quickly, didn't we?"

Givens went on to say that she wanted two or three kids, though Tyson wanted more. Also, she was partial to the name *Michael*, even if it was a girl. (Tyson, for his part, wanted to name a daughter *D'Amato*). Winning her mother's blessing had been a crucial if arduous task for Tyson, noted Givens, neglecting to mention the full proxy he'd given her mother in selecting their dream home or the $80,000 BMW he hoped would sway her affections.

What about a prenup? someone asked.

"No there isn't," said Robin. "And I'm amazed anyone would ask."

Though nobody had the nerve to mention that the 105-pound actress wasn't showing at all, she had, as Katz put it in the *Daily News*, "bobbed and weaved through questions about her pregnancy." It would take a while before reporters caught on to the idea that Robin's gravidity was a lot like her days at Harvard Medical School. You could ask all you want; she'd play along but never deny.

So when are you due? Robin was asked.

"I have no idea," she said, laughing disarmingly. "You guys are trying to get me."

On her flight back to Tokyo, Robin had read a book her sister had given her, Melody Beattie's self-help classic, *Codependent No More.* I'm not sure it helped, given what was to come, but she might've lent her copy to someone who could've used it, namely Tyson's opponent, Tony Tubbs. In many ways, Tubbs was the quintessential eighties heavyweight, which is to say, in a toxic and codependent relationship with Don King. Once an elite American amateur, a former national champion with excellent hand speed and hopes of an Olympic gold medal, Tubbs won a title under

Tyson, Robin, and some very interested sumo wrestlers

King, beating a fat Greg Page by unanimous decision, only to lose his first defense against Tim Witherspoon. By then, Tubbs was already fat and unhappy himself—as Witherspoon would soon be—over Carl King's exorbitant share of his purses. After pulling out of the rematch with Witherspoon, Tubbs sued King (as, at some point, most of those guys did) for $18 million and saw his career quickly go fallow, plummeting in the world rankings from number three to number twelve. "No promoter would touch him," noted Tim Smith in Tubbs's hometown paper, the *Cincinnati Enquirer.* "No one would risk the wrath of King."

The moment Tubbs dropped the suit, King took him back, put him on the Tyson–Pinklon Thomas undercard, announced they had "buried the hatchet," then installed Richie Giachetti as his trainer. Now here he was in Tokyo, feuding with Giachetti, whom he accused, quite reasonably, of being a King spy. Tubbs was working out sporadically and, in true heavyweight fashion—which is to say, more sensitive and self-destructive than anyone cared to realize—openly contemptuous of an incentive clause that would've paid him $50,000 for coming in under 235 pounds.

HBO's broadcast opened on the newly built Tokyo Dome, which had sold forty-three thousand tickets in anticipation of the now-international superstar. "He is a symbol of the U.S.," said one prophetic Japanese commentator. America might've lost its edge as an automotive power, but it retained hegemony in the production and export of action heroes. Tyson was not unlike the movie protagonists he'd been watching relentlessly for the past month in his penthouse suite at the New Otani Hotel: Stallone in *Rambo*, Schwarzenegger in *Commando*, Clint Eastwood, or even the primitive digital representation of Tyson himself in Nintendo's video game.

Tubbs had weighed in at what Jim Lampley—also making his HBO debut as the telecast's blow-by-blow announcer—called "a rather blubbery 238." Perhaps Tubbs thought fighting Tyson was a fait accompli. Certainly, he also wanted to stick it to King. The irony, though, is that Tubbs had both the skill and the experience to understand what was actually required to beat Tyson. The idea that you could win by merely *boxing*—meaning pick and poke, then cut an angle of escape—was a fallacy.

"Anybody can take the back way out," said Tubbs. "But if you want to win, you've got to go in and fight."

And so he did, giving as good as he got for a little more than a round. Tubbs hit Tyson with a good jab, some one-twos, and a check hook here and there as Tyson advanced. Most impressive was Tubbs's work inside, the way he planted himself, ripping uppercuts to Tyson's body.

If Tubbs wasn't especially heavy-handed, he was still a world-class heavyweight. Besides, power itself is overrated. What beats a fighter are the punches he doesn't expect. Take enough and they'll diminish one's spirit. Still, Tyson took them all, without any hesitation or perceptible sag, and kept coming. Tyson himself would say later that night, "I refuse to be hurt, knocked down, or knocked out. I can't lose. I refuse." Maybe he was speaking from a posthypnotic state, as his hypnotist, John Halpin, had accompanied Tyson on the journey. But he wasn't bullshitting. It's a great talent, the ability to get hit by a big man and remain undiscouraged.

With less than thirty seconds left in the second round, Tyson scored with his trademark combination—right hook to the body followed by a right uppercut. Now something fractured in Tubbs. At nineteen seconds, Tyson unloaded with a long left hook around Tubbs's guard, opening a gash over its intended target, the right eye itself. Suddenly, Tubbs's steps became palsied and Chaplinesque. He crashed into the ropes, then collapsed onto the canvas, a knockout recorded at 2:54 of the second.

If the postfight was notable, it was only because Bill Cayton succeeded in boxing out Don King for the preferred camera angle. Perhaps he had some help. While the Japanese loved Tyson, they were less enthusiastic about King, whose manslaughter conviction had made it difficult for him to get a visa. Once he was in Tokyo, the local Japanese promoter effectively neutered him, removing King's name and logo from all promotional materials and compensating him, per one report, with a flat fee of $50,000. The supercilious Cayton—as bad with politics as he was good with money—thought only to rub it in: "Don is not really involved in this

promotion in any sense except for the fact that he delivered the opponent," he said. "Reduced to a mere errand boy," wrote Matthews.

Don't think King would forget that.

Meanwhile, as the broadcast came to a close, Lampley noted the absence of Jimmy Jacobs, who was "back in a hospital room in New York
recovering from an illness." If Jacobs's absence distressed Tyson, the
champ wasn't letting on. "Do you realize," he asked, "how effective and
explosive I am since I became a married man?"

REWIND A YEAR OR MORE. SOMETIME AFTER TYSON BECAME THE
youngest-ever heavyweight champion, Seth Abraham, HBO CEO Michael
Fuchs, and the president of the Las Vegas Hilton threw him a private, cel-
ebratory dinner at Caesars Palace. Tyson showed up wearing all black
but for a Cartier panther—diamond-encrusted with rubies for eyes—
pinned to his leather jacket. "The size of a fist," Abraham recalls.

King made a big deal of Tyson's exquisite taste. Then, quite suddenly,
Tyson excused himself for a quick trip to the all-night jeweler catering to
high rollers and their goomars. He returned in short order with identical Cartier pins. King opened his box and triumphantly fastened his to
the lapel of his tuxedo. Abraham left his box unopened and begged Tyson's pardon. "I buy your fights," he explained. "I negotiate with Don. I
can't accept a gift of such value."

"But it wasn't that much," said Tyson. "Only ninety-five."

Ninety-five thousand dollars.

Months later, hours after the Biggs fight in Atlantic City, Gucci tem-
porarily closed its store in Trump Plaza so Tyson's entourage could shop
in peace. "I counted twelve people," said Rock Newman, then working
with promoter Butch Lewis. "And they were like 'Give me two of these,
two of those.' . . . One person rang up $2,700 in ten minutes."

All charged to Tyson, of course.

There's a lot to unpack in Tyson's largesse. He gladly paid his sister's
rent and expenses, same for Camille in her big white house: mortgage,
utilities, spending money, plus $20,000 for repairs in 1987. According to

a statement of his cash disbursements for that year, Tyson spent $17,330 on Holloway (apart from rent and utilities for their apartment in Albany), $210,819 on jewelry, $178,314 on clothing, $71,708 on limos, and $22,222 on air travel. By 1988, with the new HBO deal and several especially lucrative endorsements taking effect, Tyson's taste for the finer things had become ever more conspicuous.

There were Robin's diamonds, Ruth's car, and his own fleet of luxury automobiles, most of them German and English. Tyson spent much like he fought—in a great hurry. The causes of his impulsivity, his suggestibility, and his inability to defer gratification were long-standing and many. But the boy who had nothing except what he could steal quite suddenly had everything he could imagine, and even some things he could not. Tyson wanted to be adored, even worshipped, and, by his own later admission, to fill an emptiness within. There was a Gatsby-like quality to Tyson's acquisitions—though none more epically fraught than the Gothic Revival manor house in Bernardsville, which looked like something out of *Downton Abbey*.

"I used to look at books of homes in Scotland, England, and Ireland, and I used to say, 'I'm going to have the best house any fighter ever had,'" said Tyson. "I wanted a golden house, a house with a great dining table where you bring everyone over, the whole family, and a backyard with a tennis court and a pool, and French chandeliers. I know good things, because I never had them and I always wanted them."

The dream home was something they'd all agree on—Tyson, Robin, and Ruth, who, based on her son-in-law's descriptions, found Kenilwood, built in 1897 by George B. Post, architect of the New York Stock Exchange building. It had been home to Astors, Vanderbilts, and, for a time, FDR's undersecretary of state.

It was "Tyson's feverish desire to possess Kenilworth," as *Vanity Fair's* Leslie Bennetts wrote, that brought Ruth and Robin into Cayton's orbit. Cayton received the first call from Robin while still recovering from endocarditis. "I'm Mrs. Mike Tyson," she began, "and I'm taking over my husband's affairs." Days later, there was a letter from Roper's attorney, Michael Winston, demanding to see any and all documents relating to

Tyson's finances. Finally, on the flight home from Tokyo, in the first-class cabin on a Japan Airlines 747, Cayton had the pleasure of speaking with Robin in person.

Tyson recalled that "Robin began throwing her weight around," repeating her insistence that Cayton make available all her husband's financials. José Torres had a different POV: Ruth Roper was in the midst of an "animated conversation" with her daughter when "suddenly Robin got up and marched toward Bill." After Cayton demurred, offering only to let her see a standard contract, Tyson asked his bride to let them speak in private. "I just want her to feel that she is part of the team," Tyson explained. "That's all."

In Givens's version, Cayton approached Tyson toward the end of the flight and said he wanted to get to "know him better." Tyson brushed him off, wanting nothing to do with a condescending seventy-year-old from Larchmont. "When Bill left," writes Givens, "Michael snuggled his face in my lap like a child and said, 'Please promise me that you won't let anyone hurt me or take advantage of me. Promise me that you'll protect me!'"

Indeed, the dutiful newlywed promised.

Most of their flight, though, had been spent with the ever-solicitous King. "My wife just picked a house," said Tyson. "We're going to see it when we land. Why don't you come with us?"

Who could turn down an offer like that? Certainly not King. "Don was charming and smart and entertaining," notes Givens, "and he seemed to lighten the sadness we were all feeling."

She refers here to the sudden and horrible news of Jacobs's death. "Shortly after the fight," she said, "Michael and I lay in bed, stunned and sobbing, too grief-stricken to move."

Robin's is surely the most poignant account of the journey home. But the truth of it is Jimmy Jacobs didn't die until 7:30 a.m. on March 23—more than a day after they returned from Japan.

36

Jacobs's absence from Tokyo had been widely if discreetly reported by the New York dailies. The cause, however, remained a mystery.

"It's not a story," Cayton had assured *Newsday*'s Wally Matthews.

Not only was it a story, but Cayton was already getting played. One of King's henchmen, Al Braverman, had been calling around, telling reporters that Jacobs had AIDS and was in Mexico for a blood transfusion.

Finally, just days before the Tubbs fight, Cayton was forced to address the rumors. "He's just got pneumonia," he told reporters, still refusing to say where Jacobs was being treated. "He doesn't have AIDS, he doesn't have cancer of the colon, or any of the other things we've been hearing. He just tried to push himself too hard."

It was a wonderfully dexterous explanation, an example for anyone who wants to lie while telling the most narrow of truths, an especially useful skill in boxing. In fact, Jacobs had developed a respiratory infection within a week of his scheduled February 15 admission to Mount Sinai for chemotherapy. And while it is certain that Tyson had been lied to yet again—told that Jacobs had gone to Texas to buy rare fight films—his own sworn claim—"I didn't know he was sick at all"—defies common sense. "Mike called me from Tokyo to ask how Jim was and when we were coming," Loraine Jacobs said in an affidavit. "I told him that Jim was in the hospital. He called me once or twice after that, again to ask how Jim was." The widow goes on to claim, however, that on the fateful day Tyson received his police escort from Catskill, "neither Jim nor I believed that his death was imminent."

As it happened, Jacobs never left Mount Sinai. With his system too weak to fight the pneumonia, the infection entered his bloodstream. Immediate cause of death was septic shock. It was Robin—who'd likely heard the news from her attentive new friend, King—who told her devastated husband.

DESPITE HIS WIFE'S RELUCTANCE TO BE IN CAYTON'S PRESENCE, Tyson insisted on paying respects that night at Jim and Loraine's apartment, just a few floors down from their own. Amid the coffee and sandwiches—by both Givens's and Torres's accounts—was a palpable tension. Cayton reminded everyone they'd all be flying out to Los Angeles the next morning for the funeral, when Robin and Mike had been scheduled to close on the Bernardsville property.

"Let's change the date of the closing," Robin recalls telling Mike. "I want to be there."

It's a curious ask, as earlier that day Tyson had granted her power of attorney, an instrument her mother recommended to enable her closing the deal in his absence. But Tyson, in a show of agency rarely evidenced during his marriage, apparently instructed Robin to remain in New York, as he didn't want anything interfering with the acquisition of their dream house.

At some point, Tyson left Jacobs's apartment with Torres. "I love Robin, but I don't trust her—not yet," he said. "I guess deep inside I think all girls want me only for my money."

At twenty-one, Tyson had now lost his mother, his adoptive father, and his surrogate brother in just over five years. The death evoked familiar feelings: apocalyptic, suicidal contempt at what he saw as his cowardice, even as he wept on Torres's shoulder. "I felt like killing myself when

Cus died and I feel like killing myself now," he said. "But I don't have the guts to do it."

Tyson wasn't a fledgling pro anymore. He was the undisputed heavy-weight champion of the world, with a looming payday in excess of $20 million for Spinks—more in a single night than the combined annual payrolls of the NBA's most successful franchises, the Los Angeles Lakers and the Boston Celtics. In truth, Jimmy had been more than a brother. Tyson depended on him (or his proxy, Steve Lott) for almost everything. While Tyson and D'Amato had their rows, Tyson and Jacobs did not. In the multitude of accounts, there's but a single example of Tyson defying Jacobs—when Jimmy broached the idea of a prenuptial agreement before marrying Robin.

"Do you have one with Loraine?" Tyson shot back.

For once, Jacobs didn't bother to argue. The end was near enough. If D'Amato had been a kind of wizard, cloistered away in Catskill, Jacobs was Tyson's guide in the real world: fierce protector, strategist, apologist, confidant, and relentless advocate. But now, with the papers about to re-port that Jacobs had suffered from "lymphocytic leukemia" for the past nine years—since before Tyson had even met him!—the champion would have to reconcile his grief with his bewilderment. The man he loved and trusted was just another liar.

WHEN TORRES RETURNED HOME THAT NIGHT, THERE WAS A MESSAGE from King: *Call, no matter how late.* Torres complied, providing King with his flight number and details of the funeral arrangements.

In the meantime, one of King's friends in the clergy placed another call on his behalf. It was to Robin.

"You know Jim and I were very close," Father Clements began. "But the one thing I never understood about Jim was his relationship to Bill. And I believe in my heart that if Michael wasn't in the position he was in, he'd have nothing to do with Cayton. But it is as if Michael has been willed to him like chattel." *Chattel*, a favorite Kingism. "Do you understand?"

"Not really. I'm sorry."

"Robin, Michael deserves to be with someone who truly cares about him and really understands him. You want what's best for him, don't you?"

"Of course, Father!"

"Then you'll help me, won't you?"

"Of course, Father!"

Early the next morning, Thursday, March 24, mourners were shocked when King showed up to embrace and comfort them in the American Airlines lounge at JFK. Then they all boarded flight 3 to LAX, where, upon landing, King called attention to the lack of a limousine waiting for the champ. "These people don't know how to deal with this kid," he said within earshot of Tyson. "Ali never waited this long in any airport. Never!"

The next morning, King invited Torres to breakfast and reiterated his confidential concerns about Ruth and Robin—"a woman with larceny

Torres and Tyson arm in arm at Jimmy Jacobs's funeral

in her heart," he'd called Robin in Tokyo. King's real concern was installing a pliant executive within the Tyson camp. "He told me I should become Tyson's next manager," recalled Torres.

The idea quickly gathered momentum. "The only logical choice,"
Seth Abraham said at the time. "I would have to consider it," Torres told
Newsday's Matthews, who calculated that even Tyson's minor fights
would earn the chairman about three times his yearly salary as a public
servant. "But I would never do it for the money. I would do it for the kid,
and out of loyalty to Cus."

Jacobs was buried on the Mount of Olives at Hillside Memorial Park
and Mortuary, not far from Al Jolson's grave. Tyson dabbed at his eyes
all through the forty-five-minute service. But the star of this show was
King—even his adversaries were awed. Gene Kilroy, Ali's longtime adviser and a friend to both D'Amato and Jacobs, came not just to pay his
respects but to attest to Cayton's scrupulousness in matters of business
and warn Tyson about King. Looking back, Kilroy recognizes the futil-
ity of his undertaking. It wasn't just Cayton, who Kilroy now concedes
was "a cheap prick with zero personality," but King himself, who, despite
all the federal investigations, bad press, and finger wagging directed at
boxing's prodigy, was grossly underestimated yet again.

"King was *so* slick," says Kilroy, not unadmiringly. "You got to give
the guy some credit."

As one mourner described the way King fawned over the weeping
Tyson: "Don was hitting on him." A ceremony that began with King as
an uninvited guest would end—per Tyson's recollection—with King as a
pallbearer, making Cayton, who designated him such, the most feckless
appeaser since Neville Chamberlain. When it was over, King pulled
Mike aside and tried to kill the Spinks fight. "I told Mike that he could
do four or five fights for five million dollars apiece," King told Tyson biographer Monteith Illingworth. "He'd make a lot more money and build
up to a crescendo before Spinks."

King's argument ignored that it was Tyson himself who desperately
wanted the Spinks fight. King had another pitch: Us and Them. "We're
just niggers, Mike," he said. "You and me."

TYSON WAS ENOUGH OF A HUSTLER HIMSELF TO UNDERSTAND IT wasn't just King; everyone in his orbit was hustling for a piece. The greater their professed empathy, the more suspect they were. He was sad and tired. It had been a very long day, starting with a phone call from Robin. Armed with the newly signed power of attorney, she was with her mother and her mother's lawyer, and they were not happy. The object of their ire was Merrill Lynch vice president James Brady, a friend of Jacobs's who handled Tyson's investment portfolio.

Brady couldn't help but be impressed by Roper. "She knew her shit," he says. What she was advocating, however, wasn't financially prudent, as the money they wanted to move was in triple tax-free bonds that would come due in a matter of weeks and be used to pay the IRS. Jacobs and Cayton were sticklers when it came to taxes.

"Jim insisted on paying the IRS after each fight," says Brady. "He didn't want Tyson ending up like Joe Louis."

Nevertheless, Givens, at her mother's direction, was now demanding that Brady transfer $1.9 million from her joint account with Tyson to a new European American account, from which she would complete the Bernardsville sale. When Brady informed her that European American couldn't accept the transfer from a joint account to her newly opened individual account, Givens pitched a fit.

"I want my money," she screamed. "Where is my motherfucking money, you motherfucker?"

Then she called her husband, who instructed Brady to complete the transaction. "The lawyers had to come down," Brady recalls. "We had to tape Mike's verbal permission and everybody had to sign all kinds of documents."

Still none of it seemed to appease either Ruth or her daughter. Even as Brady completed the transfer, they kept lacing into him, vowing to take "our money" to another financial institution. "You're one of Cayton's boys," said Robin.

37

t was Finkel's wife, Beth, who had noticed Tyson's discomfort amid the crush of well-wishers after the funeral. "Mike's getting claustrophobic," she told her husband. "I think you should take him outside."

They ended up sitting on the floor somewhere in the Beverly Hilton. "I'm in love with my wife," Tyson explained. "But I'm getting nothing but grief."

For all the fear Tyson evoked, he remained in many respects a needy child—wanting to be acknowledged, accommodated, indulged, and loved. Finkel was a sympathetic listener, more than ready to pick up where Jacobs had left off. But his immediate concern was keeping his end of the Spinks deal alive before King could kill it or Cayton took it away.

"When we get back," said Tyson, "I want you to meet my wife."

Finkel was only too happy to meet Robin. They dined in the Oak Room at the Plaza Hotel shortly after returning from the funeral. Finkel found her bright, beautiful, and charming. Givens couldn't have minded that her husband had a friend so well wired in the world of entertainment. "I knew what she was, and she knew that I knew it," Finkel recalls. "I thought we could be allies."

Cayton had different ideas, though. "Bill was petrified I would somehow make a play for Mike," says Finkel.

"If you want to keep your position," Cayton told him, "stay away."

"Bill, this is the woman he sleeps with every night. This can only help you."

"Stay away."

ON WEDNESDAY, MARCH 30, JUST FIVE DAYS AFTER JACOBS'S FU-neral, the parties reconvened at the Plaza—purchased by Donald Trump only days before for a reported $390 million—for the inaugural Tyson–Spinks press conference.

This was more than Trump showing off the Plaza, where, perhaps anticipating his own marital difficulties, he'd announced his intention to install then-wife Ivana as president at a salary of "$1 a year plus all the dresses she can buy." It was also meant to signal Trump's reemergence as a sportsman. His tenure as owner of the New Jersey Generals had been disastrous, not only for the franchise but also for the entire United States Football League. As the Second Circuit Court of Appeals had concluded: "Trump's USFL merger strategy . . . ultimately caused the USFL's downfall."

In fact, he'd made a cagey move acquiring Tyson–Spinks, getting options from each fighter's camp. And while Trump's $11 million site fee shattered the previous record—the $6.8 million Caesars Palace had paid for Hagler–Leonard just the year before—certain Las Vegas hotels had been prepared to pay millions more. Trump's insistence on a Monday-night fight ensured an extralong weekend at the tables for most of the high rollers in his casinos. The drop would set records, too.

In keeping with the Trumpian obsession for bigness, the throng of 1,200 gathered in and around the Grand Ballroom that day was itself the biggest such crowd in memory, bigger even than the opening presser for Ali–Frazier. But it almost didn't happen, as the real guest of honor, Tyson, who had seemed in good spirits at dinner the night before, was now beside himself and threatening not to attend.

"He was having a fight with Robin," says Finkel, who again suggested that they step outside and get some air. The *Times*'s Phil Berger spied them on a park bench, locked in the kind of conversation it was probably best not to interrupt. Whatever Tyson's immediate problem, it was now exacerbated by his own notoriety. The day had begun with an early call for the *Today* show; then there was a photo shoot, car-wash style, one cameraman after another, back at the hotel. Now, as they sat on a bench across from the Plaza entrance, Tyson found himself besieged. There was a homeless guy, whom Tyson, after rifling through his pockets, gave a hundred-dollar bill. Then there were the Japanese tourists who wanted to take his picture. And the autograph seekers. Some were New Yorkers. But there were also Spaniards and Italians, among others, who kept rolling up on him like a tide. "Shel, Shel," he asked, "can you stop it?" Tyson, still just twenty-one, wasn't merely famous anymore. His was becoming a kind of fame that is itself a form of insanity.

While Finkel doesn't recall why Tyson and Robin were fighting, it wouldn't come as a great surprise if it had something to do with a column in that morning's *Daily News*. Bits and pieces of the Merrill Lynch episode had begun to leak out. Now here was Mike Katz's attempt to address the "ugly rumors and snide innuendos," among them the suspect nature of Givens's pregnancy. "She was hurt when she was told this rumor," he wrote after speaking with her, "but said firmly that she was still pregnant and that she had been evasive about the subject 'because of the business I'm in.'"

Eventually, Finkel talked Tyson into returning for the press conference. The show would go on, though with surprisingly little speechifying from Trump. In all, King spoke for seventeen minutes and forty-one seconds, about nine minutes longer than Butch Lewis. Tyson seethed throughout, then left without filming the agreed-upon HBO promo.

AFTERWARD, TYSON, GIVENS, ROPER, AND MICHAEL WINSTON, TYson's ostensible attorney through his mother-in-law, met with Cayton to inspect his financials. On April 1, they flew (sans lawyer) to Los Angeles. On April 4, King received a call from Tyson, requesting his presence on the Coast. Tyson said Cayton was robbing him, and wanted to talk to King about his future.

King, suddenly concerned with protocol, explained that he was obliged to run it by Cayton first.

"That motherfucker," said Tyson. "He has no respect for my wife."

Instead of immediately calling Cayton, though, King dialed Seth Abraham. Cayton might be Tyson's manager, and Givens his wife, but all the players here were drawing on the same account. After Spinks, HBO still had at least six more fights with Tyson. Whatever King did, he wasn't going to piss off his banker.

"Should I go?" asked King.

"Don, you know you're going to go," said Abraham. "Just tell Cayton."

Cayton, predictably, tried to forbid him; just as predictably, King responded that he *had* to go, as he was the kid's promoter.

King arrived in Los Angeles on April 6, a Wednesday. By Friday, he was reportedly en route to Las Vegas—with Tyson, Givens, and Roper. "Don King is making moves, I guess," Cayton told the *Times*. "It's something a lot of people told me he would try."

The next night, the four members of this new alliance sat ringside to watch Evander Holyfield—already talking about moving up in weight to fight Tyson—stop Carlos De León to become the undisputed cruiserweight champion. As the *Times*'s Phil Berger typed his story for the next day's paper, he was contacted by King's henchman Richie Giachetti.

Tyson and King were waiting for him, said Giachetti, in Barronshire Prime Rib at the Las Vegas Hilton. Berger soon found them ensconced in a remote section of the restaurant: Roper and Givens at the far end of the table, between Tyson and King. Berger pulled up a chair. Roper then whispered in King's ear.

"Ruth," King told the *Times* man, "would rather we wait until dinner is over."

IF THIS ACCOUNT SEEMS HEAVY WITH FORGOTTEN BYLINES, IT'S NOT just because I miss newspapers—which, looking back, were already mortally wounded—or the preening belligerence of the boxing beat, or even the boxing writers themselves. ("But officer," Mike Marley once famously told a rousting cop, "the curb is my pillow.") There's a forensic argument, too. As imperfect as the newspaper accounts may have been, they still comprise the most accurate record of what happened when and who said what, certainly more reliable than decades-old recollections of the larcenous or merely self-serving protagonists themselves. Deconstructing Tyson's quotes, however, requires special care. The famous nose-to-the-brain remark, for instance, was D'Amato's, delivered while Tyson was a kid under hypnosis. His rant threatening Lennox Lewis's unborn children drew from the comic book villain Apocalypse and the movie *Five Deadly Venoms*. And as noted, his postfight interview after knocking out Larry Holmes was lifted from the great welterweight Fritzie Zivic.

"You'll notice that I'm always quoting my heroes," he told his biographer Larry Sloman. "It's never me talking."

Tyson didn't consume D'Amato's syllabus cover to cover so much as snatch phrases and maxims and commit them to memory. "Mike can retain information like nobody I ever seen in my life," says Holloway. "Philosophies . . . quotes from great generals . . . old movies . . . He'd remember that shit and spring it on you ten years later."

While the world saw an unconquerable champion, those closest to Tyson recognized a very distinct kind of follower—suggestible and easily led, but with a great ego and corresponding insecurities. Reporters were accustomed to hearing D'Amato or Jacobs in Tyson's speech. But Berger's interview at Barronshire Prime Rib marked the debut of a new ventriloquist.

He professed to trust no one in boxing. That included King, who remained at his side during the interview, and Finkel, "who manages my adversaries." It was all eminently reasoned; the only problem was this Tyson didn't quite sound like Tyson: "I have a wife, a child on the way"—due that October, he believed. "It's my obligation to take control."

"There is no way I'm thinking of double-crossing Bill Cayton," he went on. "Nothing's changed. I don't know why he feels threatened. Bill sounds like he's worried that I'm going to leave. I'm no rat-fink or traitor."

It wasn't just a night at Barronshire, though, but part of a coordinated media strategy any high-powered PR firm would've envied. The same day Berger's piece ran, Marley commandeered the lead page of the *Post*'s sports section: TYSON TAKES CHARGE. Again, the message was *Trust no one*—not his manager, his promoter, or the ever-attentive Finkel, "who calls my wife ten times a day."

I ask Finkel how often he called Robin.

"That was King," he says.

It sure seemed that way. King had plenty of motive, starting with Finkel getting the closed-circuit and pay-per-view rights that normally went to the promoter. Certainly, King allayed no one's suspicions when he checked into the Hilton in Albany, where Tyson was hanging out with Holloway after returning from Vegas. But once again, King wasn't an uninvited guest. He'd gotten the call from Tyson's best friend.

"You must be Rory Holloway," King had said upon their meeting in Bernardsville.

"My man needs some help," said Holloway.

"I'd love to help you, man."

So Holloway called, after Tyson gave his blessing.

I ask Holloway if King took care of him. "Don didn't give me a dime," he says. "I was trying to help my friend."

He was only doing what Tyson wanted him to do. Then again, who knew what the credulous prince really wanted? The proliferation of conspirators made it difficult to figure. "Suddenly, Ruth was everywhere with Don King," recalls Lori Grinker. "They were like best buddies whispering all the time."

Go back to the *rat-fink* line. Was there ever a more identifiable Kingism than one of his preferred terms for rival promoter Bob Arum? Later, Marley of the *Post* found himself on the receiving end of yet another supposedly telltale quote: "If I deal with Don King, they'll slaughter me," said Tyson. "I should only deal with Bill and Shelly because they're guys who are Jewish and are good guys because they wear three-piece suits."

The line was recycled as the "Jews in suits" quote, and attributed willy-nilly to King's influence. But the only *lantzman*—one of King's favorite Yiddishisms—fitting that description was the dapper Abraham, the last guy King wanted to offend. On the other hand, Abraham had by now turned down several requests to produce Tyson's HBO contract.

"Robin, you know I can't do that," he would say. "Just have Mike call me."

"Oh, I don't want to bother him."

I recall what James Brady of Merrill Lynch told me of the day Roper came with her daughter and lawyer in tow, causing a great scene in the office.

"'Jews with suits won't give me my money.' That's what she said."

Roper? I ask. You sure?

"I was appalled." As well he should've been, an Irishman from Bay Ridge.

SO WHO WAS THE ALPHA VENTRILOQUIST?

It was she who gave King his orders in a whispered aside back at the Barronshire. The business of boxing comes with often conflicting imperatives: First, never let it look like you're not the boss (unless as a ruse). Second, pick only fights you can win. Yet here was King, the most powerful promoter in the world, the man who stood up to Shondor Birns, deferring to a woman with no experience in the game. Looking back, it reveals King's brilliance in a way that no one could yet fully understand.

"Don had an exquisite read on people," says Abraham, "but never more precise than with Robin and Ruth."

Ever since he was a kid, Tyson had been warned ad nauseum about King. Just the same, King was also the gangster father that kid had always longed for. Street cred was among King's greatest assets here. But there was still something else Tyson wanted much more.

"I think the fact that I came with a package"—with her mother—"is what he loved," Givens told *Vanity Fair*. "Michael's a baby with her; he's just 'Hug me, love me.' He wants that; that's what no one understands. He wants to be protected. He likes the fact that she fights for him, tucks him in bed, makes him stay in the house."

King could play pimp daddy all he wanted, but he couldn't smooth the covers and kiss him good night. King knew full well he couldn't compete with Roper. In that same *Vanity Fair* piece, Roper dabbed at her eyes recalling the way she set out breakfast for Robin and her sister: making faces in their cereal bowls, peaches for imaginary mouths, cherries for the eyes, and a slice of banana for the nose. It wasn't breakfast in Brownsville with Lorna Mae. "I adore my children, and Michael has become one of them," said Roper. "He calls me Ma. It's like I had a child instead of Robin getting married."

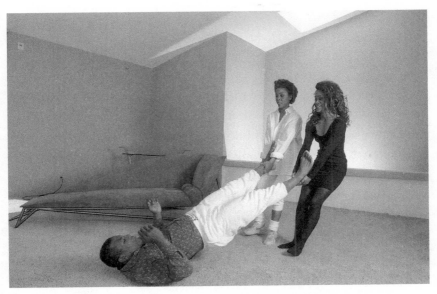

Tyson getting pulled along by his bride and her mother

38

n mid-April, Cayton boasted that while Tyson and Jacobs had enjoyed a social relationship, "the contracts that made Tyson the richest fighter in history were my baby. I think Mike recognizes that."

Cayton wasn't merely diminishing a longtime partner who had been dead less than three weeks. He was bullshitting himself. His decades in boxing had apparently failed to teach him the first precept of boxing management: *He who's with the fighter has the fighter.* For even as Cayton congratulated himself, King was babysitting Tyson in Albany.

"Mike came to see me in Catskill," José Torres recalled in an affidavit. "He asked me whether he should sign an exclusive multi-promotion contract with Don King. . . . I told him never to sign such a contract. I told him it was illegal because he had a manager, and I told him it would be the worst thing that could happen to him."

Nevertheless, Tyson soon signed a furtive agreement giving King the right to promote his next fight after Spinks, against England's Frank Bruno. No, it wouldn't hold up in court. But that mattered less than King's growing hold over Tyson.

It was often said that being Black and from the streets gave King an advantage over Cayton. Certainly, Cayton subscribed to the theory. But being an old white guy with an outsize opinion of oneself never hurt D'Amato or Jacobs with Tyson. Rather, what really injured Cayton's cause was being charmless, arrogant, and, most of all, outworked. Cayton didn't lack for allies, either. Finkel told him to be less remote. Kilroy told him to hire a Black man. For all his supposed experience in commerce, the great sage might've recognized the situation for what it clearly was and, say, taken care of Tyson's sister, Denise, who was on welfare, living with a bike messenger and their kids in Queens. But that wasn't Cayton.

The Tyson–Spinks deal was actually a series of contracts involving the principals and their reps—Tyson, Spinks, Cayton, Lewis, HBO, King, and Trump. The first of them was between King and Cayton. It's clear to see who was stepping on whose throat. Under the terms, King would "appoint" Cayton (through a corporate likeness created for the promotion) the lord of all closed-circuit and pay-per-view rights, all ancillary rights, and every conceivable concession, including the HBO rebroadcast, which Jacobs had already sold for $3.1 million. Meanwhile, King's fee would remain a flat $3 million ($500,000 from Trump's end), minus what he spent on an eight-bout undercard that was to include at least four heavyweight contenders. An addendum claiming that King was only "signing this contract under protest and as a result of economic duress" was crossed out and marked "DELETED."

"King is getting $3 million for doing very little," said Cayton. "I find his duress hysterical."

The signed contract was dated "New York, N.Y., May 7"—a Saturday, which feels odd, as Tyson could only have just returned, likely that day, from Los Angeles, where neither his manager nor his trainer knew he had been for the better part of a week. Turned out the champ and his bride were off doing a big photo shoot for *Life* magazine. Unlike its corporate siblings—*Time*, *Sports Illustrated*, and *People*, all of which would run cover stories during the lead-up to the big fight—*Life* had guaranteed Roper not just a cover but that Robin would have equal billing with Mike.

"If your pictures are published before *Life* comes out," Roper told

Grinker, then shooting the *People* piece, "I'll make sure you never work in this town again."

The *Life* spread would contain just a single photograph of the couple in what the magazine described as their "art deco house in the Hollywood hills." Most of "The Lady and the Champ: Television's Robin Givens and Boxing's Mike Tyson" had been shot back in Bernardsville: Mike in a red FILA warm-up suit cradling a white pigeon, Mike conferring with tradesmen on the renovation of his estate, Robin in heels and leather pants holding a teddy bear, Mike helping her onto a horse. The parting shot featured the couple driving away down their tree-lined private road in a silver Bentley convertible. Like so many of Tyson's purchases, the Bentley was an impulse buy. He'd seen one just like it weeks earlier, parked outside the Carriage House in Manhattan. So he called Cayton, who had it promptly delivered at a discount.

Early on the morning of May 8, the couple drove the Bentley to Gleason's Gym in Brooklyn, where a film crew of twenty-five had been left incommunicado for four days, waiting to shoot a thirty-second spot for Suntory beer. "The problem, as I understand it, is between Tyson and his wife and the management," Suntory's production manager tried to explain. "And somehow Don King is involved." By 11:00 a.m., they were done and headed in the silver Bentley to one of Robin's faves, the Pink Tea Cup.

The couple snuggled through brunch. "I couldn't recall," said Givens, "when I had felt more at peace or more happy."

Then, while snuggling, she found the rubbers in his pocket.

Though Tyson was desperately in love with his wife, and desperately insecure about it, he never stopped fucking around on her (or anyone else, for that matter). If his actions and his emotions seem difficult to reconcile, consider what the great trainer Freddie Roach once said when asked if he knew any fighters who *didn't* cheat: "Not world champions." That said, Tyson had particular challenges when it came to fidelity, starting with his own perennial difficulty in squaring right and wrong. Then there was his impenetrable sense of entitlement and, forgive me, some of the women themselves. They were there for the taking in a way that belied the strictures of Tyson's now-alternate universe, that sane, ostensibly *normal* world of the nonfamous. In the weeks to come, Givens would remark that her husband had never been "socialized."

Both Mike's and Robin's accounts have Ruth trying to calm her daughter. Nevertheless, Robin left the restaurant, jumped into the Bentley, and, blind with rage, plowed into a car on Varick Street near the entrance to the Holland Tunnel. When an apparently injured motorist emerged from his just-struck automobile, Tyson thought to give him a thick stack of cash, estimated at $20,000.

Then came two Port Authority cops, one of whom seemed to be especially impressed with the Bentley. Tyson, who volunteered that he'd been the one driving while his wife and mother-in-law hailed a cab, suggested that the officer take it, provided he didn't report the accident. After some deliberation, the cops accepted the offer and drove their new, dented Bentley to a garage in Jersey, where their fellow cops quickly ratted them out. The ensuing investigation would embarrass not only the officers themselves and Tyson and Robin (the source of her rage being duly reported in the *Post*) but also Cayton, who cited the officers' "superb professionalism" in recognizing—certainly not a bribe, as the Bentley was owned by Big Fights, Inc., and wasn't Tyson's to give away—the champ's great emotional distress, as the accident had been caused by Tyson's swerving to avoid a defenseless cat. Meanwhile, King had already gifted Tyson a new Rolls-Royce.

A FEW NIGHTS LATER, DETAILS OF CAYTON'S DISPLEASURE WERE aired on Albany's NBC affiliate, WNYT. After interviewing him by phone, longtime local sports anchor Bob McNamara quoted Cayton as saying: "King is winning Tyson with the theory that Blacks should stick together. Black trainer, Black manager, Black promoter, Black, Black, Black."

Per McNamara, Cayton was "incensed by the constant interference of Don King through the friendship King has formed with Robin Givens and her mother, Ruth."

What's more, if Tyson wanted to challenge the validity of his contract, Cayton vowed he'd take it all the way to the Supreme Court.

But in airing his beef with King, the condescending Cayton only created a greater problem for himself. "Mike is in love," he told McNamara. "And the woman he is in love with has ideas."

Going on the record about Givens and Roper was like walking into the blades of a propeller. "I'm not going to tolerate insinuations about my wife," Tyson told the *Post*'s Mike Marley, whose piece appeared under the headline SEETHING TYSON RIPS MANAGER. "He's paranoid. I've been nothing but loyal to this man. . . . Now I hear that my wife has these ideas. That's a lie. . . . Bill should be man enough to say he said it." Then the real issue: "Having Bill take one-third of my personal money, it's BS."

They were at the gym in Catskill, and Rooney attempted to defend Cayton. But it led only to a screaming match between D'Amato's disciples. "Let's just be friends," Tyson said finally. "You be the trainer."

If only it were that simple. Already, Tyson wasn't merely a fighter but among the most highly paid stars—trailing only Bill Cosby and Oprah Winfrey in that most American business of all, television. Rooney, on the other hand, was just an ex-fighter, never quite recovered from his own televised loss, a brutal knockout at the hands of Alexis Arguello in Atlantic City. The media tended to glorify him, as he seemed to have stepped out of a Schulberg script faithfully mouthing Cusisms. He was a good friend, too, drawing the highest praise from people like Brian Hamill. But he gambled, drank, and did stupid things when he drank, like getting arrested for smacking his estranged wife's boyfriend. What's more, Rooney's 10 percent cut from Tyson's purses was yet another source of Ruth Roper's ire. The real problem, however, was respect. A trainer needs his fighter's respect to do the job. But Rooney had gotten the job only because he would make compromises Atlas would not. Now those compromises were coming back to haunt him. With the biggest fight in the world now on the books, Rooney's fighter had gone AWOL for a week. And when his fighter finally did show up, just days before the Marley interview, he was 237 pounds, a listless ball of self-pity.

THE WORLD'S SINGLE GREATEST LIAR IS A FIGHTER IN TRAINING.
Basically, every interview is a variation of the following:

How's camp?

Best I ever had.

And that busted-up knuckle?

Great. Like new.

What are you walking around at?

Easiest weight cut ever.

Prediction?

You know I don't make predictions, but I can't see this going the
distance. I never felt this strong.

The bigger the fight, the more the fighter is obliged to lie, as the vocation itself requires the maintenance of a profound falsehood, the illu-
sion of invulnerability. Still, it's more difficult to be scary when word gets
out that your wife was slapping you around over the condoms, that your
mother-in-law is running you around like a flunky, that you're feuding
with your manager and yelling at your trainer. The aggravation had gotten so intense that Tyson began talking about retiring and moving to
Monaco. He'd even inquired about the tax implications.

It didn't help that the *Daily News* finally exposed Givens during that
first week of camp. Not only had she never attended Harvard Medical
School (as the latest dupe, *Essence* magazine, reported in yet another
cover story that month), but her publicist came up with the wonderfully
curious statement that her pregnancy was "not official yet." Echoing Ruth
and Robin's displeasure, Tyson had also come to see the media as agents
of his persecution.

On May 19, after a lackluster six-round sparring session, his last in

Catskill before heading to Atlantic City, Tyson stormed off to the dressing room. "I'm not talking to anyone," he said. "I'm not doing anything."

Some minutes later, though, Rooney waved in Tim Layden of the Albany *Times Union*. Tyson, sitting naked on a folding chair, was at once livid and, as Layden would recall, "choking back tears."

"Everything in my life was too good to be true, wasn't it?" he squeaked. "Now my life is so screwed up. . . . Everybody's pulling at me, this way and that way. It's all manipulative bullshit. They all want something from me; they're all making their living off me."

For all the pathos and self-absorption, at least Tyson wasn't lying to himself. "It's pretty sad when I have to go to Don King to help me explain things," he said. As for his uninspired sparring, Tyson conceded, "I'm going through the motions."

That wasn't what you wanted to hear from a fighter five weeks out from a night that was supposed to define an era in the sport. But it wasn't about to suddenly get better, either. Two days later, Oliver McCall, a journeyman heavyweight in King's employ, put Tyson on his ass.

Steve Lott tending to Tyson during a photo shoot

"He just went with the punch and rolled over on his back," said the ever-admiring Steve Lott. "I thought I was watching Bruce Lee."

Lott would just as easily have sworn that Tyson crapped crushed fruit. Still, being the champ's most dedicated acolyte, not to mention his former roommate, offered little protection when it came to the women in Tyson's life. Apparently, a reporter from *People* had prevailed upon Rooney—unaware of Roper's *Life* embargo—to ask Ruth why she couldn't have access to Tyson. Mother and daughter then took turns screaming at Rooney. But they couldn't fire him, as Tyson *did* need a trainer with the fight just weeks away. So they called Lott, the weak link, and fired him. Robin was particularly vicious, Lott recalled in Illingworth's 1991 Tyson biography: "She got me on the phone and accused me of wanting to destroy her career, called me a motherfucker and a cocksucker, and said that Mike would punch me in the face."

It turned out to be a short-lived firing. Not only was Lott paid by Big Fights—and therefore could be fired only by Cayton—but his jack-of-all-trades service and talent for mollifying Tyson in particularly stressful times were especially needed now. Cayton explained as much to Roper during an attempted peacemaking dinner and, per Katz in the *Daily News*, "came away convinced they are on the same team."

Just hours after Katz's column hit the stands, though, Tyson, Roper, Robin, and their lawyer, Michael Winston, abruptly walked off the set of a Diet Pepsi shoot where more than a hundred actors, extras, production personnel, and soft drink executives had been waiting around all morning. The deal—an easy $1 million—had been another of Cayton's babies. Diet Pepsi had also committed in excess of $3 million to advertising and ring signage for the Spinks fight. But now someone asked Tyson if he was coming back.

"Maybe," he said.

By the time Tyson was ready to return, Cayton had lowered his commission from a third to 25 percent.

Winston asked Rooney to fetch Tyson.

"I ain't gonna get him," said the trainer. "You get him."

"Take it easy, Kevin," said Cayton.

Tyson hugging Edwin Rosario

"I'm tired of this," said Rooney. "If he loses this fight, then there ain't gonna be no more commercials."

If he loses?

THERE'S A PHOTOGRAPH OF TYSON AND HIS STABLEMATE, EDWIN "Chapo" Rosario, at Johnny Tocco's gym in Las Vegas just days before the Berbick fight: each of them wearing only a white towel, Tyson grabbing Rosario in a kind of playful bear hug. I defy you to find a photograph in which Tyson looks happier. It's not just that he loves fighters but also that he empathizes with them, particularly fighters like Rosario, equal parts ferocity and tragedy.

Rosario died young, as Tyson always supposed he himself would. The immediate cause, pulmonary edema—fluid in the lungs—was likely brought on by drugs and booze, though the beatings he took across his career surely didn't help. Tyson was there the night Rosario lost by split decision to Hector Camacho at the Garden and still swears Chapo won. The following year, as the undisputed heavyweight champion, Tyson—who once refused a hooker's request for his Rosario T-shirt—volunteered to carry Rosario's spit bucket as he marched in to face the great Julio César Chávez. Rosario lost that night, his eye pounded shut. But now, seven months later—June 2, 1988—Tyson interrupted the most tumultuous camp of his life, leaving Atlantic City to attend Rosario's comeback fight at the Garden.

At ringside, Tyson and Torres exchanged warm greetings. Torres had recently resigned (encouraged by Governor Mario Cuomo, who was incensed that his commissioner had disregarded several warnings and gone to Tokyo for the Tubbs fight) to write an authorized Tyson biography for a reported $350,000—seven times his salary as chairman of the athletic commission.

Moments later in the dressing room, Steve Lott, who was working Rosario's corner, introduced Torres to the man who'd been shadowing Tyson. It was Michael Winston, Roper's lawyer. Torres soon returned to his seat, but Tyson did not. Rather, he left abruptly after making a pay-phone call, telling Rosario's trainer he had an emergency.

After the fight, which saw Rosario knock out a criminally overmatched opponent, Lott went to his Midtown apartment. There was a new message on his answering machine: "Steve, I had a problem. I'm in the hospital. Mike was kind enough to come over. I'm sorry for keeping him overnight. I'll make sure he's in Atlantic City in time for training tomorrow. I just wanted to make sure you knew where he was."

Lott was struck by the tone of the message, not merely that Robin had deigned to call him but her conspicuously good manners and her sudden care not to interfere with her husband's training routine. By the time Lott received it, however, she was likely asleep. Robin had been given an injection, after which she remembered Tyson holding her hand, leaning over the bed, and smoothing her hair. "Don't be afraid," he said. "I love you. Don't be afraid."

Months later, a Park Avenue gynecologist would attest that Robin Givens suffered "a spontaneous miscarriage" on June 3, "in the second month of her pregnancy." I'm not exactly how sure one should interpret the meaning of *second month*—medically or legally—but the understanding Givens intended to advance was that she hadn't been pregnant before the spring. Of course, that was markedly different from the understanding she'd previously advanced.

Tyson took the news hard. As he returned to Atlantic City, an already troubled training camp went fully dark. Grinker photographed him dutifully pushing a wheelchair, bearing Robin, on the boardwalk as his mother-in-law, cradling a little Yorkie in her arms, looks on. Back in the gym, Tyson was so distraught Rooney had to cancel sparring.

"We lost the baby," Tyson told Torres.

Then the bell rang anew. Tyson returned to the heavy bag as Torres studied him. Torres wasn't alone among Tyson's friends in wondering why Robin's belly never seemed to swell, but he might've been the only one to ask her, point blank, if she was pregnant.

"Of course I am," she shot back.

That was early April in Bernardsville.

Now Torres was struck by the savagery with which Tyson attacked the bag. For whatever reason, it recalled in Torres another confession.

"I like to see them run," Tyson said of his days as a mugger. "I like to see them beg."

"Please don't shoot," they said: "I'll do anything you say." But Tyson shot anyway. "I'd shoot real close to them, skin them or something," he said.

And then?

"Make them take off their pants and then go run in the streets."

39

On June 13, exactly two weeks before the fight, Wally Matthews received a call from Roper's assistant, Olga Rosario. There was more to the story of America's favorite fighter than anyone knew, she said, and it included spousal abuse and booze. Matthews was intrigued but told her he'd need a firsthand witness on the record, just for starters. Rosario said she'd be in touch. As he hung up, Matthews wondered: Why him?

"Because they thought I was anti-Cayton," he tells me now. "And I was."

Wally was "anti" a lot of things, most of them having to do with a notion of unearned privilege: rich kids, Reagan Republicans, TV "foofs," as we called them, spoiled ballplayers, and soft fighters. The boxing beat, combined with his own natural inclinations, made Wally a natural New York columnist. He was a good, swift writer, easily pissed off, and a bloodhound for hypocrisy. Of course, sportswriting was flush with its own misdirected ethics, starting with that inevitable confusion between victory and virtue. It's a dicey proposition: assessing an athlete's courage or character while typing from the press box, still burping up the pre-game meal or between wooden spoonfuls of ice cream. But covering a fight was very much like writing a column: One way or another, you found yourself grading the fighters' manhoods. The difference between Wally and most of us was in having some basis for comparison.

In the second week of February 1977, while training for the New York Golden Gloves at the Izzy Zerling Youth Recreation Center, 1720 Church Avenue, Flatbush, Brooklyn, his jaw was broken by an eventual pro named Gerald Banks. It was a left hook, and while Matthews could feel the various displacements within his mouth, it didn't really hurt. Not until he saw the puzzled expression on Banks's face did he know something was wrong.

As the doctor who wired his mouth shut proudly proclaimed, "There's no punch in the world that could dislodge this," Wally took it as literal permission to continue his quest into the Gloves' next round at the Felt Forum. "I knocked out my first two opponents," he says, "and I'm thinking there's no way I'm not winning this title."

That he was allowed to compete after sipping his meals for days, his wired jaw camouflaged by a doctored mouthpiece, identifies something at the core of boxing: not merely the psychology of the fighter but the institutional unwillingness of those around him to police the fighter's young ego. Matthews was knocked out at 1:29 of the second round by Roberto Morales of the Police Athletic League.

The experience afforded him something most of us lacked—an intimate education in boxing. But the story initiated with a call Matthews got from Roper's deputy would mark a point of no return in the story of Tyson. It would never again be about *just* boxing.

Olga Rosario called back with the number of a hotel in Madeira, Portugal, where Robin's sister, Stephanie, a tennis pro, was on tour. "Nobody knows how abusive Michael is," Stephanie told him, attributing the miscarriage to the stress brought on by her brother-in-law. Case in point, she told Matthews, was his heavy drinking on the set of Oprah's TV movie: "He started breaking the lights, using foul language, throwing things. They had to stop filming. Robin had to leave the set to calm him down."

On another occasion, she said, "He hit Robin in the head with a closed fist. He knows how to hit her, and where to hit her, without causing any real damage. We had adjoining bedrooms and I was scared so I made Robin come into my room and closed both doors. I put the latch on and the deadbolt. He just kicked the two doors in. . . . He's like a bomb. He can just explode. . . .

"My mother has dropped everything to help him, but it's no use."

The following day, Ruth Roper serendipitously dropped her objections to being interviewed and invited Matthews to her Madison Avenue office. Winston the lawyer was there and prohibited any tape recording, though Wally already had a backup device running in his coat pocket. Roper's primary concern wasn't domestic violence, however; it was concern for her son-in-law. "Michael's never really had a family," she said, "and he loves it now. He calls me 'Mom.'"

Roper merely wanted to clear up a few things. "I just feel Michael could have done more to stop Bill," she said. "He could have insisted that he stop talking to the press about his family." As for the idea that King was working through her to gain control of Tyson—"that's an insult to me, and the family," she said. "It's all being done by Bill to create a smokescreen to obscure the real issues."

Money, she meant. Matthews recalls making a mental note: *She thinks she's smarter than King.*

At some point during the interview, Robin entered, feigning surprise. "Drumming her fingertips on my shoulder as she walks in behind me," says Matthews. "The whole thing was a flirtation: *Oh, I didn't know the* press *was here.*"

Matthews asked about Stephanie's allegation of physical abuse. "I can understand Stephanie's position," she told him, echoing a line Matthews had by now already heard from Olga Rosario, Stephanie, and Ruth. "But I really feel Michael has not been socialized."

There are well-established conventions to stories as hush-hush as these, first being an expectation of exclusivity; second, one's natural trepidation at confronting someone like Tyson, about to make his debut as a full-on villain. Matthews began writing late Friday afternoon for the Sunday edition. It was Torres, despite all the pastings Wally had given him in print, who convinced Tyson to speak to him for the piece. Before he could, though, Robin Givens suddenly materialized on WNBC's *Live at Five.*

Cayton had hired private detectives to follow her mother, she charged, and offered an unnamed party $50,000 to aid in the dissolution of her marriage. "He said he'd stop at nothing less than our getting a divorce," she said. "It's like something out of *Dynasty*."

Late that night, Matthews finally got Tyson. "Well, you know, this is my wife. We have arguments," he said. "I would never bruise or beat up my wife. I never hurt my wife."

Though clearly seething, Tyson remained remarkably composed. "You can't say bad things about a person and call them an asshole, and then say that you love them," he said. "What they're saying, basically, is that I'm useless."

For Matthews, who'd been on the beat since the days of "Cus and the Kid," it was the last civil conversation he'd have with Tyson for a quarter of a century. But it ended on a note of gratitude. "You've opened my eyes to a lot of things," said Tyson.

THE EPIPHANY WAS FLEETING, OF COURSE. BY SUNDAY, TYSON WAS holed up with his wife in Bernardsville and telling the *Post*: "I'm married to Robin. Fuck everyone else." Especially Cayton, whom he, too, now held responsible for the miscarriage. "I blame Bill for that," said Tyson.

Robin, for her part, weighed in with another *Dynasty* reference, while Ruth, referring to Cayton's supposed army of dirty tricksters and private eyes, said, "People are trying very hard to intimidate me. I really have fears for my life."

On Monday, now just a week before the fight, King told his man Marley it was indeed Cayton who'd approached Father Clements: "Cayton went to the man of the Bible and the cloth and tried to bribe him. He told Father Clements he and Mike could be instrumental in building him a new church. He said he wanted to destroy their marriage at all costs and wanted the priest to help him. He also wanted Father Clements to testify against me."

Perhaps Cayton did call Clements and didn't realize Jacobs's old pal was a double agent. Then again, as a man of God, who could really blame the priest? It was King himself who that very day reduced everything swirling around Tyson into one tidy theological construct, calling Cayton "Satan in disguise."

In other news, Tyson actually sparred that day, for the first time in more than a week. While Rooney had been worried about a small cut over Tyson's left eye, he found himself more vexed with King, whom he now banished from workouts for the rest of camp.

By week's end, Winston had sent a letter on Tyson's behalf to Cayton: "Starting now, you are to take no action on my behalf." Cayton was already lawyered up, though, having hired America's preeminent litigator, Thomas Puccio, lead prosecutor in the feds' famous ABSCAM sting, who more recently had won an acquittal for socialite Claus von Bülow on charges that he poisoned his socialite wife, Sunny.

There may have been, in the long and sordid history of boxing, a more perfidious lead-up to a big fight. But never before—or since, for that matter—had the treacheries been so blatant, been made so public, and been so deeply rooted in the personal life of one fighter. For all the mournful blather wishing for *just boxing*, it was the treasons themselves that made Tyson–Spinks the most hotly anticipated fight since Ali–Frazier I. The difference was Ali–Frazier had been an almost even-money proposition. The odds for Tyson–Spinks, while narrowing, had opened with Tyson a prohibitive 5–1 favorite. Still, people couldn't get enough. The shit in the champion's life had become addictive, a global jones nourished each morning amid the acrid scent of newspaper ink. It's not difficult to imagine the week in Tyson's life as a B movie, complete with spinning headlines:

IRON MIKE'S FIGHTING MAD

CHARGE TYSON KO'D WIFE

MOM-IN-LAW SAYS SHE FEARS FOR LIFE

KING: CAYTON SOUGHT TO BRIBE PRIEST

RIVAL KING SAYS CAYTON IS A "SATAN IN DISGUISE"

TYSON STAR (VICTIM?) OF A REAL SOAP OPERA

Just as the Roaring Twenties are said to have begun with Willard–Dempsey in 1919, so can one argue that the nineties—christened "the Tabloid Decade"—began in 1988 with Tyson–Spinks. The coin of the realm in Tabloid America was celebrity, and it's not mere coincidence that the fight's guest list reads like a Cindy Adams fever dream: Frank Sinatra, Elizabeth Taylor, Oprah Winfrey, Don Johnson, Barbra Streisand, Malcolm Forbes, Jack Nicholson, Warren Beatty, Madonna and Sean Penn, George Steinbrenner, Jackie Mason, Jesse Jackson, Sylvester Stallone, Magic Johnson, Michael Jordan, and, of course, Ali. A Trump Plaza press release, listing no fewer than fifty boldface names—concludes with this rhetorical gem: "Which one of the aforementioned celebrities gets the best seat?"

Why, the future president himself, of course, whose rumored dalliance with the champion's bride, fictitious or not, was already making its way through the press room.

THE LEAST FAMOUS PERSON IN THIS ENTIRE MIX WAS THE CHAL-lenger, Michael Spinks. Tyson regarded him as just another guy. All he had to offer on the subject was a variation of what he'd told *Sports Illustrated* before the Tubbs fight: "I'll break Spinks. None of them have a chance, I'll break them all. When I fight someone, I want to break his will. I want to take his manhood. I want to rip out his heart and show it to him."

The jailhouse talk had helped make Tyson the attraction he was. But it also marked him as a bully, and Spinks, an Olympic gold medalist back in '76, had made a career of beating both bullies and long odds. He'd made it out of Saint Louis's Pruitt–Igoe projects, a thirty-three-building complex that could well have been an inspiration for the urban planners who condemned Tyson's old neighborhood—speaking of which,

Spinks had beaten Brownsville's own Eddie Mustafa Muhammad to win
his first light heavyweight title. Then, just two months after his wife died in
a car wreck, Spinks fought Dwight Qawi, a mini Tyson in style and build,
for the WBC strap. In the dressing room, Spinks's two-year-old daughter
asked if Mommy would be attending. Spinks gathered himself and won a
unanimous fifteen-round decision to become undisputed at 175 pounds.
Later, he made boxing history by beating Larry Holmes in another
fifteen-rounder, ending Holmes's bid to beat Rocky Marciano's record of
49-0 and becoming the first light heavyweight to win the heavyweight
title. In the years since, Spinks had beaten Holmes in a rematch and
knocked out Gerry Cooney. He was awkward, undefeated, and conspicuously modest, with a curiously potent right hand, the "Spinks jinx." At
31-0, just a couple weeks shy of his thirty-second birthday, Spinks was
very much unlike Tyson—a grown man both physically and emotionally.

"I've never run from anybody," he deadpanned at the final pre-
conference.

Where Tyson had the hotheaded and underobeyed Rooney in his

Tyson on his predawn run, Atlantic City, June 1988

corner, Spinks had boxing's reigning sage. The great Eddie Futch, now seventy-six, had "a big book" on Tyson's tendencies and vulnerabilities. "He'll give him angles," said Futch. "Nobody has more angles than Michael Spinks."

Futch wasn't bragging, any more than he'd bragged in 1973 when he said that his little-known fighter, Ken Norton, could beat the great Ali. Futch pointed out that Spinks, unlike Tyson, had a good, productive training camp, sparring 170 rounds. No miscarriage to deal with, and no competing claims on his body and soul. It didn't take a genius to understand why the odds on Tyson had dropped to 3–1.

TYSON'S SUITE IN THE OCEAN CLUB HAD BEEN DECORATED WITH A vast array of sepia-toned photographs featuring the all-time greats. Among them was Stanley Ketchel, who moved John Lardner to write his famous lede: "Stanley Ketchel was 24 years old when he was fatally shot in the back by the common-law husband of the lady who was cooking his breakfast."

One could easily imagine such a fate, or worse, for Tyson. Never had a kid been so explicitly warned about the mistakes that fighters make, and yet none seemed so doomed to repeat every damn one. Then again, none of Tyson's predecessors ever had the dysfunctional pieces of his interior life so ruthlessly exposed and examined on the eve of his biggest moment.

Consider him just several weeks prior: running in the 4:00 a.m. darkness along the boardwalk of a dilapidated carnival city.

"I can hear his voice," he would tell the reporters.

It was Cus's voice, and they were three reporters granted an audience after his morning workout. He didn't know them too well, but the oldest one, Jerry Izenberg of the Newark *Star-Ledger*, knew D'Amato from the old days.

"I didn't like fighting," said Tyson. "But I loved Cus."

He was choking back tears. Then he began to cry.

"I wanted to make him happy."

It's said that a happy warrior is a dangerous one. But this one was joyless.

"There's nobody to trust."

Izenberg's lede will read: "The heavyweight champion of the world cried yesterday."

Soon there was nothing left to punctuate the weeping, just a wall of sobs.

Tyson put his arms around Izenberg, who recalled thinking that his children were all older than Tyson. "Then he pulled his head back and finished the interview, almost as though nothing had happened," wrote Izenberg. "My shirt was soaked. I had to go back upstairs to my room to change it."

That was June 2, just hours before he learned of the miscarriage, before his sister-in-law alleged him to be a brute, before the spinning headlines. It should come as no surprise that Tyson's speech turned darker. But for all the talk about taking Spinks's manhood and his wanting to rip reporters' heads from their necks, Tyson's shadow self remained: confused, vulnerable, alone, and not that difficult to find. One can argue, quite reasonably, that he faced Spinks in the midst of a breakdown.

From Pete Hamill's notes at the weigh-in, the day before the fight:

In his last workouts T looked ragged, without fire.

T is a kid, his emotions close to the surface.

I remember talking to him more than a year ago, he was angry with a model who was charging limousines to his account after they had broken up. "Why does someone do that? I mean, she's got money. Why?"

When I was 21, I could swing from elation to depression within hours, depending on the progress of my love life.

I've known fighters who lost fights in order to know who their friends were.

I've known wives who wanted their husbands to lose to bring them down to earth.

The rage of the untalented against the talented is never to be underestimated.

Spinks lost wife in a car accident and two months later defended his championship brilliantly. Ali changed wives right before the Thrilla in Manila. Ray Robinson fought with grace and power and discipline no matter how complicated his domestic relations.

Others have been wrecked . . .

40

Fight day begins with Donald Trump in the ring at the convention center. He's congratulating himself on *Good Morning America*. "It turned out to be much bigger than I even thought," he says. "This has turned out to be gigantic."

Not to be outdone in her own *GMA* segment, Robin—who predicts her husband's winning by knockout in the fourth—calls Tyson-Spinks "the biggest sporting event of the century." When asked about the salacious coverage, and the depiction of her as a gold digger, she tells the host, Spencer Christian, "A lot of it's hype. I think it helps sell tickets and unfortunately, it's at our expense. . . . People don't realize we're a family—something that Michael never had before, something that I *need*."

On the bright side, however: "It has made us so much closer."

So close that years later she will write: "The day of the Spinks fight we must have made love for hours."

I'm not doubting her here, as Tyson never observed the prohibition against prefight sex. But it must've been an especially busy day for the champ, as what stands out in his recollection is finally meeting his long-time idol.

Roberto Durán is now managed by Luis DeCubas, whom Tyson grabbed by the neck after the Jose Ribalta fight. DeCubas has been asking around on Durán's behalf for tickets, not an easy request for a fighter, even a great one, then regarded as past his prime.

"Ask King," Butch Lewis tells him.

"I ain't giving that motherfucker tickets," says King, who blames Durán for ratting him out to the IRS.

Finally, DeCubas runs into Steve Lott. No problem, Lott tells him, just bring Durán to their apartment at the Ocean Club.

DeCubas doesn't want to bother Tyson the day of the fight. "No," says Lott, "*please* bring him."

They arrive in the penthouse suite sometime between noon and 2:00 p.m., as DeCubas recalls. Tyson, just emerged from a nap, becomes giddy at the sight of his idol, dancing around the room in only a Diet Pepsi towel. "I can't believe this is happening," he says. "I feel like a girl who has fallen in love for the first time."

Soon Tyson's inner fight nerd is asking, "How could Alexis Arguello

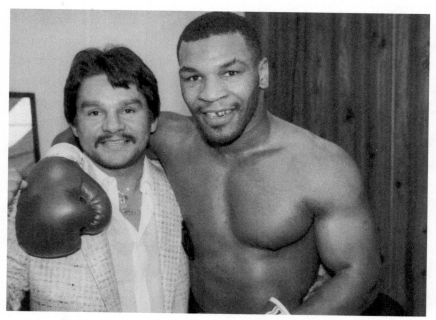

Durán visits Tyson in his dressing room before the Spinks fight.

say he could beat you, when he lost to Nato Marcel and you beat Nato Marcel?"

In fact, Durán knocked out Ernesto "Nato" Marcel in ten rounds back in 1970.

"I would've knocked him out in the first round," explains Durán, "but I was sick that day. I had a herpes in my ass."

Tyson apologizes for having only second-row seats, then asks if Durán would be kind enough to stop by the dressing room before the fight.

Ringside tickets have a face value of $1,500, a record, of course, though Trump himself had to be talked out of charging $2,000—apropos for a fight that one *Washington Post* columnist has deemed "a monument to a decade of greed." Still, there's no one who can appreciate the magnitude of this cultural moment more than the most ferocious and risk-taking entrepreneurs of the day.

Brian "Glaze" Gibbs, now between murder raps, has commissioned a stretch Mercedes to take him and members of his M & M crew from the Cypress houses to Atlantic City. Fans at the Trump Plaza entrance cheer as the men emerge from the limo, mistaking the M & M boys in their white silk suits for the group New Edition. Just ahead of them is Jesse Jackson and his coterie of Secret Service agents.

Glaze, wearing $1,500 gators, has bet ten times that much on Tyson. That's not a daring proposition, but he's got to represent. After all, he's sitting in front of Michael Jordan and the reigning Super Bowl MVP, Doug Williams. Before the year is out, he'll be arrested in the Carolinas and start talking to the feds. But the particular glories of this night will remain with him always.

"It was so beautiful," he'll recall wistfully. "Everybody was all about the money. You could smell it."

The fight will set many records, all of them measured in dollars: a $12.3 million live gate (eclipsing the previous record, $6.8 million for Hagler–Leonard the year before), a Trump Plaza pit drop of $11.5 million, $27 million from closed-circuit, and an unexpected $21 million windfall from six hundred thousand cable subscribers willing to shell out $35 a pop for the pay-per-view. "Closed-circuit is the way of the past," declares Shelly Finkel at the final presser, promising "the largest-grossing, largest-netting fight in history."

Flush with success, Finkel has gotten a call from Ruth Roper. "I made a mistake," she confides. "I let the fox in the henhouse. And now I can't get him out."

King, she means.

King is everywhere, milling about at the prefight VIP party, for which 1,200 pounds of lobster tails have been delivered, along with the endless jeroboams of Dom Pérignon. King is with Herschel Walker, then getting a hug for old time's sake from Norman Mailer, and next posing for a photographer with Trump, Jackson, and Malcolm Forbes, who's holding a crumpled dollar bill, a gift from Jackson, who wanted to say the capitalist shaman owed him money.

Even Cayton makes an appearance. Trump puts his arm around him. "Bill," he says, "I'm with you one hundred percent."

Trump, whom Cayton listed as a reference on the application for his manager's license, is about to fuck him, of course. In a matter of days, he'll volunteer his services as Tyson's "adviser." He'll mention how Tyson "respects" him, and that his end of their arrangement will all go to charity—AIDS, MS, homelessness.

NOW IN TYSON'S DRESSING ROOM, DURÁN LOOKS LIKE A GUNMAN from De Palma's *Scarface*: gold necklaces, a collared shirt unbuttoned to the solar plexus, a face grown wide from long nights at Victor's Café on West Fifty-Second Street. Durán's getting by on journeymen now. It's been months since he last fought. But Tyson, who remembers him all but ruining Davey Moore at the Garden back in '83, remains an eager audience, soliciting his advice.

"Be careful," says Durán in Spanish. "Take your time. Come in behind the jab. He's very tricky. Watch out for that right uppercut."

This doesn't sound correct to DeCubas, who, while translating, thinks Tyson might be insulted by such cautious advice.

"Durán says, 'Jump on him right away,'" DeCubas tells Tyson.

ATLANTIC CITY CAME OF AGE WITH THE MISS AMERICA PAGEANT, and a blind girl who dove on the back of a horse, a forty-foot drop into a twelve-foot-deep tub of water. But now the city has, in the words of one correspondent, the look of "decayed teeth." Its pawnshops bear signs promising CASH FOR FOOD STAMPS, GOLD. Nevertheless, scalpers are getting up to five grand for a ringside seat. By the West Hall entrance, Pete Hamill counts a line of thirty-seven limousines, along with a tour bus and an ambulance. Inside, there's a row of eight Japanese guys in the third row who could pass for yakuza.

Mailer, now sixty-five, is there for *Spin* magazine and recalls, in this very building, with its dismal armory-style architecture, the 1964 Democratic Convention and the giant photographs of the nominee, Lyndon Johnson, that hung behind the podium. A convention is, like Miss America, just another pageant, though, and so is a title fight. Instead of red, white, and blue bunting, this one's festooned with Diet Pepsi logos. It's gloriously packed—official attendance 21,785.

The celebrity introductions—featuring such boxing luminaries as Carl Icahn and Laurence Tisch—are endless. Jesse Jackson is introduced as "a friend of Donald Trump." All that makes this stretch of the evening tolerable are the boos. Yankees owner George Steinbrenner gets the very worst of it. Sean Penn, scowling throughout in his Izod polo, is also roundly jeered; his wife, Madonna, less so. Detroit Pistons center Bill Laimbeer is lustily booed—as is the ever-undeterred Don King.

"When I see Don," Larry Holmes tells Newfield, "I see the devil."

Meanwhile, a process server locates Bill Cayton in his seat and serves him with a summons and notice of claim. Tyson is suing him. Winston will file the complaint first thing in the morning, the crux of the case being paragraph 28 of Tyson's subsequent affidavit: "If I had known that Jim Jacobs was dying, and that Cayton would become my manager when Jim Jacobs died, I would not have signed."

Cayton manages an awkward smile for the TV camera.

Now there's been a delay. "Moments ago, in the dressing rooms, a major controversy erupted," booms Jim Lampley, as the broadcast cuts to a man in a white tux, no shirt, met by a phalanx of cops outside Tyson's quarters. "You're looking at a taped shot of Butch Lewis, the manager of Michael Spinks, who went wild after he discovered that Mike Tyson had had his hands taped and, apparently, had the gloves put on without a representative of Spinks' camp being in Tyson's dressing room."

In fact, Butch's brother, Nelson, had witnessed the taping and left without any objection. But it's Butch who's returned, complaining about a small "bubble" of tape near the wrist on Tyson's right glove. He demands that Rooney take it off and start over again.

"Fuck you," Rooney tells him.

"I'm God," says Tyson. "I don't have to do nothing."

"Well, you're gonna do this, God," says Butch.

Soon the cameras are following Larry Hazzard, chairman of the New Jersey commission, on his way to the dressing rooms. Hazzard understands Butch is trying to poke the bear, hoping Tyson will unravel. He can also see what the now-enraged Tyson has done to the wall.

"Put his hand right through the fuckin' Sheetrock," says Hazzard.

Still Butch won't let it go; he's holding the entire show hostage.

"Go fly a fucking kite," Hazzard tells him.

Finally, Hazzard gets Eddie Futch from Spinks's dressing room. "It's fine," says Futch, who by now has other things to worry about.

Futch has designed a game plan very much like the one Spinks carried out so well against Qawi. He's studied Tyson and believes he becomes a lesser fighter after six rounds. Spinks is to stick and move, give Tyson angles until the latter part of the fight, the so-called deep waters. Then he can drown Tyson. But Butch is in Spinks's ear, telling him otherwise. "You go right out and crack that motherfucker," he says. "You get your respect."

Futch may be as good as any trainer who ever lived. But it's Butch who convinced Spinks to leave his night shift at the Monsanto plant. It's Butch who promised he'd be a champion and Butch who got him $13.5 million.

It's Butch he believes in.

Question is, does Spinks believe in himself?

The broadcasters are saying that Spinks is playing games, delaying his ring entrance. But a visitor to his dressing room—the Hall of Fame trainer Emanuel Steward—notices something else. "They couldn't even get him to come out," Steward will recall. "He was so scared."

Recall D'Amato on the bleachers in Scranton, warning that big white kid about Tyson: *He's a killer, a monster. You've got to be very careful.* Now the fear he sought to project has finally hit its ultimate mark, seven years and one month to the day later—taking root in the imagination of Michael Spinks.

In the meantime, more introductions.

At 11:04 p.m.—per the meticulous notes Hamill is keeping on a full-page yellow pad—Jeffrey Osborne sings the national anthem.

The fans have been chanting: "Al-ee, Al-ee, Al-ee." At 11:07, their wish is granted. Ali's wearing a blue suit with a red tie, big glasses. Don King is holding his hand.

At 11:17, after a filibuster that includes the theme from *Rocky*, Robin Givens is introduced. Her dress is a vibrant, jeweled red and matches her lips. The effect is very *Dynasty*. She's booed loudly.

Finally, at 11:20, Spinks begins his ring walk, wearing a plain white Everlast robe with black trim. It's a less-than-exuberant procession for which he has selected the single corniest tune in American popular music, Kenny Loggins's "This Is It."

Wally Matthews is almost close enough to touch him as he makes his way up the ring steps.

I'm going to do the best I can, Spinks is telling himself.

Spinks waves to the crowd as if he's sending farewells from the deck of a ship now pulling away from its moorings. *Fucking guy's waving goodbye*, thinks Wally.

At 11:23 the music transitions to something vaguely techno, a deep buzzing. It's metallic, wordless, and foreboding. Tyson's on the march.

With both fighters in the ring, Michael Buffer is obliged to mention just about everyone from the New Jersey commission and the larcenous sanctioning bodies. Then there's Trump. He's orchestrated this so he can be seen with Ali.

"Ali now moved with the deliberate awesome calm of a blind man," notes Mailer, "sobering all those who stared upon him."

Except Trump.

"The man who brought this great event to Atlantic City," intones Buffer.

"Endless intro of Trump," Hamill jots on his pad.

"New Jersey thanks you, Donald Trump."

It was a new twist, thanking a guy who was selling you the fight. But it went with the Battle Royale ad blitz that had aired on TV, the bare-chested combatants, Tyson and Spinks, acknowledging their patron for this precious chance to wreck each other: "Thanks, Mister Trump."

AS HE LEAVES THE RING, ALI WHISPERS, AS BEST HE CAN, INTO Spinks's ear.

"Stick and move," he says.

The bell rings at 11:32 p.m.

Tyson strikes first, a left hook to the top of Spinks's head. He sees the fear in Spinks's eyes.

Spinks fights back, though. He fires a right hand that misses. Then another.

It's the voice of the hustler that Spinks hears, Butch Lewis over Futch, even over Ali.

But it doesn't really matter. Tyson isn't merely meaner and more re-lentless but also quicker and stronger. I'm told of a great-uncle in Poland, a cavalry officer on horseback with only a saber, who had the honor of charging at Panzers. I imagine he must've come to the same realization that Spinks did mere seconds into the fight: *There's not a damn thing I can do.*

About twenty-two seconds in, they clinch.

"Stop punching," says the ref, Frank Cappuccino. As Cappuccino moves in to separate the fighters, Tyson delivers an elbow to Spinks's head.

"Hey, Mike, knock it off, man," says Cappuccino. "Knock it off."

With a minute gone, Tyson leaps in with a massive yet compact left hook that swivels Spinks's head. Then a right to the body caroms off his solar plexus like a rubber-headed mallet. Spinks drops to a knee. It's the first time in his eleven-year pro career that he's been down.

"He had the look," writes Mailer, "of a man who had just been washed overboard in a squall."

Spinks rises, to his everlasting credit, at the count of three and assures Cappuccino he's okay. It's a noble deceit, but we're down to mere ritual now.

Tyson charges again. Spinks still wants to show he's not hurt, that Tyson can't just walk right in with impunity. Spinks cocks his right like an archer, then lets it go, dipping as he does. Tyson flings a left hook simultaneously, negating both punches but spring-loading his torso for what's to come—a counter–right uppercut, a battering ram for which Spinks's cranium is now directly in line. Spinks falls back in a heap. His head bounces on the canvas, settling just outside the ropes. His eyes look up at the lights, perhaps, or the cavernous ceiling, or, likely, nothing at all. At the count of eight, Spinks tries to rise from a crouch.

"He's not gonna make it," says Larry Merchant.

Spinks tumbles, crashing into the ropes. In that moment, he's a child capsizing on his tricycle.

The knockout is recorded at ninety-one seconds of the first round, longer than Trump's intro but still four seconds shorter than Osborne's anthem.

Tyson holds his arms outstretched, palms up, not a gladiator now so much as an emperor.

Rooney embraces him.

King rushes in, grabbing on to all he can hold, embracing them both at first, then seizing on Tyson.

Scores of pickpockets, quick and nimble as roaches, descend upon the press and VIP sections.

The ring is like a cattle car now, packed shoulder to shoulder, swaying dangerously.

"There's a near riot taking place on the apron in front of us," says Lampley.

Someone is tossed from the ring. "We just had a body fly over us here," says "Colonel" Bob Sheridan, calling the international broadcast.

Michael Spinks, a great champion, being counted out

In the midst of the scrum, Tyson finds Spinks, pulls him close, and plants a kiss by his left ear.

Buffer calls for security to clear the ring.

"I can handle chaos," says Tyson. "I've had chaos all my life."

The guy next to Hamill is looking for his wallet.

"Brownsville, all right!" yells the champion, raising a fist. "Brownsville."

On South Street, in Lower Manhattan, the presses begin to roll with a fresh proclamation, the new emperor's title, an edition of the *New York Post* declaring Tyson "the baddest man on the planet."

There's but a single dissenting opinion. Though Evander Holyfield has yet to even fight as a heavyweight, he's been watching intently from the third row. "I'm not going to let a reputation whup me," he says of Tyson. "He's got to prove it to me. Just because he beat someone else doesn't mean he beat me."

"What about Holyfield?" Rooney hollers derisively, grabbing the microphone at the postfight press conference. "There's always a hundred guys. Someone new is gonna come out every day. This is the heavyweight champ of the world! Everyone wants a piece."

Tyson's at the lectern now. King stands behind him, with Finkel hidden behind King. Robin sits to her husband's immediate right. As the session began, she clasped his hand in hers and kissed it, as if a maiden whose honor he'd just defended.

"I wasn't really appreciative of what you guys did to me," says Tyson. "You tried to embarrass me. You tried to embarrass my family. You tried to disgrace us. As far as I know, this might be my last fight."

Robin claps.

"Talk, girlfriend!" King bellows.

"He told me that this was going to happen," says Tyson.

He. D'Amato.

"You attack somebody I love, like my wife or my mother-in-law," he says. "That's the only way you can get to me."

"Here, here!" shouts King.

Tyson hugs Durán as he leaves the stage. Durán's been there the whole time, on the dais at Tyson's request. The story of Durán's giving him the winning strategy has already made the rounds. Just as children now want to be like Tyson, so does Tyson still want to be like Durán.

The reporters keep at it, mopping up, collecting quotes. "Mike Tyson is the hardest-hitting heavyweight there ever was," says Cappuccino, who, at fifty-nine, from Philadelphia, has at least some basis for comparison. "He hits harder than Marciano, Frazier, Foreman, and Jack Dempsey."

The casino is packed: high rollers working the tables. Glaze finds himself in a bathroom stall, humping someone's girlfriend.

"Hey, what you doing with my girl?"

The boyfriend. He won gold at the Olympics. He's on TV, a contender.

Still, what the fuck's he *really* going to do to a guy like Glaze? He's just a fighter.

TYSON AND ROBIN DUCK INTO THE AFTER-PARTY.

"Mike, you motherfucker."

It's his sister. She tells him to get her a diet soda.

"Let's get out of here," Tyson tells Robin. "Shelly gave me a cheesecake."

He's three days shy of his twenty-second birthday. What can he really see in this moment? His sins? The betrayals that await? The guy who'll try to shank him in prison? Or the daughter playing tennis?

Nah. None of that.

The future is a religion he cannot believe in.

There is only now: a girl in a red dress, a cheesecake from Junior's. And the voice. *Devour them both*, it commands. *And live forever.*

The back page of the *New York Post*, June 28, 1988

ACKNOWLEDGMENTS

The many debts I've incurred in writing this book begin with Mike Tyson and his wife, Kiki. Not only is Tyson's the greatest comeback I've ever seen, but also it's difficult to ignore that his improbable second ascent coincides with the years of his and Kiki's marriage. We spoke twice by Zoom—December 14, 2021, and May 10, 2022, when Kiki joined us. The meetings were wrangled by my longtime literary agent, David Vigliano, who, to my great, good fortune, just happened to have represented Tyson and his cowriter, Larry Sloman, for *Undisputed Truth* and *Iron Ambition*, unsparing self-assessments that couldn't have been easy to write.

Vigliano has come through for me before. But I've never leaned on him day in, day out as I did for this book.

The Zoom meetings weren't interviews per se, though I did use Tyson's line about D'Amato's name living through his in the prologue. After two autobiographical works, a podcast, and countless interviews, Tyson's own account is pretty clear. So, although I had no expectation he'd retell his life story again solely for my benefit, we did reach a functional understanding. He let me do my work unencumbered.

Typically, a prospective source would call Kiki and ask if it was okay to speak to me.

It was, she said.

For that alone, I'm grateful.

I'm deeply grateful, too, for Scott Moyers of Penguin Press. This didn't begin as a biographical work. I envisioned a kind of essay, a reported reminiscence not merely about Tyson but also fighters and writers, newspapers and New York. That's not what you have here, as another book revealed itself along the way. I'm still awed and somewhat overwhelmed by how much *story* Tyson generates. But it was Scott who understood what this was, or what it was becoming, long before I did. He is wise, passionate, and had more faith in me than I had in myself. Also at Penguin, many thanks to Helen Rouner.

Calling Mark Ortega a "researcher" seems inadequate. He saw narrative elements I did not, turned me to sources I knew not, and, somewhat miraculously for an old fart like me, made sense of the digital universe.

In addition to Tyson's own books, I'm beholden to his previous biographers: José Torres and Phil Berger, may they each rest in peace; boxing historian Peter Heller; and Monteith Illingworth. Ditto an old friend, the late Jack Newfield. Although I couldn't score an interview with Don King (despite countless attempts), I did make full use of Jack's masterful exposé, *Only in America*.

Here's to the Boss Scribes of New York: Wally Matthews of *Newsday*, Berger of *The New York Times*, the late Mike Marley of the *Post*, Mike Katz and Bob Raissman of the *Daily News*. Katz, who died months before publication, was incessantly profane, occasionally poetic, and impossibly patient with a younger version of myself.

There's not a writer to whom I owe more than my former editor, friend, and mentor, Pete Hamill. Whatever is good in this book is tethered, in one way or another, to him. He was a great, generous teacher, and his memory is always a blessing. His wife, Fukiko Aoki, was kind enough to gift me his old *Amboy Dukes* paperback and send on his "TYSON" file, which included Pete's contemporaneous notes from the days leading up to the Tyson–Spinks fight.

Amy Rosenbloom was invaluable, not merely in requisitioning cases from state and federal court in Manhattan but in helping me understand the voluminous filings.

Barry Weiss, Tim Brown, Jonathan Shapiro (easy work, huh?), Thomas Hauser (a source of prodigious insight and innumerable phone numbers these past few years), Bruce Trampler (Hall of Fame matchmaker and a writer himself), Ed O'Neill, and, again, Wally Matthews were kind enough to pore through different incarnations of the manuscript, offering suggestions and encouragement.

The most prescient notes, however, came from my brilliant and beautiful wife, Jenny Lumet. As my broadcast partner Tim Bradley reminds me, "Yo, you ain't even the best writer in your house."

More donors to the favor bank:

Eileen Murphy, senior editorial producer at ABC News; Mike McQuade, my boss at ESPN; Carl Moretti of Top Rank; Brian Hamill; Flo Anthony; Jeremy Schaap; Joe Tessitore; Bernardo Osuna; Jim Zirolli; Mike Mascaro; Brin-Jonathan Butler; Joe Goossen; Mike Coppinger; Jeffrey Smith; Fred Sternburg; Steve Bunce; Bob Yalen; Russ Anber; Nic Wilson; Holiday Kriegel; Nick Khan; Don Van Natta; Joe Sexton and Beth Flynn; Matt Kramer; Leslie Parke; Casey Seiler of the Albany *Times Union*; Mike Vaccaro and Chris Shaw of the *New York Post*; Tim Smith; Robert Russell; a fighter's fighter, John Scully; the ever-helpful Nadia Hujtyn; the ever-gracious Seth Abraham; the incomparable Rosie Perez; Brian "Glaze" Gibbs and the mutual friend who introduced us, Detective Joe Ponzi, long the chief investigator for the Brooklyn district attorney. Ponzi died April 18, 2022, of cancer, likely brought on by the weeks he spent as a volunteer at Ground Zero. I'll always miss him.

SOURCES

I've tried to be assiduous in the attribution of quotes, especially Tyson's. What isn't cited in the Notes comes from the following interviews. Though a good number were conducted over several days and required follow-up questions, I'm identifying them for convenience only by the date of the first session. I'm also including interviews pertaining to Tyson's life beyond the Spinks fight, as I'm appreciative not merely for the time but the way they helped inform my thinking for this volume.

Brian Hamill: July 27, 2021

Larry Merchant: July 30, 2021

Jim Lampley: August 1, 2021

Freddie Roach: August 2, 2021

Seth Abraham: August 3, 2021

Billy Keane: August 8, 2021

Greg Vicenty: August 8, 2021

Joe Spinelli: August 8, 2021

Carl Moretti: August 10, 2021

Keith Connolly: August 10, 2021

Randy Gordon: August 11, 2021

Charles Farrell: August 16, 2021

Mitch Green: August 18, 2021

Thomas Hauser: August 18, 2021

Kenny Adams: August 18, 2021

Jody Heaps: August 23, 2021

Nadia Hujtyn: August 30, 2021

Bobby Stewart: September 1, 2021

Eric Bischoff: September 1, 2021

Lee Bordick: September 1, 2021

Kilbert Pierce: September 8, 2021

Henry Milligan: September 12, 2021

Jerry Goff: September 12, 2021

John Scully: September 13, 2021

Danny Ferry: September 13, 2021

Leslie Parke: September 14, 2021

Danny Bucci: September 18, 2021

Marty Corwin: September 21, 2021

Peter Kahn: September 23, 2021

Jesus Carlos Esparza: September 24, 2021

Jeremy Schaap: September 26, 2021

Lennox Lewis: September 28, 2021

Warren Thompson: October 3, 2021

Gene Kilroy: October 5, 2021

Frank Warren: October 7, 2021

Buddy Davis: October 10, 2021

Joe Maffia: October 28, 2021

Warren Flagg: November 10, 2021

Marc Ratner: November 16, 2021

Roy Langbord: November 30, 2021

Al Evans: December 1, 2021

Robert Lipsyte: December 1, 2021

Kevin Barry: December 12, 2021

Gordy Keelen: December 18, 2021

Henry Tillman: December 19, 2021

Dave Yonko: December 22, 2021

Mike Marley: December 23, 2021

Ron Katz: December 23, 2021

Eddie Mustafa Muhammad:
December 28, 2021

Jeff Fenech: December 29, 2021

Vinny Pazienza: January 1, 2022

Tommy Brooks: January 2, 2022

Ronnie Shields: January 5, 2022

Brad Goodman: January 11, 2022

Stacey McKinley: January 11, 2022

Peter Parcher: January 14, 2022

Tim Smith: January 25, 2022

Lennie Daniels: January 26, 2022

Paul Levesque: February 2, 2022

Lou DiBella: February 3, 2022

Kimberly Heath: February 7, 2022

Bruce Trampler: February 12, 2022

Jim Thomas: February 13, 2022

Rory Holloway: February 15, 2022

Fred Dennis: May 5, 2022

Herb Cox: May 14, 2022

Tim Witherspoon: May 14, 2022

Buddy McGirt: May 18, 2022

Rick Griffith: May 18, 2022

Luis DeCubas Sr.: May 18, 2022

Shawn Michaels: May 26, 2022

Jimmie Lee Kirkpatrick: May 27, 2022

Nico Ali Walsh: June 20, 2022

Lori Grinker: June 23, 2022

Roy Jones: June 30, 2022

Barbara Trathen: July 1, 2022

Vince Phillips: July 1, 2022

Lloyd Daniels: July 2, 2022

Joe Cortez: July 10, 2022

Nic Wilson: July 22, 2022

David Vigliano: July 23, 2022

David Chesnoff: July 27, 2022

Robert Snype: September 19, 2022

Ronald "Kato" Fields: October 6, 2022

Brin-Jonathan Butler: October 25, 2022

Billy O'Rourke: January 8, 2023

Frank Mincieli: January 19, 2023

Sal Marchiano: March 14, 2023

Bob Gutkowski: April 17, 2023

Pamela Newkirk: April 21, 2023

Arlene Schulman: April 23, 2023

Rosie Perez: June 13, 2023

Brian Gibbs: July 6, 2023

Tyrell Biggs: September 19, 2023

Paul Antonelli: October 28, 2023

Rock Newman: November 10, 2023

Jim Brady: November 11, 2023

Shelly Finkel: November 19, 2023

Wallace Matthews: December 14, 2023

Larry Hazzard: December 28, 2023

Michael Spinks: April 29, 2024

Ed O'Neill: August 22, 2024

NOTES

PROLOGUE

3 **"And did I not?":** Mike Tyson, Zoom call conversation, December 12, 2021.
5 **"Dude," says the awestruck pro:** Nic Wilson, former tennis pro, interviewed July 22, 2022.

1

7 **"When I was born":** Mike Tyson with Larry Sloman, *Undisputed Truth: My Autobiography* (HarperSport, 2014), 13.
7 **"No matter how long":** Sara Harris, *Hellhole: The Shocking Story of the Inmates and Life in the New York City House of Detention for Women* (Tower Books, 1967), 8.
7 **it was not uncommon:** Edith Evans Asbury, "Mrs. Kross Bares Crowding in Jail," *New York Times*, October 25, 1963.
7 **and disproportionately Black:** Mary Perot Nichols, "The Revolving Door on Village Square," *Village Voice*, March 11, 1959.
8 **She was subjected to pitiless:** Harris, *Hellhole*, 14.
8 **"two girls holding":** James A. Wechsler, "Who Sinned?," *New York Post*, March 8, 1965.
8 **"the rats, the isolation":** Jasmine Guy, *Afeni Shakur: Evolution of a Revolutionary* (Atria Books, 2005), 94.
8 **"Homosexuality is bound":** Angela Davis, "Prison Memoirs: The Women's House of Detention," *Village Voice*, October 10, 1974, villagevoice.com/prison-memoirs-the-new-york -womens-house-of-detention.
9 **At 11:15 a.m. on Sunday:** Irving Spiegel, "Women's Prison Closed: Inmates Moved to Rikers," *New York Times*, June 14, 1971.
10 **"I so desperately wanted":** *Mike Tyson: Undisputed Truth*, directed by Spike Lee and Philip Marcus (HBO Films, 2013), Amazon Prime.
10 **Curlee's firstborn son:** Gary Schwab, "Solving the Puzzle: Jimmie Lee Kirkpatrick and De Kirkpatrick Learn How Their Families Are Linked in Mecklenburg County's Slave Era" (second of three parts), *Charlotte Observer*, February 19, 2014.
10 **born March 25, 1924:** Curlee Kirkpatrick Jr. draft card, "U.S., World War II Draft Cards for Young Men, 1940–1947," ancestry.com.
11 **Another account had her:** Michael Katz, "Rodney Tyson's Other Way Out," *New York Daily News*, November 23, 1986.
12 **She'd dose little Mike:** Tyson, *Undisputed Truth*, 419.

12 **"Screw them," said his sister:** Gary Schwab and David Scott, "Breaking Through," *Charlotte Observer*, February 24, 2013.

12 **"There was no going after":** Schwab and Scott, "Breaking Through."

12 **"the greatest I have":** Gary Schwab, "A Binding Truth" (first of three parts), *Charlotte Observer*, February 16, 2014.

13 **As a sophomore:** Kent Hannon, "The Pony Backs," *The Purdue Exponent* (West Lafayette, IN), April 19, 1968, historicalnewspapers.lib.purdue.edu.

13 **Then there was the commune:** Schwab and Scott, "Breaking Through."

2

15 **"Everyone thinks Alexander":** Mike Tyson, "Mike Tyson Explores Kierkegaard," *Wall Street Journal*, December 13, 2013, wsj.com/articles/mike-tyson-explores-kierkegaard -1386976477.

16 **"He and my mother":** Mike Tyson with Larry Sloman, *Undisputed Truth: My Autobiography* (HarperSport, 2014), 13.

17 **Perhaps, at five seven:** José Torres, *Fire and Fear: The Inside Story of Mike Tyson* (Warner Books, 1989), 18.

17 **"Did you ever":** *Piers Morgan Live*, directed by John Duber, aired November 27, 2013, on CNN, transcripts.cnn.com/show/pmt/date/2013-11-27/segment/01.

17 **"I was a little wild":** Michael Marley, "Tyson's Dad: I Don't Want Mike's Money," *New York Post*, October 14, 1988.

18 **"My mother's friends":** Tyson, *Undisputed Truth*, 14.

18 **For a time, she worked:** Monteith M. Illingworth, *Mike Tyson: Money, Myth and Betrayal* (Birch Lane Press, 1991), 4.

18 **Fires from adjacent:** Peter Heller, *Bad Intentions: The Mike Tyson Story* (NAL Books, 1989), 7.

18 **"My mother would do":** Tyson, *Undisputed Truth*, 17.

18 **Rodney, by one account:** Torres, *Fire and Fear*, 13.

19 **Rodney's platform shoes:** Torres, *Fire and Fear*, 33.

19 **"They'd drink, fight":** Tyson, *Undisputed Truth*, 17.

20 **"I knew what it was like":** *Hotboxin' with Mike Tyson*, episode 33, "Greek Billionaire Alki David," aired July 1, 2019, on YouTube, youtube.com/watch?v=syAx1T-ITTs.

3

22 **"spawning more gangsters":** Wendell Pritchett, *Brownsville, Brooklyn: Blacks, Jews, and the Changing Face of the Ghetto* (University of Chicago Press, 2002), 45.

22 **"They swaggered," writes historian:** Albert Fried, *The Rise and Fall of the Jewish Gangster in America* (Columbia University Press, 1993), 204.

23 **"brick-littered lots":** George Merlis, "Brooklyn's Amboy Street Is Now Nobody's Turf," *New York Times*, February 6, 1972.

24 **the "Supreme Godfather":** Bryant Mason, "Cops Capture 2 Youths Wanted in 2 Slayings," *New York Daily News*, October 7, 1973.

24 **claimed three quarters:** Paul Montgomery, "Gang Members Play Roles in Film on Sonny Carson," *New York Times*, October 12, 1973.

26 **eight-dollar drug debt:** Mike Santangelo and Mark Kriegel, "Basketball Star Shot in $8 Crack Dispute," *New York Daily News*, May 12, 1989.

26 **"One bullet passed":** James C. McKinley, "A Star Once, Felled First by Drugs, Now Bullets," *New York Times*, May 13, 1989.

28 **By 1974, the NYPD:** "Brooklyn Youth Gangs Concentrating on Robbery," *New York Times*, August 1, 1974.

29 **"We are like godfathers":** "Gangs Terrorizing Brooklyn Merchants," *New York Times*, February 25, 1974.

29 **"He'd have me lure":** Mike Tyson with Larry Sloman, *Undisputed Truth: My Autobiography* (HarperSport, 2014), 418.

30 **"I always imagined":** Tyson, *Undisputed Truth*, 76.

30 **"I just stood there"**: José Torres, *Fire and Fear: The Inside Story of Mike Tyson* (Warner Books, 1989), 19.

30 **"He snatched me"**: "Mike Tyson Opens Up About Sexual Abuse—Opie Jim Norton," clip from *The Opie and Jimmy Show* on Sirius XM, posted October 29, 2014, by Opie Radio, YouTube, youtu.be/6QXXUlY5rAA.

30 **"I was molested"**: Mike Tyson, interviewed by Jeremy Schaap for *E:60*, June 4, 2017. Interview transcript courtesy of Schaap.

31 **"25 tablets of Excedrin"**: Marilyn Murray, *Prisoner of Another War: A Remarkable Journey of Healing from Childhood Trauma* (Vivo, 1991), 24.

32 **"When I first met"**: Marilyn Murray, interviewed by Eileen Murphy, November 9, 2022, Scottsdale, Arizona. Interview transcript courtesy of ABC News.

4

34 **"You could go"**: Allie Conti, "Pigeon Guys Face Tough Times: 'Who Has the Money? Who Has the Roof?'" *New York Times*, February 18, 2021.

34 **"I didn't know if they"**: Mike Tyson with Larry Sloman, *Undisputed Truth: My Autobiography* (HarperSport, 2014), 21.

35 **"On the roof, none"**: Mike Tyson, "Mike Tyson Defends the Pigeon," *New York Times*, May 4, 2011.

36 **"I was screaming"**: Reeves Weideman, "Feathers," *The New Yorker*, March 6, 2011.

36 **Mad Dog 20/20 and Bacardi 151**: José Torres, *Fire and Fear: The Inside Story of Mike Tyson* (Warner Books, 1989), 21.

36 **"He could steal your underwear"**: Torres, *Fire and Fear*, 26.

37 **"I beat him"**: Tyson, *Undisputed Truth*, 31.

37 **"Everyone was afraid"**: Gary Smith, "Tyson the Timid, Tyson the Terrible," *Sports Illustrated*, March 21, 1988.

38 **"Fuck. You're only eleven?"**: Tyson, *Undisputed Truth*, 29.

38 **"We didn't talk much"**: Torres, *Fire and Fear*, 21.

40 **"I would cut their pockets"**: Mike Tyson and Eben Britton, hosts, *Hotboxin' with Mike Tyson*, podcast, season 2, episode 8, "Sportscaster Jim Gray," December 23, 2019, open.spotify.com/episode/6Zb0K4jxYkZ89Py25qN1sm?si=9445094532ff449d.

40 **"His real crimes"**: Teddy Atlas with Peter Alson, *Atlas: From the Streets to the Ring; A Son's Struggle to Become a Man* (Ecco, 2006), 71–72.

40 **"We started to scream"**: Torres, *Fire and Fear*, 23.

41 **"Afterwards, her and her friends"**: Tyson, *Undisputed Truth*, 34.

5

42 **A 1999 sentencing memo**: "Memorandum in Aid of Sentencing" (January 29, 1998), State of Maryland v. Tyson, District Court of Maryland for Montgomery County, case no. 0D00054096.

43 **"hundreds, maybe thousands of wild animals"**: "Schools and the Bad Boy," editorial, *New York Times*, December 6, 1957.

44 **For a time, there was**: Roger Wilkins, "Juvenile Center in Bronx Inspires Conflicting Views," *New York Times*, August 4, 1978.

44 **Another, made of glue and glitter**: Leslie Maitland, "No Yesterdays, No Tomorrows, It's Only Today at Spofford," *New York Times*, August 4, 1979.

44 **"where everybody knew"**: Mike Tyson with Larry "Ratso" Sloman, *Iron Ambition: My Life with Cus D'Amato* (Blue Rider Press, 2017), 7.

44 **"an institution overcrowded"**: Judson Hand, "Spofford: A House of Horrors," *New York Daily News*, November 17, 1969.

44 **There's a maintenance worker**: "Spofford Aide Charged," *New York Daily News*, May 28, 1970.

44 **A nine-year-old raped**: Judson Hand, "New Violence Reported at the Spofford Center," *New York Daily News*, April 26, 1970.

44 **"locked the doors"**: Judith Cummings, "Spofford School Guard's Arrest in Rape at Center Draws Criticism," *New York Times*, February 19, 1978.

44 **In 1972, teachers stopped:** Michael Pousner, "Teachers Rebel at Spofford in Violence Protest," *New York Daily News*, June 21, 1972.

44 **there were 130 escapes:** Edward Ranzal, "Council Panel Asks Closing of Spofford," *New York Times*, March 22, 1978.

44 **Bronx precinct cops:** Nathaniel Sheppard Jr., "20 Spofford Youths Seize a Counselor in Escape Bid," *New York Times*, February 23, 1977.

44 **was "nerve-wracking":** José Torres, *Fire and Fear: The Inside Story of Mike Tyson* (Warner Books, 1989), 29.

45 **"So I waited":** Torres, *Fire and Fear*, 30.

46 **"Then Hommo just jumped":** Tyson, *Iron Ambition*, 8.

6

51 **"I had a reputation":** José Torres, *Fire and Fear: The Inside Story of Mike Tyson* (Warner Books, 1989), 42.

51 **"Those huge redneck guards":** Mike Tyson with Larry "Ratso" Sloman, *Iron Ambition: My Life with Cus D'Amato* (Blue Rider Press, 2017), 9.

52 **"It's not that I wanted":** Tyson, *Iron Ambition*, 7.

55 **a former bookmaker:** Teddy Atlas with Peter Alson, *Atlas: From the Streets to the Ring; A Son's Struggle to Become a Man* (Ecco, 2006), 67.

56 **That same year, D'Amato:** Tyson, *Iron Ambition*, 358.

7

58 **"If a 15-year-old kid":** Jack Newfield, *Robert F. Kennedy: A Memoir* (Berkley, 1978). Originally published 1969. 224–25.

59 **"In those days, you had to":** Pete Hamill, "Up the Stairs with Cus D'Amato," *Village Voice*, November 19, 1985.

60 **"Nothing is as bad":** Gay Talese, "Suspicious Man in the Champ's Corner," *New York Times Magazine*, September 23, 1962.

61 **"Some of these enemies":** Mike Tyson with Larry "Ratso" Sloman, *Iron Ambition: My Life with Cus D'Amato* (Blue Rider Press, 2017), 362.

61 **"love and affection":** Martin Kane, "Conversation Piece: Cus D'Amato: A Very Simple Tiger," *Sports Illustrated*, April 21, 1958.

61 **"We had those horrific experiences":** Tyson, *Iron Ambition*, 24.

61 **"One of those men":** Kane, "Conversation Piece."

62 **"What you might call":** William Plummer, "Cus D'Amato," *People*, July 15, 1985.

62 **"The more pleasures":** Talese, "Suspicious Man."

62 **"I was prepared to die":** Talese, "Suspicious Man."

62 **even more egregious:** In his own autobiography, *Raging Bull: My Story*, LaMotta admits to both murder and rape.

62 **when kids stole:** Jake LaMotta with Joseph Carter and Peter Savage, *Raging Bull: My Story* (Prentice Hall, 1970), 4.

63 **"Cus never forgave Barbella":** Tyson, *Iron Ambition*, 94.

63 **a "medieval archbishop":** Budd Schulberg, "Sports' Greatest Event," *Esquire*, January 1962.

64 **"Control of the heavyweight":** Martin Kane, "The Case Against the IBC," *Sports Illustrated*, April 23, 1956.

64 **"I couldn't fight them myself":** Plummer, "Cus D'Amato."

8

66 **Floyd would rub:** Gay Talese, "The Loser," *Esquire*, March 1964.

66 **"I don't like that boy":** Floyd Patterson with Milton Gross, *Victory over Myself* (Scholastic, 1962), 7.

66 **"There was a metal ladder":** Patterson, *Victory over Myself*, 9.

68 **"intelligent and sympathetic"**: Eleanor Roosevelt, letter, May 31, 1962, Eleanor Roosevelt Papers Project, Columbian College of Arts and Sciences, erpapers.columbian.gwu.edu /may-31-1962.

68 **"I think he died"**: Nick Tosches, *The Devil in Sonny Liston* (Little, Brown, 2000), 7.

68 **President Kennedy urged**: Associated Press, "Losses Still Haunt Former Champ," *St. Louis Post-Dispatch*, August 2, 1998.

69 **"his association with persons"**: Deane McGowan, "State Commission Denies License to Liston, Ruling Out Title Fight Here," *New York Times*, April 28, 1962.

69 **"I knew if I wanted"**: Gay Talese, "Liston's Plight Shocks Patterson," *New York Times*, April 28, 1962.

70 **He didn't like going out**: Robert H. Boyle, "Hail, Hail, the Gang's All Here," *Sports Illustrated*, February 20, 1961.

70 **"I must keep my enemies"**: Gay Talese, "Suspicious Man in the Champ's Corner," *New York Times Magazine*, September 23, 1962.

70 **"Did you incur obligations"**: Gene Ward, "Inside Sports," *New York Daily News*, December 19, 1956.

71 **"I think Salerno"**: Mike Tyson with Larry "Ratso" Sloman, *Iron Ambition: My Life with Cus D'Amato* (Blue Rider Press, 2017), 446.

72 **"Never before had any"**: James Baldwin, "The Fight: Patterson vs. Liston" *Nugget*, February 1963.

73 **"For what?" asked Conrad**: Harold Conrad, *Dear Muffo* (Stein and Day, 1982), 150.

74 **Mailer occupied the stage**: Norman Mailer, "Ten Thousand Words a Minute," *Esquire*, February 1963.

74 **"If you don't have a license"**: Milton Gross, "Floyd Wants Return—'I Know I'll Do Better,'" *New York Post*, September 28, 1962.

74 **"I think that within me"**: Talese, "The Loser."

75 **Teddy Atlas likened**: Teddy Atlas with Peter Alson, *Atlas: From the Streets to the Ring; A Son's Struggle to Become a Man* (Ecco, 2006), 70.

9

76 **"It was a bitterly fought"**: Jack Smith, "Clark, Davis, Rooney Gloves Champs," *New York Daily News*, March 22, 1975.

77 **"I had gotten into a fight"**: Jonathan Rendall, *Scream: The Tyson Tapes* (Short Books, 2014), 40–41.

78 **On July 29, 1971, Cus D'Amato**: "D'Amato Files Bankruptcy," *New York Times*, July 30, 1971.

79 **province of former bootleggers**: Phil Berger, *Blood Season: Tyson and the World of Boxing* (William Morrow, Inc. 1989), 101.

79 **he'd ever call "Mother"**: Monteith M. Illingworth, *Mike Tyson: Money, Myth and Betrayal* (Birch Lane Press, 1991), 64.

79 **father was Buddy Baer**: Illingworth, *Mike Tyson*, 65.

80 **"Everything athletic that Robin did"**: Robert H. Boyle, "Really the Greatest," *Sports Illustrated*, March 7, 1966.

80 **as many as 880,000**: Stan Isaacs, "TV Sports: Jacobs Was a Legend in More Than Boxing," *Newsday*, March 25, 1988.

80 **a fourteen-year unbeaten streak**: Richard Hoffer, "Fight Manager, Collector Jimmy Jacobs Dies at 58," *Los Angeles Times*, March 24, 1988.

81 **"It was one of those maddening"**: Norman Mailer, "Ten Thousand Words a Minute," *Esquire*, February 1963.

81 **"Jimmy knew his best shots"**: Illingworth, *Mike Tyson*, 64.

81 **"He's seen so many"**: Mailer, "Ten Thousand Words."

81 **"We discuss my favorite subject"**: Boyle, "Really the Greatest."

81 **"There was a man"**: Michael Leahy, "Floyd Patterson: His Own Man," *Sports Illustrated*, June 1, 1992.

10

84 **"My life begins"**: Phil Berger, "Tyson, at Age 19, Rushes to Fulfill D'Amato Vision," *New York Times*, December 2, 1985.

85 **One morning, Tyson came down**: Mike Tyson with Larry Sloman, *Undisputed Truth: My Autobiography* (HarperSport, 2014), 51.

86 **a fifty-six-inch waist**: Donald McRae, "Me and Mike Tyson," *Guardian*, January 22, 2000.

87 **"What the white dude"**: Monteith M. Illingworth, *Mike Tyson: Money, Myth and Betrayal* (Birch Lane Press, 1991), 35.

87 **"I got turned out"**: Tyson, *Undisputed Truth*, 44.

87 **The gym above the police station**: For a sense of the gym as it was in 1980–81, and for countless other reasons, I recommend Lori Grinker's *Mike Tyson* (Powerhouse Books, 2022).

88 **"If you take a boy"**: *Watch Me Now*, directed by Michael Marton (Museum of Modern Art, June 27, 1983).

89 **"This is the one"**: Tyson, *Undisputed Truth*, 48.

90 **So what if Tyson**: Illingworth, *Mike Tyson*, 34.

90 **"The best fighter," Tyson would repeat**: Mike Tyson with Larry "Ratso" Sloman, *Iron Ambition: My Life with Cus D'Amato* (Blue Rider Press, 2017), 80.

90 **willed Rocky Graziano**: Tyson, *Iron Ambition*, 55.

90 **Leos like Teddy**: "Superstitious Side of Cus D'Amato & Boxing," posted December 5, 2019, by Valuetainment, YouTube, youtube.com/watch?v=LITwnbvUZxo.

90 **under three signs**: Tyson, *Iron Ambition*, 56.

90 **couldn't get enough UFO stories**: Tyson, *Iron Ambition*, 238.

90 ***The Denial of Death***: Robert Friedman, "Raging Calf," *Inside Sports*, August 1981.

91 **"We sat out in D'Amato's yard"**: Joseph Spinelli, "Shadow Boxing," *Sports Illustrated*, November 4, 1991.

92 **"How did you let that bum"**: Tyson, *Iron Ambition*, 73.

92 **collapsed after his morning run**: Jonathan Eig, *Ali: A Life* (Houghton Mifflin Harcourt, 2017), 486.

92 **In the ninth, the Greatest**: Eig, *Ali*, 486.

93 **"I have this young Black kid"**: Tyson, *Iron Ambition*, 73.

93 **"You have to dismantle"**: Tyson, *Undisputed Truth*, 66.

93 **Don't give him the money**: Jack Newfield, *Only in America: The Life and Crimes of Don King* (William Morrow, 1995), 164.

94 **He went through Atlas's wallet**: Tyson, *Undisputed Truth*, 44.

94 **"I got angry"**: Jonathan Rendall, *Scream: The Tyson Tapes* (Short Books, 2014), 50.

11

97 **"I was short and ugly"**: Mike Tyson with Larry Sloman, *Undisputed Truth: My Autobiography* (HarperSport, 2014), 56.

98 **"Today I sent him"**: Roberto Durán with George Diaz, *I Am Durán* (Blue Rider Press, 2016), 51.

98 **"There was an animal"**: Durán, *I Am Durán*, 5.

99 **"He would damage"**: Teddy Atlas with Peter Alson, *Atlas: From the Streets to the Ring; A Son's Struggle to Become a Man* (Ecco, 2006), 74.

100 **"You want to know"**: José Torres, *Fire and Fear: The Inside Story of Mike Tyson* (Warner Books, 1989), 56.

100 **"looking for a hundred"**: Robert Friedman, "Raging Calf," *Inside Sports*, August 1981.

101 **"I sat on the steps"**: Mike Tyson with Larry "Ratso" Sloman, *Iron Ambition: My Life with Cus D'Amato* (Blue Rider Press, 2017), 76.

101 **"Teddy Atlas literally"**: Bruce Silverglade, "Mike Tyson," introduction to *Mike Tyson*, by Lori Grinker (Powerhouse Books, 2022), 6.

103 ***There's no bass***: Steve Corbett, "Meet Billy O'Rourke, a Guy Who Nearly Derailed Mike Tyson," *Times Leader* (Wilkes-Barre, PA), June 26, 1988.

103 **"Jeff, it's up to you"**: Jack London, "Jack London Says Johnson Made a Noise Like a Lul-

laby with His Fists as He Tucked Burns in His Little Crib in Sleepy Hollow, with a Laugh," *New York Herald*, December 27, 1908.
The way London's column is often cited today includes the kicker—"The White Man must be rescued"—that's not in the original piece. The earliest source I could find for the infamous "White Race" line was in Louis Golding, "Jack Johnson: The Man with the Golden Smile," *The Sunday Mail*, Brisbane, Queensland, Australia, March 6, 1949, page 11: newspapers .com/image/1013800659.

104 **Tyson's account is straightforward**: Tyson, *Undisputed Truth*, 69–70.

104 **While Atlas's account**: Atlas, *Atlas*, 80–81.

108 **"Thor himself couldn't"**: Teddy Atlas, "Catskill's Mike Tyson Wins Jr. Olympic Championships," *Daily Mail* (Catskill, NY), July 1, 1981.

108 **"Anybody I hurt"**: Brin-Jonathan Butler, *Mike Tyson: The Kindle Singles Interview* (Amazon Digital Services, 2014).

108 **"I knew if I won"**: Peter Heller, *Bad Intentions: The Mike Tyson Story* (NAL Books, 1989), 71.

110 **"As my career progressed"**: Tyson, *Undisputed Truth*, 56.

12

111 **called his method "benevolent seduction"**: Molly Gordy, "He Gets into Tyson's Mind," *Newsday*, September 12, 1991.

111 **"I put him in a state"**: Bill Gallo, "Mind over Matters?," *New York Daily News*, February 10, 1992.

111 **"Once I was"**: Mike Tyson with Larry Sloman, *Undisputed Truth: My Autobiography* (HarperSport, 2014), 78.

112 **Trump's "elegant simplicity"**: Christopher Lehmann-Haupt, "Books of the Times," review of *Trump: The Art of the Deal* by Donald J. Trump with Tony Schwartz, *New York Times*, December 7, 1987.

112 **"He made me go back"**: Peter Heller, *Bad Intentions: The Mike Tyson Story* (NAL Books, 1989), 49.

113 **"The most insecure young man"**: Bill Gallo, "The Night Tyson's Career Went Down," *New York Daily News*, June 2, 2002.

114 **"Artie turned slowly"**: José Torres, "The Toughest S.O.B. Who Ever Lived," *Inside Sports*, February 1982.

115 **"Back then, in the dorms"**: Mark Kriegel, "Atlas Gets Shot to Bury Past," *New York Daily News*, April 20, 1994.

118 **"He couldn't have died"**: Mike Tyson with Larry "Ratso" Sloman, *Iron Ambition: My Life with Cus D'Amato* (Blue Rider Press, 2017), 44.

13

119 **"a 195-lb, 14-year-old"**: Robert Friedman, "Raging Calf," *Inside Sports*, August 1981.

122 **"I got the impression"**: W. K. Stratton, *Floyd Patterson: The Fighting Life of Boxing's Invisible Champion* (Mainstream Publishing, 2014), 67–68. Originally published by Houghton Mifflin Harcourt in 2012.

123 **proof of Tyson's age**: Dana Groff, "Tyson Celebrates Sixteenth with Second Olympic Title," *Daily Mail* (Catskill, NY), June 30, 1982.

124 **"has the potential to be"**: *Watch Me Now*, directed by Michael Marton (PBS, 1984).

124 **"When you lose"**: Mike Tyson with Larry Sloman, *Undisputed Truth: My Autobiography* (HarperSport, 2014), 80.

14

128 **"shrewd, very verbal"**: Peter Heller, *Bad Intentions: The Mike Tyson Story* (NAL Books, 1989), 56.

128 **The incident resulting**: Heller, *Bad Intentions*, 57.

128 **in whose bed:** Mike Tyson with Larry Sloman, *Undisputed Truth: My Autobiography* (HarperSport, 2014), 17.

130 **The wedding was an extravagant affair:** "About the Town & County with Betsy: Elaine Tushaj and Teddy Atlas Have Reception for 250 at Schmollinger's," *Daily Mail* (Catskill, NY), October 19, 1982.

130 **"The only one who didn't":** Teddy Atlas with Peter Alson, *Atlas: From the Streets to the Ring; A Son's Struggle to Become a Man* (Ecco, 2006), 90.

130 **"There's always someone":** Tyson, *Undisputed Truth*, 81–82.

131 **"Man, I wish I had":** Tyson, *Undisputed Truth*, 83.

131 **"I heard my boy":** Mike Tyson with Larry "Ratso" Sloman, *Iron Ambition: My Life with Cus D'Amato* (Blue Rider Press, 2017), 256.

132 **"This was a boy":** Monteith M. Illingworth, *Mike Tyson: Money, Myth and Betrayal* (Birch Lane Press, 1991), 52.

132 **"Mike was drawing attention":** Heller, *Bad Intentions*, 80.

132 **"Bill, I have a problem":** Heller, *Bad Intentions*, 81.

133 **"Look at your Black son":** Tyson, *Iron Ambition*, 258.

15

136 **"Cus always rushed":** Mike Tyson with Larry "Ratso" Sloman, *Iron Ambition: My Life with Cus D'Amato* (Blue Rider Press, 2017), 89.

136 **"one of my teachers":** Mike Tyson with Larry Sloman, *Undisputed Truth: My Autobiography* (HarperSport, 2014), 78–79.

137 **"I had three kids":** Phil Berger, *Blood Season: Tyson and the World of Boxing* (William Morrow, 1989), 130–31.

137 **"I was the fortress":** Berger, *Blood Season*, 130.

137 **"My wife tells me":** Mark Kriegel, "Atlas Gets Shot to Bury Past," *New York Daily News*, April 20, 1994.

137 **"I did something":** Tyson, *Undisputed Truth*, 86.

16

141 **"His wife, carrying his newborn":** Mike Tyson with Larry "Ratso" Sloman, *Iron Ambition: My Life with Cus D'Amato* (Blue Rider Press, 2017), 366.

142 **"I had him really frustrated":** "Jerry Goff vs. Mike Tyson," boxing match at the Ohio State Fair, August 13, 1983, uploaded August 6, 2014, by kohunting, YouTube, web.archive.org /web/20240725211743/youtube.com/watch?v=k_2CkRU8Wio.

143 **remained on the canvas:** Jonathan Field, "Mike Tyson Nice Person, Mean Guy," *Boxing Illustrated*, February 1984.

144 **"Mike beat the guy":** Rick Baker, "Tyson Loses Golden Gloves Final," *Daily Mail* (Catskill, NY), March 28, 1983.

144 **a "controversial decision":** "Boxing Champs Chosen," *Albuquerque Journal*, March 28, 1983.

144 **"Heard you fought great":** Tyson, *Iron Ambition*, 88.

146 **"I saw him get hit":** Wallace Matthews, "Holyfield: Saw Tyson Get KOd," *Newsday*, March 9, 1989.

17

147 **a thousand dollars a week:** "Affidavit of William D. Cayton," July 19, 1988, Tyson v. Cayton and Sports of the Century (New York Supreme Court, index no. 12888/88), 3.

147 **"I get my sparring":** Jonathan Field, "Mike Tyson Nice Person, Mean Guy," *Boxing Illustrated*, February 1984.

147 **"I think he was":** Lennox Lewis with Ken Gorman, *Lennox Lewis: The Story of Britain's First World Heavyweight Champion This Century*, rev. paperback ed. (Faber & Faber, 1997), 23.

148 **"She gave me a kiss":** Lewis, *Lennox Lewis*, 34–35.

149 **"He was one of these guys"**: Don McRae, "Lennox Lewis: 'I Knew I Would Meet Mike Tyson in the Ring,'" *Guardian*, November 30, 2020.

149 **"The Cus D'Amato?"**: Lewis, *Lennox Lewis*, 52.

149 **"They're joking and the best"**: Lewis, *Lennox Lewis*, 53.

150 **"We don't have to spar"**: Lewis, *Lennox Lewis*, 53.

151 **"I don't trust anybody"**: ABC Sports transcript, April 20, 1984, courtesy of ABC News; interview also available at youtube.com/watch?v=Aq9BoGZ5mB4.

152 **"It doesn't really matter who"**: Rich Baker, "Tyson Ready for Olympic Trials," *Daily Mail* (Catskill, NY), June 4, 1984.

153 **"My idols are"**: Jack Hawn, "The Old Man and the Kid," *Los Angeles Times*, June 8, 1984.

153 **"He'd beat Holmes"**: Hawn, "The Old Man."

154 **"fights like something"**: Galyn Wilkins, "Some Decisions Are Disputed," *Fort Worth Star-Telegram*, June 11, 1984.

154 **There were 4,105 in attendance**: Mike Bruton, "Winners in Olympic Ring Trials Draw a Breath, Wait for Box-Off," *Philadelphia Inquirer*, June 11, 1984.

155 **"There's more scandal"**: Wilkins, "Some Decisions Are Disputed."

156 **"Mike was robbed"**: Rick Baker, "Tyson Loses Split Decision; Fails in Bid for Olympics," *Daily Mail* (Catskill, NY), July 9, 1984.

156 **"trying to stick his thumbs"**: Peter Heller, *Bad Intentions: The Mike Tyson Story* (NAL Books, 1989), 96.

157 **D'amato wrapped him**: Earl Gustkey, "Will This Be His Crowning Glory?," *Los Angeles Times*, June 25, 1988.

157 **"Maybe Mike can knock"**: "Tyson Boxing in Houston," *Daily Mail* (Catskill, NY), July 17, 1984.

158 **"This guy's got an ego"**: Wallace Matthews, "Holyfield: I Saw Tyson Get KOd," *Newsday*, March 9, 1989.

158 **"You ain't taking this"**: Phil Berger, "Holyfield. Cooper. And in That Corner, Tyson," *New York Times*, November 19, 1991.

18

160 **"If Jimmy and Bill didn't"**: Peter Heller, *Bad Intentions: The Mike Tyson Story* (NAL Books, 1989), 95.

160 **referred to Tyson as**: Heller, *Bad Intentions*, 95.

163 **Mario Cuomo to appoint José Torres**: Thomas Rogers, "Scouting; Torres Platform," *New York Times*, November 16, 1984.

163 **"At last," Don King said**: Michael Katz, "Torres's Worlds Are United," *New York Times*, November 28, 1984.

163 **"never took a penny"**: Katz, "Torres's Worlds."

164 **"I used to always think"**: "Cus D'Amato & Mike Tyson—Making Fire Out of Fear," clip from *Sunday Morning*, aired December 2, 1984, on CBS, posted March 4, 2023, by Mike Tyson (@Boxing_Hub), YouTube, youtube.com/watch?v=YcrADvNY2L8.

168 **"I'm fighting each"**: Paul Post, "Tyson's Pro Career Appears Unlimited," *Daily Mail* (Catskill, NY), December 7, 1984.

19

169 **"I'm going to try to ruin"**: Gene Levy, "Tyson's Pro Boxing Debut Is Against Mercedes (0-2-1)," *Times Union* (Albany, NY), March 5, 1985.

170 **signed an exclusive**: "Agreement Between Michael Tyson and Reel Sports," September 28, 1984, Tyson v. Cayton and Sports of the Century (New York Supreme Court, index no. 12888/88).

170 **making Jimmy Jacobs**: "New York State Athletic Commission Boxer-Manager Contract," November 5, 1984, Tyson v. Cayton and Sports of the Century (New York Supreme Court, index no. 12888/88).

170 **"If I die"**: Tim Layden, "A Force Unleashed," *Sports Illustrated*, March 6, 2015, si.com /longform/2015/1985/tyson/index.html.

171 **whose name replaced:** A copy of Tyson's approved application appears in Peter Heller, *Bad Intentions: The Mike Tyson Story* (NAL Books, 1989), 97.
171 **"I want people":** Layden, "Force Unleashed."
172 **An old friend tells:** Heller, *Bad Intentions*, 111.
175 **"He wasn't a big guy":** Mike MacAdam, "Fascination with Mike Tyson Began in Albany," *Daily Gazette* (Schenectady, NY), November 26, 2020.
175 **"always tough":** "Mike Tyson vs Donnie Long—Best Quality Available," clip from *Top Rank Boxing*, ESPN's long-running boxing series, aired October 9, 1985, posted January 15, 2012, by GeneroEdits, YouTube, youtube.com/watch?v=EgwKlOPR8YM.
176 **Judging from news footage:** "Mike Tyson vs. Sterling Benjamin / 1985-11-01," clip from ESPN Classic's *Tyson Raw & Uncut*, posted February 10, 2017, by Mike Tyson's Fan Club, YouTube, youtube.com/watch?v=ENZRPRj-Hz8.
176 **"I had known nothing like it":** Layden, "Force Unleashed."
177 **"He have a sledgehammer":** *The 30-Minute News*, WNYT Channel 13 (Albany, NY), November 1, 1985.

20

178 **"I know," he said:** José Torres, *Fire and Fear: The Inside Story of Mike Tyson* (Warner Books, 1989), 81.
178 **dousing the grave:** Monteith M. Illingworth, *Mike Tyson: Money, Myth and Betrayal* (Birch Lane Press, 1991), 80.
180 **"Diogenes holding up":** Tommy Hanrahan, "Fight Gang Tolls a Farewell to D'Amato," *New York Daily News*, November 21, 1985.
180 **"His influence on boxing":** Hanrahan, "Fight Gang Tolls a Farewell."
180 **"I always thought there was something":** Hanrahan, "Fight Gang Tolls a Farewell."
181 **"I can't call it":** Bill Gallo, "A Special Bonding," *New York Daily News*, November 3, 1985.
182 **"The best marketing job":** Peter Heller, *Bad Intentions: The Mike Tyson Story* (NAL Books, 1989), 115.
185 **"I felt the flag":** Illingworth, *Mike Tyson*, 88.
185 **"the most electrifying":** William Nack, "Ready to Soar to the Very Top," *Sports Illustrated*, January 6, 1986.
185 **"Nothing seems to electrify":** Barry Wilner for Associated Press, "Pro Bowlers Open Jan. 11," *Star-Gazette* (Elmira, NY), January 6, 1986.
185 **And while Iger would readily:** Peter Alfano, "TV Sports: A Wedding That Wasn't," *New York Times*, December 24, 1985.
186 **a sellout crowd of 7,600:** Gordon Woodworth, "Another KO for Tyson," *Post-Star* (Glens Falls, NY), February 17, 1986.
188 **"We called it a disqualification":** "Mike Tyson v Jesse Ferguson 1985—"I Wanted to Break His Nose into His Brain!," clip from *Wide World of Sports*, aired February 16, 1986, on ABC, posted June 19, 2020, by Ultimate Mike Tyson, YouTube, youtube.com/watch?v=Lr7BYwEQNrw.

21

191 **"My dearest friend Rory":** "Mike Tyson vs Donnie Long—Best Quality Available," clip from *Top Rank Boxing*, ESPN's long-running boxing series, aired October 9, 1985, posted January 15, 2012, by GeneroEdits, YouTube, youtube.com/watch?v=EgwKlOPR8YM.
192 **"Cus told me that if anything":** José Torres, *Fire and Fear: The Inside Story of Mike Tyson* (Warner Books, 1989), 81.
193 **"He wanted me to let him":** Grinker's account of Tyson trying to grab her breast also appears in the introduction to her photographic collection *Mike Tyson*. Upon publication in 2022, Tyson's reps told the *New York Post* that Grinker and Tyson engaged in an affair when he was seventeen. Grinker denies it.
Jacklyn Hendricks, "New Mike Tyson Book Alleges Boxer 'Tried to Grab Breast' of Photographer," *New York Post*, October 13, 2022, nypost.com/2022/10/13/book-alleges-mike-tyson-tried-to-grab-photographers-breast.

193 **"made lewd and obscene"**: Pamela Newkirk, "Area Mall KOs Tyson," *Knickerbocker News* (Albany, NY), March 1, 1986.
194 **The manager confirmed**: Paul Grondahl, "Mall Official Confirms Report of Tyson Incident," *Times Union* (Albany, NY), March 2, 1986.
194 **"The Albany police commissioner"**: Monteith M. Illingworth, *Mike Tyson: Money, Myth and Betrayal* (Birch Lane Press, 1991), 93.
194 **In fact, the remark elicited**: A snippet of the postfight presser can be seen at the 31:10 mark in *Fallen Champ: The Untold Story of Mike Tyson*, directed by Barbara Kopple (Cabin Creek Films, Tri-Star Television, The Sokolow Company/NBC, 1993), youtube.com/watch?v=jMEZrQIDVN4.
194 **"I was very angry"**: *Fallen Champ*.
196 **"We partied after"**: Mike Tyson with Larry Sloman, *Undisputed Truth: My Autobiography* (HarperSport, 2014), 113.
196 **"He'd take the hardest liquor"**: Rory Holloway with Eric Wilson, *Taming the Beast* (Rough House, 2014), 5.
196 **"I had to watch him constantly"**: Illingworth, *Mike Tyson*, 93.
196 **"Jimmy was very conscious"**: Illingworth, *Mike Tyson*, 93.

22

197 **local press, as "unsubstantiated"**: Greg Luckenbaugh, "Tyson Is Good, but . . . ," *Post-Star* (Glens Falls, NY), May 3, 1986. Gene Levy, in "Caged Lion: After 7-Week Layoff, Tyson Is Ready to Tangle," *Times Union* (Albany, NY), May 1, 1986, called the incident "without substantiation."
197 **"I didn't like my performance"**: "Mike Tyson vs. Steve Zouski," Big Fights, Inc., recorded March 10, 1986, youtu.be/4K-aLcwATsQ?si=6KB8PFnY0Vg7GnIT&t=1260.
197 **Rather, his despondence**: Mike Tyson with Larry Sloman, *Undisputed Truth: My Autobiography* (HarperSport, 2014), 113.
198 **Rooney became "frantic"**: Ralph Wiley, "Winning One the Hard Way," *Sports Illustrated*, May 12, 1986.
198 **"He can hurt you"**: "Mike Tyson vs. James Tillis," *Wide World of Sports*, aired May 3, 1986, ABC, youtu.be/XsUZ1RK8TDw?si=JNsZx4pnXRVBrSDk.
199 **would've ended a draw**: Wallace Matthews, "Tillis Extends Tyson to Limit," *Newsday*, May 4, 1986.
199 **"He gave me such"**: Tyson, *Undisputed Truth*, 114.
199 **"Simply marvelous," bullshitted**: Richard Hoffer, "Tyson Wins but Not by a Knockout: Decision over Tillis Snaps a Streak by Young Heavyweight," *Los Angeles Times*, May 4, 1986.
202 **Now the World Boxing Council**: Phil Pepe, "Bigtime Spotlight on Tyson," *New York Daily News*, May 21, 1986.
202 **"this ugly little kid"**: Bill Gallo, "Green Showing Tyson No Respect," *New York Daily News*, May 8, 1986.
203 **seemed "unnaturally scared"**: José Torres, *Fire and Fear: The Inside Story of Mike Tyson* (Warner Books, 1989), 93.
203 **"There's no fighter"**: Wallace Matthews, "Tyson Takes to Stardom," *Newsday*, May 19, 1986.
203 **"I ain't no bum"**: Wallace Matthews, "Just Looking for Trouble," *Newsday*, May 20, 1986.
204 **"That's not my son's signature"**: Phil Pepe, "Mitch Erupts at Weigh-In," *New York Daily News*, May 20, 1986.
205 **"If Mitch does not"**: Pepe, "Mitch Erupts."
206 **"the whole thirty thousand dollars"**: Dick Young, "Young Ideas: Not Enough Green, So Mitch Quits King," *New York Post*, May 22, 1986.
207 **The following year, cops pulled**: James Duddy, "The Cops KO Boxer over PCP in Car," *New York Daily News*, August 28, 1987.
207 **His license had been suspended**: "Green Arrested on Drug Charge," *Newsday*, August 29, 1987.

23

208 **"Doughnuts," he said:** Mark Kriegel, "Bob Arum, Don King, Doughnuts and History," espn.com, May15, 2018.

208 **"That was a disadvantage":** "Boxing Legends Bob Arum and Don King Sit Down Together for Exclusive Interview," clip from *Top Rank Boxing,* aired March 17, 2018, on ESPN, posted March 27, 2018, by ESPN, YouTube, youtube.com/watch?v=NzbeVuqvtgQ.

210 **"Consumed by molten steel":** Christopher Evans, "The Man Who Would Be King, Part One," *Plain Dealer Magazine,* October 23, 1988.

211 **"What's your limit":** Red Smith, "King of the Ring," *New York Times Magazine,* September 28, 1975.

211 **"Tell the people":** Smith, "King of the Ring."

211 **King logged fifteen arrests:** Jack Newfield, *Only in America: The Life and Crimes of Don King* (William Morrow, 1995), 14, features a photocopied summary of King's rap sheet between 1951 and the time of his arrest for murder in April 1966. There were thirty-five arrests.

211 **On December 2, 1954, King:** Newfield, *Only in America,* 2–3.

211 **"He shot up":** Evans, "Man Who Would Be King, Part One."

212 **"He would call a stockbroker":** Evans, "Man Who Would Be King, Part One."

213 **At 3:40 a.m., King called:** "5 Now Held in Bombing of King's Home," *Cleveland Plain Dealer,* May 21, 1957.

213 **"Shondor Birns did this":** James Neff, "Searchers Unleashed," *Cleveland Plain Dealer,* July 7, 1984.

213 **His mother burned to death:** Michael D. Roberts, "Why They Blew Shondor Birns Away," *Cleveland Magazine,* July 1975, clevelandmagazine.com/in-the-cle/articles/why-they-blew -shondor-birns-away.

213 **a locker full of silk shirts:** Christopher Evans, "Mobster Mash: Shondor Birns Was Public Enemy No. 1 Before He was Blown to Bits," *Plain Dealer Magazine,* February 3, 1991.

213 **took twenty-five to thirty pellets:** "Birns Tipster Shot, Lucky to Be Alive," *Cleveland Plain Dealer,* October 6, 1957.

213 **"I knew the police":** George Barmann, "Shondor Quiet, but Capable of Quick, Violent Retaliation," *Cleveland Plain Dealer,* July 11, 1963.

213 **Birns reportedly bought:** Evans, "Man Who Would Be King, Part One."

213 **Officers Robert Tonne and John Horvath:** "Berets Nab Numbers Operator in Beating," *Cleveland Plain Dealer,* April 21, 1966.

213 **"A colored male":** Officer Tonne's incident report can be found in Newfield, *Only in America,* 7.

214 **"How much do I owe":** "Berets Nab Numbers Operator."

214 **Garrett's left eardrum:** Christopher Evans, "The Man Who Would Be King, Part Two," *Plain Dealer Magazine,* October 30, 1988.

215 **"Don," he moaned:** Newfield, *Only in America,* 6.

215 **"I was transferring guilt":** Smith, "King of the Ring."

215 **"The car was parked":** George E. Jordan, "Numbers Play Here Survives Turbulent Past," *Cleveland Plain Dealer,* May 31, 1982.

215 **"notorious clearing house":** "Lawmen Doubt Fight over Birns' Empire," *Cleveland Plain Dealer,* September 9, 1967.

215 **they'd become partners:** "Lawmen Doubt Fight."

215 **the late John Renwick:** Evans, "Man Who Would Be King, Part One."

215 **"the chief clerical employee":** Doris O'Donnell and Fred Mollenkopf, "Numbers Fronts Bared," *Cleveland Plain Dealer,* April 7, 1965.

215 **when offered immunity:** J. C. Daschbach, "Pittsburgh Hymie Refuses to Talk," *Cleveland Plain Dealer,* December 4, 1965.

216 **9:00 a.m. on April 26:** Evans, "Man Who Would Be King, Part Two."

216 **"When Sam Garrett come home":** Smith, "King of the Ring."

216 **"to buy some new grips":** Evans, "Man Who Would Be King, Part Two."

216 **"that really saved me":** Smith, "King of the Ring."

216 **$30,000 to bribe:** Newfield, *Only in America,* 12.

217 **free on $5,000 bail:** "'Kid' King Free on Bond Pending Retrial Motion," *Cleveland Plain Dealer*, February 25, 1967.
217 **Then he left:** Terrance Sherridan, "Judge Cuts Hood's Murder Penalty," *Cleveland Plain Dealer*, July 24, 1967.
217 **"The judge was a stinking bastard":** Evans, "Man Who Would Be King, Part Two."
217 **"Donald had no use":** H. Thomas Kaib, "Prisoners Have Changed, but Not Crimes, Priest Says," *Cleveland Plain Dealer*, April 24, 1978.
218 **"I had to put in":** Norman Mailer, *The Fight* (Little, Brown, 1975; repr., Vintage Books, 1997), 118–19.
218 **To others, King cited Socrates:** Evans, "Man Who Would Be King, Part Two."
219 **But the ringed construct:** Nick Khan, my former agent, now head of the WWE, is the source of this idea.
219 **"Make me big":** Newfield, *Only in America*, 28.
220 **"He needed a distinctive look":** Newfield, *Only in America*, 65.
220 **"My hair was kinky":** "Don King: The Playboy Interview," originally published May 1988, reprinted in *Wild Men: The Playboy Interview* (Playboy, 2013).
221 **"My philosophy is that all":** Newfield, *Only in America*, 143–44.

24

222 **"I was always attracted":** Mike Tyson with Larry Sloman, *Undisputed Truth: My Autobiography* (HarperSport, 2014), 485.
223 **"He just had these inhuman":** Rory Holloway with Eric Wilson, *Taming the Beast* (Rough House, 2014), 63.
223 **his friend's conquest of:** José Torres, *Fire and Fear: The Inside Story of Mike Tyson* (Warner Books, 1989), 114–15.
226 **"Greedy, overweight, suspicious":** Tim Layden, "A Savior with Nothing to Save," *Times Union* (Albany, NY), December 21, 1986.
226 **"When Tyson comes":** Norman Chad, "HBO's 'Heavyweight World Series' Looks Like a Real Lightweight Event," *Washington Post*, March 28, 1986.
227 **"I got him. He's my man":** Jack Newfield, *Only in America: The Life and Crimes of Don King* (William Morrow, 1995), 46–47.
227 **the "closest thing":** Mark Kram Jr., "'Lawdy, He's Great,'" *Sports Illustrated*, October 13, 1975.
227 **"He has an incredible name":** Torres, *Fire and Fear*, 95.
228 **"Get up, son":** Mark Kram Jr., *Smokin' Joe: The Life of Joe Frazier* (Ecco, 2019), 309.
228 **"I want them":** Pat Putnam, "Biff! Zap! It's Tyson Again," *Sports Illustrated*, August 4, 1986.
228 **"I use the fear":** "Mike Tyson vs Marvis Frazier—Best Quality Available," clip from *Wide World of Sports*, aired July 26, 1986, on ABC, posted September 19, 2012, by GeneroEdits, YouTube, youtube.com/watch?v=CRCVwsIokEw.
230 **"He did well":** Anson Wainwright, "Best I Faced: Mike Tyson," *The Ring*, April 28, 2020, web.archive.org/web/20200428222840/ringtv.com/535770-best-faced-mike-tyson-1.
231 **"The series involved":** Harry Mullan, "Bill Cayton: 'I Feel So Sorry for Mike Tyson,'" *Boxing News*, August 4, 2016, boxingnewsonline.net/bill-cayton-i-feel-so-sorry-for-mike-tyson.
231 **the Hilton's live gate:** Pat Putnam, "He's Right on Target," *Sports Illustrated*, September 15, 1986.
231 **"He has no choice":** Putnam, "He's Right on Target."

25

233 **"Enjoy this now":** Mike Tyson with Larry Sloman, *Undisputed Truth: My Autobiography* (HarperSport, 2014), 151.
233 **Liza Minnelli's apartment:** Tyson, *Undisputed Truth*, 103.
233 **He'd take them downstairs:** Tyson, *Undisputed Truth*, 135.
233 **ordered for breakfast:** "Heavyweight," Page Six, *New York Post*, August 2, 1986.

234 **"Theresa and I"**: "Greatest Boxing Interviews of All Time, | Tyson & Raging Bull," clip from Mike Tyson and Jake LaMotta interview by David Brenner on *Nightlife*, aired October 6, 1986, in syndication, posted May 22, 2020, by David Brenner Comedy, YouTube, youtube.com/watch?v=G7kpGcp7yXU.

234 **"I met Mike"**: Dan Snierson, "Q&A with Antony [sic] Michael Hall," *Entertainment Weekly*, June 18, 1999, ew.com/article/1999/06/18/qa-antony-michael-hall/.

235 **But he looked up to Tyson**: Kristine McKenny, "Movies: On the Rebound with Anthony Michael Hall," *Los Angeles Times*, April 3, 1988.

235 **"A profound communion"**: Jason Guerrasio, "Off the Ropes," *Filmmaker*, winter 2009.

235 **dread and fear**: Tim Arango, "Mike Tyson Film Takes a Swing at His Old Image," *New York Times*, May 11, 2008.

236 **"I don't think anybody"**: Scott Foundas, "Boxing, Sex and Madness: Mike Tyson, James Toback and the Ties That Bind," *LA Weekly*, April 8, 2008.

237 **She found him to be**: Beverly Johnson, *The Face That Changed It All: A Memoir* (Atria Books, 2015), 196–98.

26

238 **"I believe when someone dies"**: Hugh McIlvanney, "Mighty Mike Shoulders a Heavy Task," *Sports Illustrated*, November 24, 1986.

238 **"Those legendary tales"**: Joyce Carol Oates, "A Terrible Beauty Is Born," *Life*, March 1987.

238 **It wasn't unusual for them**: Peter Heller, *Bad Intentions: The Mike Tyson Story* (NAL Books, 1989), 150.

238 **"I'd hypnotize him"**: Bill Gallo, "Great Daze for Tyson with Aid of Hypnotist," *New York Daily News*, April 27, 1986.

239 **VHS tapes strewn about**: José Torres, *Fire and Fear: The Inside Story of Mike Tyson* (Warner Books, 1989), 111.

239 **wall of photographs**: Earl Gustkey, "A Hot Little Gym: The Top Boxers Find Their Way to Tocco's," *Los Angeles Times*, June 16, 1987.

240 **"Look at this," said Tyson**: Torres, *Fire and Fear*, 109.

241 **"Every morning at six thirty"**: Tom Archdeacon, "The Curious World of Trevor Berbick," *Miami News*, November 20, 1986.

241 **got only a third**: Associated Press, "Nevada Regulators Say Berbick Received Only One-Third of Purse After Tyson Bout," *Los Angeles Times*, January 31, 1987.

241 **"This is 'Judgment Day'"**: UPI Archives, "Mike Tyson Will Have to Pay a Minimum of . . . ," November 21, 1986.

241 **"Remember that mystique"**: Ron Borges, "Seeing Is Believing: Dundee No Tyson Fan," *Boston Globe*, November 21, 1986.

242 **low as 7–1**: Wallace Matthews, "Berbick Is Model of Inconsistency," *Newsday*, November 20, 1986.

242 **"He's not as tough"**: Wallace Matthews, "Will Pressure Get to Iron Mike?," *Newsday*, November 16, 1986.

242 **"I had to make him"**: Mike Katz, "Rodney Tyson's Other Way Out," *New York Daily News*, November 23, 1986.

243 **Tyson woke about 5:30 a.m.**: Pat Putnam, "Getting a Belt Out of Life," *Sports Illustrated*, December 1, 1986.

243 **"Steve," he yelled**: Torres, *Fire and Fear*, 111.

243 **"Kick his ass"**: Wallace Matthews, "Thirty Years After Mike Tyson Became Champion, Unfulfilled Promise Is the Lasting Memory," *Washington Post*, November 21, 2016.

243 **"I was trying to prove"**: Wallace Matthews, "Tyson Makes It to Top," *Newsday*, November 23, 1986.

244 **"I wanted to bust"**: Putnam, "Getting a Belt."

245 **Any more, said Lane**: Putnam, "Getting a Belt."

247 **"I didn't take that belt off"**: Mike Tyson with Larry Sloman, *Undisputed Truth: My Autobiography* (HarperSport, 2014), 124–25.

247 **"He was lonely"**: *Mike Tyson: The Knockout*, episode one, ABC News, aired May 25, 2021.

248 **"I want to live forever"**: "Mike Tyson vs. Trevor Berbick," clip from *World Championship Boxing*, aired November 22, 1986, on HBO, posted October 31, 2106, by Ringside Videos, YouTube, youtube.com/watch?v=ImGWr3cd9zE&t=2580s.

27

249 **"Mike was young"**: Beverly Johnson, *The Face That Changed It All: A Memoir* (Atria Books, 2015), 198.

249 **"I just wanted to have"**: Johnson, *Face That Changed*, 200.

250 **"I was there to keep"**: Rory Holloway with Eric Wilson, *Taming the Beast* (Rough House, 2014), 94–95.

251 **celebrity restaurants in *New York***: David Blum, "Where Have You Gone, Woody Allen?," *New York*, October 12, 1987, books.google.com.

251 **"I really believed"**: Mike Tyson with Larry Sloman, *Undisputed Truth: My Autobiography* (HarperSport, 2014), 134.

251 **"Damn, Wosie. You got"**: Rosie Perez, *Handbook for an Unpredictable Life: How I Survived Sister Renata and My Crazy Mother and Still Came Out Smiling (with Great Hair)* (Crown Archetype, 2014), 227.

252 **"I had a lot of bad"**: Perez, *Handbook for an Unpredictable Life*, 191.

28

254 **"Everything was Tyson"**: Monteith M. Illingworth, *Mike Tyson: Money, Myth and Betrayal* (Birch Lane Press, 1991), 168.

255 **"Buy a shirt"**: Michael Katz, "The Unification of Boxing's Shredded State," *New York Daily News*, August 2, 1987.

255 **boxing's notoriously corrupt**: In 2000, IBF founder and former president Robert W. Lee Sr. was found guilty of money laundering and tax evasion and later sentenced to twenty-two months in federal prison.

255 **"I'll have twenty thousand"**: Richard Hoffer, "Boxing: Without Spinks, Heavyweight Series Lacks Pop," *Los Angeles Times*, March 4, 1987.

255 **what he would have made**: King won the purse bid for Spinks–Tucker with a bid of $711,000. Under IBF rules, which called for a 75/25 split, the champion would have made $533,250.

256 **"Extortion," he called it**: Combined News Services, "Tubbs Out of Title Fight," *Newsday*, December 6, 1986.

256 **netted him only $1,750**: Sam Smith, "Fighters Hit Back at Kings," *Chicago Tribune*, August 10, 1987.

256 **"Bonecrusher, I want to settle"**: Matt Christie, "Meet the Bonecrusher, James Smith," *Boxing News*, April 3, 2019, boxingnewsonline.net/meet-the-bonecrusher.

257 **$400,000 payment plus**: Jack Newfield, *Only in America: The Life and Crimes of Don King* (William Morrow, 1995), 238–42.

257 **But now Carl King**: Newfield, *Only in America*, 244.

257 **"I'm telling you," Torres shot**: Michael Katz, "The Whacky Kingdom of Boxing," *New York Daily News*, December 11, 1986.

258 **"behind burly colleagues"**: Phil Berger, "Boxing Notebook: Prefight Infighting in Need of a Referee," *New York Times*, December 11, 1986.

258 **"You're taking from everybody"**: Associated Press, "Ruckus at Press Conference," *Citizen Register* (Ossining, NY), December 11, 1986.

258 **$5 million a month**: Mike Katz, "The Unification of Boxing's Shredded State," *New York Daily News*, August 2, 1987.

258 **"a walking billboard"**: Norman Chad, "HBO and Tyson: Trying Another Combination," *Washington Post*, July 21, 1989.

258 **"The only one out there"**: Joe Gergen, "Ali vs. Frazier It Ain't," *Newsday*, December 12, 1986.

258 **There were seventeen thousand**: Peter Heller, *Bad Intentions: The Mike Tyson Story* (NAL Books, 1989), 160.

258 **"I knew his mind"**: Wallace Matthews, "A Crusher for Witherspoon," *Newsday*, December 13, 1986.

258 **His $400,000 purse:** Newfield, *Only in America*, 245–46.

258 **"a clerical error"**: Phil Berger, "Witherspoon Drug Test Called Negative," *New York Times*, December 20, 1986.

259 **"A conflict of interest"**: Wallace Matthews, "No Way, Jose," *Newsday*, December 19, 1986.

259 **"The team is"**: Bob Raissman and Bill Gallo, "Squabbling Perils Tyson–Spinks," *New York Daily News*, November 12, 1987.

259 **"that brilliant boy"**: Pete Hamill, "Jose Torres: The Lost Hero," *Saturday Evening Post*, May 21, 1966.

260 **a file clerk:** Phil Berger, "Bonecrusher Smith: An Unlikely Route to Boxing Summit," *New York Times*, March 2, 1987.

261 **"Larry Merchant said"**: Wallace Matthews, "Smith Is Ready for Big Payoff," *Newsday*, March 1, 1987.

261 **"The only interesting thing"**: "Mike Tyson vs. James Smith," *World Championship Boxing*, aired March 10, 1986, on HBO, youtu.be/E2F5qB4_x7E?si=lCA6mbV8WrRaLP4U.

261 **"He didn't want"**: "Mike Tyson vs. James Smith," *World Championship Boxing*.

262 **"Who's that girl?"**: Mike Tyson with Larry Sloman, *Undisputed Truth: My Autobiography*, Kindle ed. (Penguin, 2013), 137.

29

263 **"Darlene," wrote a *People* correspondent:** Ron Arias, "If Robin Givens Can Jump from Harvard to Head of the Class, There's No Ceiling on Her Talent," *People*, May 11, 1987.

263 **her father, a bricklayer:** Billy Reed, "Robin Givens' Dad a Former Douglass High Star," *Lexington Herald-Leader*, August 20, 1988.

263 **first-team All-City:** Dave Bennett, "Dunbar Lands 2 Players on All-City Team," *Lexington Herald*, March 31, 1963.

264 **By then, Reuben had played:** Staff and wire reports, "Robin Givens' Parents Are Lexington Natives," *Lexington Herald-Leader*, October 15, 1988.

264 **"I told her I didn't want"**: Mitch Gelman and Jonathan Mandell, "Givens, Roper Have Enemies," *Newsday*, October 5, 1988.

264 **In 1969, Ruth boarded:** Robin Givens, *Grace Will Lead Me Home* (Miramax Books, 2007), 70.

265 ***Mom's been possessed:*** Givens, *Grace Will Lead*, 74–76.

265 **She would eventually:** Manny Topol, "Winfield Settles Sex Case," *Newsday*, June 3, 1988.

265 **"She worked till eleven"**: Michael Katz et al., "Left to Heart—Kayo to Love," *New York Daily News*, October 9, 1988.

265 **"I have to get her"**: Katz et al., "Left to Heart."

266 **"my first serious romance"**: Givens, *Grace Will Lead*, 138.

266 **"Do you want my autograph?"**: Arias, "If Robin Givens Can."

266 **photograph was taped:** Frank Sanello, "Robin Givens: From Doctor to Actress," *Knoxville News-Sentinel*, February 22, 1987.

266 **"Bill's confidence in Robin's chances"**: Arias, "If Robin Givens Can."

267 **"She never applied"**: Betty Liu Ebron, "Apple Sauce: To Quote an Old Vaudeville Line: You're a Doctor? I'm Dubious," *New York Daily News*, May 17, 1988.

267 **"This time last year"**: Joe Logan for Knight-Ridder Newspapers, "Cosby Takes Show to Penn Relays," *Tallahassee Democrat*, April 14, 1986.

267 **"After a year"**: Vernon Scott for United Press International, "'Head of the Class' Is a Role Familiar to Star Robin Givens," *Atlanta Journal*, June 12, 1986.

267 **"I was Black"**: Kevin Breslin, "Robin Givens," *New York Daily News*, July 27, 1986.

267 **"I called him"—Cosby:** Lisa Faye Kaplan, "At the Head of the Class," *Herald Statesman* (Yonkers, NY), October 26, 1986.

267 **"It took everything"**: Givens, *Grace Will Lead*, 150.

267 **"She only attended"**: Gelman and Mandell, "Givens, Roper Have Enemies."

267 **"Can't find any trace"**: Gelman and Mandell, "Givens, Roper Have Enemies."

268 **referring to her "parents"**: Sanello, "Robin Givens."

268 **"She was making"**: Michael Katz et al., "Left to Heart."

268 **"He was so completely hurt"**: Arias, "If Robin Givens Can."

268 **visiting her father**: Givens, *Grace Will Lead*, 105.

269 **"Harvey Weinstein, your friendship"**: Givens, *Grace Will Lead*, 330.

269 **"Cus always told me"**: Mike Tyson with Larry Sloman, *Undisputed Truth: My Autobiography* (HarperSport, 2014), 150.

269 **"What's wrong with you?"**: Rory Holloway with Eric Wilson, *Taming the Beast* (Rough House, 2014), 69.

269 **began calling frequently**: Givens, *Grace Will Lead*, 166–67.

269 **"I felt a strong sexual vibe"**: Tyson, *Undisputed Truth*, 137.

269 **"Sunset Strip power-haven"**: Anne Thompson, "Such a Deal! Industry Hangouts," *Los Angeles Times*, October 1, 1987.

269 **at least one publicist**: Leslie Bennetts, "Tyson Turmoil," *Vanity Fair*, November 1988, cites "a couple of publicists."

269 **"I was so nervous"**: Givens, *Grace Will Lead*, 172.

270 **his new Rolls-Royce**: Wallace Matthews, "Tyson Moving Up in Class," *Newsday*, April 24, 1987.

270 **It called for a million dollars**: "Promotional Agreement Between Don King Productions and Mike Tyson," November 11, 1986, Tyson v. Cayton (U.S. District Court, Southern District of New York, no. 88 civ. 8398).

271 **"You got a squeaky little voice"**: Wallace Matthews, "Tyson, Thomas Start with Battle of Words," *Newsday*, April 23, 1987.

271 **"He told me to suck"**: Ralph Wiley, *Serenity: A Boxing Memoir* (Holt, 1989; repr., Bison Books, 2000), 188.

271 **"Might have been the most vicious"**: Tyson, *Undisputed Truth*, 143.

271 **"People pay to see"**: Ralph Wiley, "Iron Mike Passes a Test," *Sports Illustrated*, June 8, 1987.

272 **worth $10 million**: Phil Berger, "Boxing Notebook: Tyson Set to Begin a Whirlwind Tour," *New York Times*, May 28, 1987.

272 **covering the event for *Newsday***: Jerry Sullivan, "Tyson Fighting for the Retarded," *Newsday*, April 1, 1987.

273 **"He wants to marry"**: Dick Young, "Tyson Hearing Wedding Bells: The Champ Falls for a Knockout," *New York Post*, May 29, 1987.

30

274 **Tyson informed Steve Lott**: Monteith M. Illingworth, *Mike Tyson: Money, Myth and Betrayal* (Birch Lane Press, 1991), 186.

275 **venerable trainer Eddie Futch**: Michael Marley, "Tyson Twins Are Double Trouble," *New York Post*, July 20, 1987.

275 **"the summer of Tyson's discontent"**: Michael Marley, "Tyson Takes Anger Out on Sparmate Broad," *New York Post*, July 27, 1987.

275 **"These people"—Jacobs, Cayton**: José Torres, *Fire and Fear: The Inside Story of Mike Tyson* (Warner Books, 1989), 130.

277 **band of six**: Phil Berger, "Tyson Crowned amid Trumpet Fanfare," *New York Times*, August 3, 1987.

277 **"prostitute his craft"**: "Hull, Las Vegas' Longtime Voice of Boxing, Dies at 75," *Las Vegas Sun*, February 16, 2000.

277 **"baubles, rubies, and fabulous doodads"**: Pat Putnam, "Only One No. 1," *Sports Illustrated*, August 10, 1987.

278 **"Sir Bonecrusher" and "Sir Pinky"**: Steve Bunce, "Steve Bunce on Boxing: When We Were Kings—the Coronation of Iron Mike Tyson," *Independent*, January 8, 2013.

280 **"catnip to the intellectuals"**: Gary Wills, "The Great Black Hope," *New York Review of Books*, February 4, 1999.

280 **"a psychic outlaw"**: Joyce Carol Oates, "A Terrible Beauty Is Born," *Life*, March 1987.

280 **"For all his reserve"**: Joyce Carol Oates, "Mike Tyson: Cockfight in the Desert," *Village Voice*, March 24, 1987, villagevoice.com/mike-tyson-cockfight-in-the-desert.

280 **Cayton even thought to trademark:** "Iron Mike Trademark Application," January 14, 1988, Tyson v. Cayton and Sports of the Century (New York Supreme Court, index no. 12888/88).
280 **"To overcome the stigma":** "Affidavit of Cayton," July 19, 1988, p. 8, no. 22, Tyson vs. Cayton and Sports of the Century (New York Supreme Court, index no. 12888/88).
281 **"In the way he's been handled":** Nigel Collins, "Mike Tyson: The Legacy of Cus D'Amato," *The Ring*, February 1986.
281 **"a fake fucking Uncle Tom":** Mike Tyson with Larry Sloman, *Undisputed Truth: My Autobiography*, Kindle ed. (Penguin, 2013), 128.
283 **In the Seventy-Fifth Precinct:** Larry Celona and Bruce Golding, "Reign of Terror When Murder Was King in NY," *New York Post*, December 17, 2014.
283 **bribed a witness:** Mary McDonnell, Adam Shrier, and Graham Rayman, "Confessions of a Crack King: I Want to Make Amends'" *New York Daily News*, March 6, 2017.
284 **"Five thousand here":** Tyson, *Undisputed Truth*, 126–27.
284 **"Those was our people":** Mike Tyson and Eben Britton, hosts, *Hotboxin' with Mike Tyson*, podcast, season 2, episode 19, "Eminem," March 19, 2020, youtube.com/watch?v=vvSyS R8RdzY.
285 **"Yo, Glaze," inmates started:** Brian "Glaze" Gibbs with Joseph Verola, *Beyond Lucky: The Brian "Glaze" Gibbs Story: Crack, Money, Murder & Redemption* (Ustar, 2015), 108.
285 **"Here's a rap group":** Daniel Brogan, "New Albums: History of New Orleans R&B Is a Primer of City's Music," *Chicago Tribune*, April 10, 1987.
286 **"They wanted me to be":** Tyson, *Undisputed Truth*, 128.

31

287 **his own promotional team:** Wallace Matthews, "Inside Boxing: Biggs' Mind Is Tough to Figure," *Newsday*, April 24, 1987.
287 **"I want to give him":** Peter Heller, *Bad Intentions: The Mike Tyson Story* (NAL Books, 1989), 176.
287 **"I was seventeen":** Bill Gallo, "Biggs Must Use Head vs. Headhunter Tyson," *New York Daily News*, October 11, 1987.
288 **"I hate Tyrell":** Phil Berger, "Boxing Notebook: Tyson Takes New Approach," *New York Times*, January 20, 1988.
288 **"She must mean":** Berger, "Boxing Notebook."
288 **"I've watched Tyrell":** Bill Gallo, "Boxing: Biggs–Tyson Picks Up Beat," *New York Daily News*, August 19, 1987.
288 **"I have a very distinct advantage":** Matthews, "Inside Boxing."
289 **"If I want the fight":** Berger, "Boxing Notebook."
289 **"About as perfect":** "Mike Tyson vs. Tyrell Biggs," *World Championship Boxing*, aired October 16, 1987, on HBO, youtu.be/Bd_gMw4LjFc?si=u7EGX0GcEWRl3qfG.
289 **"everybody has plans":** Associated Press, "Biggs: Height, Skill Will Hurt Tyson," *Record Searchlight* (Reading, CA), August 19, 1987.
289 **"I wanted to make him pay":** Bill Verigan, "Tyson Batters Biggs," *New York Daily News*, October 17, 1987.
290 **"his elbow, his head":** Michael Katz, "Tyson Wins Believer," *New York Daily News*, October 17, 1987.
291 **"I was hitting him":** "Mike Tyson vs. Tyrell Biggs—Full Fight—10-16-1987," clip from *World Championship Boxing*, aired October 16, 1987, on HBO, posted November 4, 2018, by Mike Tyson Career Bouts, YouTube, youtu.be/Bd_gMw4LjFc?si=H_T50MZUdtnn1VnT.
294 **Steve Lott would recall:** José Torres, *Fire and Fear: The Inside Story of Mike Tyson* (Warner Books, 1989), 131–32.

32

295 **"Ninety percent of":** "Mike Tyson vs. Tyrell Biggs—Full Fight—10-16-1987," clip from *World Championship Boxing*, aired October 16, 1987, on HBO, posted November 4, 2018, by Mike Tyson Career Bouts, YouTube, youtu.be/Bd_gMw4LjFc?si=H_T50MZUdtnn1VnT.

296 **"I gave him credibility"**: Dan Coughlin, "King vs. Giachetti," *Cleveland Plain Dealer*, August 3, 1981.

296 **"I was sort of an enforcer"**: Steve Bunce, "Richie 'the Torch' Giachetti: Boxing Trainer Who Rose Up from Cleveland Underworld to Assist Larry Holmes and Mike Tyson," *Independent*, March 24, 2016, independent.co.uk/news/obituaries/richie-the-torch-giachetti -boxing-trainer-who-rose-up-from-the-cleveland-underworld-to-assist-larry-holmes -and-mike-tyson-a6949276.html.

297 **Cleveland's most esteemed**: James Neff, "Rolling with the Punches," *Cleveland Plain Dealer, Sunday Magazine*, September 15, 1987.

297 **The cut took seventy-eight stitches**: Bunce, "Richie 'the Torch' Giachetti."

297 **"I treated him"**: Dan Coughlin, "Nobody Will Ever Say Richie Giachetti Is Cheap," *Cleveland Plain Dealer*, August 4, 1981.

297 **Giachetti produced six tapes**: Joseph Spinelli, "Shadow Boxing," *Sports Illustrated*, November 4, 1991.

297 **"King's got a lot"**: Spinelli, "Shadow Boxing."

297 **"The mob guys have come"**: Michael Marley, "Giachetti Fears Mob Hit," *New York Post*, August 8, 1981.

297 **"absolute paranoia from"**: Marley, "Giachetti Fears Mob Hit."

298 **"I made him understand"**: *Corruption in Professional Boxing: Hearings Before the Permanent Subcommittee on Investigations of the Committee on Governmental Affairs*, 102nd Cong. 100 (1992) (statement of Michael Franzese, Former Captain, Colombo Family).

298 **Sharpton has said he knew Pagano**: Al Sharpton and Anthony Walton, *Go and Tell Pharaoh: The Autobiography of the Reverend Al Sharpton* (Doubleday, 1996), 81.

299 **"double-crossed" the FBI**: Dan Coughlin, "'Nobody Will Ever Say Richie Giachetti Is Cheap,'" *Cleveland Plain Dealer*, August 4, 1981.

299 **"Jewish Mafia of Cleveland"**: Jack Newfield, *Only in America: The Life and Crimes of Don King* (William Morrow, 1995), 187.

299 **"Don will steal"**: *Corruption in Professional Boxing: Hearings Before the Permanent Subcommittee on Investigations of the Committee on Governmental Affairs*, 102nd Cong. 111 (1992) (statement of "Bobby," Cooperating Witness, Federal Bureau of Investigation).

299 **"Let me see"**: Newfield, *Only in America*, 184.

299 **"The rev was a great bullshitter"**: Newfield, *Only in America*, 186.

300 **"For the last five years"**: Bob Drury, Robert E. Kessler, and Mike McAlary, "The Minister and the Feds," *Newsday*, January 20, 1988.

300 **"clearly designed to discredit"**: Sharpton and Walton, *Go and Tell Pharaoh*, 83.

300 **"I don't believe"**: Jerry Capeci and Stuart Marques, "Sharpton: I Never Spied on Activists," *New York Daily News*, January 21, 1988.

302 **"Don King promotes Mike Tyson fights"**: Bob Raissman and Bill Gallo, "Squabbling Perils Tyson-Spinks," *New York Daily News*, November 12, 1987.

302 **about $10 million**: Wallace Matthews, "Inside Boxing: Holmes Says Mistrust King," *Newsday*, October 24, 1988.

302 **"Let's put it on the table"**: Associated Press, "King Presses Cooney to Sign for Title Bout," *New York Times*, April 19, 1981.

302 **Holmes would recall**: "Larry Holmes Says Don King Got Him to Fight Tyson," clip from interview of Mike Tyson and Larry Holmes at Turning Stone Resort Casino, posted June 4, 2014, by CNY Central, YouTube, youtube.com/watch?v=8UriAnwtTiM.

303 **"Har! Har! Har!"**: "Larry Holmes Says Don King."

303 **"I don't like Larry"**: Wallace Matthews, "Holmes' Wakeup Call?" *Newsday*, December 2, 1987.

303 **"You have to dismantle"**: Mike Tyson with Larry Sloman, *Undisputed Truth: My Autobiography* (HarperSport, 2014), 66.

303 **"In four or five years"**: Michael Marley, "Holmes: Tyson Will Wind Up in Prison," *New York Post*, January 5, 1988.

304 **identifying Suzette Charles**: Michael Fleming, Karen Freifeld, and Susan Mulcahy, "Inside New York: Ex-Miss with a Champ," *Newsday*, January 15, 1988.

304 **He had insisted**: Bob Raissman, "Trump: Have Ego Will Triumph," *New York Daily News*, February 14, 1988.

304 **whispering to Tyson: "Get him"**: Tyson, *Undisputed Truth*, 149.
304 **"The way you beat Tyson"**: Pat Putnam, "I Had to Come Back," *Sports Illustrated*, January 18, 1988.
305 **"He had given me a blueprint"**: Tyson, *Undisputed Truth*, 148.
305 **A delegation of humanitarians**: Phil Berger, "Tyson Keeps Title with 3 Knockdowns in Fourth," *New York Times*, January 23, 1988.
305 **"That should be"**: "Mike Tyson vs. Larry Holmes," *World Championship Boxing*, aired January 22, 1988, on HBO, youtu.be/ROqHUypvaQs?si=udy6qIB27I8Nmg4Q.
306 **"Larry Holmes was"**: "Mike Tyson vs. Larry Holmes," *World Championship Boxing*.
306 **"I was quoting Fritzie Zivic"**: Tyson, *Undisputed Truth*, 149–50.
306 **"Butch Lewis cannot"**: "Mike Tyson vs. Larry Holmes," *World Championship Boxing*.

33

308 **per a professor**: "Declaration of Ronald A. Sacher," August 15, 1991, Tyson v. Cayton (U.S. District Court, Southern District of New York, no. 88 civ. 8398).
309 **league-leading $19 million**: MLB Payrolls by Season: 1988 Payrolls, The Baseball Cube, thebaseballcube.com/content/payroll_year/1988.
309 **the additional $3.1**: "Tyson/Spinks HBO Agreement," May 24, 1988, Tyson v. Cayton (U.S. District Court, Southern District of New York, no. 88 civ. 8398).
310 **obvious pain, exhausted**: "Affidavit of Steven M. Lott," July 14, 1988, Tyson v. Cayton and Sports of the Century (New York Supreme Court, index no. 12888/88).
310 **lost twenty pounds**: "Affidavit of Loraine Jacobs," July 19, 1988, Tyson v. Cayton and Sports of the Century (New York Supreme Court, index no. 12888/88).
311 **"Miss Roper tells me"**: José Torres, *Fire and Fear: The Inside Story of Mike Tyson* (Warner Books, 1989), 149.
311 **"I realized that"**: Monteith M. Illingworth, *Mike Tyson: Money, Myth and Betrayal* (Birch Lane Press, 1991), 219.
312 **"If you walk"**: Michael Katz, "Dream Butch-ered," *New York Daily News*, January 25, 1988.
312 **Meanwhile, Cayton vowed**: Bill Gallo, "Mum's Still the Word on Tyson–Spinks," *New York Daily News*, January 27, 1988.
312 **"I still didn't get the respect"**: Mike Tyson with Larry Sloman, *Undisputed Truth: My Autobiography* (HarperSport, 2014), 170.

34

317 **"Watch this," Tyson whispered**: Robin Givens, *Grace Will Lead Me Home* (Miramax Books, 2007), 181.
317 **"I had forgotten"**: Givens, *Grace Will Lead*, 224.
317 **"Hello, Robin," he said**: Givens, *Grace Will Lead*, 225.
317 **ultimately unproven allegations**: The Illinois Department of Children and Family Services would classify an allegation that he sexually abused a child back in 1974 as "unfounded," though the Archdiocese of Chicago would eventually pay $800,000 to settle claims against Clements and four other priests.
317 **"reminded me of my story"**: Sam Smith, "Tyson: Spinks No Real Problem," *Chicago Tribune*, November 12, 1987.
317 **"stressing the permanency"**: Lisa Faye Kaplan, "Hot Stuff: Mike Tyson Takes on Heavyweight Responsibility," *Reporter Dispatch* (White Plains, NY, February 10, 1988.
318 **"Ma, we got married!"**: Givens, *Grace Will Lead*, 227.
319 **"We either agreed"**: Monteith M. Illingworth, *Mike Tyson: Money, Myth and Betrayal* (Birch Lane Press, 1991), 210.
319 **"I know Mike has been contemplating"**: Michael Katz, "Tyson Marries Real Knockout," *New York Daily News*, February 9, 1988.
319 **estimated 4,500 students**: Luther Turmelle, "Tyson Wears Kid Gloves for Central Jersey Talks," *Courier-News* (Bridgewater, NJ), February 10, 1988.
319 **The order of business**: "Official Minutes, New York State Athletic Commission," Febru-

ary 10, 1988, Tyson v. Cayton (U.S. District Court, Southern District of New York, no. 88 civ. 8398).

320 **He hadn't even applied:** "Application for Manager's License," March 8, 1988, Tyson v. Cayton (U.S. District Court, Southern District of New York, no. 88 civ. 8398).

321 **Had they known:** "Declaration of Rose Trentman," November 21, 1991, and "Declaration of James Dupree," November 16, 1991, Tyson v. Cayton (U.S. District Court, Southern District of New York, no. 88 civ. 8398).

321 **"the role of the commission":** Illingworth, *Mike Tyson*, 219.

321 **Between seven and ten inches:** "Double-Barrel Storm," *Daily Mail* (Catskill, NY), February 12, 1988.

321 **"Sit tight, Mike":** Illingworth, *Mike Tyson*, 214.

321 **"I paid very little attention":** "Declaration of Michael G. Tyson," August 18, 1991, Tyson v. Cayton (U.S. District Court, Southern District of New York, no. 88 civ. 8398).

322 **make $70 million:** Katz, "Tyson Marries Real Knockout."

323 **"I've always wanted to sit":** Robert McFadden et al., *Outrage* (Bantam Books, 1990), 209–11.

323 **"She shouldn't feel":** Hilary Waldman for Gannett News Service, "Champ Visits with Assault Victim," *Standard-Star* (New Rochelle, NY), February 16, 1988.

323 **"You know Mike":** McFadden et al., *Outrage*, 209.

324 **"Lots of children":** Michael Cottman, "Tyson Offers Tuition to Rape Victim Upstate," *Newsday*, February 16, 1988.

325 **a scheduled round of intensive chemotherapy:** "Declaration of Ronald G. Sacher, M.D.," August 15, 1991, Tyson v. Cayton (U.S. District Court, Southern District of New York, no. 88 civ. 8398).

325 **"was in Texas":** "Declaration of Michael G. Tyson," April 4, 1991, Tyson v. Cayton (U.S. District Court, Southern District of New York, no. 88 civ. 8398).

35

326 **Cayton bragged about selling:** Phil Berger, "Foreign TV Bullish on Tyson," *New York Times*, March 16, 1988.

327 **A hundred photographers:** Michael Shapiro, "Tyson Wastes No Time Retaining Title," *New York Times*, March 21, 1988.

327 **"Tyson learned his":** Paul Antonelli, "Tyson Is 'at Ease' and Ready for Tubbs," *Daily Mail* (Catskill, NY), March 16, 1988.

327 **That very morning:** Jenny Demonte, "Boxer Buys $4.2M Estate," *Daily Record* (Morristown, NJ), March 16, 1988.

327 **the $80,000 BMW:** "The Mystery of Mike Tyson's Baby," Page Six, *New York Post*, March 23, 1988.

328 **"No, there isn't":** Earl Gustkey, "Controversy Surrounds Tubbs; All Is Upbeat on Tyson Front," *Los Angeles Times*, March 18, 1988.

328 **"bobbed and weaved":** Michael Katz, "Goal: Rocky's Record," *New York Daily News*, March 18, 1988.

328 **"I have no idea":** Wallace Matthews, "Expecting the Tough Questions," *Newsday*, March 18, 1988.

328 **On her flight back:** Robin Givens, *Grace Will Lead Me Home* (Miramax Books, 2007), 235.

329 **"No promoter would":** Timothy W. Smith, "Long Wait over for Tubbs," *Cincinnati Enquirer*, May 20, 1987.

329 **sold forty-three thousand tickets:** Shapiro, "Tyson Wastes No Time."

329 **"He is a symbol":** "Mike Tyson vs Tony Tubbs—Full Fight—3-21-1988," *World Championship Boxing*, aired March 21, 1988, on HBO, posted November 5, 2018, by Mike Tyson Career Bouts, YouTube, youtube.com/watch?v=x_Hb1m3EpM4.

329 **he'd been watching:** Pat Putnam, "Tyson Takes Tokyo," *Sports Illustrated*, March 28, 1988.

330 **"Anybody can take":** Michael Katz, "Spinks Might Be Light at End of Tyson," *New York Daily News*, March 22, 1988.

330 **effectively neutered him:** Wallace Matthews, "Mrs. Tyson Gets the Power," *Newsday*, March 28, 1988.

330 **"Don is not really involved"**: Michael Marley, "Japan KOs King," *New York Post*, March 16, 1988.

331 **"mere errand boy"**: Matthews, "Mrs. Tyson Gets the Power."

331 **"Do you realize"**: Shapiro, "Tyson Wastes No Time."

331 **"I counted twelve"**: Phil Berger, "Tyson: Strong, Silent and Sometimes Scared," *New York Times*, March 20, 1988.

332 **statement of his cash disbursements**: "Mike Tyson Disbursements for the Year Ended December 31, 1987," Tyson v. Cayton and Sports of the Century (New York Supreme Court, index no. 12888/88).

332 **"I used to look"**: Leslie Bennetts, "Tyson Turmoil," *Vanity Fair*, November 1988.

332 **"I'm Mrs. Mike"**: José Torres, *Fire and Fear: The Inside Story of Mike Tyson* (Warner Books, 1989), 154.

333 **"Robin began throwing her weight"**: Mike Tyson with Larry Sloman, *Undisputed Truth: My Autobiography* (HarperSport, 2014), 161.

333 **"animated conversation" with her daughter**: Torres, *Fire and Fear*, 158.

333 **"When Bill left"**: Givens, *Grace Will Lead*, 239.

333 **"Shortly after the fight"**: Givens, *Grace Will Lead*, 238.

36

334 **"It's not a story"**: Wallace Matthews, "Managers' Health Problem for Tyson?," *Newsday*, March 10, 1988.

334 **One of King's henchmen**: Monteith M. Illingworth, *Mike Tyson: Money, Myth and Betrayal* (Birch Lane Press, 1991), 228.

334 **"He's just got pneumonia"**: Wallace Matthews, "Expecting the Tough Questions," *Newsday*, March 18, 1988.

334 **In fact, Jacobs had**: "Sacher Affidavit," September 4, 1991, Tyson v. Cayton (U.S. District Court, Southern District of New York, no. 88 civ. 8398).

334 **"I didn't know he was sick"**: "Deposition of Michael Gerard Tyson," April 4, 1991, Tyson v. Cayton (U.S. District Court, Southern District of New York, no. 88 civ. 8398).

334 **"Mike called me"**: "Affidavit of Loraine Jacobs," July 19, 1988, Tyson v. Cayton and Sports of the Century (New York Supreme Court, index no. 12888/88).

335 **"Let's change the date"**: Robin Givens, *Grace Will Lead Me Home* (Miramax Books, 2007), 242.

335 **power of attorney**: Michael Katz et al., "Left to Heart—Kayo to Love," *New York Daily News*, October 9, 1988.

335 **"I love Robin"**: José Torres, *Fire and Fear: The Inside Story of Mike Tyson* (Warner Books, 1989), 161.

335 **"I felt like killing myself"**: Wallace Matthews, "Torres May Join Tyson," *Newsday*, March 26, 1988.

336 **"Do you have one"**: Torres, *Fire and Fear*, 152.

336 **"You know Jim and I"**: Givens, *Grace Will Lead*, 243.

337 **flight 3 to LAX**: Michael Katz, "Don's No King with Tyson," *New York Daily News*, March 31, 1988.

337 **"These people don't know"**: Torres, *Fire and Fear*, 162.

337 **"a woman with larceny"**: Torres, *Fire and Fear*, 156.

338 **"He told me I should become"**: Illingworth, *Mike Tyson*, 237.

338 **"The only logical choice"**: Matthews, "Torres May Join."

338 **"I would have to consider"**: Matthews, "Torres May Join."

338 **As one mourner described**: Jack Newfield, *Only in America: The Life and Crimes of Don King* (William Morrow, 1995), 260.

338 **King as a pallbearer**: Mike Tyson with Larry Sloman, *Undisputed Truth: My Autobiography*, Kindle ed. (Penguin, 2013), 161.

338 **"I told Mike"**: Illingworth, *Mike Tyson*, 238–39.

339 **"I want my money"**: There are several versions of this episode, but the juiciest and most complete is found in Newfield, *Only in America*, 258–59.

37

341 **"$1 a year"**: Robert J. Cole, "Plaza Hotel Is Sold to Donald Trump for $390 Million," *New York Times*, March 27, 1988.
341 **"Trump's USFL merger"**: UPI, "Trump Blamed for USFL's Lost Suit," *Daily Item* (Lynn, MA), March 11, 1988.
341 **certain Las Vegas hotels**: Ron Borges, "In This Card Game, Trump Beat Vegas," *Boston Globe*, March 13, 1988.
341 **throng of 1,200**: Bill Gallo, "Punchout at the Plaza," *New York Daily News*, March 30, 1988.
342 **"Shel, Shel," he asked**: Phil Berger, *Blood Season: Tyson and the World of Boxing* (William Morrow, 1989), 249.
342 **"ugly rumors and snide innuendos"**: Michael Katz, "Honeymoon's Not Over," *New York Daily News*, March 30, 1988.
342 **In all, King spoke**: Gallo, "Punchout at the Plaza."
343 **"That motherfucker," said Tyson**: Monteith M. Illingworth, *Mike Tyson: Money, Myth and Betrayal* (Birch Lane Press, 1991), 247.
343 **"Don King is making moves"**: Phil Berger, "Cayton and King Battling over Tyson," *New York Times*, April 10, 1988.
344 **"You'll notice that I'm always"**: Mike Tyson with Larry Sloman, *Undisputed Truth: My Autobiography*, Kindle ed. (Penguin, 2013), 150.
344 **"I have a wife"**: Phil Berger, "Tyson Has Big Questions About Money," *New York Times*, April 11, 1988.
344 **due that October**: Michael Marley, "Tyson Takes Charge," *New York Post*, April 11, 1988.
344 **"There is no way"**: Berger, "Tyson Has Big Questions."
345 **"who calls my wife"**: Marley, "Tyson Takes Charge."
345 **"If I deal with Don"**: Michael Marley, "Seething Tyson Rips Manager," *New York Post*, May 18, 1988.
346 **"I think the fact"**: Leslie Bennetts, "Tyson Turmoil," *Vanity Fair*, November 1988.

38

348 **"the contracts that made Tyson"**: Wallace Matthews, "The Tug-of-War over Tyson," *Newsday*, April 14, 1988.
348 **"Mike came to see me"**: "Affidavit of Jose Torres," p. 6, no. 17, September 26, 1991, Tyson v. Cayton (U.S. District Court, Southern District of New York, no. 88 civ. 8398).
349 **was on welfare**: Michael Marley, "Who's in Champ's Corner?," *New York Post*, June 24, 1988.
349 **at least four heavyweight**: "Agreement between William D. Cayton, Sports of the Century, and Don King Productions," May 7, 1988, Tyson v. Cayton and Sports of the Century (New York Supreme Court, index no. 12888/88).
349 **"King is getting $3 million"**: Michael Marley, "Spinks Can Handle 'Relative,'" *New York Post*, May 16, 1988.
349 *Life* **had guaranteed**: Robin Givens, *Grace Will Lead Me Home* (Miramax Books, 2007), 250; José Torres, *Fire and Fear: The Inside Story of Mike Tyson* (Warner Books, 1989), 184.
350 **the Carriage House**: Michael Marley, "Tyson Will Be Riding in Style," *New York Post*, April 13, 1988.
350 **crew of twenty-five**: Wallace Matthews, "Tyson Watch: Mystery Grows," *Newsday*, May 9, 1988.
350 **"I couldn't recall"**: Givens, *Grace Will Lead*, 253.
351 **never been "socialized"**: Wallace Matthews, "Tyson's Troubled Times: Family Goes Public with Personal Matters," *Newsday*, June 19, 1988.
351 **officers' "superb professionalism"**: Jerry Nachman, "Champ Blames It All on Cat," *New York Post*, May 13, 1988.
351 **"King is winning"**: Wallace Matthews, "Tyson's Manager Takes It Back: 'Just Kidding,'" *Newsday*, May 16, 1988.
352 **"I'm not going to tolerate"**: Michael Marley, "Seething Tyson Rips Manager," *New York Post*, May 18, 1988.

352 **Cosby and Oprah Winfrey:** Dave Anderson, "Mike Tyson's Toughest Opponent," *New York Times*, April 19, 1988.
352 **arrested for smacking:** Wallace Matthews, "A Chip on Shoulder of Tyson's Trainer," *Newsday*, December 17, 1987.
352 **was 237 pounds:** Matthews, "Tyson's Manager."
353 **moving to Monaco:** Michael Katz, "Love Backs Tyson into Own Corner," *New York Daily News*, May 26, 1988.
353 **"not official yet":** Betty Liu Ebron, "Apple Sauce: To Quote an Old Vaudeville Line: You're a Doctor? I'm Dubious," *New York Daily News*, May 17, 1988.
354 **"choking back tears":** Tim Layden, "A Force Unleashed," *Sports Illustrated*, March 6, 1985, si.com/longform/2015/1985/tyson/index.html.
354 **"so screwed up":** Tim Layden, "Frustrated Tyson Says Changes Coming," *Times-Union* (Albany, NY), May 20, 1988.
355 **"He just went with the punch":** Wallace Matthews, "Inside Boxing: Tyson Knocked Down, Sort Of," *Newsday*, May 26, 1988.
355 **Apparently, a reporter:** Torres, *Fire and Fear*, 185.
355 **"She got me":** Monteith M. Illingworth, *Mike Tyson: Money, Myth and Betrayal* (Birch Lane Press, 1991), 256.
355 **"came away convinced":** Katz, "Love Backs Tyson."
355 **Just hours after Katz's column:** Dave Anderson, "'If He Loses This Fight, No More Commercials,'" *New York Times*, May 29, 1988.
355 **easy $1 million:** "Letter of Agreement Between Reel Sports Inc. and the Pepsi-Cola Company," May 26, 1988, Tyson v. Cayton (U.S. District Court, Southern District of New York, no. 88 civ. 8398).
355 **"I ain't gonna get him":** Anderson, "'If He Loses This Fight.'"
357 **a hooker's request:** Mike Tyson with Larry Sloman, *Undisputed Truth: My Autobiography* (HarperSport, 2014), 105.
357 **encouraged by Governor Mario Cuomo:** Wallace Matthews, "Did Cuomo KO Torres?," *Newsday*, May 19, 1988.
357 **"Steve, I had a problem":** Torres, *Fire and Fear*, 175.
357 **"Don't be afraid":** Givens, *Grace Will Lead*, 259.
357 **"a spontaneous miscarriage":** Stuart Marques and Michael Katz, "Doc: Robin Lost Baby," *New York Daily News*, October 13, 1988.
357 **"the second month":** Amy Pagnozzi, "Givens' Pregnancy: Was Mike's Proposal Ill Conceived?," *New York Post*, October 13, 1988.
358 **"We lost the baby":** Torres, *Fire and Fear*, 176.
358 **"Of course I am":** Torres, *Fire and Fear*, 167.
358 **"I like to see":** Torres, *Fire and Fear*, 176–77.

39

360 **Matthews was knocked:** "Gloves Results," *New York Daily News*, February 16, 1977.
360 **"Nobody knows how abusive":** Wallace Matthews, "Tyson's Troubled Times: Family Goes Public with Personal Matters," *Newsday*, June 19, 1988.
362 **"He said he'd stop at nothing":** Associated Press, "Givens: Cayton Seeks Tyson Divorce," *Press of Atlantic City*, June 18, 1988.
362 **"I'm married to Robin":** Michael Marley, "Iron Mike's Fighting Mad," *New York Post*, June 20, 1988.
362 **"People are trying very hard":** Amy Pagnozzi and Flo Anthony, "Mom-in-Law Says She Fears for Life," *New York Post*, June 20, 1988.
362 **"Cayton went to the man":** Michael Marley, "King: Cayton Sought to Bribe Tyson Priest," *New York Post*, June 21, 1988.
363 **"Satan in disguise":** Stan Hochman, "Round II: Rival King Says Cayton Is a 'Satan in Disguise,'" *Philadelphia Daily News*, June 21, 1988.
363 **While Rooney had been worried:** Michael Katz, "King Rips Cayton as Tyson Spars," *New York Daily News*, June 21, 1988.

363 **banished from workouts:** Michael Katz, "All Tyson Doors Are Ajar," *New York Daily News*, June 22, 1988.

363 **"Starting now, you are":** Michael Winston to Bill Cayton, June 24, 1988, Tyson v. Cayton (U.S. District Court, Southern District of New York, no. 88 civ. 8398).

363 **Cayton was already lawyered up:** Michael Marley, "Heavyweight Lawyer in Cayton's Corner," *New York Post*, June 16, 1988.

364 **"the Tabloid Decade":** David Kamp, "The Tabloid Decade," *Vanity Fair*, February 1999.

364 **"Which one of":** Trump Plaza Hotel and Casino, Don King Productions, Butch Lewis Productions, Inc., "Tyson/Spinks June 27 Bout at Trump Plaza Attracting Big Names in Sports, Politics and Show Biz," news release, June 20, 1988, from Pete Hamill's personal papers, courtesy of Fukiko Aioki.

364 **"I'll break Spinks":** Gary Smith, "Tyson the Timid, Tyson the Terrible," *Sports Illustrated*, March 21, 1988.

365 **"I've never run from anybody":** Associated Press, "Spinks Gets Courage from Brother Leon," *Sunday News* (Lancaster, PA), June 26, 1988.

366 **"a big book":** Pat Putnam, "The Big Showdown," *Sports Illustrated*, July 27, 1988.

366 **sparring 170 rounds:** Michael Marley, "Tyson Packs Punch in Sparring Session," *New York Post*, June 21, 1988.

366 **sepia-toned photographs:** Tom Callahan, "Boxing's Allure," *Time*, June 27, 1988.

366 **"I can hear his voice":** William Gildea, "Victory Without Joy," *Washington Post*, June 7, 1988.

367 **"champion of the world cried":** Jerry Izenberg, "Inside Mike Tyson," *Star-Ledger*, June 3, 1988.

367 **"Then he pulled his head":** Jerry Izenberg, *Once They Were Giants* (Skyhorse, 2021), 182.

40

369 **"bigger than I even thought":** Donald Trump and Robin Givens, interview by Spencer Christian, *Good Morning America*, ABC, June 27, 1988.

369 **"The day of the Spinks fight":** Robin Givens, *Grace Will Lead Me Home* (Miramax Books, 2007), 262.

371 **of charging $2,000:** Dave Anderson, "Donald Trump's $1,500 High-Roller Ringside," *New York Times*, May 1, 1988.

371 **"a monument to a decade":** Judy Mann, "Fight Is Monument to a Decade of Greed," *Washington Post*, June 29, 1988.

372 **"the largest-grossing":** "Rare 1988 Throwback: 'Tyson vs. Spinks' Press Conference!," footage of press conference at Trump Plaza in Atlantic City, New Jersey, March 30, 1988, posted May 21, 2019, by Hezakya Newz & Films, YouTube, youtube.com/watch?v=7iS3xARn47Q.

372 **"Bill," he says, "I'm with you":** Phil Berger, "Cayton Is Shocked by Trump's Move," *New York Times*, July 13, 1988.

373 **of "decayed teeth":** Sally Jenkins, "Atlantic City and Its Mr. Big Play Their Trump Card," *Washington Post*, June 27, 1988. Her lede is spectacular: "Behind the great chrome and glass casinos, the city looks like decayed teeth, and the signs on the crummy little money shops say 'Cash for food stamps, gold.' The impending heavyweight title prizefight between Mike Tyson and Michael Spinks is taking place amid indiscriminate spending and mesmerizing squalor, an ambiance that was summed up by Spinks' manager Butch Lewis, who wore his tuxedo with no shirt."

373 **"a friend of Donald":** Phil Mushnick, "Mr. Trump's Chumps," *New York Post*, June 29, 1988.

373 **"When I see Don":** Jack Newfield, *Only in America: The Life and Crimes of Don King* (William Morrow, 1995), 149.

373 **"If I had known":** "Affidavit of Michael Tyson," June 29, 1988, Tyson v. Cayton and Sports of the Century (New York Supreme Court, index no. 12888/88).

374 **In fact, Butch's brother:** José Torres, *Fire and Fear: The Inside Story of Mike Tyson* (Warner Books, 1989), 198–99.

374 **"I'm God," says Tyson:** Mike Tyson with Larry Sloman, *Undisputed Truth: My Autobiography* (HarperSport, 2014), 170–71.

374 **"Put his hand right through"**: John Florio and Ouisie Shapiro, *One Punch from the Promised Land* (Lyons Press, 2013), 211.

375 **The broadcasters are saying**: "Mike Tyson vs. Michael Spinks," directed by Marc Payton, *World Championship Boxing*, aired June 27, 1988, on HBO, youtube.com/watch?v=TRtYaFa_eXg.

375 **"They couldn't even"**: Florio and Shapiro, *One Punch*, 212.

376 **"Ali now moved"**: Norman Mailer, "Fury, Fear, Philosophy: Understanding Mike Tyson," *Spin*, September 1988.

376 **"The man who brought"**: Wallace Matthews, "New Fodder for a Towering Ego," *Newsday*, July 10, 1988.

376 **"New Jersey thanks"**: Mailer, "Fury, Fear, Philosophy."

376 **"Stick and move"**: Florio and Shapiro, *One Punch*, 213.

376 **He sees the fear**: Pat Putnam, "'I'm Gonna Hurt This Guy,'" *Sports Illustrated*, July 4, 1988.

377 **"He had the look"**: Mailer, "Fury, Fear, Philosophy."

377 **Spinks still wants**: Michael Marley, "The Baddest Man on Earth," *New York Post*, June 28, 1988.

377 **walk right in**: Walt MacPeek, "Visit from 'Idol' Durán Helped Tyson Focus on Task at Hand," *Star-Ledger*, June 28, 1988.

377 **"He's not gonna"**: "Mike Tyson vs. Michael Spinks," *World Championship Boxing*.

377 **four seconds shorter**: Marley, "Baddest Man on Earth."

378 **"I can handle chaos"**: Pete Hamill, "A Raging Bull from Brownsville," *New York Post*, June 28, 1988.

378 **declaring Tyson "the baddest man"**: The *Post*'s back-page headline reads "The Baddest Man on Earth," but Mike Marley's lede refers to Tyson, for the first time, as best I can tell, as "the baddest man on the planet."

378 **"I'm not going to let"**: Rich Hoffman, "Two Views of the Destruction," *Philadelphia Daily News*, June 28, 1988.

379 **"Mike Tyson is the hardest-hitting"**: William Gildea and Sally Jenkins, "Court Next Arena of Battle for Tyson," *Washington Post*, June 29, 1988.

379 **She tells him to get her**: Tyson, *Undisputed Truth*, 172.

379 **"Let's get out"**: Givens, *Grace Will Lead*, 263.

SELECTED BIBLIOGRAPHY

Ali, Dr. Rita. *Triple Jeopardy*. Words Matter Publishing, 2021.

Anderson, Dave. *In the Corner: Great Boxing Trainers Talk About Their Art*. William Morrow and Company, Inc., 1991.

Atlas, Teddy, with Peter Alson. *Atlas: From the Streets to the Ring; A Son's Struggle to Become a Man*. Ecco, 2006.

Berger, Phil. *Blood Season: Tyson and the World of Boxing*. William Morrow and Company, Inc., 1989.

Berger, Phil. *Punch Lines: Berger on Boxing*. Four Walls Eight Windows, 1993.

Brenner, Teddy, as told to Barney Nagler. *Only the Ring Was Square*. Prentice-Hall, 1981.

Brown, Ethan. *Queens Reigns Supreme: Fat Cat, 50 Cent, and the Rise of the Hip-Hop Hustler*. Anchor Books, 2005.

Bunce, Steve. *Bunce's Big Fat Short History of British Boxing*. Bantam Books, 2017.

Butler, Brin-Jonathan. *The Domino Diaries*. Picador, 2015.

Butler, Brin-Jonathan. *Mike Tyson: The Kindle Singles Interview*. Amazon Digital Services, Inc., 2014.

Calder-Smith, Dominic. *The Long Round: The Triumphs and Tragedies of the Men Who Fought Mike Tyson*. Yellow Jersey Press, 2004.

Conrad, Harold. *Dear Muffo*. Stein and Day, 1982.

DiSanto, John, and Matthew H. Ward. *Boxing in Atlantic City*. Arcadia Publishing, 2021.

Donaldson, Greg. *The Ville: Cops and Kids in Urban America*. Ticknor & Fields, 1993.

Durán, Roberto, with George Diaz. *I Am Durán*. Blue Rider Press, 2016.

Duva, Lou, with Tim Smith. *A Fighting Life: My Seven Decades in Boxing*. Sports Publishing, 2016.

Early, Gerald. *Tuxedo Junction: Essays on American Culture*. Ecco, 1989.

Eig, Jonathan. *Ali: A Life*. Houghton Mifflin Harcourt, 2017.

Evans, Gavin. *Mama's Boy: Lennox Lewis and the Heavyweight Crown*. Highdown, 2004.

Farrell, Charles. *(Low)life: A Memoir of Jazz, Fight-Fixing, and the Mob*. Hamilcar Publications, 2021.

Florio, John, and Ouisie Shapiro. *One Punch from the Promised Land: Leon Spinks, Michael Spinks, and the Myth of the Heavyweight Title*. Lyons Press, 2013.

Fried, Albert. *The Rise and Fall of the Jewish Gangster in America*. Columbia University Press, 1993.

Gibbs, Brian, with Joseph A. Verola. *Beyond Lucky: The Brian "Glaze" Gibbs Story: Crack, Money, Murder & Redemption.* Ustar Publishing, 2015.

Gifford, Dr. Justin. *Street Poison: The Biography of Iceberg Slim.* Skyhorse Publishing, 2015.

Givens, Robin. *Grace Will Lead Me Home.* Miramax Books, 2007.

Gonzalez, Rudy, with Martin A. Feigenbaum. *The Inner Ring: The Set-Up of Mike Tyson and the Uncrowning of Don King.* Surfside Six Publishing, 1995.

Gordon, Randy. *Glove Affair: My Lifelong Journey in the World of Professional Boxing.* Rowman & Littlefield, 2019.

Green, Peter. *Alexander of Macedon, 356–323 B.C.: A Historical Biography.* University of California Press, 1991.

Grinker, Lori. *Mike Tyson.* Powerhouse Books, 2022.

Guy, Jasmine. *Afeni Shakur: Evolution of a Revolutionary.* Atria Books, 2005.

Hamill, Pete. *Flesh and Blood.* Random House, 1977.

Hamill, Pete. *Irrational Ravings.* G.P. Putnam's Sons, 1971.

Hannigan, Dave. *Drama in the Bahamas: Muhammad Ali's Last Fight.* Sports Publishing, 2016.

Harris, Sara. *Hellhole: The Shocking Story of the Inmates and Life in the New York City House of Detention for Women.* Tower Books, 1967.

Hauser, Thomas. *The Black Lights: Inside the World of Professional Boxing.* Simon & Schuster, 1991. Originally published 1986.

Hauser, Thomas. *Chaos, Corruption, Courage, and Glory: A Year in Boxing.* Sport Media Publishing, 2005.

Hauser, Thomas. *Muhammad Ali: His Life and Times.* Simon & Schuster, 1992.

Heinz, W. C., and Nathan Ward, eds. *The Book of Boxing.* Total Sports Publishing, 1999.

Heller, Peter. *Bad Intentions: The Mike Tyson Story.* NAL Books, 1989.

Heller, Peter. *"In This Corner . . . !": 42 World Champions Tell Their Stories.* Da Capo Press, 1994.

Hoffer, Richard. *A Savage Business: The Comeback and Comedown of Mike Tyson.* Simon & Schuster, 1998.

Holloway, Rory, with Eric Wilson. *Taming the Beast: The Untold Story of Mike Tyson.* Rough House, 2014.

Holyfield, Evander, with Lee Gruenfeld. *Becoming Holyfield: A Fighter's Journey.* Atria Books, 2008.

Hurt, Harry, III. *Lost Tycoon: The Many Lives of Donald J. Trump.* W. W. Norton, 1993.

Illingworth, Monteith M. *Mike Tyson: Money, Myth and Betrayal.* Birch Lane Press, 1991.

Izenberg, Jerry. *Once They Were Giants.* Skyhorse Publishing, 2021.

Johnson, Beverly. *The Face That Changed It All: A Memoir.* Atria Books, 2015.

Kimball, George, and John Schulian, eds. *At the Fights: American Writers on Boxing.* Library of America, 2011.

Kram, Mark, Jr. *Smokin' Joe: The Life of Joe Frazier.* Ecco, 2019.

Kriegel, Mark. *Bless Me, Father.* Doubleday, 1995.

LaMotta, Jake, with Joseph Carter and Peter Savage. *Raging Bull: My Story.* Prentice-Hall, 1970.

Lane, Mills, with Jedwin Smith. *Let's Get It On.* Crown Publishers, 1998.

Layden, Joe. *The Last Great Fight: The Extraordinary Tale of Two Men and How One Fight Changed Their Lives Forever.* St. Martin's Press, 2007.

Lewis, Lennox, with Ken Gorman. *Lennox Lewis: The Story of Britain's First World Heavyweight Champion This Century.* Faber & Faber, 1997. Originally published 1993.

Lipsyte, Robert. *The Contender.* Harper, revised paperback edition, 2018. Originally published 1967.

Mailer, Norman. *The Fight.* Vintage Books, 1997. Originally published 1975.

Mailer, Norman. *The Presidential Papers.* Bantam Books, 1964.

Malinowski, Scoop. *Heavyweight Armageddon!* Zumaya Publications, 2008.

McAlary, Mike. *Cop Shot: The Murder of Edward Byrne.* G.P. Putnam's Sons, 1990.

McFadden, Robert, Ralph Blumenthal, M. A. Farber, E. R. Shipp, Charles Strum, and Craig Wolff. *Outrage: The Story Behind the Tawana Brawley Hoax.* Bantam Books, 1990.

McIlvanney, Hugh. *The Hardest Game: McIlvanney on Boxing.* Contemporary Books, 2001. Originally published 1996.

McNeil, William F. *The Rise of Mike Tyson, Heavyweight.* McFarland, 2014.

McRae, Donald. *Dark Trade: Lost in Boxing.* Hamilcar Publications, 2019. Originally published 1996.

Miller, James Andrew. *Tinder Box: HBO's Ruthless Pursuit of New Frontiers.* Henry Holt, 2021.

Mitchell, Kevin. *Jacobs Beach: The Mob, The Fights, The Fifties.* Pegasus Books, 2010.

Murray, Marilyn. *Prisoner of Another War: A Remarkable Journey of Healing from Childhood Trauma.* Vivo Publications, 1991.

Newfield, Jack. *Only in America: The Life and Crimes of Don King.* William Morrow, Inc., 1995.

Newfield, Jack. *Robert F. Kennedy: A Memoir.* Berkley, 1978. Originally published 1969.

Oates, Joyce Carol. *On Boxing.* Doubleday, 1987.

Oates, Joyce Carol, and Daniel Halpern, eds. *Reading the Fights.* Henry Holt, 1988.

O'Connor, Daniel, ed. *Iron Mike: A Mike Tyson Reader.* Da Capo Press, 2002.

Patterson, Floyd, with Milton Gross. *Victory over Myself.* Scholastic Book Services, 1962.

Perez, Rosie. *Handbook for an Unpredictable Life: How I Survived Sister Renata and My Crazy Mother and Still Came Out Smiling (with Great Hair).* Crown Archetype, 2014.

Pritchett, Wendell. *Brownsville, Brooklyn: Blacks, Jews, and the Changing Face of the Ghetto.* University of Chicago Press, 2002.

Remnick, David. *King of the World: Muhammad Ali and the Rise of an American Hero.* Random House, 1998.

Rendall, Jonathan. *Scream: The Tyson Tapes.* Short Books, 2014.

Roberts, James B., and Alexander C. Skutt. *The Boxing Register.* McBooks Press, 1997.

Roberts, Randy. *Jack Dempsey: The Manassa Mauler.* University of Illinois Press, 2003. Originally published 1979.

Roberts, Randy, and J. Gregory Garrison. *Heavy Justice: The Trial of Mike Tyson.* University of Arkansas Press, 2000.

Ryan, Hugh. *The Women's House of Detention: A Queer History of a Forgotten Prison.* Bold Type Books, 2022.

Schulberg, Budd. *Ringside.* Ivan R. Dee, 2006.

Schulberg, Budd. *Sparring with Hemingway.* Ivan R. Dee, 1995.

Sharpton, Al, and Anthony Walton. *Go and Tell Pharoah: The Autobiography of the Reverend Al Sharpton.* Doubleday, 1996.

Shulman, Irving. *The Amboy Dukes.* Pocket Books, 1971. Originally published 1947.

Slim, Iceberg. *Pimp: The Story of My Life.* Holloway House, 1967.

Snyder, Todd D. *Beat Boxing: How Hip-Hop Changed the Fight Game.* Hamilcar Publications, 2021.

Stratton, W. K. *Floyd Patterson: The Fighting Life of Boxing's Invisible Champion.* Mainstream Publishing, 2014. Originally published 2012.

Talese, Gay. *Frank Sinatra Has a Cold and Other Essays.* Penguin Books, 2011.

Thomas, James J. *The Holyfield Way.* Sports Publishing, 2005.

Toback, James. *Jim: The Author's Self-Centered Memoir on the Great Jim Brown.* Rat Press, 2009. Originally published 1971.

Torres, José. *Fire and Fear: The Inside Story of Mike Tyson.* Warner Books, 1989.

Tosches, Nick. *The Devil in Sonny Liston.* Little, Brown, 2000.

Turkus, Burton B., and Sid Feder. *Murder, Inc.: The Story of "The Syndicate."* Bantam Books, 1960. Originally published 1951.

Tyson, Mike. *Iron Ambition: My Life with Cus D'Amato.* Blue Rider Press, 2017.

Tyson, Mike, with Larry Sloman. *Undisputed Truth: My Autobiography.* HarperSport, 2014. Originally published 2013.

Valenti, John, with Ron Naclerio. *Swee'Pea and Other Playground Legends.* Michael Kesend Publishing, 1990.

Vogan, Travis. *The Boxing Film: A Cultural and Transmedia History.* Rutgers University Press, 2020. Kindle.

Wiley, Ralph. *Serenity: A Boxing Memoir.* Bison Books, 2000. Originally published 1989.

Willis, George. *The Bite Fight: Tyson, Holyfield, and the Night That Changed Boxing Forever.* Triumph Books, 2013.

IMAGE CREDITS

166 Ken Regan/Camera 5
171 Ken Regan/Camera 5
179 © Lori Grinker/Contact Press Images
180 © Lori Grinker/Contact Press Images
199 *The Ring* magazine via Getty Images
204 William E. Sauro/*The New York Times*/Redux
206 *The Ring* magazine via Getty Images
210 Cleveland Press Collections, courtesy of the Michael Schwartz Library Special
     Collections, Cleveland State University
214 Cleveland Press Collections, courtesy of the Michael Schwartz Library Special
     Collections, Cleveland State University
223 Linda Platt
228 Ken Regan/Camera 5
236 © Lori Grinker/Contact Press Images
239 Linda Platt
244 AFP FILES/AFP via Getty Images
246 *The Ring* magazine via Getty Images
247 © Lori Grinker/Contact Press Images
260 © Lori Grinker/Contact Press Images
264 © American Broadcasting Companies, Inc. All rights reserved.
     (credit: ABC Photo Archives)
272 Richard Mackson/*Sports Illustrated* via Getty Images
275 © Lori Grinker/Contact Press Images
279 Front Page/Tor Lindseth
282 © Lori Grinker/Contact Press Images
291 Chris Smith/Popperfoto via Getty Images
301 Sonia Moskowitz/Getty Images
302 © Lori Grinker/Contact Press Images
306 *The Ring* magazine via Getty Images
318 © Lori Grinker/Contact Press Images
324 © Lori Grinker/Contact Press Images
328 © Lori Grinker/Contact Press Images
337 Mike Mullen, Herald Examiner Collection/Los Angeles Public Library
347 Anthony Barboza via Getty Images
354 © Lori Grinker/Contact Press Images
356 Official Boxing Gods
365 © Lori Grinker/Contact Press Images
370 Official Boxing Gods
378 *The Ring* magazine via Getty Images
380 *The New York Post*/NYP Holdings, Inc.

INDEX

Italic page references indicate photos